Designing AN

DESIGNING COMMUNITY

Charrettes, master plans and form-based codes

David Walters

AMSTERDAM • BOSTON • HEIDELBERG • LONDON • NEW YORK • OXFORD
PARIS • SAN DIEGO • SAN FRANCISCO • SINGAPORE • SYDNEY • TOKYO
Architectural Press is an imprint of Elsevier

ELSEVIER

Architectural
Press

Architectural Press is an imprint of Elsevier
Linacre House, Jordan Hill, Oxford OX2 8DP, UK
30 Corporate Drive, Suite 400, Burlington, MA 01803, USA

First edition 2007

British Library Cataloguing in Publication Data
A catalogue record for this book is available from the British Library

Library of Congress Cataloging-in-Publication Data
A catalog record for this book is available from the Library of Congress

ISBN: 978-0-7506-6925-2

For information on all Architectural Press publications
visit our website at www.architecturalpress.com

Typeset by Charon Tec Ltd (A Macmillan Company), Chennai, India
www.charontec.com
Printed and bound in Italy

07 08 09 10 11   10 9 8 7 6 5 4 3 2 1

Contents

Acknowledgements

As with any enterprise of this nature, I wish to thank several people for all kinds of help and advice. First and foremost my wife, Linda Luise Brown, usually my co-author, but in this case my ever present editor and helpmate-in-chief while pursuing her other career as a painter and affiliate artist-in-residence at the McColl Center for Visual Art in Charlotte, NC, for 18 months during the writing of this book.

Second are my colleagues in practice at The Lawrence Group in Davidson, NC, especially Craig Lewis, Dave Malushizky (whose skilful perspective drawings grace the cover and several pages of this book), Chad Hall and Catherine Monroe (now moved on to other employment – we miss you!). Craig Lewis was especially helpful in providing much useful material for Chapter 7 regarding charrette organization and budgeting, and indeed was the managing genius behind the book's case studies. However, the opinions in this book are mine alone and should not be imputed to any of my colleagues. If I got things wrong, it's my fault.

At the College of Architecture at the University of North Carolina at Charlotte, I would like to thank my graduate assistant, Lacey Wolf, for prompt and invaluable help with library research and image scanning; Chair of Instruction Betsy West, AIA, for providing some partial release time from teaching for one semester, without which this book would not have been completed on time; and Dean Kenneth Lambla, AIA, for supporting my research trips back to my native England with travel money squeezed from a tight budget.

To this list I would add friends and colleagues in the UK, Joe Holyoak and Polly Feather in Birmingham, for continued advice and encouragement; my son Adrian Walters, an architect in Boston, MA, for taking several much needed photographs in his adopted hometown; and Laura Sacha at the Architectural Press for always being helpful in patiently answering all my questions.

All photographs and drawings are reproduced by permission of the author and/or The Lawrence Group, Town Planners & Architects, unless otherwise noted.

Drawings illustrated in Chapter 8 are reproduced by permission of the Town of Huntersville, NC, and in Chapter 9 by permission of the City of Concord, NC.

David Walters
Charlotte, NC

Credits

HUNTERSVILLE (Case Study I)

Project Team

The Lawrence Group: Town Planners & Architects
Craig Lewis, AICP, CNU
David Walters, RIBA, APA
Dave Malushizky, AIA
Paul Hubbman, AIA
Catherine Monroe, LEED
Chad Hall

Kimley-Horn and Associates: Transportation Planners and Engineers
Stephen Stansbery, AICP
Roger Henderson, PE, AICP

Rose & Associates, Inc.: Land Development and Real Estate Advisory Services
Kathleen Rose, CCIM
Diane Carter, CCIM

Henson-Harrington, Inc.: Landscape Architecture and Land Planning
Tom Harrington, RLA

Arnett Muldrow & Associates: Branding and Marketing Design
Ben Muldrow
Tripp Muldrow

Town of Huntersville Board of Commissioners

Kim Phillips, Mayor
Teri Leonhardt
Sara McAulay
Jeff Pugliese
Brian Sisson
Jill Swain

Town Staff

Jerry Cox, Town Manager
Greg Ferguson, Assistant Town Manager
Jack Simoneau, Planning Director
Bill Coxe, Transportation Planner

CONCORD (Case Study II)

Project team

The Lawrence Group: Town Planners & Architects
Craig Lewis, AICP, CNU
David Walters, RIBA, APA
Dave Malushizky, AIA
Catherine Monroe, LEED
Chad Hall
Ellen Cervera

Kimley-Horn and Associates: Transportation Planners and Engineers
Stephen Stansbery, AICP
Nik Nikolaev, ASLA, RLA

Rose & Associates, Inc.: Land Development and Real Estate Advisory Services
Kathleen Rose, CCIM
Diane Carter, CCIM

Henson-Harrington, Inc.: Landscape Architecture and Land Planning
Tom Harrington, RLA

City of Concord Elected Officials

J. Scott Padgett, Mayor
David W. Phillips
Jim Ramseur
Allen T. Small
Alfred M. Brown, Jr
W. Lamar Barrier
Dr Hector H. Henry II
Randy Grimes

City Staff

Brian Hiatt, City Manager
Jim Greene, Deputy City Manager
Annette Privette, Public Information Officer
Jeff Young, Director of Business and Neighborhood Services
Steve Osborne, Deputy Director of Business and Neighborhood Services
Karl Fritschen, Urban Design Manager
Catherine Russo, Executive Assistant

Introduction

Planning and urban design: the postmodern crisis in planning and the role of urban design in reformulating planning practice

This is a book for architects, landscape architects, planners and students of all three professions. It aims to show planners how urban design is once again central to their profession, and it seeks to inform architects and landscape architects about the public policy and theory-based content of planning that governs their work as urban designers. As a lens to bring these issues into focus, the book utilizes comparative studies of British and American theory and practice about urban design and planning, for the two countries have many urban issues in common: the legacy of failed modernist architecture and planning concepts, the regeneration of central cities, the battle against urban poverty and the crisis of affordable housing, and improving the dismal design standards of much suburban development are just four of the most obvious ones. But for all these professional similarities, the political context in which architects, urban designers and planners work in the two countries is radically different, both structurally in terms of the political framework for planning in a democracy, and ideologically regarding the relative roles of the state and private capital. As an English architect working in America, the author has first-hand experience of both sets of conditions, and is able to examine issues 'from the inside,' using his own work in America as case studies where appropriate.

But first a word about the title: *Designing Community*. This places equal emphasis on design (in this context conceptualized as the act of creating city spaces as sites and containers of human activity) and on the concept of community. Community is a term loosely bandied about by everybody from politicians to planners and urban designers to developers to members of communities themselves, and it means different things to different people. At the most minimal level 'community' is a term coined by developers to cast a superficial romantic gloss over their latest mass-produced subdivisions or housing estates, usually called into being by photographs of happy families in front of their new homes. A particularly egregious use of the term could be found in August 2006 in a developer's advertisement for a subdivision amidst the sprawl that surrounds Charlotte, NC, in the USA, which offered a 'new way of life' in a 'full brick community.' For British readers, 'full brick' means a housing estate where the detached houses are built of light timber frame faced with brick on all sides instead of simply a veneer on the front. Brick is a sign of status in American house building, as opposed to cheaper vinyl siding, and here the potentially rich concept of community is reduced merely to a marketing ploy of snobbish aesthetics.

To residents of a neighborhood, 'community' is often a way of defining their shared values (or shared income levels) as distinct and separate from adjacent areas, and the term may be used for either positive or exclusionary purposes. To ethnic minorities, 'community' can be a rallying cry of unity and identity linked to a specific locality, or it can become an element in a political ideology, as witnessed by British Prime Minister Tony Blair's use of the term in a speech in January 1999:

A modern idea of community is one which applauds and nurtures individual choice and personal autonomy and which recognizes the irreducible pluralism of modern society. (Holden and Iveson: p. 61)

This idea of community as a dialectic between the individual and society, especially when linked to physical space in the city, has a long lineage in planning and urban design practice, and this book examines relationships between physical urban form and the social activities and attitudes of citizens as they affect, guide and challenge the work of design and planning professionals in Britain and America. The role of public participation in planning and urban design is crucial in this regard. The days of the detached 'expert' handing down his plan to a grateful and awed public are long gone, and deservedly so. However, in their place are confused and often bruising debates between planners, politicians, designers and the public about priorities for urban growth or infill development, open space, traffic, schools, parks, affordable housing and a host of other urban issues. To help resolve these issues, this book describes and highlights some effective techniques using the design 'charrette' format of public involvement in planning decisions. The American usage of this term is roughly equivalent in the UK to 'action planning' and 'planning weekends,' and is most directly equated to the process of 'Enquiry by Design' promulgated by the Prince of Wales' Foundation. All the terms mean broadly the same thing: intensive, inclusive workshops, lasting several days, that involve a variety of professionals, elected officials and citizens from the community working together to hammer out concrete design proposals or master plans for future action.

By pairing the two words 'Designing' and 'Community,' I mean to highlight intersections between the act of physical placemaking and larger issues of society and culture. The book's subtitle, *Charrettes, master plans and form-based codes,* identifies a secondary juncture between planning and architecture as the site of a revived and important professional discourse about urbanism and methods of creating and regulating development to promote good quality design. After several decades of separation, in both theory and practice, the two professions are once more converging, led in part by architects and urban designers who have restructured the leading edge of planning practice around theories and principles of physical urban design. In Britain this is part of structured government policy, while in the USA these changes have evolved through the professional activism of architects and planners themselves, often in the face of government neglect or opposition.

This book also builds upon a few basic presumptions about urbanism. First and foremost is that the *form* of physical places needs to be considered long before conventional planning standards about uses of space and buildings. Buildings and urban spaces last a lot longer than do fleeting patterns of use, which might change every year or two, or several times within each generation. In everyday life, old buildings are retrofitted for new uses and comparatively new buildings can be left vacant after only a few years; whole neighborhoods cycle through decline and decay, followed by periods of renewal and gentrification by new people with fresh priorities and different lifestyles. For the last 50 years, in the USA especially, understanding this importance of urban form has been exactly what planning has *not* been about. Considerations of use have been paramount, to the exclusion of almost everything else; America is cluttered with examples where the zoning codes that control development have made the urban form of traditional American towns illegal by outlawing the commonsense practice of mixing uses

within the same building, and by forcing single-use buildings to space themselves widely apart. By contrast, the new form-based American zoning codes discussed in this book put form first and use second.

The destructive capacity of conventional zoning is a familiar story, more pertinent in the USA than Britain, where the 'townscape' school of civic design and the tradition of 'town planning' with its physical design implications never quite faded from view. But this traditional emphasis on urban design in British planning has been markedly lacking in most new developments constructed around the edges of British towns and cities since the 1950s, and especially since the 1980s. Part of the reasoning behind the British government's recent push for design codes to become an integral part of the planning and development system has been the desire to improve the poor quality of design that has become part of the normative British suburban experience. In this regard, Britain and America have much in common, and can usefully learn from each other's experience in attempting to reformulate their planning systems around concepts of good urbanism.

Depressingly mediocre developments like the example shown in Figure I.1 are common across Britain and have been constructed in this miserable manner despite the flood of government guidance for good urban design that promotes improved urban standards. Paul Murrain, a figure at the heart of recent discussions in Britain about traditional urbanism and

Figure I.1 Mediocre contemporary British suburban development. This housing estate adjacent to the new Upton development in Northampton, UK, illustrates sloppy design qualities typical of much British suburban housing. No attention is paid to creating defined urban spaces or good detailing of the public realm. Compare to Figures 3.5, 5.11 and 5.34.

design codes, asks the question simply: 'Why are we still building this rubbish?' (Murrain: p. 133). This inability of design standards to take hold bears witness to the fact that guidance is not enough. As in America, the detailed rules, or codes, that govern urban development need to be changed. Unfortunately, good design needs to be mandated, not simply encouraged.

This leads to the second principle of urbanism upon which much of the urban design theory and most of the practical examples in this book are based: 'traditional urbanism' provides the best armature for diverse and multicultural civic life to flourish, as envisioned both by British government policies for 'sustainable communities' and American New Urbanists' ambitions for more socially just and environmentally sustainable cities. Spaces such as the street, the square, the boulevard and the park fulfill this role because they are inherently human scaled yet neutral and non-deterministic. Their universality as common spatial types allows them to fade into the background and permits public life in all its diverse forms to take center stage. This is important – the only real point in making urban spaces is to provide places where people of all types and ages can live out full and interesting lives as citizens in a now globalized society. The myriad of small, diverse acts that together create community are best achieved as pedestrians, meeting and interacting with friends, acquaintances and strangers in the street, in the square, on the campus, in the park. The Danish urbanist Jan Gehl celebrates this most clearly in his book *Life Between Buildings*, where he documents the social and cultural richness that is possible in a well-designed pedestrian world (Gehl, 1987). To paraphrase Gehl, 'Life takes place on foot.' Casual encounters in shared spaces are the heart of community life, and if urban spaces are poorly designed, people will hurry through them as quickly as possible, with no thought of stopping, pausing or resting. If the public spaces are attractive, perhaps lined with housing, shops and offices, people may linger and engage in what Gehl calls 'optional activities,' like sitting down in the shade for a moment, or enjoying a sunny corner in the winter (Gehl: pp. 11–16). Perhaps our pedestrians might pause to admire a view, a statue or a fountain, or buy a cup of coffee and chat to acquaintances. It is from these sorts of activities, meeting people while doing something else, that sociability amongst members of a neighborhood can be affirmed and consolidated, and sociability is at the core of community.

It is clear from recent history that the undefined, 'universal' spaces of modernist urbanism did not facilitate this kind of sociable interaction. Nor do the parking lots of contemporary suburbia! Urban designer Jonathan Barnett explains the American dilemma well:

> In most US cities and towns, necessary activities take place using a car, and the opportunities for any kind of casual interaction are much diminished. The commute goes from the garage at home to the garage or parking lot at work. Only the journey from the car space to the lobby takes place on foot. Shopping and errands are done by car to individual destinations. Schools, churches, country clubs, movies – each is a separate destination reachable only by car. The Courthouse Square is empty. People drive to the health club and do their walking on a treadmill. (Barnett, 2003: p. 22)

Some designers, such as Dutch architect Rem Koolhas, believe that modern transportation and the Internet have made traditional urban spaces obsolete; other critics such as Michael Dear have gone so far as to say that 'the phone and the modem have rendered the street irrelevant' (Dear, 1995: p. 31). But many urbanists and critics believe the opposite. Even Kevin Kelly, a leading prophet of the 'geography is dead' theme, qualifies this assertion by admitting that distinctive places retain their value, and that this value will increase despite the non-spatial dimension of information technology (Kelly: pp. 94–95, in Florida: p. 219).

Author Joel Garreau, best known for his seminal book *Edge Cities*, noted that cities are changing faster today than at any time for 150 years, and that computers are reshaping our urban world to favor places that provide and nourish face-to-face contact. Garreau expressed his belief that the urban future could 'look like the 18th century, only cooler.' Edge cities and downtowns 'that are sterile and charmless will die.' Garreau believes the primary purpose of future cities will be to provide optimum conditions for face-to-face contact, an ancient but still primary human need (Garreau, 2001). In similar vein, Bill Mitchell argues in his book, *E-Topia: Urban Life, Jim – But Not As We Know It*, that physical places and urban spaces will retain their relevance in the Internet society specifically because people still care about meeting face-to-face and gravitate to places that offer particular cultural, urban, scenic or climatic attractions that cannot be experienced at the end of a wire and a computer screen (Mitchell: p. 141). In strong opposition to influential designers such as Koolhas and his followers, whose work has been characterized as 'Post Urbanist' (Kelbaugh, 2005), the position in this book is decidedly 'Re-Urbanist,' or New Urbanist – without the

Figure I.2 Housing at Park Hill, Sheffield, UK. These gargantuan exercises in brutalist formalism from the 1960s were highly regarded by architects but despised by most residents. The concrete housing blocks have been listed as Grade II historic buildings and are due for a major refurbishment by the development company Urban Splash whereby 1000 original flats will be converted into 867 new apartments, and the public spaces completely revamped and reconnected to the city center.

overtones of pseudo-historical architecture applied by several American practitioners that obscure and distort New Urbanism's founding aims and intentions.

As background and context to these discussions about the importance of traditional urban space, *Designing Community* examines the uneven relationship between urban design and planning during the 20th century and into the 21st, and affirms the return to physical design as a core discipline of city planning. This remarriage is not as easy as it might sound, for not only has American zoning ignored the design elements of city planning, but more than two decades of postmodernist planning theory in both countries have sought to distance the profession from urban design – generated by antipathy to the sort of urbanism practiced when modernist ideas held sway in the mid-20th century (see Figure I.2). This book charts the transition away from the modernist doctrine of design-based 'blueprint planning' to postmodernist sensibilities of 'planning process over product' and to the most extreme articulations of the postmodern critique, namely that planning is an impossible and illegitimate act in postmodern, post-industrial urban conditions.

To counter this nihilism, the book specifically examines planning and urban design theories that reaffirm the relevance of the discipline, and which support a reintegration of urban design at the forefront of new planning practice. This argument uses postmodernist critiques of planning and design to transform and reinvigorate modernist ideals and ambitions for a better society, informed now by clearer understandings of cultural difference and diversity, and the text examines how this shift has changed the ways we think about cities and the ways in which we design and plan them. Looking at these issues within comparative British and American contexts provides a sharp contrast between the aforementioned government initiative for 'sustainable communities' in Britain and an almost complete antipathy by the American federal government to any form of progressive planning agenda. In the USA it is generally left to individual towns and cities to tackle complex social, cultural and environmental issues on their own, with only a little help, occasionally, from state legislatures.

The term 'urban design' is used so often throughout the book that a brief definition is necessary. This design activity can best be summarized as:

> The relationship between different buildings; the relationship between buildings and the streets, squares, parks, waterways and other spaces that make up the public domain; the nature and quality of the public domain itself; the relationship of one part of a village, town or city with other parts; and the patterns of movement and activity which are thereby established: in short, the complex relationships between all the elements of built and unbuilt space. The appearance and treatment of the spaces between and around buildings is often of comparable importance to the design of buildings themselves … (DETR, 1995: available at www.planning.odpm.gov.uk/ppg/ppg1/02.htm.03)

In short, urban design is about 'designing cities without designing buildings' (Barnett, 1982: p. 55). This definition is important for two reasons. First, it points out the importance of design codes and guidelines in creating mechanisms to control and guide the future work of architects. Master plans of the type discussed in this book are important for setting the vision and direction for a community, but it is the zoning ordinance or design code that actually regulates the form, massing and placement of future buildings within that plan as it eventually 'builds out,' inevitably with some changes from the layout envisaged at inception. Second, much of this book has to do with the pragmatic practice of urban design in communities, creating plans that often have a timeline of 20 years to build-out. The fruits of such work, using charrettes to involve the community in making master plans, the

Figure I.3 Residential tower block, Benwell, Newcastle-upon-Tyne, UK, 1971. Le Corbusier's grand vision of 'towers in the park' translated into cut-price public housing. The poorly defined spaces between isolated buildings quickly became unloved and unlovely.

master plans themselves and the regulating codes with which to guide implementation of the plans, are discussed and analyzed throughout the book in case studies from the British author's own American experience.

This work is prefaced by a review of the major movements and ideas in planning and urbanism that have provoked and prompted planners and designers in Britain and America for the last 100 years. With the wisdom of hindsight, it is easy to identify the 'failings' of modernism from the 1950s through the 1970s: the demolition of whole communities in the name of progress; empty windswept urban landscapes of unloved and unlovely spaces between the 'brutalist' concrete buildings so beloved by architects and so hated by the public; and housing lower-income citizens in ghettoes of bleak high-rise residential towers (see Figure I.3). These are just a few of the most obvious blunders. But these massive miscalculations were perpetrated not by an evil or careless corps of professionals hell-bent on destroying society; they were largely the result of honest, sincere attempts to create a better society by architects and planners who took their jobs very seriously. If there was an overarching problem with the modernist worldview, it was that we, as planning and design professionals, did not listen. We did not listen to what history had to teach us, and we were so convinced we were right that we did not pay attention to what people in communities and neighborhoods were telling us; nor did we take heed soon enough of the critical discourse that was building up within the professions and in parallel and tangential disciplines

in the social sciences and cultural studies during the 1960s onwards. This book makes efforts to avoid those mistakes, and accordingly, the early chapters review the historical development of ideas and methods in Anglo-American planning and urban design during the 20th century, together with an overview of the main theoretical arguments that highlight the intellectual shift from modernist to postmodernist thought.

It is the nature of the complex subjects covered in this book that many topics are inextricably intertwined, and appear at various places within the text, but for clarity the book is organized around a simple framework. It begins by setting the scene for planning and urban design in Britain and the USA with some brief cross-cultural comparisons of the two political cultures and systems of professional discourse. This is followed by three sequential sections: History, Theory and Practice, including two detailed case studies. This straightforward order reinforces one of the author's central contentions: history, theory and practice should be consciously interrelated in the minds of architects and planners. In this regard, the words of philosopher George Santayana provide essential professional guidance: 'Those who cannot remember the past are condemned to repeat it' (Santayana: p. 284). The need for these linkages can be seen in the crises that occurred within the architecture and planning professions during the 1970s as modernist doctrine collapsed and modernist buildings were demolished by dynamite, and in the subsequent, often feverish search for theories that could instigate and justify a rejuvenated practice. Much like architects before them, planners in the 1980s looked outside the profession for clues about how to reconceptualize their tasks and roles in society; this book tells part of the story of that search – and of the return to traditional concepts of physical urban design that are once again at the forefront of planning practice.

This book deals with matters of planning history and theory for two other specific reasons. First, the planning professions in Britain and America are faced with significant changes as urban design becomes once more a central concern to planners not trained in that discipline for several decades. These incursions of design theory and practice are being led by architects, who, acting as urban designers, are challenging planners to rethink the abstract and procedural ways they have conceptualized the city in recent years, and instead to consider urbanism in terms of physical settings, three-dimensional places for social, economic, political and recreational activities. Some postmodern planning theorists view theses developments with dismay, fearing a return to didactic planning where grandiose plans are imposed on communities by well meaning but imprudent designers. Setting out the historical and theoretical context for the revival of urban design as a central discipline of planning enables readers to judge for themselves whether such fears are well founded.

Second, while architects are challenging planners to learn design techniques traditionally associated with the architectural profession, architects themselves are in danger of falling victim to hubris, dismissing decades of planning history and theory as misguided or irrelevant. If architects are to earn credibility from planners, and to avoid repeating modernism's mistakes, designers have to be aware of planning's main traditions and typologies, and be especially cognizant of that discipline's contemporary theoretical debates.

This book thus has some grand ambitions, but in more immediate terms, it has other more modest points of origin rooted in practice and education, not least of which is the author's desire to dispel the common misconception, at least in America, about what constitutes a charrette. The term entered the jargon of American planning in the 1990s from the pioneering architect-planners of the New Urbanist movement, who used it to describe the foundation of their master planning process. As the term 'charrette' and the intensive design process it represented became more widely accepted, the word became more and more abused, and its definition stretched to the point of breaking. At the time of writing in America, it is not uncommon for any meeting organized to discuss some design or planning matter to be called a charrette.

The origins of the term 'charrette' are well known in architectural circles in Britain and America – although a British reviewer of the author's previous book, *Design First: Design-based Planning for Communities* (co-written with his wife, Linda Luise Brown, in 2004) affected for some reason not to be aware of it. Briefly, the word derives from the French for 'little cart,' particularly the one that traveled the streets of Paris in the 19th century collecting the final architectural drawings prepared by students at the Parisian École des Beaux Arts. The students worked on their design projects in different locations around the city, often in the ateliers of their professors, and when they heard the clatter of the little cart's iron-rimmed wheels echoing on the cobblestone streets, they knew their design time was almost up. The sound and the imminent arrival of the cart induced frantic, last minute efforts by the students to complete the drawings. The term has since evolved in architectural jargon to mean any fast-paced design activity that is brought to a conclusion at a fixed time.

The distinction about what constitutes a proper and effective charrette is more than simple semantics. The process itself comprises an important planning tool that is especially relevant in resolving contentious planning and architectural issues in the diffuse, confusing, contradictory and politically charged world of the post-industrial city. Therefore, a more profound reason for writing this book, which in many ways is a follow-up to and elaboration of themes in *Design First*, is to expound the relevance of the charrette as a planning and design methodology particularly well suited to the complex and conflicted planning issues in contemporary American and British urban development.

But charrettes are only one topic examined in this book. They are the public participation component of a tripartite urban design and planning methodology whose companion techniques are a renewed focus on urban design master plans, and the resurgence of 'form-based zoning' (USA) or 'design codes' (UK) whereby the design contents of community master plans are given legal weight. Charrettes provide the forum for meaningful public participation in planning; master plans derived from these charrettes establish and communicate the community's vision in detail; and form-based codes provide the legal framework for implementation of the visions. This last item is particularly important: the codes provide citizens with some reasonable confidence that their community's efforts cannot be easily subverted by developers and errant politicians. Developers also profit from a higher degree of certainty in the planning process and local politicians gain from having very clear guidelines by which to measure future development and change in their community.

In the USA, these three techniques combine to provide the most optimistic way forward in America's struggle to create liveable, sustainable cities in the face of growing environmental and social problems. In the UK, the introduction of form-based coding into that nation's more centralized planning system is a very relevant practical topic, and this book seeks specifically to provide workable advice and examples for the British reader in translating American practice for British conditions. At issue is the extent of detail contained in design codes. In the USA, form-based zoning is constrained in many instances by state laws that limit the amount of architectural detail allowed in development control regulations; typical zoning codes based on urban design principles tend to remain at the level of urban morphology – building massing, siting and the creation of a well-designed public realm of urban spaces. In the UK, initial examples of design coding reveal a desire to move beyond this urbanity and include a level of detail that begins to resemble a 'pattern book' for builders which describes architectural styles in detail. There are many examples of such strict controlling documents in the USA, but they are almost always a function of private, not public codes, and there is a major question concerning the appropriateness of this level of control as part of any public planning regime.

In both countries, these working methods of charrettes, master plans and design codes raise important issues regarding the intellectual 'fit' between planning's renewed emphasis on physical design and postmodernist approaches that are more 'communicative,' whereby plans are not created as finite documents but as flexible constructs of community empowerment based around many diverse viewpoints. Physical master planning carries some overtones of the once-discredited modernist techniques of 'blueprint' planning, where old attitudes of 'the expert knows best' led to many failed urban renewal schemes. This potential trap illustrates the importance of understanding history, but we cannot just start this story in the second half of the 20th century as modernism loosed its grip and postmodern critiques took center stage. Many postmodernist theories focus on greater citizen empowerment and activism, allowing diverse voices to influence, even control, the community planning process, but the roots of community participation in planning and design go much deeper historically, well back into the 19th century and to the European anarchist philosophers and geographers of the period – people like Peter Kropotkin and Elisée Reclus. These thinkers and theorists in turn influenced visionaries such as Ebenezer Howard and Patrick Geddes who were more focused on physical planning for community ideals. To this end, the text takes a brief journey back into the 19th century, examines the patterns of thought that linked these disparate personalities, and establishes their relevance to our more recent and contemporary activities in community planning and urban design.

The intellectual lineage from these 19th and early 20th century European precursors of citizen-powered community design can be usefully connected to several more recent 20th century figures. Large amongst these is American community activist Jane Jacobs, who, in her stingingly critical book, *The Death and Life of Great American Cities* (1961), demolished many modernist planning practices and reputations in the 1950s and 1960s, and avidly promoted learning from existing community patterns instead of abstract planning ideals. Other important protagonists are people

whom we now might regard as the shock troops of postmodernism, the young and idealistic 'advocacy planners' and 'community architects' in America and Britain, respectively, who, like the author, worked in poor communities against the ravages of municipal bureaucracy in the 1970s. Central to the practice of 'community architecture' was the belief that each community had within itself the seeds and capacity for its own revival. From this perspective, what a threatened neighborhood needed was activist professional guidance from architects and planners who identified strongly with the community, perhaps even lived there themselves, and were the catalysts not only for design and planning ideas, but for an upsurge of community energy and direct action – usually directed against city hall and official planning policies.

A unique blending of this kind of assertive community leadership combined with official city policy – what in the USA became known as 'equity planning' – was provided in the UK by Anglo-Swedish architect Ralph Erskine's revolutionary community participation process at the working-class suburb of Byker, in Newcastle-upon-Tyne, England, from 1968 to 1982. This text examines Erskine's work in detail, and no review of community design would be complete without mention of Christopher Alexander's deceptively simple and empowering 'pattern language,' dating from 1977.

These and other precedents feed into the story of communities helping to shape their local environment, a fundamental premise of the charrette process as it has evolved in recent years. When properly designed and managed, charrettes create dynamic public forums where diverse points of view from community interest groups, developers and public officials can be openly discussed. Most importantly, contradictory ideas from these groups can be evaluated by means of quick design explorations and illustrated within a few hours for public comment. In many instances, people's ideas can change when they are able to see what words and planning concepts mean when translated into plans of streets and buildings and three-dimensional renderings of various options; the design drawings enable people to visualize more accurately potential changes for the actual places they know and understand. *It is this quick feedback loop of design testing that distinguishes real charrettes from poor imitations.*

The design explorations from a charrette are then sifted and compiled into a coherent master plan that provides and depicts the vision that is necessary to guide a community's future growth. However, the master plans discussed and illustrated in this book are much more ambitious than the two-dimensional maps that comprise the planner's normative graphic depiction of colored land use zones, and which have sufficed for many decades, in America at least, as the outcome of community visioning and comprehensive planning. The master plans also offer some important advantages over the British system of 'planning and development briefs,' which summarize in graphic form the public authorities' expectations for specific sites. These briefs are very useful in establishing performance requirements to be met by private development and in highlighting particular contextual and/or programmatic factors to be incorporated. However, master plans properly prepared from a charrette process go further: they present potential *solutions* in terms of built form, spatial infrastructure, building uses and the economic development impact of the project – all criteria needed by a community if it is to manage future change effectively.

It is an aphorism that even the best master plans are of little use without regulations specifically formulated to guide their implementation, and the discussions on form-based codes may be of particular interest to British readers. These regulations, as they have been developed in America over the past decade, primarily embody the three-dimensional characteristics of an urban area and its buildings and spaces by means of a series of building and spatial typologies; then, as a secondary level of control these codes regulate the appropriate range of uses within the various building types. Form-based codes put form first and use second, a complete reversal of the use-based zoning that has been the unwitting agency of so much urban and suburban degradation in American cities since World War II. Use-based zoning rarely considers the urban form of communities; everything is a function of use and convenience, with little or no consideration given to what it would actually look and feel like to inhabit new developments and subdivisions. Any mechanism for creating a distinctive sense of place is completely absent from this outdated kind of zoning, common since the 1950s and still the most potent regulatory force in American cities today. These harmful and obsolescent practices, referred to as 'conventional zoning' throughout the text, have no real equivalent in the British system, but in America such zoning regulations have hamstrung many communities' attempts to manage growth effectively, or to promote meaningful infill development.

But before dealing with these technicalities, let us make sure that readers in Britain and the USA have a reasonable grasp of the similarities and differences that pertain to politics, planning and urban design in both countries. That is where we begin.

Cultural comparisons

Setting the scene: Cultural and professional comparisons between planning and urban design in Britain and America

1

SYNOPSIS

Planners and urban designers in the USA and Britain hold many concepts and techniques in common. The political context, however, contrasts sharply, and this chapter examines some of these differences to enable readers in both countries to see their professional interests from the perspective of different political systems. Despite the common language, history and general similarity of the two nations and their capitalist democratic structures, there are deep divisions in political emphasis and culture between them.

Some of the national disparities between social and cultural attitudes in Britain and America are most clearly expressed in urbanism by the effects of differing government policies upon the form of towns and cities. These disparities have profound impacts on the work of planners in both countries, and have been well documented by British authors J.B. Cullingworth, R. Wakeford and John Punter. Briefly they may be summarized under two headings: the extent to which planning systems operate within a framework of constitutionally protected property rights; and the ways in which both nations' history and culture have framed the hierarchies of national, regional and local governments (Cullingworth and Nadin: p. 9). For the British reader, this chapter outlines the basic structure of planning and zoning as practiced in most American towns and cities. For the American audience, the text explains the British concept of a 'plan-led' system, whereby the plan, although not a legally binding document as in some other European countries, provides clear and explicit guidance to be followed about the amount, character and location of desired development. Additionally, the more unified British planning system now places 'sustainable development' at the heart of its policies to an extent unknown in American practice, where this ambition exists only in fragmented instances across that large country.

LEGAL AND POLITICAL FRAMEWORKS IN AMERICA

The Fifth Amendment to the American Constitution states that private property shall not be 'taken by the government for public use without just compensation,' and since all regulation of land use affects property rights, land use and urban design plans can be subject to powerful legal challenge as being in violation of the Constitution. From one point of view, any restriction on the development potential of land by a zoning classification is a 'taking' – an action that takes away value from property owners who may otherwise develop their land for more profitable uses. Despite decades of rulings by the US Supreme Court that land regulation through zoning is legal, the most common American sentiment in regard to property rights remains the oft-quoted injunction that 'nobody can tell me what to do with my land!' In many areas of the country, the idea of controlling land use and urban form is accepted only grudgingly, if at all. Paradoxically, American citizens welcome land use regulation and government action to forbid other people's actions they find objectionable, for example, building an asphalt plant in or near their residential neighborhood. This attitude towards land development is very different from attitudes and expectations in Britain, where, since 1947 the ownership of land has not automatically included any rights to develop it.

To the British observer, the most salient characteristic of the American planning system is its local scale

3

and administration. Whereas the British system extends over the whole country, controlled by central government policies and requirements, and coordinated at a variety of regional and local levels, no such integrated system exists in the much larger USA. (The USA is roughly 40 times the size of Britain, but has only approximately 5 times its population). Indeed government in America was deliberately designed to be 'inefficient' by the framers of the Constitution, with a complex series of checks and balances between federal, state and a multitude of local governments. This system was designed precisely to ensure that power could not be concentrated in the hands of one particular group, thus avoiding the type of centralized control experienced by the colonies under British rule before the Declaration of Independence in 1776. Over more than two centuries this attitude has morphed into a deep public distrust of government, and accordingly, planning in the USA is almost exclusively a local matter. This devolution of power is so localized that even today, many local governments in America – usually smaller towns in rural areas – have only the most minimal planning systems, and some proudly have none at all. Some states do have statewide regimes of planning and growth management to varying degrees, but these comprise only about 25 percent of the total, and from a British perspective even these powers are limited. There is a tangible dislike by a majority of the American public and their elected officials for any large-scale state or regional planning authority.

This condition of contemporary American politics owes much to the founding theories of liberalism developed in Britain during the 18th century. These ideas portrayed an 'atomistic conception of human society,' where human beings were seen as 'rational actors who are the best judges of their own private interests' (Fainstein and Fainstein: p. 281). Liberalism of this type seeks to keep government small, and to diffuse power within society. (This classic meaning of 'liberal' differs from the term in normative American usage at the time of writing, where 'liberal' has for several years been a pejorative term for someone holding ideas that could in any way be classified as left-wing.) Under this theory, social progress is not decided explicitly, but is the result of multiple decisions by many parties, only some of them government agencies, and the government's role is intentionally kept small so as not to influence individual interests unduly.

For more than two decades, since the ascendancy to power by President Ronald Reagan in 1980, Americans have been taught to see government as 'the problem' in this sense and to define progress as commercial success

in the private sector. Specifically, Reagan and his lieutenants engineered a rejection of the welfare society and its social safety net promulgated in the 1960s by President Johnson, and also sought to dismantle the older, activist 'social democratic' approach of President Franklin D. Roosevelt's New Deal policies of the 1930s. With only a partial hiatus under the more progressive administration of President Clinton from 1992 to 2000, this ideology has dominated American politics to the extent that even a populist president like Clinton was forced to retreat from several of his more activist policies.

Under this anti-regulation, anti-government ideology, all solutions to environmental problems, for example, must be 'market-based,' i.e. framed and instigated by companies for their pecuniary gain. In line with the US government's refusal to ratify the 1992 Kyoto international protocols to reduce global warming, federal regulation of pollution by the Environmental Protection Agency has been intentionally weakened by President George W. Bush and Congress after the election in 2000. For example, euphemistically worded legislation such as the 'Clean Skies Initiative' allows power generation companies to increase their profits by rescinding the requirement to install the more advanced pollution control technology mandated by the previous administration of President Clinton.

In the context of similar federal government apathy or antagonism toward socially and environmentally progressive policies in the planning arena, it has been left to individual towns and cities to craft programs of reform and resistance as they seek to define themselves as oases of social and environmental responsibility in the desert of federal indifference or denial. Fortunately, there are many individual municipalities in the USA that take their planning responsibilities seriously, and a good proportion of these are constantly trying new ideas and methods, involving in several cases detailed design thinking in the preparation of new plans. Progressive American communities like these provide the case study examples in this book, which make instructive comparisons with emerging British practice under new planning legislation passed in 2004.

From the perspective of the centralized and hierarchical British planning framework, the diversity of American experience and practice seems almost to refute any idea of a coherent system. As Cullingworth and Punter have pointed out, there are over 40 000 different local governments with sometimes radically divergent ideas about planning that operate within 50 different states that have distinct histories and legal systems. Punter quotes F.J. Popper in describing the American system of land use controls as:

> ... so loose, so deliberately disjointed and open ended, that it is barely a system in the sense that the European elite civil service bureaucracies understand the term. The right to make regulatory decisions shifts unpredictably over time from one level to another. No principle of administrative rationality, constitutional entitlement, economic efficiency, or even ideological predisposition truly determines the government locus of decisions. It is more often a matter of the inevitably uncertain catch-as-catch-can pluralism of ... power politics. (Popper: p. 299, in Punter: p. 7)

There can be no better example of this unpredictability in planning than the passage of 'Measure 37' in the state of Oregon, which since the 1970s has been considered one of the most, if not the most, progressive state in America regarding environmentally sensitive planning concepts and techniques. At a single stroke in the November 2004 state elections, Oregon voters scuppered this planning practice by approving a new law that places individual property rights above any planning legislation and exacts financial penalties from municipalities that zone long-held private properties in ways that diminish their market value for uncontrolled development.

This new property rights law is on the brink of wrecking Oregon's best-in-the-nation record of reining in sprawl and sets up a collision between two radically different visions of how American cities should grow. On the one hand is the concept of managing growth by careful planning, where a high priority is placed on environmental conservation and the long-term public good. On the other is the argument that cities should evolve simply from the self-interested actions of individual property owners, building whatever kinds of development short-term market forces will support. Property rights advocates argue these development rights should be unconstrained by planning of any kind, which many regard as social engineering for socialistic purposes. From this perspective, planning restricts individual freedom and is thus, by definition, anti-American.

This assertion of the primacy of private property rights has its roots in England, going back as far as the middle ages and the development of English common law, which progressively curtailed the power of centralized government to control land for its own purposes and premiated the rights of personal property owners

(Lai, 1988: p. 15–18). This primacy of private rights over state power was well illustrated after the Great Fire of London in 1666, when King Charles II lacked the legal authority to rebuild London on a well-conceived, efficient and beautiful modern plan such as the one proposed by Sir Christopher Wren. In the absence of government power to overcome individual property owners' desires to rebuild what they had before the fire, and faced with strong middle-class opinion that would brook no interference from the king, Charles' government settled for pragmatic regulations to oversee the city's rebuilding that focused mainly on improved construction, materials and building type classifications without any comprehensive master plan that affected private property.

In some ways Measure 37 is a distant echo of this English sentiment and it illustrates a nationwide paradox in American public opinion – although voters favor protection of farmland and rural open space by a large margin, they vote down these protections if they perceive them as restrictions on personal rights. As an article in *The Washington Post* explains:

> The law compels the government to pay cash to longtime property owners when land-use restrictions reduce the value of their property – or, if the government can't pay, to allow owners to develop their land as they see fit. Because there is virtually no local or state money to pay landowners, Measure 37 is starting to unravel smart-growth laws that have defined living patterns, set land prices and protected open space in this state for more than three decades. Although the unraveling is being watched with alarm by smart-growth advocates across the country, it is exactly what local backers of the new law say they want as recompense for what they describe as years of arbitrary bossiness in the enforcement of land-use restrictions. Smart-growth laws attempt to direct development to areas served by existing roads and utilities and curtail new housing and business construction that will sprawl out to rural areas.
>
> 'If you are going to restrict what someone can do with his land, then you have to pay for it,' said Dale Riddle, vice president for legal affairs at Seneca Jones Timber Co., an Oregon firm that was the largest donor to the campaign for Measure 37. Measure 37 was sold to voters last year as a matter of fairness. On ubiquitous radio ads, the frail, woebegone voice of Dorothy English, who bought land in 1953, explained how land-use laws had blocked her from dividing her 40 acres for her children. 'I'm 91 years old, my husband is dead and I don't know how

much longer I can fight,' she said. The ballot measure won with 61 percent of the vote.

State financial records, though, show that small family farmers contributed virtually nothing to the Family Farm Preservation political action committee that bankrolled Measure 37. Most of the money came from timber companies and real estate interests that stand to profit if, as many here expect, large tracts of forests and farmland are unlocked for development. (Harden, 2005)

This unethical marketing and financing ploy reflects a national pattern, where property rights campaigns are often sold to voters as compensation for struggling small landholders against 'big brother' government bureaucracy, while in fact the campaigns are instigated and supported by large companies seeking ways around regulations that limit mining, logging and large-scale property development.

Oregon's new law, which was challenged and reversed in the lower courts before being upheld by the state supreme court, has spawned copycat legislation elsewhere, and galvanized opponents of planning and 'Smart Growth' across the USA. (Smart Growth is the generic term for attempts at creating more sustainable alternatives to untrammeled suburban expansion around American towns and cities.) In neighboring Washington State, another state with progressive environmental legislation, a 'Property Fairness Initiative' has been introduced in the legislature that would mandate compensation be paid to property owners for all government regulation since January 1996 that decreased land value. Under this proposed law a wide array of land use and environmental laws and regulations, including landscape buffer requirements, habitat designations, building codes or zoning restrictions, would be rendered invalid, as no local government would have enough money to pay every land owner for every decision that affected property values. Like Measure 37 in Oregon, the Washington initiative poses a major threat to state and local planning; indeed proponents of this kind of legislation make no secret of their desire to dismantle or destroy land use planning as a function of government in America. Similar anti-planning initiatives are being considered or enacted in Wisconsin, Illinois and California. Four other states, Louisiana, Texas, Mississippi and Florida (all in the politically conservative American South) already have differing forms of regulatory compensation laws that take aim at the same progressive planning practices as Measure 37 (Homsy: pp. 16–19). In October 2006, the American House of Representatives went one

step further and passed the Private Property Rights Implementation Act, which makes it easier for developers and property owners everywhere in the USA to claim financial compensation from local councils for any zoning or environmental regulation that reduces the development potential of a site. The head of the National Association of Home Builders gleefully referred to this measure as 'a hammer to the head' of American local government. Property rights advocates are expected to seek Senate approval for a similar measure in order to make this fundamental attack on planning the law of the land.

The fractious and fractured nature of local government in America is itself an issue in any comparative study with British practice. Some British commentators have variously described American local government as 'fiercely localist, fragmented, balkanized, participative, corrupt, financially autonomous, lean and under-resourced; each of these words encapsulates one key aspect of a system that has evolved over two centuries largely without state or federal direction' and one where 'corruption is regularly rewarded' (Wakeford, 1990; Cullingworth, 1993, in Punter: p. 7). Local governments are often fiercely competitive with their neighbors over the issue of new development because each town's finances rely extensively on local property taxes and sales taxes for their sources of income. However, uncritical popular belief continues to support generic suburban growth, seemingly unaware of the difficult financial consequences looming around the corner. Commercial development usually brings in more money in taxes than a municipality spends to provide services such as water, sewer, police and fire protection to that development, and thus office parks and shopping centers are much sought after by elected officials and town staff; by contrast, most low-density housing estates or subdivisions (except the most exclusively expensive versions) cost considerably more to service than a town can recoup in local taxes because household members expect and require civic amenities such as schools, libraries and parks, all of which are expensive to construct and maintain (Burchell *et al.*, 2005). These financial equations cause local taxes to rise to support the costs of growth, and despite holding strong views about the primacy of property rights there is often a pervasive and contradictory anti-growth sentiment amongst citizens.

Many municipalities are chronically under-resourced to be able to deal with these conflicting pressures, and in several towns where the author has worked as a consultant, there have been neither sufficient financial resources to match the town's ambitions for growth management, nor town staff with the time or experience to administer zoning plans or regulations. For this reason, amongst others, many small American communities undertake little or no planning or zoning functions, and if plans are made and adopted, they often fall by the wayside for lack of administrative expertise or the ability to pay for the necessary staff.

Despite the variable conditions of planning across America, and with the caveat that national and most state governments in America lack agendas for the kind of sustainable development promoted avidly by British authorities, the broad policy objectives and operational techniques in much American planning would be familiar to most British professionals: analyzing communities, setting a vision for future patterns of development and infrastructure provision, and managing the changes as they occur. The most fundamental variation between the two national systems resides in the relationship between planning for the future and the regulation of development to achieve that goal. In Britain, and in Europe generally, the two functions are indivisible: control of development is carried out in accordance with the adopted plan. This is far from the case in America, where the creation of strategies to guide development (planning) is crucially sundered from the mechanisms of development control (zoning). Planning provides the vision, but zoning, based in pragmatic and political realities (which often do not match the plan vision) is what actually controls development. The potential for ambiguity and conflict is ripe.

The 'Great American Divide': The Divorce of Planning from Zoning

This divorce between planning and zoning has been discussed elsewhere (Walters and Brown: pp. 109–112; Cullingworth, 1993, 1997), but in summary, conventional zoning is site specific and rarely considers any criteria beyond the boundary of a specific site or project, whereas planning, by contrast, concerns itself with large-scale issues and future possibilities over larger areas. But public plans in America are usually generalized and advisory only; they have no force of law and are frequently ignored when influential people or wealthy developers apply to build projects that contradict the official plan. This relative impotence of planning is partly explained by the fact that zoning became a practice with the force of law earlier than any planning legislation.

The precepts of the Constitution have always colored American attitudes to land ownership and land use planning, and are central to that nation's concepts of personal independence and its version of democracy. For Americans, land is a 'replaceable, tradable, exploitable commodity like any other' (Punter: p. 9) and zoning evolved in the early 20th century as a device for protecting the interests of property owners from development they considered undesirable. This exclusion was achieved by separating uses and prohibiting those that could reduce the value of existing properties. The constitutionality of this practice was securely established by the Supreme Court decision of *Village of Euclid et al. v. Ambler Realty Co.* in 1926 and the Standard State Zoning Enabling Act passed that same year provided a model for individual states to set up their own statutes to allow individual municipalities to create zoning regulations. The act stated that such zoning regulations should be made in accordance with a 'comprehensive plan,' but this meant simply that zoning regulations should cover the whole area of a municipality, not that the town or city should have a plan that dealt comprehensively with future visions for community development or urban form (Lai, 1988: pp. 118–119).

Since their inception, zoning regulations have controlled the 'kinds of activities that can be accommodated on a given piece of land, the amount of space devoted to those activities and the ways that buildings may be placed and shaped' (Barnett, 2004: p. 2). Conventional zoning has therefore dealt in some ways with three-dimensional issues of building placement on sites and the shape and massing of buildings, but in only the most prosaic and crude manner. Most crucially, these timid essays into issues of form and massing usually consider the building as an object unto itself, with little or no regard for the ways that structures relate to each other in terms of creating meaningful, attractive and useful public spaces between buildings. This bland and bureaucratic division of space is also facilitated by American subdivision ordinances, which control the details of dividing properties into smaller parcels. Standards that specify the size and shape of plots of land, the design and engineering criteria for streets and rules governing open space are generally all located in subdivision ordinances. In practice, most of these ordinances are based on generic engineering concepts of excessively wide streets and turning radii, which, when combined with restrictions of the angle streets can slope, have led to excessive and destructive clear cutting and flattening of development sites across the nation. All sense of place and distinctive geography is lost in this process, and American man-made habitats often assume a dull and dreary sameness. Despite more sophisticated planning legislation, new developments around the edges of British towns and cities suffer from similar symptoms of this place-less condition. A major ambition of the British government's move to incorporate form-based codes into British planning legislation is precisely to overcome the aesthetic and environmental problems caused by the poor design of new developments (see Figure I.1 in the Introduction).

Another primary partner to conventional zoning ordinances in America is the zoning map, a two-dimensional representation of a city, town or neighborhood with colored areas representing zones of different and segregated uses. Because each purpose has a different zone, allowing uses to mix together would create a graphically confusing mishmash of different colors, giving the appearance of random disorder. Thus for conceptual and pragmatic reasons, conventional zoning leads to ever larger, more simplified single-use zoning districts that are easy to grasp and simple to administer. Each function is buffered from its neighbor and a clear logical system is put in place. Unfortunately, this system destroyed most, if not all of the character that gave life and distinctiveness to American urban places. In creating a simple bureaucratic vision of the world, the much-loved America of the older towns, cities, or streetcar suburbs became illegal. In short, as Jonathan Barnett has pithily stated, 'unnecessarily exclusive zones, plus mindless mapping of these zones over large areas, is a big part of the recipe for suburban sprawl' (Barnett, 2004: p. 3).

By the latter half of the 20th century, zoning had morphed from being a rigid and predictable division of land that protected property values into a commodity as tradable as the land it regulated. It became the primary bargaining chip in the legal and financial game of property development: rezoning land to facilitate a more profitable use is one of the main objectives of any American developer, while neighborhood groups usually line up to oppose such changes. Most of the work done by planners in high-growth cities like Charlotte, NC, takes the form of dealing with rezoning petitions, where developers or property owners want to change the types or density of development on parcels of land from that originally prescribed by the city's plan. The growth pressures in places like Charlotte are so great, and the political influence wielded by developers over politicians so powerful and commonplace, that most rezoning requests are granted, often against the advice of the

city's professional planners. Sometimes compromise can be agreed with neighboring residents, but this process of constant revision renders plans prepared by the city mostly worthless, as zoning changes can radically change the pattern of urban development from that envisaged by planners.

In an attempt to bring some order to this runaway process, a North Carolina state legislator promoted new legislation that now requires all city and town councils in North Carolina to state explicitly whether a proposed zoning change is consistent with the relevant city plan before voting on the change. The intention of the new state law was to make elected officials think twice before going against an adopted plan and to make zoning decisions more transparent to the public, but at a council meeting in January 2006, the Mayor of Charlotte, one Pat McCrory, angrily denounced this modest impediment to the city's longstanding practice of ignoring adopted plans in favor of developers' desires as 'bureaucratic junk.'

In this rezoning process, many conflicts between developers and neighborhood groups devolve into merely a squabble over numbers. Say, for example, a developer wants to raise the density on a site from four dwellings per acre to eight (from 10 to 20 units per hectare). Neighborhood activists automatically oppose the new number, suspicious from the outset that it constitutes overdevelopment of the site from the community perspective. A compromise may be reached at, say, a density of six dwellings per acre (15 per hectare) but design is often not a factor; indeed, because design is rarely an integral element of conventional, use-based zoning categories, it has little legal impact. Generally, the main variables under discussion are the numbers, dwellings per acre in residential development or building areas in commercial projects. This is one of the crucial problems that American form-based zoning confronts directly: design criteria for building form, massing and public space design are embedded by drawings, diagrams, photos and text of form-based zoning codes, and thus become matters of legal fact rather than easily ignored suggestions or guidelines.

To overcome the problems caused by lack of design concepts within conventional zoning regulations, several progressive American municipalities have made strenuous efforts to integrate design into their planning policies in other ways. San Francisco, San Diego, New York and some other major cities developed complex policies that incorporate urban design standards; mid-size communities like Austin, TX, have created form-based codes as optional categories, but applied only at the request of developers; and in the mid-1990s a few bold places, often smaller towns such as Belmont, Huntersville, Cornelius and Davidson, all in North Carolina, completely rewrote their zoning codes according to form-based principles and in pursuance of new, community-based and comprehensive planning visions for more sustainable urban growth. Since then, form-based coding has made strides in other states, notably California, but most American towns and cities have made few changes to their conventional, use-based policies and practices that have been the norm since the 1950s, and continue to develop in inefficient and wasteful patterns of low-density sprawl. In this context, while American politicians and voters are passing new laws that stringently limit the effectiveness of planning in some areas of the country, an increasing number of individual towns and cities across the nation are reviving the practice of comprehensive planning as communities seek to manage their own futures, seeking more transparency and accountability in government. It is left up to these municipalities and to individual planners, architects and urban designers to reform a planning system that until recently has mandated suburban sprawl in preference to more compact urban patterns. The New Urbanist movement was born from such small-scale initiatives, and with it came the revival of charrettes, master plans and form-based codes as a methodology for working towards more sustainable cities.

This new generation of comprehensive plans is more ambitious than earlier versions that fell into disrepute during the 1950s and 1960s after the failures of urban renewal. In particular, there is now a far greater emphasis on public participation, and a growing sense on the part of American planners that three-dimensional urban design has a much larger role to play than simple, old-fashioned two-dimensional land use maps. This mini-renaissance in comprehensive planning provides the opportunity for communities to rid themselves of the outdated thinking about land use encapsulated by simplistic colored maps and related zoning legislation based solely on use. By incorporating more advanced concepts of design and sustainability into new plans, American planning practice is beginning to converge with its British counterpart.

But anti-planning initiatives such as the new law in Oregon and the Private Property Rights Implementation Act seek to strip all effective planning powers from local authorities, and at the time of writing in 2006, opinion in America is divided as to whether this major challenge to planning and growth management will spread nationwide, or whether public opinion will wake up to the inevitable damage to the American landscape caused by giving market forces free rein. In this latter case, the public could use its referendum power to place pro-planning measures on an election ballot or public opinion could pressure legislators to reverse course and maintain a workable apparatus for growth management and environmental protection.

While these significant cultural questions are pondered by American public and political opinion, most planners in the USA remain facilitators to the development industry and the political will of their local elected officials, who largely remain committed to unrestrained growth and free market capitalism. This local condition is mirrored at state and national levels: there is little appetite in Washington or state legislatures for political intervention in the marketplace to advance social or environmental agendas. Some modest environmental gains were made by some states such as Maryland and Georgia with attempts at regional planning, while the Clinton administration's design-oriented HOPE VI program for reviving defunct public housing and integrating affordable and subsidized housing into market-rate developments achieved significant successes (see Figure 1.1). However, President George W. Bush and his conservative advisors have dismantled this particular program, while the reformist governors of Maryland and Georgia were defeated in subsequent elections and replaced by politicians sympathetic to special interests from the building and development industries responsible for generic sprawl-type development. In the face of government lethargy

Figure 1.1 First Ward HOPE VI project, Charlotte, NC. A crime- and drug-ridden public housing project close to the city center was transformed into a safe and attractive place to live for people with a wide range of incomes.

or more usually, hostility to coordinated planning initiatives, it was left to a small number of individual towns and cities to create their own progressive agendas. Portland, OR, was for years the city most highly regarded by some (and the most hated by others) for its regional transit planning and urban growth boundary, or conserved green belt, around the urbanized area. Of all American cities, Portland is the one whose policies most resemble normative British practice: now these decades of sophisticated planning are severely threatened by Measure 37.

THE BRITISH PLANNING SYSTEM

Apart from a period during the 1980s when British Prime Minister Margaret Thatcher led that country on a parallel path with the neo-liberal approach of her friend and ally President Reagan — one that actively curtailed the scope and objectives of public sector planning — Britain has retained a more socially democratic platform with stronger policies for providing public services such as health care, transportation, energy and housing. This British view meshes with the predominant European belief that 'democracy includes social as well as political rights' (Fainstein and Fainstein: p. 280). Since Tony Blair won the 1997 general election, he and his colleagues have sought to combine elements of Europe's social democratic model with America's brand of private enterprise inherited from Thatcher, but for all its 'Americanization' and privatization of key sectors of the economy, British policies in many areas, including planning and the environment, are more socially aware and progressive than their American federal counterparts.

Without a constitution to define the hierarchy and roles of government, the British system relies heavily on precedent, but the major difference between the planning systems of the two countries can be traced back to the extensive physical damage British cities sustained during World War II and the subsequent need for a massive national rebuilding campaign (see Figure 1.2). Before the war, development and planning in Britain during the 1920s and 1930s showed several similarities to American practice today inasmuch as development was controlled by zoning maps that indicated where land was zoned for industry, open space, residential development at certain densities and so forth. These zoning maps were part of local authority 'planning schemes' originally mandated under the 1909 Housing, Town Planning, Etc. Act of Parliament (the first British legislation to use the phrase 'town planning') with a

view to improving public health and housing standards in new development. This practice was reinforced by the 1919 Housing and Town Planning Act and again in the Town and Country Planning Act of 1932, but the administration of this legislation was cumbersome, convoluted and full of loopholes that enabled crafty developers to build cheap suburban developments along arterial roads around the edges of towns and cities without having to obtain permission or comply with the plan.

The economic depression of the 1930s in Europe and America further complicated conditions, with large areas of Britain suffering great economic hardship and industrial decline. The response to similar economic difficulties in the USA took the form of President Roosevelt's 'New Deal' program of extensive public works and social policies to reduce suffering: in Britain, several urgent reports were produced, the most significant being the Barlow Report, developed in the late 1930s, but not published until the early days of World War II in 1940. This document argued for a clear national policy of government intervention to secure effective economic development and stable employment, and while the report was temporarily shelved due to the outbreak of war, it established an important shift in national thinking about economic development, employment and regionalism that influenced post-war British attitudes about planning and the urban form of cities.

The onset of war in 1939 drastically changed planning and the management of land use in Britain. In the wartime economy, nearly three-quarters of the land area of England was subject to interim emergency development controls, and during the immediate post-war years this practice was extended nationwide so that the development potential of all land was taken into public control to facilitate national rebuilding efforts. Landowners retained ownership of their land at existing (1947) values, with the rights in place at that time, but new laws placed future decisions about development in the hands of democratically elected local authorities. While this has become normal and established precedent for all Britons, for American readers coming from a very different historical and cultural perspective, it is worth quoting from a British wartime report — the 1944 White Paper *The Control of Land Use* (Cmd 6537), written when Britain, Russia and America were clearly winning the war against Germany, and victory was only a matter of time. This report demonstrated the thinking behind national reconstruction in a forthcoming time of peace, presaged the formation of post-war planning legislation and set forth a view for the

Figure 1.2 Plymouth city center after the aerial bombardment by the Luftwaffe in 1941. In seven fearful nights in April and May 1941, nearly 1000 British civilians were killed and another 1000 maimed. The city center was devastated, with almost every building destroyed or badly damaged. The buildings left standing in this photo were burnt-out shells. *(Reproduced by permission of Plymouth City Museum & Art Gallery)*

role of government that has remained widely accepted in the UK to this day:

> Provision for the right use of land, in accordance with a considered policy, is an essential requirement of the government's programme of post-war reconstruction. New houses ... the new layout of areas devastated by enemy action or blighted by reason of age or bad living conditions ... the new schools that will be required ... the balanced distribution of industry ... a healthy and well-balanced agriculture ... the preservation of land for national parks and forests ... the assurance to the people of enjoyment of the sea and countryside in times of leisure ... a new and safer highway system ... [all these things] involve the use of land, and it is essential that their various claims on land should be so harmonized as to ensure for the people of this country the greatest possible measure of individual well-being and national prosperity. (Quoted in Cullingworth and Nadin: p. 22)

This desire for efficient 'harmonization' of land use, so that the urgent task of rebuilding Britain's shattered cities could proceed quickly and efficiently, resulted in the revolutionary change in the concept of land and property rights in the UK embodied in the landmark Town and Country Planning Act of 1947. To this day, private property owners hold legal title to their land as a physical entity, but the rights to develop that land are held communally and dispensed by local government in accordance with detailed community plans that are required to follow key principles established by central government policy. More than anything else, bringing the development rights of property into the public rather than the private domain allowed the British government to instigate and manage widespread, comprehensive planning across the nation on a scale never before attempted, and because of its comprehensiveness, the British planning system has usually included a significant urban design component.

In contrast to Americans believing that government is 'the problem,' Britons by and large still perceive that progressive government action is the best mechanism for solving urgent environmental problems in their now globalized, post-industrial society, and for protecting their social rights as citizens in the face of the often harsh policies of unfettered capitalism. The observation of British political philosopher T.H. Marshall from 1965 that '[s]ocial rights imply an absolute right to a certain standard of civilization which is conditional only on the discharge of the general duties of [democratic] citizenship' (Marshall: p. 103) is still relevant in this regard, and summarizes British sentiment.

Within this framework of rights and responsibilities, the British government can require powerful interest groups to limit or surrender their privileges for the good of other sections of society (Fainstein and Fainstein: p. 280). Whereas the pursuit of private profit shapes the American environment, with government in Washington and state capitals increasingly controlled by the purchasing power of private corporations and well-connected lobbyists, the driving force behind British urban form since 1947 has been a more objective brand of public policy. American urban designer Jonathan Barnett noted wistfully:

> In Great Britain, and in many other European countries, there is a simple solution to the uncertainties created by private real estate development. The planning authorities would simply publish a general plan, and reserve judgments about individual projects until they were ready to be built. In the United States, we are reluctant to give this much discretion to our public officials, as we have not built up the same traditions of professional, and trustworthy, government service. (Barnett, 1974: p. 47)

Planning practice in Britain today is shaped by detailed guidance notes on planning policy issued by the central government; these establish the objectives and preferred mechanisms for action, and local government is required to follow these mandates in drawing up their own detailed plans. In this kind of 'plan-led' system, private developers are expected to follow these directives if they want to get projects approved, and only in exceptional circumstances will developments that do not comply with the plan be permitted. British plans also contain their own integral layers of development control; the specificity of the plans, particularly at the local level, enables definitive guidance and standards to be built into the plan documents from which planners control development. At least that is the theory. The main reason the government has radically overhauled the planning system, and is seeking to guarantee better design in new development through design coding, is because so much suburban development in Britain has fallen well below expected standards.

This government push for better urban design is not a new phenomenon. Beginning in the 1990s, British planning policies began to embrace urban design concepts in a serious manner after more than a decade of government and professional hostility towards such ideas (Punter *et al.*: pp. 12–14). This occurred initially under the leadership of two progressive Ministers for the Environment in Conservative governments, first Chris Patten (whose 1990 speech to the Royal Fine Art Commission 'Good Design is a Good Investment' was a transformation of previous government policies) and later John Gummer, under whose auspices two reports promoting the issue of better urban design were published in 1994 and 1995 (DoE, 1994, 1995).

In the foreword to the 1995 report, Gummer addressed a topic that is key to urban design as a discipline and to the concept of design coding:

> Too much of our debate about development focuses on architecture but ignores urban design. As a result, too much of that debate revolves around a handful of one-off landmark buildings which, by their nature, will not be repeated. These are important, but surely what matters much more is the typical development taking place every week in the streets and squares of England. It is here that so much local character is created or destroyed. (DoE, 1995, unpaginated Preface)

The debate begun by Patten and Gummer over the future form and social context of British cities, and ways to improve the design quality of new developments, was stimulated further by a series of broadsides by HRH The Prince of Wales (notably in his book *A Vision of Britain* and accompanying TV series in 1988) whereby he set forth '10 commandments' that must be considered for harmonious development: place, hierarchy, scale, enclosure, materials, decoration, art, signs, lights and community. Prince Charles argued that architectural and urban designs should always be developed around these issues if new buildings were to harmonize with existing town and cityscapes (HRH Prince of Wales, 1988), and his impassioned advocacy catalyzed a national debate about the role of design guidelines and policies.

In the same year, 1988, Francis Tibbalds, a leading British urban designer, was elected to the presidency of the Royal Town Planning Institute. Significantly, Tibbalds had promoted better urban design in the planning system as a major theme of his election campaign, and he particularly emphasized the quality of the public realm as the primary component of attractive, safe and vital places. Drawing on the 1985 book *Responsive Environments*, a practical handbook of good urban design principles (Bentley *et al.*, 1985), Tibbalds applied these ideas, together with American precedents from excellent urban design studies produced in San Francisco during the 1970s and 1980s, in his landmark *Birmingham Urban Design Study* dating from 1990 (Tibbalds *et al.*, 1990).

Tibbalds' analysis and others like it emphasized concepts of contextual design and the redefinition of the public space of the street as the basis for renewed emphasis on urban design in British planning and development control (Punter *et al.*: p. 13). Over the next few years a national campaign was instigated for better urban design, including a series of government policy guidelines and a good practice guide (DoE, 1995, 1996, 1997, 1999). This was followed in 2000 by further notes on the importance of good urban design with the publication by the DETR (the Department of the Environment, Transport and the Regions) and CABE (the Commission for Architecture and the Built Environment) of the detailed manual *By Design: Urban Design in the Planning System: Towards Better Practice.* This document outlined basic urban design concepts and contained sophisticated guidance on how good urban design can 'shape urban form and generate activity' (DETR, 2000: p. 51). The same year (2000) saw the publication of an even more detailed handbook on urban design, the *Urban Design Compendium*, prepared by the firm of Llewelyn-Davies in association with Alan Baxter and Associates for the government-sponsored bodies English Partnerships and the Housing Corporation. This was followed in 2001 by the guide to the government's Planning Policy Guidance Note 3 entitled *By Design: Better Places to Live* that focused especially on urban housing layout design (DTLR and CABE, 2001), and in 2002 by *Urban Design Guidance: Urban Design Frameworks, Development Briefs and Master Plans*, prepared by the Urban Design Group (Cowan *et al.*, 2002). The last four publications contained a host of urban design information from which an entire urban design program could be taught. In particular, the *Urban Design Compendium*

was intended specifically as a companion volume to *By Design: Urban Design in the Planning System*, and it comprised a source of best practices under six headings: the Fundamentals (of urban design), Appreciating the Context, Creating the Urban Structure, Making the Connections, Detailing the Place, and Implementation and Delivery.

This major move towards greater emphasis on urban design as an arm of government policy was highlighted in Britain by one further key policy document, *Our Towns and Cities: the Future: Delivering an Urban Renaissance* issued by Prime Minister Tony Blair's government in 2000, and based on the 1999 report of a government-appointed Urban Task Force, led by the architect-peer Lord (Richard) Rogers of Riverside. This initiative came not a moment too soon, as British cities faced serious problems of revitalization of poor, blighted urban areas complicated by increasing ethnic tensions, and country towns grappled with creeping suburbanization and the loss of previously protected countryside. Over the past 20 years, Britain's suburban landscape has grown to resemble a five-eighths scale model of American sprawl. Everything is slightly smaller than its American precedent, the stores, the shopping trolleys, the people, the cars, the parking lots, the street widths and so on, but the pattern is strikingly and depressingly similar. Edge-of-town shopping areas comprise isolated 'big box' stores, large barren car parks and stand-alone fast food restaurants all accessed only by car – or just occasionally by bus. Nobody would walk willingly to these places (see Figure 1.3).

In the face of this swathe of mediocrity that threatens England's green and pleasant land, the British

Figure 1.3 British suburbia. This bleak edge-of-town shopping center in Harlow, Essex, could be anywhere in Britain.

...ommitment to improving standards in ...ronment through its planning and urban design ... is evident in another mountain of recent publications from the government-appointed body, the Commission for Architecture and the Built Environment. In addition to *By Design: Urban Design in the Planning System: Towards Better Practice* (DETR and CABE, 2000), these include *The Value of Urban Design* (CABE, 2001), *Protecting Design Quality in Planning* (CABE, 2003a), *The Councillor's Guide to Urban Design* (CABE, 2003b), *Making Design Policy Work* (CABE, 2005a) and several others. These initiatives were gathered together into a package of changes to the British system enacted under the Planning and Compulsory Purchase Act, 2004. In particular, this new legislation emphasized the concept of 'spatial planning,' which restored design as a central component of planning. Spatial planning is essentially comprehensive planning in a new, improved form; it 'goes beyond traditional land use planning to bring together and integrate policies for the development and use of land with other policies and programs which influence the nature of places and how they function' (ODPM, 2005: para. 30). Spatial planning 'aims to reconnect planning with physical outcomes' by means of design thinking integrated across all levels of planning, from visual to social and environmental. Issues as diverse as open space management, road design, parking, traffic calming, social infrastructure, educational provision, health facilities, transportation, transit, recycling, waste management and the organization of the public realm all have design implications (CABE, 2005a: pp. 5–8).

Design is integral to this new system at a variety of levels: new plans are required 'to express the strategic spatial vision' of the planning authority; to establish the desired standards for development, and to provide site specific guidance comprising 'development frameworks, masterplans and design codes' to maintain high design quality in new urban projects (CABE, 2005a: p. 4). Central to this new system are Local Development Frameworks (LDFs), portfolios of development documents comprising plans and design policies ranging from strategic proposals for the whole area administered by the local authority to detailed development plans for specific local sites. These LDFs are also required to include implementation strategies and mechanisms for public participation: the emphasis is on the timely delivery of well-designed development by the private sector with appropriate and site-specific allocations of land for this development clearly identified by the public planning authority (Collins and Moren: p. 19). For American readers, this bears

repeating: the local planning authorities in Britain decide, with public consultation, where development will take place and what kind of development it will be (see Figure 3.7). Then private developers create new developments to match the plan.

At the heart of the LDF process and documentation is the physical master planning of key development areas in three-dimensional detail. These studies integrate with other Supplementary Planning Documents (SPDs), which encompass several levels of detail regarding such items as sustainability appraisals (SAs), Strategic Environmental Assessments (SEAs) and Statements of Community Involvement (SCIs) (Collins and Moren: xviii). Within the depths of this murky alphabet soup lurks the solid commitment to improved urban design, based around the traditional concepts of urbanism discussed throughout this book. Most importantly for the topics in this book is the requirement that each LDF must contain SPDs, which include master plans, design or development briefs and in some areas, design codes (see Chapter 5). In this new context, the British government sees design codes as tools for defining good design and then for delivering it as part of the development control process.

COMPARATIVE SUMMARY

This brief comparison between the British and American planning systems can be summarized as the difference between American efforts that try to anticipate trends and market forces, and British desires 'to bend [these trends and forces] in publicly desirable directions' (Cullingworth and Nadin: p. 10). Historical and cultural factors play a large role in determining the objectives and techniques of planning systems, and the British regime, with its attendant focus on sustainability and urban design, is rooted in a strong ethic of land preservation, originated by the husbandry of the aristocratic land-owning class, but taken forward more recently by semi-public bodies such as the Council for the Protection of Rural England (see Figure 1.4). Popular attitudes in favor of preserving the countryside and containing suburban sprawl in the UK are also related to factors such as the early onset of industrialization in the late 17th century with its attendant vivid and visible history of squalid urban development; the small size of the country, where land is manifestly a finite resource; the long history of parliamentary governance; and the integrative power of the professional civil service in national and local government. In this context the restraint of urban growth is a top priority in

Figure 1.4 Ashburton, Devon, UK. This small town nestles within a landscape protected from development by its classification as an 'area of outstanding natural beauty.' The fields surrounding the town have been farmed at least since Saxon times (*c.* 700 AD). This picturesque setting now supports the local tourist economy to a significant extent.

the public's mind; land is something to be conserved and husbanded, and national and local government structures exist to make this a feasible possibility.

In comparison, 'land in the USA has historically been a replaceable commodity that could and should be parceled out for individual control and development; and if one person saw fit to destroy the environment of his valley in pursuit of profit, well, why not? There was always another valley over the next hill' (Cullingworth and Nadin: p. 10). This 'frontier' mentality was forcibly expressed to the author in recent years by a local right-wing politician in Charlotte, NC, who maintained with equanimity that an ugly, polluted city was an acceptable price to pay for the free exercise of individual property rights. The American concept of property rights is founded on the belief that the owner has the right to earn a profit from his land, and to drastically change its character in the process (Cullingworth and Nadin: p. 10). By any reasonable measure, this makes the planner's job in America far more difficult than the equivalent professional role in Great Britain.

Despite these yawning differences in the operational contexts for the planning professions in Britain and America at the outset of the new millennium, urban designers and planners on both sides of the Atlantic find themselves utilizing very similar precepts and typologies for traditional urban forms and spaces in their work. Whatever the differences in origin and philosophy, one consistency has emerged between the two professional cultures: urban design is once again an important topic at the forefront of planning. With this constructive thought in mind, let us now turn our attention to some other historical dimensions of planning and urban design in the two countries.

History

The evolution of the planning process and the changing role of urban design

SYNOPSIS

To an architect, a plan is a drawing; to a planner, it is a written document. From such small but vital distinctions, the two professions have grown apart dramatically over the 60 years since the end of World War II. However, incursions by architects into the field of planning during the last 10 years, particularly under the leadership of New Urbanists in America, are returning the discipline to its roots in physical design. To place this renewed interest in urban design and master planning in its proper perspective, it is necessary to review the main strands of planning theory and practice during the past 100 years, especially the many changes since the heyday of physical and comprehensive planning in the 1950s. This broad historical overview includes perspectives by urban design and planning professionals, social and political scientists, and cultural theorists; it discusses briefly how the different types of planning – social, economic and physical – have been practiced during the 20th century, and how architects and planners have responded to new challenges and opportunities.

This chapter demonstrates how planning theory and practice abandoned its original concepts and methods of physical design and master plans in favor of a quasi-scientific, open-ended systems approach to problem solving. Planning theory then shifted towards 'communicative' planning, where public participation became the most important element, and this people-centered approach has been followed most recently by a revival of form-based master planning as the means to instigate, improve and control new development. Four overlapping critical perspectives capture the richness of this urban history that crosses many different disciplines, including design, sociology, public administration,

economics and politics. First, the scene is set by a brief summary of the normative historical review of some major figures and movements in planning. Second, a broader theoretical view examines the transition from modernism to postmodern thinking about planning and urban design. Third, physical planning and design are placed in the context of their companion disciplines of economic planning and policy analysis. The final and fourth frame of reference examines the six main categories of planning that have been theorized and practiced in British and American cities over the past 100 years.

For planners, some of the material contained in this story may be familiar, but for architects much will be new information, witness again to the bifurcation of the two professions from their common point of origin and early development. The renaissance of physical design gives hope that both professional groups can reconnect their skills to deal effectively with the stark social and environmental challenges embodied in the post-industrial landscapes of both nations. As a first step in this process, and to avoid any ambiguity about the term, it is necessary to define 'urban design' more specifically, beyond the brief characterization established in the Introduction.

DEFINITIONS OF URBAN DESIGN

The term 'urban design' was first coined in America in the 1950s. In 1956, José Luis Sert, Dean at Harvard's Graduate School of Design and a pupil of modernist master architect Le Corbusier, convened the first Urban Design Conference at Harvard and set up the first American urban design program at that university (Shane: p. 63). One year later, in 1957, the American

Institute of Architects set up a committee on urban design (Rowley: p. 306). Other versions of the profession's origins note the University of Pennsylvania's Civic Design Program begun in 1957 and place the date of Harvard's urban design program at 1960 (Barnett, 1982: p. 13). (All three accounts of alleged American professional precedence in this subject area oddly omit mention of the founding in 1909 of the very first Department of Civic Design at the University of Liverpool in England half a century earlier.)

Early definitions of the discipline were similarly ambiguous, and ranged from the design of regional infrastructure to the particulars of street furniture. The great American urbanist Kevin Lynch sought (unsuccessfully) to distinguish between 'urban design,' which he considered to be project-based and limited to the primarily aesthetic arrangement of buildings and spaces, and 'city design', by which he meant a larger, participatory, interdisciplinary and interconnected framework that dealt with all the physical parts of the built environment to which the public had access. By the mid-1960s, when Jonathan Barnett and others operated the innovative and politically ground-breaking Urban Design Group as part of the New York City Planning Commission, Lynch's larger definition had been co-opted into the preferred term 'urban design,' to the extent that in his important book *Urban Design as Public Policy* (1974) Barnett felt no need to provide a specific definition, other than to imply that urban design was the central discipline of civic improvement efforts involving physical design, public policy and political action.

This concept of urban design as a larger framework of spatial and functional design for whole communities quickly crossed the Atlantic, and merged with the existing British 'townscape' traditions of design-based town planning promulgated by Gordon Cullen, Frederick Gibberd, William Holford and Thomas Sharp, amongst others (Rowley: p. 306). British practice since the early years of the 20th century had focused on the clear-cut concept of functional and aesthetic harmony in town design, and this professional craft was practiced by well-meaning but detached experts with little thought for public participation. With the wisdom of hindsight, this kind of urban design modeled on architectural practice might have been limited in its scope, but it did provide a deliverable public service and a defined end product.

The term 'urban design' as used in this book draws on these historical precedents, but is expanded to include more recent understandings of environmental issues and the social dynamics of places. In straightforward terms, urban design means 'the art of making places for people. It includes the way places work and matters such as community safety, as well as how they look. It concerns the connections between people and places, movement and urban form, nature and the built fabric …' (DETR, 2000: p. 8). Urban design therefore 'involves the design of buildings, groups of buildings, spaces and landscapes in villages, towns and cities, and the establishment of frameworks and processes which facilitate successful development' (DETR, 2000: p. 93). More specifically, urban design:

> … draws together the many strands of place-making – environmental responsibility, social equity and economic viability, for example – into the creation of places of beauty and distinct identity. Urban design is derived from but transcends related matters such as planning and transportation policy, architectural design, development economics, landscape [design] and engineering. [It] is about creating a vision for an area and then deploying the skills and resources to realize that vision. (Llewelyn-Davies, 2000: p. 12)

Although these are English definitions, they apply equally to American practice, and this intertwining of Anglo-American procedures extends to many facets in the history of planning and urban design over the last century.

MAJOR HISTORICAL MOVEMENTS IN PLANNING

Planning's formative history is usually constructed around three separate movements that occurred at the end of the 19th century, framed as reactions to urban squalor and harsh living conditions: the Garden City movement originating in the UK, the City Beautiful movement founded in the USA and the major push for public health reform that was common to both countries (Campbell and Fainstein: p. 5). The profession's history is then usually classified into three main periods: (1) the formative years (late 1800s to *c.* 1910) dominated by figures such as Garden City pioneer Ebenezer Howard and City Beautiful designer Daniel Burnham; (2) the modernist period (*c.* 1910–1970) encompassing the birth, development and consolidation of the profession of planning, during which time regional and national initiatives were formulated in both countries and schools of planning were created in British and American universities; and (3) the postmodern era (1970 to the present) characterized by recurring crises where planning as a civic enterprise has been attacked from within the profession and from without. These difficulties were spurred initially by the collapse of the 1960s 'Great Society' ambitions in America and the failure of 'comprehensive' urban renewal on both sides of the Atlantic, and fuelled by consequent low professional esteem and major shifts of professional opinion about the proper processes and products of planning. This condition was compounded in Britain and America during the 1980s by attempts from the Thatcher and Reagan administrations to restrict the roles of governments and planners in urban development and economic affairs. Planners' dilemmas have also been complicated since the 1990s by an upsurge of environmental concerns about sprawl, pollution and the degradation of the landscape, and overall, the last few decades of the 20th century have been characterized by an intense theoretical debate over the roles of planning and urban design in the postmodern period, even to the point of questioning their whole validity.

In contrast to this marked diversity of contemporary opinion, there was a common foundation to all 20th century planning based in the reactions to the evils of the 19th century industrial city. As the 19th century drew to a close, daily life for millions of poor people in the industrial cities of Europe and America was miserable and wretched. Some improvements to the filthy, festering slums of previous decades had been made in Britain as a result of the historic 1875 Public Health Act; increasingly large areas of cities outside London were provided with basic public health facilities such as sewer systems and water supply, but the urban environment in which millions of impoverished families lived and worked remained desolate and depressing – drab, monotonous, still riddled with polluted air and water, and lacking any green spaces or natural areas conducive to relaxation or recreation. Frederick Law Olmsted's urban parks for all classes in American cities such as Boston and New York were the exception rather than the rule; the famous London parks were sited in the more prosperous western areas of the city, and few green spaces penetrated the dark, dank working class terraces that spread for mile after mile east of the city center. Victorian industrial cities may have been powerful economic engines for the expansion of the British Empire and the production of new wealth, but living conditions for the lower classes were still shameful in the extreme. Conditions had improved, it is true, from the utter misery

described by Frederick Engels in his 1845 writings on the conditions of the working poor in Manchester, England, but the publication in 1883 of a pamphlet entitled *The Bitter Cry of Outcast London*, written by a clergyman, Andrew Mearns, provoked a sensational response from the public and led to the formation of the Royal Commission on the Housing of the Working Classes in the following year, 1884, which in turn led to a new batch of legislation aimed at mitigating the terrible situation (Hall, P.: p. 16).

Because the planning profession has some of its roots in these efforts to improve the horrific conditions in which millions of poor Americans and Britons lived during the latter decades of the 19th century, it is worth quoting a passage at length from Mearns' anguished pamphlet to give some sense of the realities he encountered:

> … you have to penetrate courts reeking with poisonous and malodorous gasses arising from accumulations of sewage and refuse scattered in all directions and often flowing beneath your feet; courts, many of them which the sun never penetrates, which are never visited by a breath of fresh air, and which rarely know the virtues of a drop of cleansing water. You have to ascend rotten staircases, which threaten to give way beneath every step, and which in some cases have already broken down, leaving gaps that imperil the limbs and lives of the unwary. You have to grope your way along dark and filthy passages swarming with vermin. Then, if you are not driven back by the intolerable stench, you may gain admittance to the dens in which these thousands of beings … herd together … Every room in these rotten and reeking tenements houses a family, often two. In one cellar a sanitary inspector reports finding a father, mother, three children and four pigs! In another, a missionary found a man ill with small-pox, his wife just recovering from her eighth confinement, and the children running about half naked and covered with filth. Here are seven people living in one underground kitchen, and a little child lying dead in the same room. (Mearns: p. 4, in Hall, P.: pp. 16–17)

Conditions were no better in American cities such as New York or Chicago, where social and religious reformer Jane Addams set up Hull House in 1898, the first of more than 400 Christian settlements in various American cities armed with a missionary zeal to save the poor. In New York, two Housing Tenement Commissions, in 1894 and 1900, sought to improve matters, and reforming legislation was passed in 1901 after a political battle against vested interests and the 'unrestrained greed' of developers. A section of the Commission's report of 1900 described housing conditions in New York as follows:

> The tenement districts of New York are places in which thousands of people are living in the smallest places in which it is possible for human beings to exist – crowded together in dark, ill-ventilated rooms, in many of which the sunlight never enters and in most of which fresh air is unknown. They are centers of disease, poverty, vice and crime ... (DeForest and Veiller, I.: p. 112, in Hall, P.: p. 39)

Reaction to this state of urban squalor provided one of the main catalysts for the development of planning during the early years of the 20th century on both sides of the Atlantic. These urban problems were seen as disastrous consequences of unchecked capitalism and political corruption, and the planning profession's political roots thus lay in the concept of progressive reform, whereby wider concepts of public interest were premiated over narrow, often conflicting interests of individuals and groups. The profession's parallel origins in architecture and landscape architecture formed early views of planning as extending architecture's purpose of improving amenities from the scale of a building to the city as a whole (Klosterman, 1985).

Planning thus combines several technical, social and aesthetic origins, which accounts for the profession's 'eclectic blend of design, civil engineering, local politics, community organization and social justice' (Campbell and Fainstein: p. 5). Underlying these various interests and disciplines was a belief in the power of professional expertise in design and engineering allied to scientific method and purposeful, rational thinking. The possibility of violent revolution by the discontented and distressed working classes was a significant worry to the political and business elites in the major cities of Europe and America, and early planners were convinced that this combination of professionalism and rational planning would promote economic growth and political stability more effectively than the uncoordinated activities of private capital.

The formative years of city planning were thus shaped by the overarching sense of the industrial city as symbol of social disorder that had to be tamed and reconfigured, but efforts to do so generally took the form of uncoordinated municipal or voluntary initiatives without clear government commitments. Planning

techniques were heavily influenced by the fledgling profession's architectural lineage and the predominant method was the physical design 'blueprint,' where the main themes comprised a lowering of residential densities to provide more daylight and sunlight into dwellings, more green space integrated into neighborhoods, and controlled suburban expansion combined with new garden cities. In America the City Beautiful movement, though short-lived, provided a clear civic design vision at the beginning of the 20th century, while in Britain, Raymond Unwin's massive tome *Town Planning in Practice* (1909) and his influential pamphlet *Nothing Gained by Overcrowding* (1912) were seminal texts that molded planners' thinking.

After the tragic interlude of World War I, the planning profession's formative phase transitioned into a period of consolidated growth on both sides of the Atlantic. In Europe, the 1920s and 1930s fostered the heyday of modernism as an avant-garde movement in both architecture and planning. Energy and innovation in new social housing in Europe, typified by the excellent work of Ernst May in Frankfurt from 1925 to 1933, was matched across the ocean by farsighted attempts at regional planning led by the Regional Planning Association of America (RPAA). This body was created in 1923 under the leadership of urban critic Lewis Mumford, architect-planners Clarence Stein, Henry Wright and Frederick Lee Ackerman, environmentalist Benton MacKaye (founder of the Appalachian Trail), economist Stuart Chase, developer Alexander Bing, architectural editor Charles Whitaker, and housing activist Catherine Bauer. Although brief, the influence of the RPAA was considerable on American government policy in the 1930s, creating the intellectual framework for massive 'New Deal' projects, such as the Tennessee Valley Authority's restructuring of large parts of middle America, and the innovative but ultimately doomed new towns movement.

World War II brought this period of heady avant-garde experimentation to a brutal close, and after the war the huge task of rebuilding Europe's cities and the economies of its member nations was the catalyst for institutionalizing the pre-war initiatives into government policies. Most dramatic was Britain's New Towns program, a state-financed version of Howard's Garden City vision and, despite its flaws, one of modernism's resounding success stories in its scope and efficiency. Much as in Howard's cooperative vision decades earlier, urban dwellers were transplanted from densely packed, older and often damaged areas of London and other industrial cities into new, lower-density towns created in the green belts beyond the urban periphery, and linked by roads and railways. The architecture and urban design of these new towns was generally regarded as less successful, being rendered in a timid and half-hearted modernism blended with a touch of the English vernacular (the exception being Milton Keynes, constructed later in more uncompromising architectural modernist fashion). But time has been kind to these boldly conceived yet modestly constructed environments, and 50 years on, most new towns provide pleasantly low key and effective places to live a decent life.

Planning and city design thus became elements of state policy in Europe, while in America the intellectual heritage of the RPAA was sadly frittered away as public policy promoted massive programs of suburban expansion coupled with redevelopment of inner city areas under the misconceived urban renewal program. In these frenzies of building and demolition, little thought was given to regional, environmental or social consequences. Despite these national differences, comprehensive planning to tackle large-scale urban problems came to the fore as the dominant methodology in both countries, marrying the physical design blueprint techniques inherited from previous decades to new techniques of social and economic management. Together they aimed at creating a unified, or 'unitary', vision for city development that stressed order, coherence and rationality.

These new, radically improved cities were to be created by scientific and rational planning methods and given form by new, crisp and functional architecture; all traces of the old, dirty, corrupt and decadent cities of the past were to be wiped away. In both countries, during the 1950s and 1960s, the logical, rational and forward-looking precepts of modernism seemed unrivalled as the signposts to a better future. In post-World War II Britain, the promise of a new, post-colonial era beckoned, fraught with ambiguity, but also full of potential for a fresh, more egalitarian society. In America, the country woke up to the fact that it had emerged into the post-war period as the most powerful nation on earth as the British Empire dissolved into memory. But in both countries, the visions for transforming their squalid industrial environments into shining utopias perversely created as many problems as they solved.

By the 1970s, cracks were appearing in this structure of modernist ideas and methods, and their intellectual sheen was tarnished by failures on the ground that could not be ignored. The massive scale of the social and environmental predicaments created during the 1960s by wholesale urban redevelopment in Britain and equivalent urban renewal in America (sharpened there by that country's attendant issues of race and discrimination) brought about a crisis of confidence in the aims, objectives and methodologies that were at the heart of the modernist agenda so dear to architects and planners.

FROM MODERNISM TO POSTMODERNISM

Many books have described the problems and eventual collapse of modernism in architecture – most dramatically illustrated by the demolition of dozens of high-rise housing towers during the 1980s and 1990s following the first such spectacle at Pruitt-Igoe in St Louis, MO, in 1972 (Nairn, 1955, 1957; Pawley, 1971; Blake, 1974; Jencks, 1977; Gold, 1997; Hall, 2002; Walters and Brown, 2004; *et al.*). In the vacuum created by these failures, architects cast a wide net outside the profession looking for new ideas that could inform and reinvigorate their efforts now that everything they had most recently learned about architecture from within its own discourse had proved false or useless. Ideas from French literary theory, semiotics, linguistics, philosophy, post-structuralist and deconstructionist cultural studies, and even chaos theory were all fed into the hopper in the search for new paradigms. The superficial result was a rash of buildings whose willful forms and gratuitous historical detail visibly distanced themselves from their modernist forbears. At a deeper and more useful level, new outward-looking pluralist thinking and a more open-minded approach to relationships between 'high' architecture and popular culture replaced the ossified dogmas of modernist theory. But an equally interesting development was the renewed interest in finding validation once more from within the historical depth and technical rationale of architectural discourse. This inward search, bred in part by an aversion to the callow superficiality of many postmodern endeavors and the incomprehensible nature of much writing about architecture from positions within critical studies and cultural theory, proceeded along two axes: a deeper study of the history and theory of architecture and urbanism, and a revived interest in advanced contemporary building technology.

In the latter direction, this refreshed focus on technology spawned the refinement of high-tech architecture in the work of designers such as Norman Foster, Richard Rogers and others during the 1980s and 1990s, leading today to exciting new interests in sustainability and 'green' design. In a kindred avenue of exploration, sophisticated computer technologies have

Figure 2.1 The Sage performing arts center, Gateshead, in northeast England, 2004; Norman Foster and Partners, Architects. One of the better examples of 'blob' buildings dropped into cities as a means of urban regeneration by eye-catching architecture. In the hands of less talented designers, such buildings can destroy cohesive urban space by their obsession with their own form.

opened up a whole new range of formal vocabularies and three-dimensional fabrication techniques, relevant at scales varying from interior design to whole buildings. Although fascinating and important in many respects (see Figure 2.1), this tendency towards wild new forms, created largely for no other reason than they are now possible, raises doubts amongst many urbanists, who see in this outburst of blob-like formalism a return by architects to the anti-contextual object worship that was so problematic during the modernist period.

At the other end of the spectrum from this technologically motivated search for newness, a revived appreciation developed for certain architectural types and urban patterns that have retained their usefulness throughout history. Beginning in the 1970s, these typological and morphological approaches offered architects and urbanists more substantial bases for design than the fleeting newness of modernism or neo-modernism, however technologically seductive. Building types and urban morphologies manifested themselves in the work of European architects such as Aldo Rossi and Rob and Leon Krier during the 1970s with their advocacy for the urban forms of traditional European cities. These interests spread to American academia in the 1970s and 1980s through the pioneering work of teachers such as Michael Dennis and Colin Rowe at Cornell University and Vincent Scully at Yale, where they combined with a renewed interest in American urban vernacular types. This heady mixture affected a new generation of young architects, including Andres Duany and Elizabeth Plater-Zyberk who catalyzed widespread American interest in traditional urban forms through their innovative work on

Traditional Neighborhood Development (TND) from the 1980s onwards. This revival of traditional urbanism on the east coast of the USA melded with the more ecologically driven Transit-Oriented Development (TOD) concepts of Peter Calthorpe, Douglas Kelbaugh and Daniel Solomon on the west coast to form the contemporary movement of New Urbanism in the early 1990s. Beyond this confluence of ideas, the international origins and growth of New Urbanism have been dealt with at length in this author's previous book *Design First* (Walters and Brown: pp. 53–73), which illustrated how many of the ideas about urban design that are now labeled 'New Urbanist' were in fact, as Seattle architect and activist Michael Pyatok has also explained, 'the natural convergence of ideas incubating among thousands of my peers who, over the past 30 years, have been rethinking, experimenting, and practicing … better ways of organizing humanity' (Pyatok: p. 803).

In the same way that architects cast a wide net searching for new paradigms of theory and practice about working in the city after the failure of modernist doctrine, planners followed a similar pattern. First came the grudging acceptance of the collapse of modernist ideas and techniques; second came the quest outside the discipline for other means of validation; and third, the renewed interest in reappraising some older ideas from within planning's own professional discourse. Common to several strands of planning practice in the 1960s and 1970s was the increasing reliance on the social sciences for information and techniques of operation, particularly in what became known as 'systems planning' and 'democratic planning.' Despite the potential usefulness of social science material, planners were faced with the fact that this approach had not greatly improved their practice, and so by the early 1980s '[f]urther digging among the social sciences or returning to planning's design origins seemed less likely to bear fruit than exploring other domains, especially in the humanities. The places to which planners turned [in the second phase of their search] described the intricate interweaving of social practices, norms, behavior and language, and ... showed that ... reality is a social construction' rather than a physical one (Moore Milroy: p. 182). Examples of these postmodern searches for ways to apply broader cultural principles into a revived planning practice can be found, for example, in phenomenology (Bolan, 1980; Lim and Albrecht, 1987), in critical theory (Albrecht and Lim, 1986), in pragmatism (Hoch, 1984) or in feminism (Moore Milroy, 1991).

Moore Milroy's point about reality now being considered a social construct, and therefore subjective and variable, is an important one for architects and planners alike, because modernist theory and practice operated from the opposite assumption, that empirical methods of observation and analysis into human behavior could reveal quantifiable and useful 'objective' information to guide designers and planners. This simplistic thinking, known as architectural determinism – the belief that the design and layout of buildings could influence behavior – fell into academic disrepute during the 1960s, but it remained a potent concept in urban design at least through the mid-1980s, when Alice Coleman's widely read study of that decade's urban riots in Britain linked this violence directly to the failures of modern architecture and planning (Coleman, 1985). Although the social, racial and economic situation in 1980s Britain that bred the riots was far more complex than the cause-and-effect argument about the physical environment, the simplistic connection was a compelling one in the public mind. It was easier to blame architecture and planning than to deal with the deep-seated problems of social inequity and racial tension.

The self-assurance and belief of planners 'in their right and ability to shape urban and regional space through the application of ... scientific ... rationality' (Harrison: p. 3) was challenged in several ways: first by left- and right-wing critical theories about urban affairs; second by postmodernism and different views about culture and society; third by globalization and its attendant economic uncertainties as money moved freely around the globe in search of profit, leaving behind once prosperous places now mired in decay; and fourthly by the 'irrational' forces of urban politics,

fed by individual and diverging concepts of 'value, difference, power and identity' within communities (Harrison: p. 3). The idea that empirical analysis of social phenomena could still provide useful 'hard' information for planners and designers retained its operational power within the planning profession, but new and contrasting postmodern perspectives began to suggest that 'soft' information about how people defined and perceived their environment was more important, even if it revealed circumstances that were more diffuse, ambiguous and sometimes contradictory. These new insights were derived largely through cultural and communication studies, paralleling architecture's search for new sources of theory external to the discipline. During the 1990s, therefore, a lot of planning theory revolved around the dilemma created between modernism and postmodernism, between planning's historical purpose of creating the 'ideal city' in terms of physical order, functional efficiency and social homogeneity, and the new realization that society and its urban forms were complex, contradictory, flexible, discontinuous and fragmentary – resistant to the idea of a single, consensual viewpoint about what was ideal or what constituted the 'public interest.'

While planning theorists were preoccupied with these more abstruse issues, planning practitioners were running the gamut of various techniques, seeking valid and useful ways to process this newfound complexity. Almost all these methods, in their rejection of modernist comprehensive planning, turned their backs on physical design as a priority, concentrating instead on planning as a communicative process, trying to recast the planner as a facilitator in a shifting social and cultural conversation about urban issues. Process became more important than product, but in many ways the urban condition showed no measurable improvement. In both Britain and America, social and ethnic tensions increased in central cities and some older suburbs, the economic and social gaps widened between the 'haves' and 'have-nots,' air and water pollution worsened, caused by new development and increasing automobile use, and precious countryside around towns and cities came under increased development pressure.

Contrasted with this list of problems, there were some success stories, with several older urban areas reinventing and rejuvenating themselves, attracting new investment and populations. Urban regeneration and city living became fashionable on both sides of the Atlantic, a welcome counterpoint to the ever-widening rings of low-density suburbia that exacerbated environmental problems (see Figure 2.2). The physical design of places became an important factor

Figure 2.2 Uptown Housing on the Green, Charlotte, NC; FMK Architects. High-density urban living is now commonplace in the center of mid-size American cities such as Charlotte. This good example is constructed over an underground parking garage topped by a landscaped park, providing the city with good public space replete with public art.

in this largely market-driven urban revival, returning planning once again to its roots of civic design.

This return to physical planning was prompted by a dramatic incursion into planning by architects such as this author and many others beginning in the 1980s. As planning theory and practice meandered away from physical design in search of new paradigms, architects, acting as urban designers, took over this vacant territory and reinvented this once-traditional arm of planning practice. In America, architects loosely organized under the banner of what became New Urbanism preached a radical, conservative revolution, setting forth a new design-based vision of walkable, compact, transit-supportive communities that offered a real alternative to car-dominated, energy expensive suburbia. Most importantly, these architects did not stop at designing this vision; following the example of Andres Duany and Elizabeth Plater-Zyberk, they branched out into the unlikely field of writing and illustrating zoning ordinances, up till that point almost exclusively the domain of planning professionals.

The power of zoning codes to shape urban form is well illustrated by the American landscape in 2006, which is still dominated by sprawling, segregated, single-use, low-density developments, the products of old-fashioned ordinances that mold development into the car-dependent patterns first created in the 1950s. No changes could be wrought on this inefficient and

often ugly landscape without altering these regulations, and in a rallying cry to his fellow architects (and calling up references from his Cuban-American heritage) Duany urged the new corps of avant-garde urban designers to go out 'and capture the transmitters,' i.e. rewrite the zoning codes.

This author helped create such form-based zoning ordinances in several towns around the Charlotte, NC, region during the mid-1990s and has continued that work to the present time of writing in 2006 – creating master plans and design codes that instigate and regulate new development, and engaging in public participation exercises that help validate such plans. More recent British initiatives, comprising attempts by national government to translate this American experience into the British planning system through design codes for new developments, provide fertile ground for comparisons and contrasts between the two countries and their systems of development and planning regulation. These circumstances also provide a very interesting commentary on the continuing dialectic between modernist ideas and postmodern practices. For example, the official British government policies to promote better urban design in new development and to create 'sustainable communities' – ones that aim to revitalize local economies, reduce energy use, protect the environment, promote diversity, and improve education, health and housing – place the technique of master planning at the center of the whole enterprise. While reiterating the postmodern demand for effective participation of diverse client and user groups, government guidance defines master planning as 'coordinating and developing information so that [it fits] together as a coherent whole,' a very modernist ambition (English Partnerships, 1999: unpaginated). In his Foreword to *Creating Successful Masterplans: A Guide for Clients*, Jon Rouse, then Chief Executive of CABE (the Commission for Architecture and the Built Environment, Britain's government-appointed advisory body on architecture and planning), states clearly that urban design master planning is a core element of the government's urban renaissance strategy for Britain's towns and cities:

The good news is that the importance of master-planning *is now understood once again*. Indeed, it would be almost unthinkable for a significant new development to proceed without a masterplan. *This is a remarkable shift in a short period of time* but it introduces important questions. How can we be sure we are good at this process of masterplanning? How should we go about drawing up and adopting masterplans that will result in places where people want to live, work and play? (CABE, 2004a: p. 3)

The phrases this author has italicized for emphasis indicate an unmistakable return to modernist principles of a coherent spatial strategy that brings order to an urban area by providing a clear and authoritative vision. Successful master plans, Rouse goes on to argue, are those that combine 'clear three-dimensional representations of how a place can change, backed up by solid social and economic analysis and a clear, useful set of design principles' (CABE, 2004a: p. 3). Repeated use of the word 'clear' refutes the notion of ambiguity so central to postmodernist worldviews, and as if to hammer home the point of a return to modernist thinking in the UK regarding the role of the professional expert in creating new plans, an advertisement for a major conference in 2006 on the future of European cities, entitled 'Masterplanning and the European City,' proclaims that 'masterplanning is governing the development and regeneration of our cities … The future success of our European cities relies *upon the professionals who shape our attitude* to built form and context' (Flyer for the Fifth Annual *Architectural Review* Conference, 2006; this author's italics added again for emphasis).

These sentiments clearly indicate a return to modernist concepts of civic design in planning, but now (one hopes) somewhat refreshed and improved by a postmodern awareness of the importance of public participation and diversity. As Prince Charles famously said: 'Planning and architecture are much too important to be left to the professionals' (HRH The Prince of Wales, 1998). However, while the CABE document, *Creating Successful Masterplans*, has sections on public participation, the sentiments about 'consulting and communicating with stakeholders' retain much of the 'command and control' concepts of unreconstructed modernism: 'Time should be given to consultation but not so much that the project is submerged by it. The right amount of information is needed at the right time. Input at the wrong level offered at the wrong time results in unnecessary frustration and delay' (CABE, 2004a: p. 66). By contrast, other British techniques for public participation in planning, such as the 'Enquiry by Design' process promulgated by The Prince's Foundation or 'Planning Weekends,' a staple of community planning practice, have a lot in common with the American charrette process described and illustrated in this book. The charrette's open-ended and inclusive process confers many benefits on the master planning process, and offers a workable

methodology to reconcile modernist and postmodernist concepts that stress contrasting ideas of unity on the one hand and pluralism on the other.

This attempt to mediate between modernism and postmodernism situates this book in a particular place regarding the continuing dialogue between the two paradigms. Various critics have identified a series of viable positions for planning in this context (Lee, 1973; Jameson, 1984; Huyssen, 1986; Habermas, 1987; Flax, 1987; Klotz, 1988; Friedmann, 1989; Murphy, 1989; Beauregard, 1989, 1991; Harvey, 1989; Healey, 1992, 1997; Smart, 1992; Irving, 1993; Sandercock, 1998; Ellin, 1999; Kunzmann, 1999; Taylor, 1999; Nylund, 2001; *et al.*), but the various possibilities can essentially be boiled down to three main alternatives:

1. Postmodernism as a revision of modernism, making adjustments to compensate for modernism's failings, but retaining some core beliefs.
2. Postmodernism as a more radical displacement of some major tenets of modernism, brought about by economic and cultural changes resulting from the globalization of the economy.
3. Postmodernism as a complete and differentiated successor to modernism, a whole new way of understanding society not commensurable with Enlightenment values such as logic, progress and scientific rationality that have been at the very core of modernism. (Moore Milroy: pp. 182–233)

The working methods for urban designers and planners discussed in this book fall largely within the first category, i.e. learning from postmodernist critiques of modernism's failings in order to revise modernism substantially as part of a continuous process of revision and renewal. The methodologies and case studies described in this book illustrate how modernist beliefs can be modified in quite dramatic but realistic ways to reflect new knowledge, to accept ambiguities, and to understand the demands of pluralism and diversity, while at the same time maintaining belief in the continued validity of rational, technical discourse focused on notions of human progress. To this extent, the methodology sometimes occupies territory staked out in the second, more radical option, but it is consistent in rejecting the third interpretation.

However, a simple marriage of rational planning with improved public participation is only one, relatively simplistic, step towards the goal of a newly effective planning framework. The ideal of 'communicative planning' embodied in the charrette format – planning through processes of democratic discussion to uncover meanings and priorities that would otherwise remain invisible – reflects the postmodernist comprehension of the importance of multiple voices and helps to validate any master plan. But the process of democratic argument by itself does not necessarily guarantee equitable urban outcomes: communicative processes are always shaped by the exercise of some kind of power, and the most powerful groups or individuals in a community can often distort the outcome. American and British experience with powerful middle-class NIMBY (Not In My Back Yard) groups are commonplace; there are always people who want to block certain kinds of development out of selfish, exclusionary motives, e.g. a homeless shelter or a facility to help pregnant teenagers, or even housing for people who earn slightly less money than themselves. Planners and designers thus have to exercise ethical judgment in an activist manner to help bring about social justice, or to achieve larger aims such as social and environmental sustainability, and these ethical judgments have to be informed by normative views about what is good and right.

To this trio of planning skills – rational design-based planning, communicative planning to uncover diversity and different viewpoints, and ethical judgment to offset imbalances of power in communities and support social and environmental – should be added a fourth technique: public prophecy. This is 'the ability to envision alternative and better futures, and then to influence myriads of decisions towards those futures … [B]ringing new possibilities for the future into the realm of popular imagination may help make possible what otherwise might not be' (Harrison: p. 12). This future vision will necessarily be fragmentary and provisional; lots of unanticipated consequences and intervening contingencies will interject themselves in the process, 'but the very process of visioning makes a different future more likely' (Harrison: p. 12). Creating visions of the future is at the core of the master planning process, and the recent revival of master planning as a mainstream technique focuses firmly on physical planning and urban design. However, physical planning rarely stands alone; it is most usually related to its companion disciplines of economic planning and policy analysis.

PHYSICAL PLANNING AND URBAN DESIGN IN CONTEXT

Comprehensive planning and its associated urban design vocabulary comprised a cornerstone of modernism,

and the period of transition from this era of unified certainty in the principles and techniques rational analysis and plan-making to the quagmire of uncertainty, relativism and discord that characterizes the recent postmodern period needs to be charted very carefully. The first thing to remember is that physical planning never stands alone. It is preceded by economic planning that decides where, when and how to direct public and private investment, with consequent effects on the physical environments of towns, cities and countryside. Physical planning then orchestrates this development of towns and cities primarily to promote (as British planner Patrick Abercrombie set out in 1933) 'health, economy, convenience and beauty in urban settings' (Healey, 2002: p. 490). Hand in hand with physical planning, policy analysis provides a rational framework for decision making by setting goals and then measuring effectiveness and efficiency in meeting those goals.

Contemporary interest in economic planning derives from critiques of industrial capitalism, most directly from Karl Marx's 19th century attack on the social costs of industrial development, where the drive for maximum profit by entrepreneurs and corporations exploited the work force and severely damaged the environment (see Figure 2.3). More recently, the sense of need for economic planning was enhanced by the repeated experience of market failures, such as a series of economic slumps in the 20th century, most dramatically illustrated by the Depression of the early 1930s. These experiences 'fostered ideas which suggested that economies could be "managed" to avoid market failures' (Healey, 2002: p. 492). In Britain, this tendency was most clearly expressed through government policies based on the ideas of John Maynard Keynes, who argued that economies slumped because of lack of consumer demand, and this crisis could be offset by targeted public expenditures by the state to stimulate demand through maintaining full employment. This 'mixed economy' often took the form of large-scale programs of public works to create more jobs and to pump money back into the economy, all backed by a comprehensive welfare state that took care of public needs of health care, housing and education at the state expense. This state provision enabled companies to keep their labor costs relatively low, as they did not have to provide expensive benefit provisions from within the private sector.

By the 1970s, however, 'these demand-stimulation strategies seemed to have run out of steam' (Healey, 2002: p. 492) as other, non-western countries in the developing world with lower labor costs were able to

Figure 2.3 Power station at Gateshead, UK, seen from the Benwell area of Newcastle-upon-Tyne, 1970. Now demolished, this power station polluted the environment for thousands of working class residents.

undercut the high wage economies of Europe and America. The economic slowdown and rising inflation provided a fertile ground for the seeds of a new set of economic ideas, particularly in Britain and the USA, where neo-liberal economics based on 'free market' ideas and minimum government regulation came to the fore under the ideological leadership of Margaret Thatcher and Ronald Reagan. Here, the role of government was reversed – instead of being an active manipulator of economic conditions to even out the problematic highs and lows of unconstrained capitalism, and minimize the disadvantage experienced by lower-income groups, government was now seen as 'the problem,' a source of regulatory impediment to business. The aim now was to minimize the role of government economic planning, limiting it to managing the money supply and keeping inflation under control, while relying on private enterprise to create new wealth by means of competitive innovation, free from the 'burden' of bureaucratic oversight.

From this point of view, spatial and environmental planning were considered flagrant examples of these 'burdens,' and policies for balancing growth with resources and using public money to stabilize regional economies by promoting development and job growth in declining areas were rejected as 'blockages to supply-side activity.' The adverse social and economic consequences to communities affected by this approach were dismissed as the 'necessary costs of transition to a more soundly-based economy which would generate the wealth to put them right in due course. Planning … was seen not just as unnecessary, but as counterproductive' to this market-based economic strategy (Healey, 2002: p. 493).

However, in a dramatic 'road to Damascus' moment in 1988, Margaret Thatcher underwent a surprising conversion to environmental thinking and the emphasis in economic planning shifted. Thatcher astonished her fellow Conservatives with a resounding endorsement of environmentalism, declaring that Conservatives were 'not merely friends of the earth' but also 'its guardians and trustees for generations to come.' She continued: 'The core of Tory philosophy and the case for protecting the environment are the same. No generation has a freehold on the Earth. All we have is a life tenancy – with a full repairing lease' (Cullingworth and Nadin: p. 168).

Whatever the reasons for Thatcher's change of heart, her speech placed a spotlight on environmental policy, but it provided no clues about how the right-wing government would reconcile its free enterprise philosophy with its newfound environmental stewardship. As Cullingworth and Nadin point out:

[t]he former is characterized by a market orientation, with profits as the reward; the latter revolves around much broader ideas. Market forces do not necessarily work well with environmental protection. Quite the contrary: individuals may be rewarded for actions which harm the environment (and, indeed, they may be subsidized to do so – as with some agricultural policies). Attempts can be made to adjust or influence the market … but there is a limit to the extent to which a government wedded to market ideals can provide incentives (or rewards) for actions which protect the environment … (Cullingworth and Nadin: p. 169)

For this and other reasons, the push in Britain for massive deregulation of economic activity so typical of the 1980s had morphed by the mid-1990s into a renewed interest in regulatory reform, fuelled by increasing public distress with the social consequences of unrestrained 'free market' policies, so poignantly illustrated by the yawning gaps of social and economic inequality exposed in British society. These apprehensions were matched by increasing levels of concern about environmental problems and the nation's 'disappearing countryside,' and by the end of the century the new Labour government led by Prime Minister Tony Blair was advocating the strategic management of change and development in the various regions of the country. Economic planning was back on the agenda, and physical planning was close behind, with urban design now positioned as the main policy instrument for urban regeneration.

Without equivalent government initiatives for managing economic development and patterns of growth, the form of America's cities has devolved to an aggregation of fragments with little cohesive physical form as market forces have been allowed more or less free rein, and planners have been effectively reduced to facilitators of private development. American cities thus represent fascinating but problematic maps of society – landscapes marked by pockets of great wealth and great poverty, sprawling across a schizophrenic panorama of great beauty mixed with development that is often ugly and environmentally harmful. Simultaneously, in some fortunate cities, downtown cores have reinvented themselves as active and popular hubs of culture, entertainment and high-class living, but the economic energy of central urban areas is always in conflict with competitive activities around ever-expanding urban peripheries. To large sections of American populace, any form of regional planning that might resolve this unhelpful dilemma is stigmatized as 'big government' and therefore ideologically unacceptable, allowing these negative tendencies to go unchecked, and the normative cycles of 'boom-and-bust' capitalism remain unhindered. Any economic planning that does occur is usually localized and competitive between individual municipalities as they fight to attract new investment, and physical planning is therefore very limited in its scope and content, rarely rising above the scale of individual projects.

In contrast to the British renaissance in planning and urban design as primary mechanisms within the government's national policies of urban regeneration, planning in America has largely remained the handmaiden of private sector development. Forced by policy and circumstance to play this minor role, American planning has accordingly focused less on visionary projects and major initiatives, and more on modest, strategic agendas regarding 'doable' small changes in

policy. This technique of planning as policy analysis and public administration grew out of American experience in business corporations, and this economic-based logic was transferred to the public sector as a way of making the workings of local government more efficient and effective. Local municipalities were and still are much more fragmented and competitive than their British counterparts, and historically have been much more open to the vagaries of local politics. Research into the workings of American local government illustrates many instances where local politicians have colluded with private interests to promote development that was very profitable to those concerned but detrimental to the larger public interest. While this kind of corruption is certainly not unknown in Britain, it is much more common in the USA, and because of that nation's legal system which equates the spending of money in politics with freedom of 'speech,' the ability of private money and corporate influence to 'buy' laws, policies and decisions from grateful lawmakers is not even illegal, unless this practice reaches excessively blatant proportions and falls foul of some legal technicality. One particular study (Logan and Molotch, 1987) argued that 'US local governance was dominated by property development and investment interests' (Healey, 2002: p. 496); more recently, nationally syndicated columnist Neal Peirce described American democracy as ' a partisan brew of spin, scandal [and] money chasing' (Peirce, 2006). Many planners have experienced instances where chummy relationships between developers and elected officials, often reinforced by gifts of money in the form of 'campaign contributions,' have resulted in the approval of development projects that contradicted established plans, overrode the advice of the professional planners and inflicted damage on the natural environment.

As a means of countering this kind of corruption in America's local politics, techniques of policy analysis were introduced to provide a framework whereby actions by elected officials could be more easily measured against relevant criteria, and individuals held more accountable for their actions. This framework offered rational, objective methods of identifying goals, creating policies, implementing them by making decisions that were guided by these policies and monitoring results. Similar ambitions were achieved in British central and local government by the presence of a solid professional class of civil servants whose expertise could keep politicians in check. In mainland Europe, administrative action by local government is often controlled by legal rules derived from the

Napoleonic code, and both systems help 'constrain the play of political power games and to limit the subversion of administrative systems to private and party political objectives' (Healey, 2002: p. 495).

Understanding something of the national contexts within which planning and urban design take place in Britain and America is an important theme of this book, and underlying this international perspective is the history of city planning in Britain and the USA over the past 100 years. We have examined some of the main origins and periods of planning and we have noted how physical design-based planning is part of a trilogy comprising economics, physical design and policy. Within this broad framework, it is appropriate now to summarize six types of planning that have emerged over the course of the 20th century in Britain and America and which embody the various shifts in theory and practice noted above.

SIX TYPOLOGIES OF PLANNING

These different types can be described as follows:

1. *Traditional* or *comprehensive planning* held sway for most of the first half of the 20th century and was characterized by politically neutral experts, who, it was believed, could take a long-term, dispassionate and rational view of new urban development. This type of planning focused on producing clear statements about the form and content of new development.
2. *Systems planning* flourished from the late 1950s through the 1970s, and resulted from the failure of comprehensive planning to deal effectively with the unforeseen growth that marked the post-World War II period in Britain and America. It promoted a more scientific and analytical view of the city as a set of complex processes, and was less interested in any form of final, physical plan.
3. *Democratic planning* arose on both sides of the Atlantic during the 1960s onwards as a result of transformations in society derived from loosening the traditional, repressive barriers of class and race, and giving more people a voice in the formation of their future.
4. *Advocacy and equity planning* were more activist strands of democratic planning, and sought specifically to address burning social issues of social inequality and injustice in American and British cities. These planning movements were again born during the 1960s and continued through the 1970s.
5. *Strategic and incrementalist planning* focused on small-scale objectives and acknowledged pragmatic real-world constraints. Practiced first in the world of private corporations from the 1950s onwards, these techniques were transferred to the public sector in the 1960s and are still influential today, particularly in America.
6. *Environmental planning* has its roots as far back as Howard's Garden City, but most directly evolved during the 1960s and 1970s when 'many of the ecological and social implications of global development were first widely understood' (Wheeler and Beatley: p. 1). The growing environmental crises of climate change and global warming evident at the beginning of the 21st century have lent an extra edge of urgency to this approach.

Comprehensive Planning

Comprehensive planning, so called because of its roots in the comprehensiveness of architectural and civic design, was the unifying paradigm of planning practice immediately after World War II in both America and Britain. It was generally defined by large-scale, overarching physical visions of urban changes and guided by the conception of a unified, knowable public interest. Its objectives were summed up pithily in 1933 by British planner Patrick Abercrombie in his famous triad of 'beauty, health and convenience' (Abercrombie: p. 104), making clear reference to the Roman architect Vitruvius' celebrated statement that architecture was concerned with 'firmness, commodity and delight.' Frederick Law Olmsted, the unofficial leader of the emerging city planning profession in America stated similar aims in 1909, when he defined city planning in terms of 'efficiency … economy … beauty' (Klaus: p. 457).

This kind of planning relied implicitly on a non-political stance by an impartial expert who weighed competing objectives with rational, intellectual detachment. While this approach flourished for the first half of the 20th century, later critics have regarded this detached stance and these twin precepts of large scale and a singular, unified public interest as unwieldy and impractical at best, and unrealistic and paternalistic at worst in a fast-changing, increasingly diverse society. Typical critiques argue that this approach to planning 'perpetuates a monopoly over planning power and discourages participation. If planning is to be inclusive it cannot pretend that a single planning agency can represent the interests of a divergent and conflicted society' (Campbell and Fainstein: p. 262).

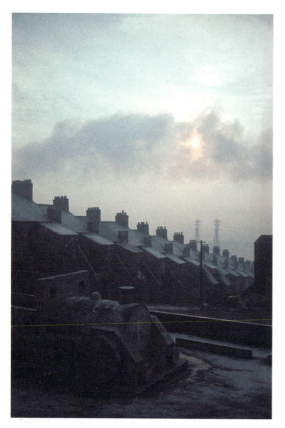

Figure 2.5 Thamesmead, East Greenwich, London, 1977. The architects' vision of towers in the park replaced decayed industrial housing in many British cities, but this brave new world soon fell into disrepute; parts of this quasi new town – built in this instance on drained marshland east of central London – provided the setting for the film version of Anthony Burgess' dystopian novel *Clockwork Orange*.

Figure 2.4 Terrace Housing at Benwell, Newcastle-upon-Tyne, UK, 1970. These grim 19th century terraces were eventually demolished and the residents rehoused.

This criticism of comprehensive planning was something new and unexpected in the post-war world. During most of the 1950s in Europe and America, comprehensive planning theory and practice was united in a straightforward, stable view of the world. In Britain, rebuilding its cities and economy after the struggles and devastation of World War II, and with several major urban areas in ruins from the German Luftwaffe's aerial bombardment (see Figure 1.2), the task was urgent and massive. Comprehensive planning on a large scale was the only approach that could get the job done.

Besides their concern with rebuilding bomb-damaged city centers and industrial districts, British architects and planners were faced with the legacy of the industrial cities themselves, where millions of people still lived in poverty in bleak and forbidding physical environments. Even as late as 1970, photographs of endless acres of grim, soot-grimed British terrace

housing dating from the 19th century without a single tree in sight and blanketed by an ever-present pall of pollution, reminded planners and architects just how bad those conditions were (see Figure 2.4). No wonder architects and planners wanted to obliterate those miserable conditions and the past that created them, and a new city of bright, modern buildings sited amidst a park-like landscape with plenty of sun and clean, fresh air presented a compelling vision of urban improvement (see Figure 2.5).

Public participation did not enter the picture in any meaningful way; the scale and complexity of planning rendered it 'somewhat mystical, or arcane' to the general public, and its practice stayed firmly in the hands of objective, rational experts. 'The job of the planner was to make plans, to develop codes to enforce those plans, and then to enforce those codes' (Hall, P.: p. 355). Change was afoot and little time was spent thinking beyond the end state of the new utopia; it was more important to get there. Town planning and architecture were essentially regarded as two branches of the same profession, and the Royal Institute of British Architects initially resisted the establishment of a separate professional body for town planning on the grounds that architects already had this covered. Typical of the textbooks of the time was Lewis Keeble's *Principles and Practice of Town and Country Planning* (1959; 4th edn 1969), which set out the key techniques for town planning as 'architecture writ large' (Taylor, 1999: pp. 330–331).

American cities were spared the physical havoc and destruction of aerial bombardment during World War II, but comprehensive planning was also well ensconced in that country during the decade of growing prosperity after the victory celebrations in 1945. As late as 1964, a leading authority, Professor T.J. Kent Jr, at the University of California at Berkeley, could assure students reading his book *The General Urban Plan* that it was possible and desirable to produce some kind of optimal land use plan. This planning was conceived as generally a steady-state condition, achieved by rational expertise; however, in a slim foreshadowing of the changes to come, Kent warned his readers that 'because the planner's basic understanding of the interrelationship between socio-economic forces and the physical environment was largely intuitive and speculative' the objectives of the plan should be continually adjusted as time passes (Hall, P.: p. 357).

By the 1960s, many physical conditions in British cities had been substantially improved, with hundreds of thousands of city dwellers 'decanted' to new lives in various government-planned new towns constructed around London and other metropolitan areas. But countless acres of old terraced housing stood as silent witness to the grim, industrial past, and to architects and planners alike these neighborhoods impeded progress; their continued demolition was a way to cleanse society of the residual evils of the industrial city. It did not really matter if the buildings and streets were not technically slums. It was sufficient that they were old, decaying and overcrowded by the new, lower density standards of the day. The possibility that the housing could be refurbished and the neighborhoods brought back to life was not one that students or qualified professionals were encouraged to pursue by prevailing doctrine. Similar attitudes reigned in American cities under the aegis of urban renewal and these well-meaning but disastrously misconceived professional attitudes were accurately skewered by American critic Jane Jacobs in her 1961 polemic, *The Death and Life of Great American Cities*. Jacobs' relentless and unforgiving decimation of professional ideologies and expertise at the core of comprehensive planning exposed once and for all the weaknesses of this approach and opened the way for major reform over the next several decades.

But Jane Jacobs was by no means a lone voice in the critique of post-war planning and architecture; the authority of physical and comprehensive planning was also shaken, and ultimately demolished, during the 1950s and 1960s by social scientists who had recently joined the ranks of academic planners. American political scientist Alan Altshuler published two devastating

analyses of comprehensive planning in 1965 (Altshuler, 1965a, 1965b) and radical geographers such as Henri Lefebvre in France added their voices to the growing chorus of complaint. In his essay 'Reflections on the Politics of Space,' Lefebvre argued against the rational, objective views of urban space that were central to conventional comprehensive planning, maintaining instead that space was neither neutral nor a formal abstraction of the type imagined by traditional town planners and urban designers. He argued that space was not a separate, 'scientific object' removed from ideology and politics; it has always been shaped and molded by political processes (Lefebvre, 1970: p. 341).

Learning from this wide variety of criticisms, a new breed of planner evolved during the 1960s and 1970s who viewed the profession's primary concern with the physical city as overly restrictive, and the conventional perceptions of the urban development process as politically naïve. To these new critics, the emphasis on technical, physical design solutions reflected views of city life that were predominantly middle class, and planners' attempts to formulate a clear statement of the public interest ended up as no more than a reflection of the priorities held by the civic and business elites at the expense of other viewpoints. Life beyond the planner's drawing board was a lot more complex and diverse than professional planners realized and they came to believe that the old-fashioned physical design methods missed the true intricacies of society in the evolving, modern city. Instead of concentrating on physical design and a fixed vision of future improvement, the new generation of planners instituted an approach that was more flexible and (allegedly) value-neutral in its application of a highly systematic methodology which focused on handling a flow of information rather than creating physical solutions: the planner now identified problems, defined goals, analyzed information, implemented solutions (usually policies rather than designs) and evaluated the results (Klosterman, 1985).

The Rise of Systems Planning

Rapid population growth and the post-war economic boom in both Britain and America exposed the weakness of steady-state planning methods and gave rise to a rash of new criticisms. As Hall points out, the once-stable world of planners' assumptions fell apart; it no longer corresponded to a new, fast-paced and changing reality, and planners possessed few tools to deal with these novel and unexpected circumstances:

Everything began to get out of hand. In every industrial country there was an unexpected baby boom, to which the demographers reacted with surprise, the planners with alarm … [E]verywhere it created instant demands for maternity wards and childcare clinics [and] only slightly delayed needs for schools and playgrounds … [A]lmost simultaneously, the postwar economic boom got underway, bringing pressure for new investment in factories and offices. And, as boom generated affluence … countries soon passed into the realms of high, mass-consumption societies, with unprecedented demands for durable consumer goods: most notable among these, land-hungry homes and cars. The result everywhere – in America, in Britain, in the whole of western Europe – was that the pace of urban development and urban change began to accelerate to an almost superheated level; the old planning system, geared to a static world, was overwhelmed. (Hall, P.: p. 359)

If these radical circumstances were not enoughto force the planning system to change, there were other shifts within the intellectual world of planning theory during the mid-to-late 1950s, particularly in America, that set the discipline on a different course. Academics discovered relatively obscure German texts from earlier decades on locational theory and spatial distribution, translated them, and began to apply them to contemporary problems in attempts to understand and manage the unprecedented rates of economic and physical urban growth. In America, planning was infused by a newly invigorated geographic discipline created by merging human spatial analysis and location theory with new techniques of transportation analysis, while in Britain these new insights began to enter the curricula of planning schools along with a greater emphasis on social sciences (Hall, P.: p. 360). The urgency and pace of these changes was such that by the late 1960s, a student friend of the author enrolled in a planning degree program at a prestigious British university could proudly proclaim her disdain for the 'old-fashioned' emphasis on physical design that characterized architecture: she was proud that her planning studies contained almost no instruction about physical design, concentrating instead on concepts of the city as a complex web of systems, monitored and guided by entirely new 'scientific' and computer-aided techniques. In just over 10 years, planning had changed from a design-based craft into a coolly scientific process of complex data management.

The old master plan approach, which derived fixed assumptions about the desired objectives, and then set about producing designs and regulations to bring

that vision to reality, was thus replaced by the concept of planning as an open-ended process, where a fixed master plan was irrelevant. The process itself became more important than the product, which by definition would constantly change through continuous monitoring and adjustment. This process 'involved a constantly recycled series of logical steps: goal-setting, forecasting of change in the outside world, assessment of chains of consequences of alternative courses of action, appraisal of costs and benefits as a basis for action strategies, and continuous monitoring' (Webber, 1968/9: p. 278, in Hall, P.: p. 362). This systems approach was derived initially from military research, where the planners controlled all aspects of the system and its variables, and systems planners, despite their antipathy towards old-fashioned 'blueprint' master plans, unwittingly adopted some of the same apolitical, even Olympian positions regarding the relationship between planning practice and politics. They saw the new systematic process of planning as much more active and kinetic than static master plans, but they still imagined the political system as passive, 'benign and receptive to the planner's advice' rather than an active element of their systems analysis (Hall, P.: p. 363).

During the 1970s crucial differences began to be recognized between the tightly controlled military context and the shifting world of urban planning, where the planners were definitely *not* in control of external political and social forces, and in many cases were controlled by them. This inconsistency in the system planner's position proved ultimately fatal to the movement as politics played an increasingly large role in city planning from the 1960s onward and the city as a system of variables refused to stay quietly under the control of the new breed of scientific planners. By the mid-1970s this radical new systems approach to planning had largely collapsed, partly under the weight of its own unfulfilled ambitions, but its demise was also aided by the introduction of new planning paradigms that sought to deal directly with the ebb and flow of political currents that affected urban policy. Three new paradigms emerged, from the center and the opposite poles of the political spectrum, but all shared the desire to increase the participation of the public in the planning process. These three new approaches are best categorized as centrist *democratic* planning, which sought to change the 'top-down' approach inherent in comprehensive and systems planning in favor of more open political debate; *incrementalist* or *strategic* planning, derived from right-wing political thought and corporate policy that began with the modest but practical assumption that planning was the art of the possible, rather than a venue for major societal reform; and finally, *advocacy* or *equity* planning, born from a passionate left-wing critique of the social injustice embedded in the contemporary city in Britain and America, and which imagined planning could and indeed should become the agency for social change and social justice.

Democratic Planning

During the 1960s, critics of traditional comprehensive planning, whatever their own personal prescriptions for reform, were often united in demanding a change from top-down, 'Olympian' methods of city planning to ones that featured more citizen participation, and more reliance on knowledge and techniques from the social sciences. Indeed this call for public participation remains a rallying cry today; it is certainly a fundamental tenet of the charrette methodology described in this book. Susan and Norman Fainstein, in their seminal essay 'City Planning and Political Values: An Updated View,' quote Herbert Gans from 1968, arguing that planning 'ought to be determined by whatever goal or goals the community considers important' (Gans: pp. 102–103), and to make the point of this argument's continued relevance, they call on influential planning theorists John Friedmann and John Forester from the late 1980s. Friedmann recommended planners seek out knowledge from those 'in the front line of action – households, local communities, social movements' (Friedmann: p. 327), while Forester exhorted planners 'to develop a set of community relations strategies.' Forester specifically suggested that community networks should be actively cultivated, e.g. by alerting less-organized interest groups to significant issues and assuring community groups were engaged in debate about policies affecting them. Planners needed to exercise skills in conflict management, and try to compensate for unbalanced political and economic pressures (Forester: p. 155).

The desire to make up for uneven political and economic pressures indicates clear leanings towards advocacy and equity planning's ambitions to correct social inequality, but democratic planning in its ideal form should not seek to privilege any one group over another. In theory, democracy is predicated on the axiom of majority rule; this is the mechanism by which citizens control government. Indeed the famous 19th century French political theorist Alexis de Tocqueville stated in his classic work *Democracy in America* that 'the very essence of democratic government consists in

the absolute sovereignty of the majority' (Tocqueville, 1848: 1957 edn, p. 264). The corollary to this position of power is that the citizenry become educated about the relevant issues and the democratic planner must therefore seek to educate the public as well as take direction from them.

The planner's desire for greater democracy and citizen participation in planning faces critical problems in practice, chiefly because of the relative ignorance and selfishness of the citizenry, and general apathy on the part of the public. These are the most common conditions in everyday planning practice, but lurking in the shadows is a larger and more sinister fear – that 'the rule of the majority leads to social mediocrity and even to fascist authoritarianism' (Fainstein and Fainstein: p. 277).

It is a fact of life that people are frequently unwilling to take decisions that benefit the community in the long-term if these decisions involve delaying the gratification of their own short-term convenience. Many worthwhile planning policies fail to gain public acceptance because of this common circumstance. Democratic governance and planning suffer from the well-known tendency for people to act in their narrow self-interest instead of giving priority to the overall well-being of their larger community. These perennial and frustrating planning problems are captured by the well-know acronyms NIMBY, BANANA (Build Absolutely Nothing Anywhere Near Anything) and LULU (Locally Unwanted Land Use). Moreover, unless there is a matter of vital and immediate importance to a community, few individuals take the time to involve themselves in the local political and planning process, leaving the democratic planner with only a small minority of citizens to work with – and there is no guarantee that this group is representative of general public opinion.

These dilemmas clearly illustrate major weaknesses of democratic planning, and the gap between theory, where the public is regarded as the ultimate authority in the preparation of plans, and the political realities of practice where this same public contains bias, ignorance and competing special interests of unequal power. In practice, there is no unified public voice, so which group or groups should planners heed the most? When planners promote the right of community members to participate in the planning process, they are faced with the necessity of making judgments between various segments of society. In making these decisions, it is often difficult for a planner to set aside his or her own value systems, with the likely outcome that the planner ends up (unintentionally) imposing a vision of a somewhat idealized, middle-class, bourgeois world (Fainstein and Fainstein: p. 268).

Historically, planners sought to resolve this dilemma either by reducing the scale of planning objectives to suit political realities, and borrowing strategies from the corporate sector to regain some sense of detached objectivity; or by committing their full professional efforts to the cause of society's most disadvantaged groups. These divergent courses gave rise to incrementalist and strategic planning, on the one hand, and advocacy and equity planning, on the other.

Incrementalist and Strategic Planning

Planners of this persuasion sought to mitigate the dilemmas of comprehensive and democratic planning by borrowing a methodology from the private corporate sector that emphasized incremental, small-scale changes that could combine eventually into a larger, more substantial set of improvements. This method sought to resolve two problems: (1) to avoid the perceived pitfalls of over-ambitious and unrealistic comprehensive planning, incrementalism intentionally limited the scope and ambition of each planning proposal; and (2) to sidestep the crippling political choices faced by democratic planners trying to tackle large, difficult problems over which public opinion was divided, smaller, less-contentious problems were selected at the margins of public policy where limited success was achievable.

In focusing on small-scale objectives and real-world constraints, incrementalist and strategic planning created a direct critique of the large-scale, often utopian visions of comprehensive planning. Proponents regarded this piecemeal approach – using resources to improve what could be fixed in terms of the political realities – as more nimble and realistic than comprehensive planning, and the related belief that this series of continuous small-scale adjustments to public policies could eventually lead to a discernable improvement in physical, social and economic conditions was linked directly to classic 19th century liberal political theories of limited government. This mirrored the dominant beliefs of the private, capitalist sector that the 'invisible hand' of market forces would promote prosperity by a similar series of continuous, small-scale, self-interested adjustments. But because incrementalism primarily benefited those social groups already most privileged and able to manipulate policy to their best advantage, the capacity to create social and environmental change was

very limited within this style of planning. Thus, for example, 'efforts at environmental preservation and conservation of energy resources founder as a result of a process of incremental decision making that strictly limits the scope of change' (Fainstein and Fainstein: p. 282).

In their defense, incrementalist planners argued that even with its faults, incrementalism offered a more realistic and effective approach than comprehensive planning. They claimed comprehensive planning could be easily ignored by the public by its very nature of large-scale visions and remoteness from the immediate concerns of everyday society. Indeed trenchant critics such as American theorist Charles Lindblom went further and argued in his influential 1959 article 'The Science of Muddling Through,' that 'attempts at superhuman comprehensiveness' were 'futile' in a complex society such as post-war America; such comprehensiveness required a mountain of data and a level of complexity that was simply beyond the grasp of planners, and the unlikely process of 'muddling through' was in fact superior in outcomes and technique (Lindblom: p. 302).

The origins of strategic planning lie in the private sector and date from the mid-1960s, a period when American corporations like General Electric recognized the need to plan effectively and manage their futures at a time when the future itself appeared increasingly uncertain (Kaufman and Jacobs: p. 325). At the heart of strategic planning lies the 'SWOT' analysis methodology – a mechanism for analyzing the Strengths, Weaknesses, Opportunities and Threats that apply to any particular organization or topic. As a measure of this method's continued relevance, the author used it in 2005 in a planning study for the small town of Mineral Springs on the suburban fringe of Charlotte, NC, which was becoming surrounded by generic and mediocre sprawl development. The town sought advice from the author and Ken Chilton, a planning colleague at the University of North Carolina at Charlotte, on updating and changing its planning policies to control new development and retain its rural environmental character (see Figure 2.6). Amongst other planning and design studies, a mixed graduate class of architects and planners under the instruction of the two professors conducted a SWOT analysis on the town's zoning ordinance as follows:

- *Strengths.* Elements of the existing zoning ordinance that promoted the preferred community vision of a compact rural community with preserved open space.

Figure 2.6 Farmland in Mineral Springs, NC. Across America, landscapes like this are under constant threat from suburban sprawl.

- *Weaknesses*. Sections of the zoning ordinance that needed to be strengthened or changed to realize this community vision.
- *Opportunities*. The chance to implement new and improved zoning regulations that could promote the preferred types of development before the onset of major new urban growth.
- *Threats*. Loopholes in existing regulations that could allow the small town to be overwhelmed with standardized suburban sprawl and strip development.

This planning exercise was strategic and incrementalist in as much as it sought to affect only what it could change, namely the conditions within the town's own boundaries. Mineral Springs was powerless to affect the rate and quality of development taking place around its borders within other jurisdictions that did not share its concerns; not only does this area of North Carolina have no effective framework for regional planning of the kind taken for granted in the UK, but many elected officials are openly hostile to the idea of coordinated planning as an 'un-American, socialist concept.' Citizens of Mineral Springs were themselves equally critical of major new planning initiatives, seeing them as 'big government' and likely to require tax increases to implement. Accordingly, the student planning team consciously reined in their more ambitious proposals derived from extensive geographic information systems (GIS) studies and conservation design plans to focus on a series of modest, incremental changes to local ordinances that stood a

good chance of being accepted by elected officials and their constituents. When taken together, these changes could effect some useful and important modifications in town policy to achieve several of the community's goals, but larger, urgent issues of environmental degradation in the surrounding regional area were not tackled at all.

This example shows clearly the strengths and weaknesses of a strategic planning approach. On the positive side, it is a process that achieved some real improvements in a political environment that was hostile to larger, more ambitious ideas. From the negative perspective, by not challenging the political *status quo*, this approach failed to achieve any major improvement in environmental conditions beyond the boundaries of the small community, and so this limited success is just that, a drop in the bucket when compared to the flood of poor developments taking place in surrounding communities which lack the understanding or motivation to improve the standard of new development. A major problem that is almost impossible to overcome in contemporary America is the aforementioned divisive fragmentation of local government, whereby adjacent municipalities usually compete for development and actively resist any form of meaningful collaboration around larger goals. In this context, the kind of long-range, regional planning required by law in the UK is impossible to achieve and so the short-term strategic planning of the type discussed in this example often becomes the only option for American planners.

Critics of strategic and incrementalist planning, particularly those concerned with advocacy and equity planning, have always complained that the former were too timid and conservative, 'reinforcing the *status quo* and neglecting the power of ... social change,' and replacing long-term vision and theory with overly pragmatic short-term stimulus and response techniques (Campbell and Fainstein: p. 262). Whereas strategic planners usually sought to avoid confrontation by limiting their objectives to what was achievable by small, incremental policy changes and local consensus, advocacy and equity planners by contrast sought out conflict by directly challenging those policies and institutions they thought responsible for promoting social and economic inequality.

Advocacy and Equity Planning

Advocacy and equity planners in America firmly rejected the idea of the planner as the disinterested, objective technician. Paul Davidoff, in his classic

1965 article, 'Advocacy and Pluralism in Planning,' specifically argued that 'planning action cannot be prescribed from a position of value neutrality … [and] values are inescapable elements of any rational decision-making process' (Davidoff: p. 306). He went on to say that planners should be advocates of what they deem proper and that they should 'engage in the political process as advocates of the interests of both government and other groups, organizations, or individuals who are concerned for proposing policies for the future development of the community' (Davidoff: p. 307).

The activist position inherent in advocacy and equity planning was born from the social revolution of the civil rights movement in the USA during the 1960s, and the consequent demands for social justice and political equality. From this position, Davidoff attacked not only the notion of the planner as an objective expert, detached from the political process, but also the presumption there could be a single, common public interest in a nation deeply divided by class and economic inequality.

Given this oppositional stance to traditional planning methods and assumptions, it is no surprise that advocacy planners began working outside the bureaucratic system of public government, championing instead the rights of individual communities and taking their fight to city hall. Advocacy planning starts, by definition, at the grassroots, neighborhood level. In Britain, similar activities fell under the rubrics of 'community action' and 'community architecture,' bred not by a cataclysmic change like the civil rights movement in the USA, but by the build-up of festering discontent with British urban policies of the 1960s, where, like urban renewal in America, large-scale redevelopment destroyed familiar environments and broke apart communities. Protest swept through Britain's inner cities in the mid-to-late 1960s, and this direct community action opposed the seemingly unbridled power of local councils to clear away older parts of British cities, and the mercenary corporate interests that sought to capitalize on this generally arid and soulless urban redevelopment (Towers: p. xiv). Young British professionals working as 'community architects,' the equivalent of American advocacy planners, organized demonstrations and protests to draw attention to the real needs of deprived urban areas and helped communities to participate in shaping their futures through active lobbying, media events, and the creation of alternative development plans. Davidoff once again provided a rallying theme across the Atlantic when he wrote: 'If the planning process is to encourage democratic urban government, then it must … include rather than exclude citizens from participating in the process' (Davidoff: p. 307). Idealistic young architects and planners, often students rather than qualified professionals, focused their efforts on poor neighborhoods and low-income families, trying to assist areas and populations that were powerless in the face of insensitive bureaucracies with fixed ideas about city redevelopment (see Figure 2.7).

Davidoff also pointed out that advocacy of alternative plans prepared with and for communities by these young designers and planners could stimulate and reenergize city planning. The adversarial nature inherent in advocacy planning and community architecture would, he argued, have the beneficial effect of forcing government planners to be more careful in their research and their approach to problems, seeking solutions that reflected actual conditions rather than uncritically following traditional methods. In advancing his argument for a much more interventionist style of planning, Davidoff also advocated a shift from land-use to socio-economic planning, specifically so that the profession could deal first and foremost with issues of social injustice and redistribution of resources, and only later move on to physical issues of city form. He argued that planners proposed unsatisfactory physical solutions because of insufficient knowledge and without the benefit of social and economic methods of analysis that would have enabled them to gain a more accurate understanding of urban conditions (Davidoff: pp. 316–317). The failures of the urban renewal program, where whole neighborhoods were demolished and communities split asunder all in the name of ill-defined civic improvement, spurred Davidoff's insistence that planning would become more successful when it focused on social and economic issues instead of concentrating heavily on physical design.

This was a call echoed by many others. Advocacy planning spawned a 'kinder, gentler' cousin – equity planning – which also promoted the interests of disadvantaged groups within society but with the important difference that planners like Norman Krumholz in Cleveland, OH, or architects like Ralph Erskine and his partner Vernon Gracie in Newcastle-upon-Tyne in the UK, worked for local government bureaucracies, trying to reform the system from within. These planners and architects walked a difficult line between activism for communities and the promotion of a larger, more objective notion of the public interest. Whereas democratic planning emphasized the participatory process, trying to reach broad

Figure 2.7 Community action poster for Benwell, Newcastle-upon-Tyne, UK, 1970. This poster in the window of the community action office, where the author worked part-time while a graduate student, seeks volunteers to collect information about unfair rent practices and harassment by private slumlords.

consensus and thus validate the planning effort, equity planning focused on redistributing civic resources to those groups and communities most in need. It particularly sought to expose and oppose the hypocrisy of public policies that benefited private capital while espousing the public interest; many projects for downtown renewal trumpeted as promoting economic development and new employment opportunities in fact did little more than garner taxpayer subsidies for developers. To add insult to injury, such schemes often displaced low-income workers from their homes without improving their employment situation in any way.

Correcting social injustice was a central tenet of equity planning. It sought to add a dimension of urgency that was lacking in the limited objectives of strategic or incrementalist planning, and return to a more progressive path of both promoting the larger public interest and directly addressing urban inequalities. Equity planners thus combined a socialist's belief in material equality with a 'democrat's faith in government by the people' (Fainstein and Fainstein: p. 280), and equity planning asserted 'a greater faith in finding

common ground of public interest and working within the system of public sector planning' (Campbell and Fainstein: p. 263). The most vivid example of ambitious, committed and fully-fledged equity planning in America can be found in the efforts of Norman Krumholz, Director of the City Planning Commission in Cleveland, during the 1970s (Krumholz, 1982).

In that decade, Cleveland suffered from an extreme version of a common American urban condition: a failing, older city hemorrhaging population and economic resources, and surrounded by prosperous, newer municipalities in the suburbs. Traditional land use planning and local politics had failed to make any impression on these circumstances, so, spurred by an ethical imperative, city planners set out to try to improve urban conditions the city. Quoting from the Code of Ethics of the American Institute of Planners to the effect that a planner 'shall seek to expand choice and opportunity for all persons, recognizing a special responsibility to plan for the needs of disadvantaged groups' (the wording itself was a result of lobbying within the profession by Paul Davidoff), planning staff worked to deemphasize traditional concerns with zoning, land use and urban design, and to highlight instead issues of social justice such as access to jobs, public transportation and housing conditions. However, in retrospect, it must be acknowledged that equity planning in America made little impact due largely to its socialist roots. Its left-leaning philosophy regarding the redistribution of power and resources away from the capitalist elite, and its emphasis on material equality rather than simply legal and political equality, remains deeply antithetical to much American public opinion.

Environmental Planning

The desire by many American planners to combat social inequality remains an active motivation in the opening years of the 21st century, but this sense of urgency has been joined by another: the environmental degradation resulting from badly considered patterns of suburban development. During the 1990s, Americans' understanding of the physical and environmental problems associated with conventional patterns of suburban development expanded into a sense of potential environmental crisis. However, environmentalism and its overarching concern of climate change and global warming remains a hotly debated political topic in the USA, with bitter disagreements between the right and left of the political spectrum. As evidence of the resistance to scientific knowledge by right-wing American politicians, a Republican member of the North Carolina State legislature who is also a member of the state's Legislative Commission on Global Climate Change wrote an editorial in *The Charlotte Observer* newspaper in 2006 stating flatly that global warming did not exist (Pettinger, 2006). These extreme views are widely held at the right wing of American political opinion, but some modest degree of consensus has emerged in the public-at-large on the need for greater environmental sensitivity regarding the ecological impact of new development. However, even this fragile agreement is threatened by the federal government's disinterest in environmental matters, and this political resistance is a far cry from the attitude most prevalent in Britain and the rest of Europe, where government bodies and the public agree in principle on the urgent reality of this environmental threat, and the need to develop policies and design strategies for cities and buildings to become more energy efficient and 'sustainable.'

In these contrasting national contexts, a new strand of environmental planning has come to the fore during the last 10 years. Because the impact of development on the environment has many wide-ranging effects that are not easily managed or improved through the limited goals of strategic planning, or by the singular, adversarial focus of advocacy planning, or even from the activist position within city government represented by equity planning, the increasing sophistication of environmental planning has brought about a return to the once discredited idea of comprehensive planning, albeit in a more advanced form than the type practiced 50 years ago. Planners are encouraged once again to think in terms of the big picture, and the effects of various types of growth and development on the natural environment in a regional context. One of the standard texts on environmental planning in the USA argues that planners 'can be effective in promoting proactive, comprehensive planning that seeks to avoid water and air pollution and land use problems before they happen, and thus protect the community's quality of life and potential for economic growth' (Daniels and Daniels: p. 4).

Environmental planning takes a holistic view of physical land and development issues in order to balance the management of natural resources with economic development to promote the kind of growth that is sustainable over the long term. It involves 'shaping a community or region by protecting and improving air and water quality; conserving farming, forestry, and wildlife resources; reducing exposure to natural hazards; and maintaining the natural features and built environment that make a place livable and desirable' (Daniels and Daniels: p. xix). However, the regional sweep of environmental planning faces many difficulties in the USA because of the fragmented and competitive (sometimes even combative) nature of local governments. This fragmentary democracy whereby municipalities are pitted against each other makes any kind of consensual, regional planning very difficult.

Despite these obstacles, environmental planning is slowly gaining ground in America, and opening up new approaches for planners. Its founding concept is the notion that any sector of land has a certain 'carrying capacity' that can support a spectrum of human, animal and vegetative life in relative harmony, and, consequent to this, each generation has the responsibility not to upset this balance. This is a far cry from the conditions that pertain in all industrialized nations today; even in (relatively) environmentally conscious Britain, where a host of government policies support sustainable design and planning, the ecological impacts of new development and existing lifestyles are a long way from being sustainable. Environmental planning is thus perhaps the most urgent branch of planning theory and practice at the current time, and planners working in this sector, particularly in the USA, often find themselves taking on advocacy roles in attempts to influence public policy.

In this position, American planners find themselves at odds with the public's perception of their place in society. Because American political thought and popular mythology is dominated by the 18th and 19th century liberal tradition of deference to market mechanisms and the incrementalism inherent in the continuous small-scale adjustments of Adam Smith's 'invisible hand,' America has generally preferred planners to serve as arbiters of conflict rather than proactive shapers of the built environment. This accounts for the continued practice of incrementalist planning, but because of its aversion to contentious changes in public policy, this type of planning is singularly unable to instigate the critical actions needed to deal with fast-growing environmental problems in America's cities and suburbs. To overcome these limitations, and to engage the urgent environmental issues inherent in the ubiquitous sprawling patterns of suburban growth in the USA, many American architects and planners have combined a renewed activist approach with environmentalism to promote a 'smart growth' agenda since the mid-1990s.

The smart growth movement for more sustainable and less environmentally damaging forms of development is an important stimulant that has prompted a renewal of interest in the once-condemned practice of comprehensive planning. In reality, despite all the theoretical and political opprobrium heaped on this practice from the 1970s onwards, planners in Britain and America never completely abandoned this approach to managing the urban environment. In the USA, planning law in various states requires communities to create some form of overall comprehensive or master plan as the basic legal framework

for development control decisions. This requirement is by no means uniform across the nation, but in the states of Oregon, Florida, Washington, New Jersey and Rhode Island, for example, comprehensive planning at the municipal level is standard procedure (Meck, 1997). Many cities, large and small, across the USA follow similar mandates, with varying degrees of firmness and exactitude, and this commitment, or lack of it, derives from the highly political nature of such planning activities. As witness to the depth of this ideological fervor, the author was a member of a planning team for a comprehensive plan in a rural county north of Charlotte, NC, in 2004, when the process was scrapped halfway to completion by new county commissioners who had been elected on a 'no planning' platform. In the resulting highly charged emotional and political setting, the planning consultants were publicly upbraided in vitriolic terms by these newly elected officials and told that their presence in the county was not wanted under any circumstances. The new chairman of the commissioners then proudly announced that in the future, all 'socialist' ideas about planning and design were to be banned from discussion at county commission meetings.

The political dimensions of almost all planning activities thus require a discussion of major movements and ideas in 20th century planning through one other lens: the ubiquitous dialectic between the private interests of capital and the markets on the one hand and the public interest of the state on the other; between the planner as someone who aims to uphold the public interest and correct social imbalances, and as a facilitator of property development and capital accumulation by the private sector (Campbell and Fainstein: p. 148). These inherent contradictions are embedded in the planner's role, and markedly affect the function of urban design within public policy. This complex duality is the topic of the next chapter.

Political theory, postmodern planning and urban design

3

SYNOPSIS

A discussion of political theory may seem a long way from the daily workload of practicing planners and architects, but heated local debates over public and private concerns in future land development are framed in almost every case by the larger dialectic between the state and private capital. Within a capitalist economy, planners and architects help shape the built environment so that it operates efficiently, and maintains the existing social and economic order – a prime requirement for continued and efficient capitalist production and profitability. This mission can often conflict with planning's other main goal of advancing and protecting the common good and the collective interests of the community, including the welfare of deprived groups or others threatened or harmed by development.

This complex duality is a cause of stress to practicing professionals on the ground, and a fertile field of contention to academics in schools of architecture and planning. The demise of traditional, comprehensive planning in the 1950s led to a rash of new planning movements during subsequent decades, each of which sought to express or manufacture its own legitimacy, a process that generally involved developing a body of intellectual theory as the backbone to practice. Planning during the decades of the 1970s and 1980s was thus characterized by competing theories, often increasingly arcane and couched in academic jargon that removed them, sometimes by their authors' design, from the everyday world of practice. Architectural theory suffered a similar fate during that same time, a condition from which it has barely recovered. But that is another story!

This new academic landscape was mapped most effectively by scholars who sought to explain the new stresses and opportunities in the fast-changing politics of global capitalism in ways that could suggest new and sometimes radical roles for planning and planners. A summary of this political analysis is followed by a deeper examination of the related and concurrent theoretical swing in planning and urban design from modernism to postmodernism. The chapter concludes by examining how, within this shifting theoretical and political context, urban design and master planning returned as key components of planning practice – as mainstream national government policy in Britain and as a technique utilized piecemeal by progressive local governments in the USA.

THEORY, PRACTICE AND POLITICS

The increasing distance between theory and practice in planning was marked by a move away from theories *of* planning to theories *about* planning. Less intellectual effort was applied to instrumental theories of *action* and much more to speculative theories of *explanation* (or, because of the dense language that characterized much of the writing, theories of obfuscation might be a more appropriate term). In the 1950s, viewed by many as the utopian heyday of comprehensive planning, planning was a well-founded academic discipline in Britain and America, but one that was founded on established techniques rather than any coherent body of theory. Planners operated much like architects and engineers; they followed the design processes of those professions for buildings or public works, and applied them to the design of towns and cities (Hall, P.: p. 355).

In this process, a somewhat naïve belief in architectural determinism – the credo that well-designed places could improve people's lives and standards of behavior – was bolstered by a smattering of social science and economics. This somewhat amateur methodology worked for a profession operating in a relatively static society, but not in one that was changing fast with many new sets of social circumstances and demographics. As we have noted, new theories of systems planning promised to provide new tools to manage this complexity, but when these theories also failed to meet real world challenges posed by society and culture in the 1960s and 1970s, the field opened up for other intellectual attempts to set out workable paradigms for effective planning.

The intellectual landscape of the 1970s was dominated initially by Marxist theory, some of which is still pertinent today. While there are many variations of Marxist urban theory, in essence it states that the form of the capitalist city is the result of money moving around in pursuit of profit. But because capitalism on its own is characterized by its recurring 'boom and bust' cycles, which can become more extreme in the current phase of global capitalism, private companies call on government at local, state and national level to help mitigate the effects of their own dysfunctional patterns of activity. Government can do this by providing transportation infrastructure, schools, and social services to help maintain a coherent and relatively conflict-free society (Hall, P.: p. 369). At the same time, capital does not want government to limit its profit-making potential by interfering too much.

In America, the general public fails to distinguish between communism, socialism and Marxism, lumping all three together under the catch-all category of anti-American ideas, and outside academia there is little awareness of the importance of intellectual Marxist studies to the modern planning profession. The work of British geographer David Harvey, for example, who explained urban growth in economic terms of the movement of capital, and the writings of Parisian intellectual Manuel Castells, who concentrated on social theories of collaboration between the bureaucratic state and private capital interests to reduce the possibility of class conflict, were typical of studies that laid the groundwork for more realistic understandings of the planner's role in today's society.

At the heart of the dialectic between state and capital is the paradox that while capitalist enterprises want government 'to get out of their way,' at the same time they need the public sector to do things for them that they are unable or unwilling to undertake themselves. Private companies and individuals often feel unjustly constrained by government intervention in the market through zoning and other land use controls, but developers and property owners need government action to provide and maintain the infrastructure of urbanization necessary for the efficient working of private commerce. The private sector does not want to pay for highways, bridges, public transportation and sewage systems, but it needs them to maintain and expand the private production of goods and services, and it expects the state (and taxpayers) to provide these expensive items and maintain them in perpetuity (see Figure 3.1). To this list of public provisions can be added libraries, schools, parks and other environmental amenities that attract and retain the stable and contented workforce necessary to maintain production in the private sector, and to reduce the potential for class conflict.

Figure 3.1 Construction of the outerbelt freeway around Charlotte, NC. This 60-mile circular freeway around the city has taken more than 10 years to build and cost more than a billion (US) dollars.

This conundrum has been characterized as the contradiction between the social character of land, i.e. land construed as a social resource for the collective good, and its more easily understood value as a private commodity with rights of personal ownership and control (Foglesong: p. 171). Private capital also needs government for another reason: if land is treated exclusively as a private commodity there is no effective mechanism for dealing with what economists call 'externalities,' those consequences of private development – social and public costs – that affect properties and conditions beyond the boundaries of of any particular project. These social and public costs are 'external' to the private costs and benefits of that development, and classic examples are pollution from a factory that burdens neighbors with extra healthcare costs and the loss of property values due to a degraded environment, or the costs imposed on an existing neighborhood by traffic congestion, increased noise and a loss of privacy caused by adjacent new developments (Klosterman, 1985).

Not all externalities are negative; the construction of new roads or transit systems by government agencies, for example, can increase land values without individual property owners having to expend any effort or money to reap this reward. In this context, planning agencies on both sides of the Atlantic try to recoup some of this increased private value for the public coffers by imposing on developers who gain from such economic windfalls various demands for the construction of public facilities associated with new developments or payments *in lieu* of construction costs.

In a somewhat perverse way, private capital in America has a strong interest in government increasingly 'socializing' the use of land by putting it under public control to cope with these externalities – by enacting regulations to provide environmental amenities such as clean air and water, or building new parks and other facilities to mitigate the negative effects of some private development on other property owners and businesses. Indeed the world of private capital wants and needs government to go beyond building and maintaining the transportation infrastructure. It wants the public sector to coordinate the spatial arrangement of this infrastructure with associated land uses to provide the most efficient circulation possible; this allows the private sector to maximize profitable production by reducing the costs of moving goods and services around. This increased public control of land necessary for capitalist urbanization is in direct contradiction to the basic premise of American private property rights and this so-called 'property

contradiction' is one of the forces that has structured the development of planning in America (Foglesong: p. 171).

This 'property contradiction' is vividly exposed in the USA by increasingly common right-wing activism to get government out of planning, and allow the free market to 'solve' urban and suburban problems by permitting property development to operate with little or no regulation – exactly the reasoning behind Oregon's Measure 37. This sounds like a simple conservative idea, but behind the rhetoric lurk many unanswered, and perhaps unanswerable, questions. For example, government-financed freeways have opened up hundreds of thousands of acres in America for development; would the same profitable development have occurred if these roads had been privately built and financed as pay-as-you-drive tollways? If water supply and sewer systems were built by private companies and paid for with user fees high enough for the companies to make a profit instead of being built using public money, would the private sector be developing extensively in arid areas of southwestern states like New Mexico, Arizona and parts of California? What would happen if there were no government-financed tax deductions for mortgage interest payments to underpin the private house building industry? All these measures are public subsidies to private development in America, and the rhetoric about government getting off the backs of business is usually a smoke screen for the repeal of specific regulations irksome to a particular group (Barnett, 2003: pp. 9–10). However, the overwhelming success of the anti-planning Measure 37 in Oregon funded by big business shows that public opinion in America is easily manipulated, and often cannot penetrate a slickly presented message to see the real facts and issues.

The relationship between private capital and the state is framed somewhat differently in the UK, where the development rights of all land have been held in the public domain since the landmark Town and Country Planning Act of 1947, which nationalized the development potential of private land to make possible the coordinated process of rebuilding national infrastructure and urban areas following the devastation of British cities by aerial bombardment during World War II. However, the issue of externalities and the dialogue between private capital and the state is still relevant; it just takes place with somewhat different rules and in a different political climate where many decisions regarding the location of new development are taken by government. The private developers' role remains similar in terms of trying to wring concessions from government while government still tries to exact money or land for community facilities from developers as part of the planning approval process.

The fact that rules change according to cultural conditions brings up another important point of clarification in the understanding of planning's historical development: it is not appropriate to think of 'capital' as a monolithic entity. There are several clear, distinct interest groups within the structure of private capital, and only some of them are inherently opposed to greater government intervention in the control and use of land. Those most clearly resistant to public control of property comprise what has been referred to as 'property capital,' i.e. people who 'plan and equip space – real estate developers, construction contractors and directors of mortgage lending institutions' (Foglesong: p. 172). These companies comprise a very powerful lobby: in the 2002 election cycle in North Carolina, for example, political action committees representing real estate agents and home-builders gave nearly half-a-million dollars to legislative candidates, making these interest groups the largest contributors in the state, well ahead of lobbyists for health care companies, bankers and lawyers (Hall, R., 2003). The lobbying efforts of these special interest groups are continuous and effective. For example, writing about the activities of the North Carolina Home Builders Association (NCHBA), the *North Carolina Builder* magazine reported that:

[d]espite the best efforts of environmental and other special interest groups to advance their anti-growth elitist agenda, NCHBA emerged from the 2005 legislative session with major victories … Of the 2984 bills introduced this session, 1181 (40%) directly affected the residential construction industry in one way or another [but] not a single bill opposed by the NCHBA was enacted. (Wilms: p. 7)

This example reveals to the British reader the impressive power that private industry groups hold over American governments and illustrates the huge difficulties in advancing any progressive agenda for sustainable development or smart growth in that nation. However, the development lobby represents only a portion of private capital interests; individual property owners often want government to curtail the property rights of those same companies in quite dramatic fashion when it comes to protecting their own residential property against encroachment from new developments. The ways in which private property and capital interests

create, disband and reform alliances around various property rights and development issues is inherent in the capitalist structure of American society, and planners often find themselves as mediators in these intra-capitalist conflicts rather than activist agents of change for social progress.

From a British perspective, planning in the 1970s was often seen as a struggle between class-based forces on the left and right of the political spectrum for the control and management of the urban environment (Healey, 1992: p. 235). Ultimately the conservative right wing won out, ushering in a decade of Thatcherism in the 1980s when an attack was launched on the whole enterprise of planning and urban management from the standpoint of conservative, market-based economics. In a famous and much-quoted comment, Margaret Thatcher claimed that 'there is no such thing as society; there are only individuals and families.' This statement symbolized the shift in the language of British politics during the 1980s from 'the public good' to 'individual choice' (Thornley, 1991: p. 2). Under the social consensus that held for three decades after World War II, British planners saw their role as guardians of the public good or community interest, but this traditional view of state intervention in the marketplace became increasingly at odds with successive Thatcher governments. Planning in Britain was caught in an ambiguous position between the egalitarian view of the welfare state and the individualist impulses of private capital, and the response to Thatcherite policies by British planners and urbanists varied between three different positions (Thornley, 1991).

First came the belief that despite the rhetoric, little would change. The main beneficiaries from the planning regime had historically been the middle classes in prosperous urban areas, the suburbs and the rural towns, and it was thought no government would risk offending that major swathe of the electorate. A second position agreed that while the planning framework would remain in place for the reasons noted above, shifts of emphasis would rephrase the dialectic between the state and private capital in favor of private development interests. Planners taking this position argued that their job had always included helping developers, and under the new regime this role received more visible legitimization.

By contrast, the third perspective emphasized more substantive alterations in the politics of planning brought about by the change to a market-driven system. This view argued that whereas planning in previous decades had been defined by policies that included social objectives, and that the relationship between developers and planners had been built around bargaining and mutual negotiation within this policy framework, under Thatcherism such policies were radically deemphasized. Social objectives were eliminated in favor of drastically simplified physical controls over development.

A key element of this shift was a centralization of planning control within national government and a diminution of local government authority. A clear example of this change could be seen in the early stages of redevelopment in London's docklands, where planning control was taken out of the hands of elected local governments and placed in the care of unelected agencies, or Urban Development Corporations (UDCs) appointed by central government. The task of these UDCs, such as the London Docklands Development Corporation (LDDC), was to smooth the way for the kind of redevelopment that suited central government's ambitions but ran counter to local government priorities and objectives. For many planners and other critics, this transformation went far beyond a mere shift of emphasis in the planning system towards development: it comprised a deliberate severance of planning from its roots in post-war welfare state consensus and the denial of social criteria and local democratic control in decision-making (Thornley, 1991: p. 4).

The case of London's docklands has been discussed and evaluated by many critics, both for its uncoordinated aesthetics and urban form and for its ideological, market-driven disregard for social policy (Ledgerwood, 1985; Brindley *et al.*, 1989; Brownhill, 1990; Thornley, 1991; Church, 1992; Edwards, 1992; Ambrose, 1994; Fainstein, 1995; Rogers, 1997; Hebbert, 1998; Hall, P., 2002; *et al.*). Hall and Thornley quote a famous statement by Michael Heseltine, Thatcher's Secretary of State for the Environment, justifying the taking away of local planning powers from the London Borough Councils whose territory encompassed the docklands area:

… we took their powers away from them because they were making such a mess of it. They are the people who got it all wrong. They had advisory committees, planning committees, inter-relating committees and even discussion committees – but nothing happened … UDCs do things. More to the point they can be seen to do things and they are *free from the delays of the normal democratic process* (Hall, P.: p. 393; Thornley: p. 181; this author's italics added).

Although the development in the London docklands is not complete (government plans call for 200 000 new homes and all related social and commercial infrastructure along a 40-mile stretch of the River Thames estuary in the ambitious Thames Gateway project), interim evaluations cast the docklands project as both a success or sobering failure. From one perspective, 'the environment has been transformed, the population has grown, there are new jobs, road and rail construction continue at a frenetic pace; London docklands has become almost a symbol of a certain style of development' reflecting the culture and politics of the 1980s and 1990s (Hall, P.: p. 398). However, there are dissenting voices, ranging from that of one London architect who confided his opinion to the author that the Canary Wharf area with its underground shopping malls and generic skyscrapers was 'a lot of American crap, well-built, but still crap,' (see Figure 3.2) to more sober analyses that pointed out that most of this new prosperity bypassed local communities who found themselves locked out of the job and property markets which were dominated by financial services sector professionals with relatively high incomes and buying power. Other criticisms examined the huge financial problems derived from a whole series of development bankruptcies in the slump of the 1990s, including the most massive one of all, the Canadian developer, Olympia & York (Fainstein,

Figure 3.2 Canary Wharf, London, from North Greenwich, 2006. Improved public transportation and road links with other parts of London have enhanced the livability of the Docklands but much of the architecture remains generic and uninspired, creating an 'American' downtown in the midst of the British capital.

1995). Perhaps most famously, the architect-peer, Lord (Richard) Rogers, described Canary Wharf as:

… unsustainable development without real civic quality or lasting communal benefit. [It was] an extremely expensive fiasco for the taxpayer, who subsidized big business but had no say in how the money was spent … Instead of gaining a vibrant and humane new borough that would have taken its place within the larger framework of the metropolis and enriched the poorer communities in its vicinity, Londoners acquired a chaos of commercial buildings and … footed the bill for one of the most spectacular bankruptcies of the 1990s. (Rogers, 1997: p. 109)

The British government used the power of the newly created Enterprise Zones and UDCs to by-pass local democracy and negotiate directly with developers. Decisions were often made in secret with minimal consultation with local authorities or community groups, and this new form of planning and development control redefined politics in Britain for several years. Thatcher's government defined local democracy negatively as parochial and small-minded, and considered it detrimental to the kind of large-scale development deemed important to the national interest and national economic progress (Thornley: pp. 183–184). In fairness, there was ample evidence to support this uncomfortable contention about local democracy. In 1977, the local boroughs quashed a visionary attempt by the Greater London Council to hold the 1998 Olympics in the docklands (now of course, they will be held a little further to the east in 2012), and the 1976 plan for the docks area was based on a dull and banal vision of the future with extensive municipal land holdings earmarked for undetermined and naïve expectations of some future, unspecified industrial use. There was no interest from private developers, and meanwhile, younger residents of the area were leaving in droves (Hebbert: p. 189).

At first, the central government's sweeping new powers brought little dramatic change, as the strategy was simply to clean up the sites, lay down new infrastructure, and offer significant tax concessions to developers. However, one important transformation did take place immediately. The previous mundane plan for the area had intended to drain and fill in the dock basins to create featureless new industrial sites, but the LDDC realized it would be cheaper to leave the water in place and more effective to capitalize on its immense evocative ambience. But development

still proceeded at a lackluster, piecemeal pace; the LDDC had little in the way of a visionary plan (a beautiful townscape-inspired urban design master plan for the Isle of Dogs by Gordon Cullen and David Gosling had been rejected by the Corporation in 1982 (Gosling: pp. 124–145); see Figure 3.3) and the government was content to await action according to market preferences. To stimulate private investment further the government did invest £77 million in a new light rail link (the Docklands Light Railway) in 1982, but the predominant vision in the private sector was still a low-density business park with trees, ample parking and 'crinkly tin sheds … a convenient backyard to the real London west of the Tower' (Hebbert: p. 192).

When change came, it did indeed come from the private sector, and in a fortuitous way. The chairman of the international bank Credit Suisse First Boston was looking for space to expand his company's operations in London in anticipation of the explosion in financial services that was about to occur in the city (the so-called Big Bang of 1986). He found London's planning policy of trying to squeeze all the new office development into the historic medieval core absurd, especially as the open vistas of the docklands lay 10 minutes drive to the east, where planning permission was virtually guaranteed by central government along with 10 years of property tax relief (Hebbert: p. 193). Other American banks and developers were brought in, and in consultation with the LDDC, new plans were announced for over 12 000 000 square feet (1 110 000 square meters) of new office space in 1985.

Five million square feet of office space was ready by 1992, along with urban squares and boulevards, but road and rail transportation infrastructure was still sadly lacking, and this, combined with a severe slump in the office market, led to collapse of these grand ambitions and the massive bankruptcy of the lead developer, Olympia & York. At one time Olympia & York was the largest development company in the world, but in 1993 it folded in financial ruin with debts of over $20 billion (Hebbert: p. 195). Ironically, the collapse came just as new highways and a more efficient and dependable docklands railway improved accessibility. Work was also set to begin on the long-awaited Jubilee Line Underground line extension and a nearby terminal (at Stratford) for the new high-speed rail link to the Channel Tunnel and Europe. In 1995, the developer Paul Reichman, once head of Olympia & York, returned to lead an international consortium of investors to revive the project and by the following year work was back on track, with new offices, restaurants and shops.

Figure 3.3 Sketch for development on the Isle of Dogs, near Canary Wharf, London, 1982; Gordon Cullen. Cullen's evocative renderings of urban spaces framed by mixed-use development were too advanced for the crude, market-based thinking that ruled in official circles during the early stages of Docklands development. His vision, as part of plans prepared by Edward Hollamby and Professor David Gosling, was rejected by the London Docklands Development Corporation. *(Reproduction courtesy of Mrs Jacqueline Cullen)*

A decade later, the whole Docklands episode can be viewed as an encapsulation of postmodern planning and urban design, full of contradiction and ambiguity. Today, London Docklands is one of the most thriving urban areas in Britain and across the European continent, but for all its innovation and prosperity, the architecture and urban design are often undistinguished. The buildings and plazas are generic design products of multinational capital rather than works of architecture and urban design that demonstrate responsiveness to the local specifics of place. However, amongst the mediocrity are sprinkled genuine jewels, such as Norman Foster's heroic underground station at Canary Wharf, several other Jubilee Line stations and CZWG's idiosyncratic 'ski-slope' housing. On the economic front, the opinions are similarly mixed: despite the millions of pounds invested in the

Docklands, the 'trickle-down' effect to surrounding underprivileged areas in the East End has been limited and sluggish (Ambrose, in Hebbert: p. 196). How this disappointing design and economic performance can be ameliorated by the next waves of massive developments in the Labour government's Thames Gateway project and the extensive remediation and building frenzy for the 2012 Olympics remains to be seen, and will undoubtedly be the subject of much critical analysis. In the meantime, the profiles of state control, local politics, global capitalism and postmodernism – and their implications for planning, development and urban design – are all present and available for study in the Docklands saga.

These political and planning dramas were by no means unique to Britain. Writing about developments in New York City at about the same time during the

1980s, American geographer Susan Fainstein could be describing London's Docklands when she noted:

> The lead public institutions, in implementing the development projects of the era, operated in isolation from democratic inputs. By focusing on the construction of first-class office space, luxury housing and tourist attractions, and short-changing the affordable-housing, small-business and community-based industry sectors, they prompted developers to engrave the image of two cities – one for the rich and one for the poor – on the landscape. Redevelopment took the form of islands of shiny new structures in the midst of decayed public facilities and deterioration in living conditions for the poor. (Fainstein, 1995: p. 133)

American cities are still dealing with the legacy of these policies and their consequences, and in Britain, the radical shift in priorities from local to central government that the Thatcher administration engineered to jumpstart the Docklands development had immense repercussions for planning across the country. Government ministers intentionally 'dismembered the strategic planning system that had been painfully built up by successive governments during the 1960s and maintained during the 1970s' (Hall, P.: p. 401). First to go were the Regional Economic Planning Councils, abolished in 1979. The 1980 Planning Act radically diminished the potency of county Structure Plans, a major element of coordinated regional planning, and a government policy paper in 1986 proposed abolishing this level of planning altogether. An Act of Parliament in 1986 did indeed disband the regional planning authority for London, the Greater London Council, controlled at that time by elected left-wing politicians opposed to Prime Minister Thatcher's agenda for the capital.

The unabashedly right-wing agenda of the Thatcher government to dismantle planning was heavily influenced by American writers whose work was praised and publicized by conservative think-tanks in the UK, such as the Centre for Policy Studies and the Adam Smith Institute. Among these writers was Edward Banfield, whose book *Unheavenly City Revisited* (1974) comprised a normative libertarian diatribe against government intervention in the 'natural processes' of demographic change, economic growth and individual aspirations to improvement in class status (Thornley: p. 98). A more interesting choice of reference material was the seminal book

The Death and Life of Great American Cities (1961) by Jane Jacobs, in which the author crucified large-scale municipal planning and praised instead, small-scale local communities, full of local businesses and enterprises free of ham-handed government intervention. Whereas *designers* then and today focused on Jacob's descriptions and prescriptions for the physical environment of thriving neighborhoods and districts (mixed uses, small blocks, walkable neighborhoods, eyes on the street, etc.), *political theorists* seized upon the simplistic political message of the book, to the effect that central government planning was bad; local free enterprise was good. Today, progressive planners and urban designers extol Jacob's prescriptions for good, lively and attractive urban places; 20 and 30 years ago conservatives used the same writings to fashion arguments designed to eliminate planning as a public function. Therefore, the criticism of Docklands development being 'Americanized' strikes a much deeper chord than simply the roles of American bank executives, or the American and Canadian nationalities of major developers, or even of the American architecture firms who designed several of the buildings: American thinking went right to the core of the British government's policies. Perhaps as repayment for all this trans-Atlantic beneficence, Britain promptly gifted the idea of Enterprise Zones to America, where it was embraced, oddly enough by left-leaning politicians, and enacted into law in 26 states (Hall, P.: p. 400).

The reversal of Thatcherism from the early 1990s to the present day is quite remarkable in the fields of British planning and urban design. While several changes to the economic fabric of British society (both good and bad) wrought during her period in power have remained a decade-and-a-half later, many aspects of city planning have been significantly transformed. Successive British governments halted the process of dismantling planning before it had gone too far, although from a pro-planning perspective much damage had already been done, both to the British countryside, with extensive development in the formerly protected green belt areas around towns and cities during the 1980s, and to the fabric of planning itself – with low morale in the profession and previous policies in disarray. More recently, many reforms have been implemented, particularly under Tony Blair's administrations and the leadership of Deputy Prime Minister John Prescott, whose Office of the Deputy Prime Minister (ODPM) oversaw environmental and planning matters at a national level until its disbandment and reorganization into the

Department for Communities and Local Government in 2006 following a sex scandal involving the unlikely Mr Prescott. These planning reforms aim to foster a greater sense of environmental sustainability and greater citizen involvement allied with a push for good urban design as prerequisites for new development. For at least one critic, this transformation of the British planning system cannot come a moment too soon.

The American New Urbanist, Hank Dittmar, now the Chief Executive of the Prince's Foundation in London, wrote an opinion piece in the *RIBA Journal* in 2005 stating that while the debates about urban styles and precedents 'rumble on, the British city is being rebuilt as trash-space, dominated by cul-de-sacs and indifferent high-rises … [I]t is time we united to work out why it is so hard to build walkable, mixed-use places and what we can do about it' (Dittmar: p. 26). Clearly reform is on the way. At a 2006 conference on the new Local Development Frameworks (LDFs) and the role of master planning within the new British planning regime, the participants, architects and planners alike, were united about their commitment to improve urban design. The major reservations concerned whether the planning profession possessed the right skills to administer a design-led system. This is a serious concern on both sides of the Atlantic where for years planners have been educated in almost everything except urban design; postmodern critiques of planning viewed the physical design component of planning in very negative terms, considering it to be symptomatic of insensitive bureaucracies that suppressed diversity and difference in pursuit of a fixed and finite plan.

POSTMODERN CRITIQUES OF PLANNING

In part, planners' lack of design skills can be traced back to the harsh curtailment of planning in Britain during the 1980s and the profession's equivalent low status in the USA at that same time. This difficult and barren period led to soul-searching about planning methods, the profession's objectives and even its legitimacy. Planners sought some clear ideological base for action; they wanted to improve democratic representation within planning, and tried to come to terms with the plethora of new and often confusing postmodern critiques of planning. Amidst this enquiry, interest in the physical design of urban places was marked by its absence. Whereas postmodernism in

architecture focused on trying to create new aesthetics and design principles, but generated little more than a change in stylistic preferences combined with much unintelligible writing, postmodern thought in geography and planning had more profound but negative effects, giving rise to arguments that challenged the legitimacy of the whole planning enterprise.

This conclusion from academics generally of a left-wing persuasion played into the hands of right-wing Thatcherite and Reaganite policies that aimed to reduce planning to little more than a mechanism to facilitate private development, and it has taken a couple of decades for the planning system in Britain to enlarge its scope to become again an agency of proactive government policy. In America, with the honorable but fleeting exception of the soon to be defunct HOPE VI program for affordable housing, this renaissance has not occurred at national level; it has been left to individual cities such as Portland, OR, or a coordinated collaboration of small towns in north Mecklenburg County, NC, to instigate smart growth initiatives that mold urban and suburban growth into more sustainable patterns of compact development and preserved open space. While such instances of innovative public policies at the scale of individual communities are numerous in America, they still constitute only a small minority of municipalities; elsewhere, planning still remains the handmaiden of private development. As a working planner in the Charlotte region who was a student in one of the author's graduate seminars during the writing of this book remarked: 'All I do is make the developers' lives easier. It's what my elected officials want. They don't seem to care about the future.'

While right-wing Conservative and Republican politicians aimed during the 1980s to reduce or eliminate planning for commercial and ideological purposes, left-wing postmodernist and deconstructionist critics paradoxically sought the same ends, but for very different reasons. These critics saw modernist planning as the repressive hand of a paternalistic, exclusionary political structure, and plotted its downfall by intellectually dismantling the belief in scientific rationalism that was the heart of modernist, comprehensive and design-based planning concepts. These patterns of logical, positivist and progressivist thinking were derived from the great European period of the Enlightenment during the 17th and 18th centuries – and it was Enlightenment principles themselves that bore the brunt of postmodernism's attack.

In historical terms, Enlightenment thought aimed to free individuals from the twin tyrannies of its time – dogmatic religious faith and capricious political despotism – and these liberated individuals, it was believed, could combine in democratic association to manage their collective affairs and build a better world with the help of scientific knowledge and reason. Such thinking framed the attitudes of America's Founding Fathers, the authors of that country's Constitution, in their search for independence from Great Britain, and this same philosophy nurtured the growth of western democracies in the 19th and 20th centuries. This paradigm links capitalism, democracy and progress in a setting where they may comfortably coexist, and planning becomes the mechanism and framework in which citizens can act together to manage issues concerning private ownership and public sharing of space (Healey, 1992: p. 236).

Despite the undeniable benefits brought to society and culture by this great intellectual revolution, the generation of thinkers in Europe and America during the 1970s and 1980s opposed this modernist project with verve and vigor; they considered the internal coherence and consistency of belief that characterized modernist approaches to problems oppressed and suppressed divergent worldviews and ideological positions – particularly those of minorities and underprivileged sections of society. In terms of city planning and design, critics pointed to the failures of city development during the period of urban renewal where big plans led to the further deprivation of the poor, and to the dysfunctional zoning of the city into separate zones that made sense on planners' diagrams and corporate balance sheets, but caused social hardship and financial stress on poorer workers and women trying to balance home and work lives. At a more abstract level, British geographer David Harvey characterized the shift from modernism to postmodernism as a break with 'large-scale, metropolitan-wide, technologically rational and efficient urban plans backed by no-frills modern architecture' and a move towards 'fiction, fragmentation, collage, and eclecticism, all suffused with ephemerality and chaos' (Harvey, 1989: p. 66).

Within this new fragmented view of culture, deconstructionist arguments broadly held that whatever form planning took, it could never be a legitimate act in a postmodern world. Planning was inevitably predicated on some form of modernist thought, with all the unified, logical and synthetic rationality that implied, and this cohesive paradigm had been rendered obsolete in the new era and fractured universe of divergence, discord and difference (Healey, 1992: p. 237). In this intellectual context, planning, with its

quest for measurable improvement in urban conditions based on a focused vision of a better society, including better designed buildings and urban spaces, was considered at best irrelevant, because a singular vision was no longer appropriate for the new diverse society; or at worst, oppressive, as the imposition of a dominating world view by those with power upon those without it. By this reading, privileged and powerful factions (capitalist corporations, government bureaucracies and heterosexual white males) were always in a position to usurp and dominate the efforts of less powerful, or powerless groups such as minorities, ethnic cultures, immigrants, women, gays, lesbians and poor sections of society, and to mold the planning process to fit their own controlling agenda. From this perspective, physical planning and urban design were the expression in concrete form of these oppressive, controlling objectives.

As articulate as some of these critiques were, even those with strong arguments provided little help to planners and urban designers trying to do a job in the complex world of practice. There was open disagreement amongst academic planners about how to proceed with planning once traditional Enlightenment views had been challenged and to some extent dethroned by postmodernist critiques, and much intellectual effort has been expended over the last 20 years to define and elaborate this disjuncture between modernism and postmodernism in planning (Beauregard, 1990, 1991; Goodchild, 1990; Milroy, 1991; et al.). The appeal of this critical enterprise was understandable: 'The modernism–postmodernism divide provided an overall framework in which to critique the whole era of modernist planning. It therefore allowed postmodernist analysts to distance themselves from modernism's monolithic … master narrative in place of multiple discourses' and thus 'provided theoretical support for the emerging interest in multiculturalism' and diversity (Campbell and Fainstein: p. 149). But like Marxist analysis of previous decades, these critiques offered insight into cultural themes but little useful guidance for practicing planners. Indeed, as Peter Hall has suggested, postmodern planning theory, with few exceptions, 'moved planners towards a total relativism, a denial of any kind of norms' (Hall, P.: p. 375).

In this rudderless void, practicing planners tended to veer between various styles of planning on a contingency basis, applying whichever techniques seemed most appropriate for particular challenges and tasks. This disconnect between planning theory and practice did not stop academics from trying to bring intellectual order to the confusing landscape of postmodern planning, and some of this analysis is useful. Less extreme deconstructive arguments can combine with those encouraging plurality and difference to correct those modernist certainties that turned out to be false, e.g. about urban form (such as the compositional principle of separated object buildings isolated in free-flowing, 'universal' space) and dogmatic 'top-down' planning procedures that told people what was good for them. Likewise, challenging the modernist belief that ideas held to be true in western democracies must be universally correct in other religious, ethnic or cultural contexts also produces an important check on oppressive intellectual hegemony. Additionally, understanding that knowledge of the world gained through non-scientific means, such as mythologies, art and ethnic or cultural traditions, can be as valid as information acquired by means of rational and technical procedures provides a worthy line of enquiry likely to enrich professional conversations.

However, using this critical approach to demolish any conceptual structure that incorporates norms about communal standards or rational decision-making, and replacing those standards with a completely non-hierarchical relativism (e.g. Dear, 1995), strikes at the very heart of planning and urban design; both these disciplines depend at some point on rational criteria and consensus. From a reading of Lyotard (1988), Simonsen (1990) argues in a similar vein to Dear, suggesting that postmodernism places equal value on 'milliards' of small narratives 'weaving the web of daily life' which leads to the breakdown of consensus and the fragmentation the communal realm, undermining the basis for collective action. But if there can be no valid criteria by which to judge the relative merits of one theory over another (or one design proposal against alternatives) 'then it would follow that there can be no reasoned debate … at all (Taylor, 1999: pp. 338–339).

In a more positive vein, English planning theorist Patsy Healey (following the path sketched out by David Harvey, John Forester and Jürgen Habermas) has countered these trends towards complete relativism by suggesting that some aspects of the postmodernist challenge to planning must be 'actively resisted … as regressive and undemocratic' (Healey, 1992: p. 238). Healey outlines several strategies for planning to capitalize on some postmodernism insights while resisting others, seeking either to create new forms of postmodern practice or to reformulate the modernist project in some way so that it remains valid (Healey, 1992: pp. 238–249). Paraphrasing Healey's

longer list, there are two approaches among these possibilities that are particularly relevant:

1. Bolstering the belief in scientific rational discourse by bringing the incremental logic of the marketplace into planning as a replacement for the grand social and physical visions of traditional planning.
2. Reforming modernist planning and urban design by capitalizing on new postmodern appreciations for the importance of diversity and difference by focusing the planning process around greater communication, tolerance and respect between divergent interest groups. This comprises the so-called 'communicative planning' approach, a theory and technique that is gaining considerable credibility and support in contemporary planning practice.

These potential courses of future action look like new versions of existing types of planning and design that have framed the last 50 years of urban effort; incrementalist, democratic, equity and advocacy planning are all represented here. For example, refiguring planning around the logic of the market is a very incrementalist approach, dependent upon many individual developments to create the future in an organic manner without any overall cohesive master plan or strategy. Physical design master plans may exist, but only at the local project level; regional strategies have little place in this approach, as they require public intervention in the marketplace to redirect investment according to social rather than financial criteria.

Augmenting the emphasis on scientific, rational thought by incorporating market economics into planning essentially resists the whole postmodern critique of planning, and reinforces its modernist principles. In this scenario, planning comes into play only to ensure that the actions of individuals (or private companies) do not impose excessive costs on neighbors, communities and environments – 'the external costs' or 'externalities' noted earlier in this chapter. As far as possible, this kind of planning uses pricing strategies that require these external costs to be internalized, i.e. paid for by the people or companies deriving benefit from their actions (Healey, 1992: p. 239). One example of this strategy is Mayor Ken Livingstone's Central London Congestion Charge, whereby motorists who drive in the heart of Britain's capital have to pay for that convenience. This limits the number of drivers who choose to use their own private vehicles, with the consequence that more people are redirected onto public transport, thus reducing congestion and air pollution, while money is raised through the charges to defray the costs of improved bus and train services.

Other examples can be found in American cities, where these ideas of pricing and 'internalizing' the costs of development are debated vociferously. Developers are united against these concepts, wishing to retain the *status quo* whereby the public sector carries as many of the external costs associated with development as possible, especially constructing roads, providing water and sewer service, and, most importantly in high growth areas, building enough new schools to keep pace with the surge in population. But as cities grow, the ever-increasing costs of providing these municipal services outstrip the revenues collected through the primary funding sources of local property and sales taxes, leading to continual tax increases on existing citizens to pay for facilities required by newcomers. The unfairness of this equation has sparked major protests and angry public arguments, pitting newcomers against existing residents and suburbanites against people living in central neighborhoods. These debates include calls for tax reform, especially the ideas of 'impact fees' levied on new development to defray the costs of new and improved facilities needed to cater to the newcomers. (This is similar in some respects to the British concept of 'planning gain,' where developers are charged a fee to help fund public services, based on the increase in value to their land brought about by new development.) Another American idea, 'Adequate Public Facilities Ordinances' (APFOs), comprise regulations that link and limit the rate of new development to the capacity of community facilities like schools, parks and sewage systems to handle the new growth. In situations where facilities are insufficient to accommodate new development, these ordinances provide local authorities with a mechanism to halt or slow growth, but, importantly, like British provisions, these regulations usually include opportunities for developers to pay sums of money to public authorities to offset the costs of new schools and other services, and thus gain permission for new residential subdivisions or commercial developments to proceed.

Because developers have no intention of reducing their profits by paying the impact fees themselves, they inevitably pass the costs onto new homebuyers and thus increase the price of new housing. This can lead to a slow down in housing purchases and the construction of new homes, something that developers are at pains to avoid. APFOs are seen by right-wing

opinion in America as flagrant mechanisms to intervene in the marketplace to delay development to an artificial pace determined by public bureaucrats, and as a means of exacting money from the private sector to pay for public facilities. In cities like Charlotte, where historically private developers have been able to influence elected officials to do their bidding – by financial contributions to their election campaigns and by assiduously cultivating personal relationships to curry favors in return – these more progressive ideas have been stillborn. Moves by various activist groups or by city planning staff to move such ideas forward on the agenda tend to get stifled by elected officials on the City Council and County Commission. This is a familiar story in towns and cities across America.

The second approach for creating a new planning methodology, one that extends modernity's tolerance and expands the process to include a more activist recognition of diversity and disadvantage (Healey, 1992: p. 241), can be illustrated by a brief discussion of the British government's overarching planning strategy for 'sustainable communities.' The approach set out in Deputy Prime Minister John Prescott's Five-Year Plan 'Sustainable Communities: People, Places and Prosperity,' (ODPM, 2005c) is a mixture of modernist and postmodernist ambitions and sensibilities. The government's vision of sustainable communities for all is expressed clearly in the document: 'A flourishing, fair society based on opportunity and choice for everyone depends on creating sustainable communities – places that offer everyone a decent home that they can afford in a community in which they want to live and work, now and in the future' (ODPM, 2005c: p. 4).

In postmodern critical terminology, this is a 'totalizing meta-narrative,' i.e. a large-scale vision for social progress that, in this instance, embraces all of British society. This is the kind of utopian modernist thinking that postmodern theorists decry on the grounds it unduly subordinates other worldviews beneath this dominant paradigm. However, the government's policy document also indicates an awareness of difference, a postmodern trend: 'Not all communities are the same: different places have different strengths and needs' (ODPM, 2005c: p. 4). A more detailed definition of sustainable communities also bridges between modernist and postmodernist thought: 'Sustainable communities … meet the diverse needs of existing and future residents, are sensitive to their environment, and contribute to a high quality of life. They are safe and inclusive, well planned, built and run, and offer equality of opportunity and good services for all.' Such places are also 'diverse, reflecting their local circumstances.' They offer, amongst other attributes, 'a sense of community identity and belonging ... social inclusion ... (and) tolerance, respect and engagement with people from different cultures, backgrounds and beliefs.' They are ' well run – with effective and inclusive participation, representation and leadership' (ODPM, 2005c: pp. 56–7). Physical design makes a major comeback in these policies: plans for sustainable communities also include expectations for environmentally sensitive architectural and urban design, affordable housing and transportation choices, as well as access to good schools and health care.

Similar notions exist in the urban policy statements of the Conservative opposition party in Britain. A position paper, entitled *Renewing Suburbia: Creating Suburban Villages*, sets out how Tory leader David Cameron wants to revive suburban housing estates into living and working urban villages that have a master planned mix of uses and types of housing that enable people to live, work and shop in close proximity. These urban villages would be safe and attractive places for people to bring up families (Woolf: p. 27). In an encouraging contrast to America, both main political parties in the UK are vying to become the leading champions of green design.

But the notion of sustainability needs to be defined very carefully. Australian critic Leonie Sandercock has examined the concept from postmodernist and modernist viewpoints, in what she calls 'critical and utopian perspectives.' She argues from a postmodernist (critical) position that sustainability is only:

> ... the latest in a long line of totalizing thought since the Enlightenment which claims to be *the* only true and moral way of looking at and analyzing the world ... [such as] The Garden City to the Regional City to Decentralization/New Towns to Designing with Nature, to Systems Theory, Radical Planning, and the current rages, Communicative Action and the New Urbanism... Underlying this ... approach is the suspicion that sustainability might yet be another way of screwing the poor in rich countries, and poor nations in a global context. (Sandercock, 2004: unpaginated)

At the same time, Sandercock admits to the attraction of the utopian impulse by framing two 'great questions' for the future of human society: 'how might we live with each other in peaceful intercultural coexistence in the cities ... of the 21st century? And how might we live well and sustainably on the earth?

[These are] very much urban questions.' She goes on to suggest a way forward:

> What is a sustainable approach to urban development? It is *not* the model that most cities have adopted in the past 15 years or so to cope with restructuring, where the notion of urban development is one of transforming the physical fabric in order to attract transnational capital, investing in megaprojects, infrastructure, convention centers, etc., and improving a city's international image and credit rating, but paying little or no attention to its own neighborhoods and communities (place *marketing* rather than place *making*). Actually, improving the physical environment of central cities is very important in attracting investment, but in itself, this is not sufficient; it is not the road to sustainable development. To be sustainable, urban development has to be based on [investment in] a city's own resource endowments, which includes human, social, cultural, intellectual, environmental and urban capital, and needs to be guided by a long term vision of the good city that enjoys popular support because it has been put together through extensive discussion. So a model of inclusive democracy seems to be central to such a vision, as well as a local state which is attentive ... (Sandercock, 2004: unpaginated)

The British government's approach seems to understand and encourage this process, but the question must remain: to what extent can any top-down initiative, however well intentioned and 'attentive,' be compatible with bottom-up, community-driven ingenuity that might challenge the ethos of the overall program?

Despite Sandercock's apparent dismissal of 'communicative action,' or 'communicative planning,' as others have called it, the suggestions for 'extensive discussion' and 'local democracy' within the overall vision of 'the good city' sound very much like the planning approach advocated by British academic Patsy Healey, as 'Planning as a Communicative Enterprise' (Healey, 2006).

This 'communicative' way of revitalizing planning in the postmodern era capitalizes on new awareness of diversity and difference by increasing the debate and dialogue between all groups affected by the planning effort. This approach means a lot more than adding a few public meetings to the schedule; it tries to create new and site-specific knowledge by active communication and sharing perceptions and experiences between all participants, and avoiding pre-formulated

Figure 3.4 Typical charrette in progress, Huntersville, NC, 2004. Residents talk and consultants listen during the early stages of a community design charrette.

or generic concepts. During this process, nothing is off the table or inadmissible in the debate except claims that certain topics cannot be discussed. By bringing as many different participants together as possible, communicative planning confronts the challenge of 'making sense together while living differently,' and creates a new paradigm of 'future seeking,' rather than the 'future defining' model more common in the traditional comprehensive master planning process (Healey, 1992: pp. 240–252).

British planner Sir Peter Hall has pointed out that this all seems very useful, except that 'stripped of its dense Germanic philosophical basis' it sounds very much like the democratic planning theories of the 1960s and in particular akin to Paul Davidoff's proposals for advocacy planning: 'cultivate community networks, listen carefully to the people … educate the citizens in how to join in, supply information, … emphasize the need to participate (and) compensate for external pressures' (Hall. P.: pp. 371–372). In fact, this sounds very much like what takes place in a public design charrette (see Figure 3.4). Despite this historical recycling of concepts and methods, there is one important difference. The often abstruse theoretical discursions of Marxists and postmodernists have allowed attentive planners and architects to 'penetrate the mask of capitalism,' (Hall, P.: p. 372) and understand more accurately the forces at work in their professions. This enables self-aware professionals to be more effective in assisting citizen groups and the general public to act and change their own lives and environments for the better. As part of this effort, skills in urban design are increasingly perceived as relevant to mainstream planning policy and objectives.

MASTER PLANNING AND URBAN DESIGN AS PUBLIC POLICY

Despite the frenzy of intellectual activity in defining and demolishing planning theories over the last 40 years, in Britain at least, vestiges of planning as physical design never quite went away. The 'townscape' school of civic design exemplified best by the English urban designer Gordon Cullen (see Figure 3.3) whose eponymous book encapsulated this approach in simple text and beautiful drawings, remained a critical counterpoint to mainstream modernism, and prompted the picturesque 'neo-vernacular' revival in the 1970s in many housing and urban development projects (Cullen, 1961). During that period, this author was a senior associate in a small west country practice in the UK that won several national awards for housing that was heavily influenced by Cullen's work (see Figure 3.5), and the publication of the *Design Guide for Residential Areas*, by the County Council of Essex in 1973 (see Figure 3.6) formalized this approach and marked a determined attempt by architect-planners to 'place their practice of design control on a clearer theoretical footing by articulating "principles" of good design' (Taylor, 1999: p. 333).

In practice, therefore, as Taylor has clearly pointed out:

… at the level of 'local' planning, at least, many planners continued to believe that the physical form and aesthetic appearance of new development were important concerns of town planning. And although there were lessons for small area 'local' planning in systems and rational process

Figure 3.5 Oaklands Park, Dawlish, Devon, UK, 1975; Mervyn Seal and Associates, Architects. The picturesque creation of views, setting up a specific sequence of visual experiences, closely followed Gordon Cullen's townscape design principles. This example demonstrates that suburban housing can be the venue for good design; compare with Figure I.1 in the Introduction.

thinking … these lessons could be accommodated within an essentially traditional design-based conception of planning. (Taylor, 1999: p. 333)

Taylor supports one of the main contentions of this book, that the physical, design-based conception of planning continues to have relevance to planning theory and practice today, as witnessed by the revival of interest in urban design since the 1980s (Taylor, 1999: p. 333). This process can only be helped by ideas derived from communicative planning; fostering greater public participation can only enrich the physical design process.

The new, mandatory Local Development Frameworks (LDFs) – required of every planning authority in England by the Planning and Compulsory Purchase Act of 2004 – reinforce the importance of physical design by establishing detailed spatial, economic and environmental strategies for all types of new and infill development within their jurisdiction. Additionally, all local authorities are required to set up increased opportunities for public participation in deciding the content of new plans. Once approved, these plans control all new developments unless there is a very unusual circumstance judged worthy of an exception. A typical LDF (from the author's former home of the South Hams area in the county of Devon) defines its overarching aim as improving the wellbeing of all people in its planning area through sustainable development. In a very proactive manner, the document states

that 'planning shapes where people live and work, and has a critical role to play in achieving balanced housing markets and sustainable improvements in the economic performance of the area' (South Hams District Council, 2006: p. 5). Far from merely facilitating development, as is commonplace in the American system, English planning practice operates on the clear assumption that *it will guide development*; the market will follow. In the South Hams' Area Action Plans produced as part of their LDF, new housing is specified both by the number of new homes and the specific sites on which these homes will be built (see Figure 3.7). Other objectives focusing on physical design include protecting the environment; regenerating existing towns and villages; providing more affordable housing mainly through a 'new town' proposal (for which a detailed urban design master plan has been prepared); and above all, developing in a sustainable manner. This mantra of sustainability is repeated over and over, and is proudly defined as '*the underlying purpose of the planning system*' (South Hams District Council, 2006: p. 5, 8; author's italics).

The American experience with physical planning and urban design has been somewhat different. Without a comparable professional tradition like the British townscape school, issues of physical design largely disappeared from planners' agendas from the 1960s onwards, especially with development control in the USA being administered through zoning ordinances that dealt almost exclusively with land and building

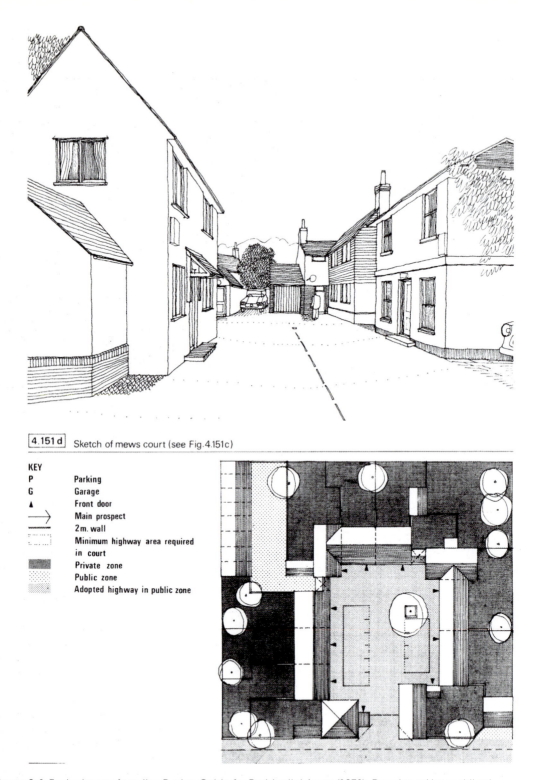

4.151 d Sketch of mews court (see Fig. 4.151c)

KEY
P   Parking
G   Garage
▲   Front door
→   Main prospect
           2 m. wall
           Minimum highway area required
           in court
           Private zone
           Public zone
           Adopted highway in public zone

Figure 3.6 Typical page from the *Design Guide for Residential Areas* (1973). Developed by architect-planner Melville Dunbar for Essex County Council, in southeast England, this document became a model for later design codes using neo-vernacular (or neo-traditional) styles of housing. *(Reproduction courtesy of Essex County Council)*

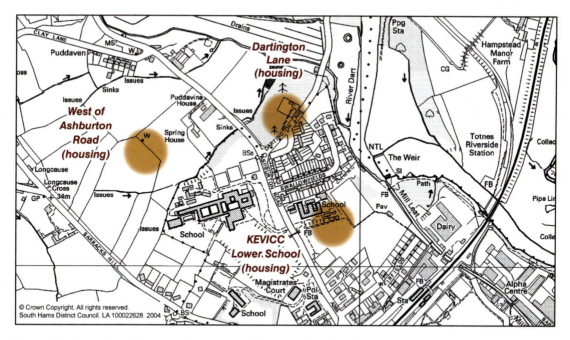

Figure 3.7 Extract from the Local Development Framework for the South Hams district of the county of Devon, England, 2006. This is a typical example of an English local plan delineating specific locations for new development based on sustainable criteria such as adjacency to existing development and infrastructure, including public transportation. *(Reproduction by permission of South Hams District Council and the Ordnance Survey on behalf of HMSO © Crown Copyright 2006. All rights reserved. Ordnance Survey licence number 100046395)*

use, with little or no mention of architectural or urban design. Fortunately, this was not quite universal across the nation. The work of Jonathan Barnett in New York and that city's local plans created during the 1970s and 1980s included rigorous urban design thinking, encapsulated in planning guidance and development control (zoning) regulations. Barnett's work as a teacher and founder of the Graduate Program in Urban Design at New York's City College in the 1970s also continued to support the idea that physical design retained an important role in planning. Students in that program were architects who received 'intensive education in the context of urban design: law, public administration, real estate, the sociology of cities, environmental psychology, as well as theories and case studies of urban design.' Students were expected to 'transfer their design skills from buildings to the city as a whole' and urban designers were expected to work 'with other professionals on the design of cities in the same way as the architect works with other professionals in the design of buildings' (Barnett, 1974: p. 190). However, this was a special case particular to the place and key individuals in

positions of authority, and was not replicated to any great extent in other American cities except progressive west coast metropolitan areas such as Portland, Seattle and San Francisco where sophisticated urban design concepts were also incorporated into local legislation (Punter, 1999).

While urban design did not often figure as an important component of American planning, the practice of comprehensive planning did receive renewed stimulus through a 1996 article by American planner Judith Innes. Innes made a case for a return to comprehensive planning by relying on the recently promoted theory and techniques of communicative planning, and used this new approach to rebut perhaps the most famous critique of comprehensive planning, by Alan Altshuler in 1965. Innes argued persuasively that new public participation techniques developed under the rubric of communicative planning enabled the process of consensus building to be reinvigorated, and a usable definition of the public interest to be achieved. This specifically countered Altshuler's main criticisms of comprehensive planning, that the public interest is not something fixed,

59

but fluid and changing through political will and political action, and as such, it is not discoverable by planners' normative techniques of rational observation, analysis and argument (Altshuler, 1965a: p. 303).

Whether stimulated by the theoretical arguments of Innes' article (which was based on extensive practical experience over several years in California) or simply by the persistence of old comprehensive planning ideas that would not die, comprehensive planning for communities in America is alive and well once more, with towns and cities all across the nation engaged in such ventures. Austin, TX, provides one good example (Beatley and Brower, 1994), and more locally to this author's region, Salisbury, NC, a town of some 40 000 people 40 miles north of Charlotte, is also typical in this regard, having recently completed a 20-year vision plan. Ironically, Salisbury is the seat of the county government that threw the planners out in the fit of libertarian pique noted in Chapter 2. The town is an independent municipality, separate from the administration of its surrounding county, and by contrast, a very progressive place (see Figure 3.8).

The primary difference between the planning documents from the South Hams and Salisbury, NC, lies in the clear presumption by planners in Salisbury that growth will occur wherever developers build rather than in places chosen by the planners. The only guidance regarding patterns of growth is a map indicating primary and secondary growth areas; the primary area comprises the existing zoning jurisdiction, while the secondary area consists of outlying agricultural land interspersed with low-density housing subdivisions over which Salisbury has no control (see Figure 3.9). The plan states its preference for infill development in the primary area, and where new development takes place on greenfield land in the secondary area, the document suggests that it take the form of compact 'Neighborhoods and Village Communities' (Salisbury: p. 185). Because the Salisbury planners cannot control where growth will occur, their community's plan relies more on detailed policy recommendations with New Urbanist design guidelines for streets, house design and landscaping to improve the generic and mediocre design of new developments. Whereas the South Hams LDF is full of proactive strategies to guide development, there is a sense throughout the Salisbury document that the town authorities are setting out an admirable vision for their town, but that it is one that they doubt the development industry will take seriously. Accordingly, the Salisbury plan is heavy on detailed recommendations because it is largely impotent on the major issues.

One setting where Salisbury does have a larger measure of control over its future is its historic downtown core, where the town has successfully used charrette-based master plans in smaller projects designed to bring the private and public sectors together. The author and a colleague, Robin Davis, led one such master plan effort in 1998 for three blocks in the town center. A public design charrette was held on site, and a new three-dimensional master plan produced for the conversion and revitalization of existing buildings and the insertion of new infill buildings. The town adopted the plan immediately, and within 6 years, most of the recommendations were implemented, with the new buildings matching the plan's vision very closely (see Figures 3.10 and 3.11).

This illustrates the type of project wherein urban design master planning is returning to the fore of American practice. The last 10 years have seen a marked resurgence of these techniques as architects have reentered the planning field, bringing with them their training in design and their concern with product as much as process. Examples such as the Salisbury plan illustrate how cross-disciplinary urban design has shifted the debate between modernist and postmodernist viewpoints: master planning has been removed from its traditional place within conventional comprehensive planning and recontextualized through the charrette process of communicative planning whereby different groups can be brought to the negotiating or drawing table, with the result that the resulting verbal and drawn communication will help

Figure 3.8 Town center, Salisbury, NC.
Redevelopment of sites in the historic downtown has been controlled by master plans and historic district regulations to promote compatibility with older buildings.

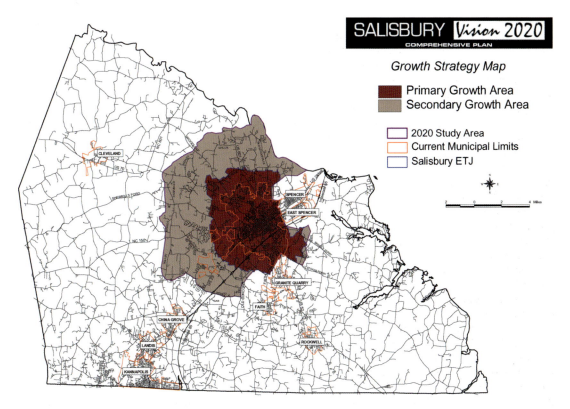

Figure 3.9 Growth Strategy Map, Salisbury, NC, 2001. In contrast to the English example in Figure 3.7, growth management in a progressive American community is limited to the identification of hierarchic preferred areas of development, most of which are not even controlled by city zoning. These controls are limited to the dark brown areas within the city's boundaries and its limited extra-territorial jurisdiction (ETJ). *(Reproduction courtesy of the City of Salisbury, NC)*

Figures 3.10 and 3.11 Downtown redevelopment site, Salisbury, NC, before (left; 1999) and after redevelopment (right; 2005). In contrast to the vagueness of its overall growth management plans, specific urban redevelopment sites are controlled by detailed master plans. The new development in Figure 3.11 matches the project master plan very closely.

identify the best possible solutions for all concerned (Storper: p. 169). In this process, the totalizing scope of modernist planning has given way to a more post-modern, fragmentary vision constructed from issues of diversity, differences, and sometimes conflict; within this fragmented context, master plans still aim for a degree of comprehensiveness but in smaller, discontinuous increments of the city such as town center revitalization projects and efforts to restructure the suburbs on a site by site basis.

In some ways the fluctuating discourse championed by postmodern theorists was anticipated by none other than Patrick Abercrombie, one of the profession's leading practitioners and teachers, and an early champion of comprehensive planning in Britain. In 1927 he warned about the dangers of conceiving master planning as a static exercise in physical typologies, crediting Patrick Geddes with enriching the process of town planning and avoiding the discipline becoming merely a sterile and mechanical mix of typological clichés such as the Parisian boulevard or the English garden village (Mellor: p. 157).

Abercrombie went on to say that Geddes shattered this formalist dream by the famous Scottish polymath's insistence on a planning process that sought out environmental, social and economic factors specific to each region as the basis for planning instead of using empty formal formulas. This exhortation from 80 years ago has clear implications for our postmodern age. First, that the master planning process should be shaped by the particular physical, environmental, economic and social conditions pertinent to the particular community under discussion rather than simply being a vehicle for the designer's preferred set of physical forms; and second, that the master plan has to find the right balance between vision, prescription and flexibility.

The master plans produced by the charrette process described in this book are much more detailed in their urban and architectural content than many examples encountered within normative American planning practice. In parallel with good British examples, they take two-dimensional thinking into the third dimension of real places, and are specific, detailed and thorough enough in their depiction of urban qualities to create agreement about the architectural, urban and environmental character of an area. At the same time, they are robust enough to facilitate change over time, particularly when their implementation is managed by form-based zoning ordinances. Any examination of a pleasant neighborhood, town or city reveals the buildings and urban

spaces that generate the place's character last much longer than uses. Master plans that set out the components of urban form and space needed to create and develop this 'sense of place' provide a much more profound and reliable framework for a community's evolution than do abstract maps of transitory uses.

Master planning and form-based zoning create interesting challenges and opportunities. The whole concept of master planning usually involves the definition of some future state of urban development, most often in the form of an economically realistic build-out study of the land in question, but the examples in this book do not imply a static or finite vision. To different degrees, the plans function as *illustrations* of what can be achieved rather than blueprints for precise implementation, although the case study illustrated in Chapter 8 is very much rooted in developmental reality. Many master planning projects have a time scale of 10–20 years for realization, and no set of drawings can fix everything about the future. Instead, the detailed master plan acts both as a signpost and a map, pointing in a clear direction and providing plentiful information about how to reach the chosen destination. It is detailed and specific because signposts and maps are useless if they are vague and ambiguous. The best master plans are always accompanied by implementation documents, including form-based zoning in the USA and the design code equivalent in the UK. These codes, along with detailed programs of public works improvements, public and private sector investments or administrative actions that are prioritized in the project report, provide the tools municipalities need to manage development over time, keeping it on track and handling variations that may arise.

This characterization of master plans is very similar to the definition established by Britain's Urban Design Group for CABE, the government's advisory body on architecture and the built environment. In the 2002 document *Urban Design Guidance*, author Robert Cowan writes:

The purpose of a master plan is to set out principles on matters of importance, not to prescribe in detail how development should be designed. But a master plan should show in some detail how the principles are to be implemented. If the master plan shows an area designated for mixed-use development, for example, it should show a layout (of buildings, streets and other public spaces) that will support such uses ... by ensuring that the footprints of the buildings are appropriate ... (Cowan: p. 13)

Figure 3.12 Charrette Discussion, Wake Forest, NC, 2003. Communicative planning strategies must include people who may not normally involve themselves in planning discussions. Here, a meeting is attended by a specially invited local women's group.

This is also comparable to the 'design in detail' philosophy at the heart of the charrette process, and another integral charrette principle, the fast feedback loop, satisfies an important criterion set out by Healey in her exposition of communicative planning (Healey, 1992). Healey is at pains to point out the necessity for formal techniques of urban analysis and design to be supplemented by wide-ranging discussions of moral, social, economic and aesthetic issues and experiences, expressed in many forms and listened to with equal seriousness (see Figure 3.12). The ability of the charrette process to give tangible design form to ideas as they are raised in this free flowing critique and learning experience, enables the concepts to be debated more accurately and helps individuals and groups understand and agree on plan proposals without necessarily having a unified point of view.

In this way assumptions by participants can be critiqued and the process demystified through openness and transparency without simplification (Healey, 1992: p. 248). The site specificity of project design work strongly suggests that the design code for any project's implementation should also be tailored to the specifics of that place and community. For example, the form-based code connected with the master plan for redevelopment of a predominantly African-American community in Greenville, SC, in 2001, followed this pattern. Writing about this in our book *Design First*, my wife, Linda Luise Brown, and I explained that:

Because our master plan [produced from a week-long community charrette] is a realistic build-out

'study' rather than a firm development proposal, it's necessary to enact a new zoning code tied to the specific design principles of the plan in order to guide actual development projects as they are prepared. Our Neighborhood Code was written to provide for the development of property as shown in the master plan, but it has the inherent flexibility to adapt to future market conditions and more site-specific studies. In addition, the code provides predictability and assurance to potential investors that any future development will be consistent with the master plan. (Walters and Brown: p. 215)

This principle of site specificity is a vital one for community buy-in to the overall project. Any suggestion of preconceived, 'one size fits all' ideas being laid over a community's needs, desires and expectations can kill community interest quickly, and can fall into the trap of the discredited 'expert planner knows best' mentality of old-fashioned comprehensive planning. This requirement for site specificity raises important questions regarding the current American fascination with the 'Smart Code,' invented and promulgated by Andres Duany and Elizabeth Plater-Zyberk, and designed to replace at a stroke the out-of-date and sprawl-inducing zoning ordinances that control development in most American communities.

The intentionally broad range of applicability, and the urgency of solving the problem of sprawl development across the USA, lends credibility to the central premise of the Smart Code – that sound principles of civic design are universal and with only minor variation can fit almost any community in America. This is a powerful ambition, bred of the desire to bring substantial and speedy physical improvements to towns and cities often in dire need of such assistance, but the process for achieving these goals is open to substantial critique in terms of the search for new, participatory paradigms of planning that meld the objective expertise of planning and design experts with the subjective experiences, histories and expectations of individual communities. Accordingly, before returning to this issue in Chapter 5, which reviews form-based coding and other design regulation mechanisms in detail, it is important to examine the history and contemporary practice of the field of public participation. Only through meaningful public participation can master plans and codes have any validity in the modern world.

Planning, urban design and citizen power: community participation in planning from 19th century anarchist roots to today

SYNOPSIS

Public participation in planning and urban design is a topic important enough to merit its own chapter, which reviews its origins in 19th century anarchist philosophy, its development through a diverse group of planning pioneers including Patrick Geddes and Ebenezer Howard at the start of the 20th century, and its impact across a wide range of planning and design efforts, culminating in the charrette methodology advocated in this volume. Among the leading proponents of citizen activism and community power during recent decades are Jane Jacobs, Christopher Alexander, Ralph Erskine and Rod Hackney, the British pioneer of community architecture, along with many young architects and planners involved in the community architecture and advocacy planning movements of the 1970s and 1980s. This chapter puts the work of these individuals and groups in historical and political context.

Public participation in planning and urban design master plans has become a stock in trade of government planning policies promulgated by the British government since the turn of the century, and the process has raised its profile in the USA as local government increasingly sees the benefits conferred on its planning efforts by active community involvement. Academic theory has also focused on public participation through the promotion of 'communicative planning' as a means of providing legitimacy to new planning efforts in a postmodern world. This emphasis on planning as process devalued product-oriented master planning from the 1970s to the 1990s, but allied with design charrettes, master planning has revived in a community-based format that effectively melds process and product. At the start of the 21st century, this revival of master planning has reintegrated urban design directly into the core of planning practice.

ANARCHIST ORIGINS OF COMMUNITY DEVELOPMENT

Events and circumstances in the modern world sometimes have unexpected roots, and the whole concept of public involvement in planning towns and cities is no exception. Important in the evolution of public participation in planning are a couple of disparate historical events, far removed in place and time from our present study. During the summer of 1876, a 34-year-old Russian prince by the name of Peter Kropotkin (1842–1921), 'by birth a member of Russia's most privileged aristocracy but by choice a revolutionary propagandist,' escaped from the prison hospital in St Petersburg, fled the imperial troops and spies of Tsar Alexander II, and boarded a ship bound for England, seeking refuge and intellectual freedom to pursue his radical anarchist agenda (Hulse: p. 1). Nearly two decades later, in 1894, during the widespread arrest of anarchists in France, and the state suppression of that ideology, the eminent French geographer Elisée Reclus (1830–1905), a well-known member of the international anarchist movement, was allegedly saved from imprisonment by the fact that Britain's prestigious Royal Geographical Society 'had crowned his international reputation' as the world's foremost geographer 'by awarding him its gold medal' (Woodcock: p. 21).

These evasions of imprisonment by two of the most important intellectuals in the anarchist movement of the late 19th century kept alive and accessible two strands of thought concerning people, politics and power that have proved of great importance to the history of 20th century planning and urban design. They continue to resonate powerfully today: first, people should be empowered to plan their own cities 'from the bottom up'; and second, that communities in their 'natural' state function best as 'collectivist, small scale societies ... living in harmony with their environments' (Hall, P.: p. 150).

Kropotkin envisaged self-sufficient cities with food grown on surrounding farms. Factories and shops would provide goods and services for local needs, and city parks would be created on land requisitioned from the once private estates of the defunct aristocracy. In similar vein to contemporary 19th century reformers William Morris and Ebenezer Howard, Kropotkin regarded buildings – and by extension, neighborhoods and cities – 'as the product of collective skills ... produced by many hands' (Hulse: pp. 57–59). The sentiment of these social reformers and activists held that society must restructure itself based on cooperation among free individuals and not by the imposition of strictures from a centralized authority, however benign or well intentioned those may appear to be.

In his 1898 book *Fields, Factories and Workshops*, Kropotkin extended this thesis into the concept of 'mutual aid' as a defining premise for the new community. This collaboration, he argued, would resist the centralized authority of the state or major capitalist corporations that he saw as the main cause of suppression of individual freedom in the industrial city. Kropotkin illustrated his premise by an analysis of the medieval city in Europe, where each neighborhood or parish was often the province of a self-governing craft guild; the city was 'the union of these districts, streets, parishes and guilds' (Hall, P.: p. 151; see Figure 4.1). Stripped of its medieval trappings, this is similar to a core belief of New Urbanists, which they in turn updated from New York sociologist Charles Perry's concept, published in the First Regional Plan of New York in 1929, to the effect that a city is a collection of neighborhoods, each with its own character and sociospatial definition.

Kropotkin's French colleague, Elisée Reclus, reinforced the proposition that freedom and justice 'can be found wherever free thought breaks loose from the chains of dogma ... wherever honest people ... join freely together in order to educate themselves, and to reclaim ... the complete satisfaction of their needs' (Reclus, in Clark and Martin: p. 62). Reclus believed that 'patriarchal, authoritarian, power-based institutions of society' conspired against human freedom and nature, and that social and environmental justice could be achieved only when people rediscovered and experienced connectedness with others and with nature through 'engaged, transformative activity.' Reclus 'pointed toward the regeneration of a rich, highly individualized yet social self (and) the regeneration of a free, cooperative community' (Clark and Martin: p. 114).

Another important figure involved in this alternative and communitarian vision of urban development and city design was Patrick Geddes (1854–1932), the famous Scottish geographer. Geddes, who has become justly recognized as the father of regional planning, was an acquaintance of Reclus and Kropotkin, and is best described as an 'unclassifiable polymath' with far-flung interests in geography, biology and social sciences (Hall, P.: p. 143). Most importantly for our enquiry, the idiosyncratic Scotsman drew on his knowledge of the work of Reclus, Kropotkin and others, and contributed to contemporary planning theory 'the idea that men and women could make their own cities' in order to escape a world of mass production and centralized authority (Hall, P.: p. 263).

Geddes took the position that 'society had to be reconstructed not by sweeping governmental measures ... but through the efforts of millions of individuals' (Hall, P.: p. 152). In this way ordinary people could form neighborhoods, collaborate on cities and come together to create and manage geographically defined regions. Included in Geddes' vision was the enhanced role of nature, promoting an ecological viewpoint first described by Reclus in his philosophical

Figure 4.1 Siena, Italy. View from *il Torre Mangia*, the bell tower at the heart of the medieval city. Although not always evident to the modern tourist, each neighborhood or *contrade* is socially well defined and often focuses around a local parish church. *(Photo by Adrian Walters)*

approach which posited that human beings are insep-
arable from their environment, its geographic features, and the flora and fauna of defined natural
regions (Clark and Martin: p. 5). Describing urban
conditions in 1915, Geddes wrote that 'the children,
the women, the workers of the town can come but
rarely to the country … [W]e must therefore bring
the country to them' (Geddes: pp. 48–49). Geddes
imagined an organically evolving urban form where
nature was inextricably combined with urbanity, produced from the collaborative efforts of the communities themselves, and all set within a geographically
and ecologically defined region. This was, in effect,
Ebenezer Howard's Garden City vision writ large.

Howard of course had developed themes similar to
this anarchist-derived philosophy for his Garden City,
involving local management, self-government and
community identity. Howard published his radical
proposal for Garden Cities in 1898, under the title
Tomorrow: A Peaceful Path to Real Reform, the same
year as Kropotkin's *Fields, Factories and Workshops*.
Born in Britain in 1850, Howard lived in America,
notably Chicago, for several years during the 1870s,
and came to understand the implications of new suburbs in Britain and America very well. He appreciated
that the railway had made rural areas directly accessible

to existing towns and cities, a factor which was fundamentally changing the longstanding rationales of
static urban location and form: large populations
could now be shifted to and from remote rural areas
if efficient mass transportation was provided. One of
the most powerful reasons for moving outside cities
was the availability of cheap land in the countryside,
and in Howard's time this land was especially under-
valued. In addition to urban problems of industrial
overcrowding and squalor in British cities, poverty in
rural areas was also endemic. Britain's agricultural
industry at the end of the 19th century was plagued
by recession, and Howard's intention was not only to
relieve urban crises, but also to alleviate rural poverty
by the transformation of depressed rural areas into
prosperous new towns.

Howard's practical scheme created revenue by the
conversion of cheap farmland to urban use, and utilized this money to finance the development of new
cities by reinvesting these profits in the public infrastructure of the community. Despite Howard's unwill-
ingness to commit to any specific town plan, his
famous diagrams clearly illustrate the importance he
placed on this public infrastructure (see Figure 4.2).
He located public institutions at the heart of the community, surrounded them by a park, and this open

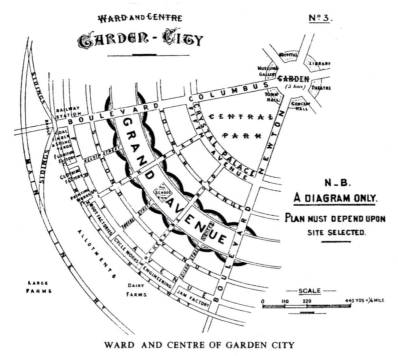

WARD AND CENTRE OF GARDEN CITY

Figure 4.2 Garden City
Diagram, Ebenezer Howard,
1898. This drawing is not a
definitive plan, but a diagram
to illustrate the relationships
of uses and infrastructure.
*(Reproduction courtesy of
MIT Press)*

space was bordered by a linear glass-roofed structure enclosing all the retail functions of the city, very much the precursor of today's shopping mall. Radiating from this center, residential areas incorporated sites of all sizes for a mixture of social classes, and beyond these lay the industrial and manufacturing zone. This was served by a railway ring and bordered by farmland that functioned as a greenbelt to define the edges of the community and to limit growth in accordance with the proposed population figure of 32 000 people.

More important to Howard than the physical form of the new city were its processes of social and economic construction and management. In his famous 'three magnets' diagram, the final words under his new 'town–country' paradigm are 'freedom' and 'cooperation,' twin pillars of the anarchist philosophy of Reclus and Kropotkin (see Figure 4.3). As Hall points out, these words 'are not just rhetoric; they are the heart of the plan' (Hall, P.: p. 95). Once the original mortgage debt was paid off by the self-governing community, the continuing income stream from improving land values and selling off sites for new development could be invested in funds to provide a sort of local welfare

state. The increased land values would flow back into the community 'to found pensions with liberty for our aged poor, now imprisoned in workhouses; to banish despair and awaken hope in the breasts of those that have fallen; to silence the harsh voice of anger, and awaken the soft notes of brotherliness and goodwill' (Howard: p. 13).

The Garden City has been an inspiration to urban designers and planners for over a century, and this economic, social and environmental blend of city and nature still serves as a set of guiding principles today, particularly for New Urbanists. It is surprising therefore to remember that another hero, or rather heroine of New Urbanism, American author and urban critic Jane Jacobs, was caustic in her criticism of Howard's ideas. In recent years it has become fashionable to elevate Jacobs to near sainthood for her passionate and articulate defense of cities and scathing attacks on conventional planning contained in her 1961 landmark book *The Death and Life of Great American Cities*. This *magnum opus* was indeed a stunning work of insight that laid bare and sliced apart many myths of conventional planning; its timeless advice for planners

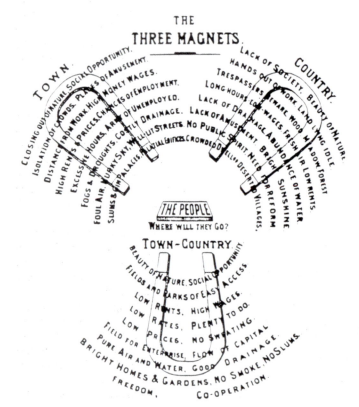

Figure 4.3 The 'Three Magnets' diagram, Ebenezer Howard, 1898. Compare with an updated version in Figure 6.9. *(Reproduction courtesy of MIT Press)*

and urban designers about how neighborhoods and cities actually work as opposed to theories about how they are *supposed* to work are still relevant today. But not everything Jacobs wrote in her otherwise wonderfully irascible and passionate critique of city planning was correct.

PEOPLE VERSUS THE PLANNERS: JANE JACOBS AND THE NEIGHBORHOOD

In particular, Jacobs introduced one fundamental misconception of Howard's vision, calling his view of planning 'essentially paternalistic, if not authoritarian' (Jacobs: p. 29), and dismissed his ideas of smaller towns in a constellation as contrary to the only concepts she recognized as holding promise for cities – dense, mixed-use urban neighborhoods within a great metropolis (see Figure 4.4). While this criticism of paternalistic authoritarianism could be justly applied to the contrasting designs and theories of Le Corbusier and his disciples, Jacobs misconstrued the motivations of Howard and other anarchist-inspired reformers. This serious misreading might be one reason for the great American urbanist Lewis Mumford's trenchant critique of Jacobs, and his defense of the Garden City in his famous 1962 essay in *The New Yorker*, 'The Sky Line: Mother Jacobs' Home Remedies' (Mumford, 1962, 1968). Mumford's own great work, *The City in History* had been published in 1961, the same year as Jacobs' book, and contained a sustained, although not uncritical, paean of praise to city planning

Figure 4.4 Greenwich Village, New York. Although gentrified from the 1950s and 1960s when Jane Jacobs lived in the Village, the neighborhood in 2006 retains much of its vitality and diversity.

and design in its various forms. Jacobs' intemperate criticisms of planning of all stripes thus struck at some of Mumford's core beliefs, and to get a sense of Mumford's barely controlled anger over what he saw as Jacobs' betrayal of profound and valid principles of planning, it is worth quoting at length a passage of his critique. Note Mumford's dismissive use of the appellation 'Mrs' as if to emphasize Jacobs' gender and lack of professional qualifications (she was an associate editor at *Architectural Forum* magazine).

> Ebenezer Howard, Mrs Jacobs insists, 'set spinning powerful and city-destroying ideas. He conceived that the way to deal with the city's functions was to sort and sift out of the whole certain simple uses, and to arrange each of these in relative self-containment. He focused on the provision of wholesome housing as the central problem to which everything else was subsidiary.' No statement could be further from the truth. Mrs Jacobs' wild characterization contradicts Howard's clearly formulated idea of the garden city as a balanced, many-sided urban community. In the same vein, Mrs Jacobs' acute dislike of nearly every improvement in town planning is concentrated in one omnibus epithet expressive of her utmost contempt: 'Radiant Garden City Beautiful.' Obviously, neither radiance (sunlight), nor gardens, nor spaciousness, nor beauty can have any place in Mrs Jacobs' picture of a great city. (Mumford, 1968: p. 189)

Mumford's support of the Garden City concept was well established; he had previously written in praise of the urban dimension of Howard's vision in his Introduction to the 1946 edition of Howard's book, where he stressed: 'The Garden City, as Howard defined it, is not a suburb but the antithesis of a suburb: not a mere rural retreat but a more integrated foundation for an effective urban life' (Mumford, 1946: pp. 29–40).

Patrick Geddes also received a brisk brush off by Jacobs, who ridiculed his regional vision. Based on her antipathy to Howard's Garden City, Jacobs decried Geddes' notion that 'garden cities would be rationally distributed throughout large territories, dovetailing into natural resources, balanced against agriculture and woodland' (Jacobs: p. 29). From today's more ecological viewpoint developed in response to pervasive suburban sprawl, Jacobs' critique seems errant and capriciously misconceived; Geddes' vision seems sensible, even praiseworthy to us today. As a call to action in the face of diminishing natural resources and badly planned suburban growth, Geddes' foresight retains its relevance, with as much or more urgency than at the time of its original declaration nearly a century ago.

For Jacobs, no network of smaller towns could ever rival the cultural and social energy of the big city, and were always inferior in her mind. She refused to see them as complementary to the metropolis, as did Howard and Geddes, and instead saw them as threats to urban vitality, bleeding city life away in pursuit of some rural utopia. She may have been unaware of Kropotkin's thesis that the city was an agent of state and capitalist domination of the individual, and that human freedom and dignity demanded an alternative to the industrial conurbation. Jacobs thus misread much of the Garden City movement, both in its ideology and its physical form, developed primarily through the work of the English architect-planners Raymond Unwin and Barry Parker, who are absent from her critique except for a brief misreading of Unwin's 1912 polemic pamphlet *Nothing Gained by Overcrowding!*

Where Jacobs struck home was in her defense of the urban neighborhood and the street as essential components of city life and city space. She rounded on Le Corbusier for his attack on traditional urban forms and his famous disparagement of the street as a foul and primitive place (Le Corbusier, 1922, 1925), and on his slavish disciples for their refusal to appreciate the character and potential of older, shabby but still functional urban neighborhoods.

In a brilliant passage Jacobs compared the actual evolving state of Boston's North End in the late 1950s to the blinkered perception of planners and bankers who rejected the evidence of their own eyes and preferred instead the dry dogma of their planning theories and financial *pro formas*. Jacobs described how, in the years after World War II, the neighborhood slowly transformed itself from an overcrowded slum to a place characterized by an 'atmosphere of buoyancy, friendliness and good health.' The streets of houses were being improved by the sweat equity of the residents with little financial assistance from city banks, and mingled among the housing were 'an incredible number of splendid food stores, as well as such enterprises as upholstery making, metalworking, carpentry [and] food processing. The streets were alive with children playing, people shopping, people strolling, people talking' (Jacobs: p. 19) (see Figure 4.5).

Jacobs recounted a conversation with a Boston planner who understood her attraction to the neighborhood but was unable to reconcile its character

Figure 4.5 Sidewalk café, North End, Boston, MA. Crowds spill onto the sidewalk watching one of the Italian football team's matches in the 2006 World Cup. *(Photo by Adrian Walters)*

with his ideas developed from his professional training; his data told him it was a high-density slum, ripe for demolition and redevelopment. 'I know how you feel,' the planner told Jacobs. 'I often go down there myself just to walk around the streets and feel that wonderful, cheerful street life … You ought to come back in the summer if you think it's fun now. You'd be crazy about it in the summer. But of course we have to rebuild it eventually. We've got to get those people off the streets' (Jacobs: p. 20).

Jacobs delighted in pointing out to her readers the obvious disconnection between this planner's response as an ordinary person and as a professional. 'My friend's instincts told him the North End was a good place … [b]ut everything he had learned as a physical planner about what is good for people and good for city neighborhoods, everything that made him an expert, told him the North End had to be a bad place' (Jacobs: p. 20).

In terms of our current agreement with Jacobs concerning the street as the fundamental building block of urbanism, whether via New Urbanism in the

USA or from different traditional sources in the UK, Mumford's modernist dismissal of the street in his writings and his preference for 'superblocks' preferably with pedestrian and vehicular segregation, strikes a discordant note. Clearly both Mumford and Jacobs had much to learn from each other, but sadly, this meeting of minds never took place. Having complimented Jacobs early in his essay for her insights into the evils of urban renewal, Mumford's bruising counter-attack over the Garden City and other planning disagreements essentially stifled communication between them, and today's urban designer is forced to pick and choose pieces of advice and theory from each author, and to discard other sections of their writings as unsound.

Even though Jacobs made some errors in her critique of city planning, her work has lasting popularity and relevance – not so much for her sideswipes at historical figures and pioneers of Anglo-American city design in the 20th century – but for her relentlessly pragmatic focus on places in cities that work well as social and economic entities. Jacobs taught architects and planners to look at these places with open minds and objective eyes, and relearn the lessons embodied in these locations, particularly the physical and functional relationships of space, density and human activity. She urged architects and planners to disregard the prevailing academic and professional theories about cities, and to study instead the actual forms and circumstances of successful neighborhoods on the ground.

In practice, Jacobs' analysis of the places that nurtured successful city life helped turn architects' attention away from the wide open, 'universal' spaces of modern city development with its 'sorted out' partitioning of urbanism into separate compartments, and towards the older, traditional urban typologies of streets, blocks, squares and parks where all sorts of different uses mixed companionably together. Instead of urban space being designed merely as the setting or foreground to show off new buildings, such as the plaza in front of Kallmann McKinnell and Knowles' Boston City Hall (see Figure 4.6), Jacobs chided architects to create something far more important: spaces for people, or 'outdoor rooms' where the daily patterns of life could be lived in functionally rich, convenient, and pleasant surroundings made safe by the constant presence of 'eyes on the street,' neighbors and passers-by who provide casual but continual visual supervision of public space (see Figure 4.7).

Jacobs' focus on mixing uses and designing public space with traditional urban typologies enshrined her

Figure 4.6 City Hall Plaza, Boston, MA. The public art cow sculptures are the only inhabitants of this over-scaled and under-used public space typical of modernist urbanism. *(Photo by Adrian Walters)*

Figure 4.7 Street in Athens, GA. Students, faculty and staff from the adjacent campus of the University of Georgia support local shops, and maintain an active and pleasant street life. This is the archetypal urban space of New Urbanism.

in the pantheon of New Urbanism some 30–40 years after she wrote her influential book in 1961. More immediately, during the late 1960s and 1970s, her praise of local citizen activism to fight monolithic plans produced by centralized bureaucracies provided impetus to many neighborhoods and left-leaning activists in Britain and America to become more aggressive in taking their own battles to City Hall. By a perplexing twist of historical irony, as we noted earlier, Jacobs' same writings were being used by right-wing think-tanks in Britain to bolster arguments for the complete dissolution of planning.

This reaction to centralized authority and state bureaucracy returned 'the anarchist strain of planning thought that had so heavily infused the early garden city movement and its regional planning derivative' to the forefront of planning theory and practice (Hall, P.: p. 263). These early seeds of citizen power, which had lain dormant for decades, flowered energetically during the late 1960s and 1970s through the work of young, activist 'advocacy planners' and 'community architects' in America and Britain respectively. This was a time when young, idealistic professionals put their skills and talents at the service of disempowered communities, helping them resist the 'top-down' plans and strictures of local and state government. By a combination of direct action and cheap or *pro-bono* professional advice, these young idealists helped struggling and stressed communities defy city or corporate redevelopment plans that threatened to sweep away local places, buildings and livelihoods under the guise of urban renewal.

COMMUNITY-BASED ARCHITECTURE AND PLANNING

Like most political movements, this upsurge in community politics and action did not arrive on the scene *ex nuovo*; it was presaged 20 years earlier at a meeting at London's Architectural Association school of architecture in 1948, when amidst the formal heroics of Corbusian towers that were then fashionable, the Italian anarchist architect Giancarlo de Carlo was invited to speak on ways to improve the standard of housing for the urban poor (Hall, P.: p. 271). Echoing Kropotkin and Reclus, de Carlo stated, 'The housing problem cannot be solved from above. It is a problem of *the people*, and it will not be solved, or even boldly faced, except by the concrete will and action of the people themselves' (de Carlo, 1948, in Hall, P.: p. 271).

This oppositional stance was primarily against cumbersome, inflexible and often hostile public bureaucracies, along with insensitive and greedy developers, but in some instances, attitudes within the architectural profession itself were the cause of community ire. The architectural profession was, and still is caught up with the preoccupation of innovative design and eye-catching forms, leaving 'little room for the recognition of the social value of design ideas and processes' (Towers: p. ix). Innovation itself was assumed to be the result of creative individuals, which in turn gave short shrift to the many circumstances where the cooperative efforts of volunteers produced important new initiatives.

Community architecture and advocacy planning became true forces in inner city redevelopment politics when young professionals entered the fray and bolstered local groups' resistance to development plans with their valuable technical expertise. This idealistic, local activism was sometimes confused in its aims and ambitions, and often reactive rather than creative, but activists were united in believing that the residents and users of new housing, workplaces and other community facilities should be involved in their planning and design. By this means, young professionals sought to improve the lot of the poor, not by means of the kind of well-meaning paternalism that had been one of the downfalls of modernism, but by directly empowering socially disadvantaged groups and individuals. Over several years of hard-fought battles with local authorities and private developers, this kind of alternative professional practice developed three main sets of concerns – social awareness, environmental sensitivity and democratic participation – and in Britain certainly, brought about several significant changes. Rehabilitation of older buildings and the retention of communally important structures have become more common than the previous formula of demolition followed by comprehensive redevelopment. The design of new developments has become more sensitive to social and physical contexts, and 'consultation' is now relatively normal in the development process – but without necessarily developing to the point of true democratic participation.

The community movements and activism of the 1960s gave rise to several important legislative milestones in Britain, including the Urban Aid programme in 1968; the 1969 Housing Act, that established the concept of General Improvement Areas (GIAs) where grants for rehabilitation and improvement of older housing were promoted as alternatives to demolition; and the more effective Housing Action Area legislation that followed in 1974. Under the Urban Aid legislation, the British government funded new Community Development Projects (CDPs) in distressed urban areas, where each project was set up in collaboration with the appropriate local authority and included a 'research team' and an 'action team,' staffed usually by enthusiastic young professional planners, architects and students. The author was one such participant in the teams for the Benwell area of Newcastle-upon-Tyne (see Figures 2.3, 2.4 and 2.7), one of 12 such CDPs established in the early 1970s (Towers: p. 63).

The 1969 Housing Act also led to progressive efforts by enlightened professionals and authorities in various British cities – such as the SNAP project in Liverpool where the national housing charity Shelter set up a groundbreaking Neighbourhood Action Project involving 740 terraced houses in the Toxteth area at the invitation of the city council. Here, within a 3-year period, owner occupation increased by 33 percent and over half the houses in the project area were renovated. Meanwhile, in 1972, in the modest industrial town of Macclesfield, 15 miles south of Manchester in northwest England, an unknown young architect took issue with that council's plans to demolish his small terraced house (Towers: p. 55). The architect's name was Rod Hackney.

In 1971, Hackney had bought a run-down 19th century house at 222 Black Road, Macclesfield for £1000 ($1875). [Currency conversions throughout this book at based on the May 2006 exchange rates.] A few months later he applied for a Home Improvement Grant to refurbish the bathroom, only to be refused on the grounds that the house had a life of only around 5 years before it would be demolished as part of a redevelopment plan. Hackney refused to accept the council's argument that because the 160-year-old houses lacked basic amenities such as indoor plumbing, they should also be classified as structurally unsound and devoid of merit. Hackney's professional expertise told him that his property and those of his neighbors 'could be improved at a reasonable cost to provide sound and comfortable homes' (Towers: p. 77). In his book, *Building Democracy*, Graham Towers describes what happened next:

> A residents association was formed, the local press was alerted, councillors and the local MP were lobbied, and a detailed structural and condition survey was carried out. A cost study was prepared showing that the houses could be improved for only 35 percent of the cost of redevelopment. Eventually, over a year later, the campaign succeeded when Rod Hackney's house, together with 32 of his immediate neighbours, was declared the first Black Road General Improvement Area (GIA). During the course of the prolonged struggle, many of the residents had managed to buy their homes through various arrangements of loans and mortgages. A group of houses that had been 70 percent tenanted 4 years earlier had become 90 percent owner-occupied by the time the GIA was declared … To keep within budget, residents decided to do much of the building work themselves. Rod Hackney's house was improved first and became a model, not just of what could be achieved, but how to go about self-build. Over the next year the other houses were

improved with the Residents Association acting as general contractor. Residents worked on their own houses and collectively on the improvement of the common area in the centre of the block. Specialist subcontractors were employed for the more difficult tasks, and friends and relatives helped out the elderly who were unable to do the work themselves. The work to each house was purpose-designed to meet individual requirements and to keep within the various budgets of what each household could afford. (Towers: p. 77)

The Black Road scheme was small in area but hugely influential (see Figure 4.8). The innovations pioneered by Hackney evolved into a new model for urban regeneration – a powerful alternative to the traditional wholesale demolition of older housing areas. Good public relations had been an important ingredient in the success of the Black Road project, and Hackney possessed a flair for publicity. Black Road became nationally famous, and spurred many similar projects in the older industrial towns and cities of Britain and Northern Ireland. Hackney's successful formula relied on the residents' own efforts and finances being enhanced by money raised from outside agencies and private funds through well-orchestrated community campaigns and supported by the technical expertise of Hackney's fast growing architectural staff. As his practice expanded to keep pace with the wave of community self-build projects, Hackney would usually employ an architect to live and work in the area,

Figure 4.8 Refurbished terrace houses, Black Road, Macclesfield, UK. The end of this row of houses is marked by a plaque commemorating the successful efforts of architect Rod Hackney in 1974 to forestall demolition and obtain local government grants for the conversion and renovation of older housing.

'whose job was to lead the self-build process by example, teach basic building skills, organize the supply of materials, and bring in specialists for the difficult tasks' (Towers: p. 80). By 1985, Hackney ran a firm with 12 offices and 70 employees, and he had expanded traditional architectural services into construction and development. Hackney's philosophy expanded similarly: community architecture, he argued was not simply about housing; it was about re-creating wealth. Towers' account again provides a clear example:

> Take an area of run-down housing with poor residents, many of whom are unemployed. Property values are low and so is the income of the neighbourhood. There is a culture of dependency on subsistence level welfare benefits. Lack of work and very low incomes create a breeding ground for crime, which further stigmatizes the area. Individually these families can do nothing to change the situation … [but] cooperative action … can work wonders. First, the residents need to band together and organize. Next, they need to acquire their homes. In a depressed area they are worth next to nothing, and mortgages can be arranged even for the unemployed. Then they have an asset against which they can borrow or apply for grants. With the assistance of the community architect they can learn skills – not just building trades but organizational and communication skills as well. Using their own free labour – which is paid for by state [unemployment] benefits – they repair and improve their houses or build new ones. During the process the local economy benefits because specialist builders are employed and builders merchants increase their trade. Residents end up owning a house that is worth twice as much as it cost. They have gained confidence in their ability to achieve. They also have skills they can use to get employment or to set up a small business. The poverty cycle is broken and the area and its residents increase in value. (Towers: p. 81)

There are problems with this approach, however. In periods of rising property values, lenders can be persuaded to invest in assets that will appreciate; in flat or declining housing markets, this is rarely the case. The determination of the participants is also crucial; they have to possess extraordinary resolve and stamina to complete this kind of heavy, hands-on project, and relatively few people enjoy this level of energy and commitment. Location and housing type are also very important: the ideal venues for this kind of work are small-scale terraced houses suitable for occupation by single families and with depressed property values. This self-help, rehab approach is far less feasible in city districts where building types are more likely to be high-density flats and multi-occupancy buildings and where land values are too expensive for the funding formulas to work.

Nonetheless, Hackney's success was remarkable in changing attitudes in Britain towards older housing stock and validated the whole notion that local people can play a major role in the creation of their urban environment. His efforts were acknowledged by his election to the Presidency of the Royal Institute of British Architects in 1987 and rewarded in a different way by patronage from none other than Prince Charles. That same year, Prince Charles and Rod Hackney sat together at the RIBA awards ceremony for outstanding community architecture. This recognition of working-class, community architecture by the British monarchy provides an ironic twist to this self-build success story. It was the anarchist vision of Kropotkin and Reclus come to some small fruition a century later, and honored by an establishment figure those pioneers would have despised.

While the British government was stimulated into action during the mid-1960s and 1970s, enacting the series of housing initiatives noted above, the American federal government was similarly occupied with trying to solve the intractable problem of poverty and decayed housing in poor urban areas of the nation's cities. In 1964, with President Lyndon Johnson in the White House and campaigning for reelection, criticisms of misconceived urban renewal projects reached deafening levels. When a series of riots broke out in several cities that summer, new urban policies to resolve the burgeoning problems became an urgent priority. The result was Johnson's 'Model Cities' program, designed to eliminate the worst slum areas and increase the supply of decent, low-cost housing by harnessing the anger and frustration of poor neighborhoods for constructive purposes (Hall, P.: p. 283).

The key idea was to involve local communities in the process of change through Community Development Agencies (CDAs), structured initially to facilitate inclusive citizen participation. However, bad experiences with fractious local participation under previous legislation to tackle the 'War on Poverty' led city bureaucracies to retain overall power in this new program instead of sharing it equitably with citizen groups. The program proved very difficult to coordinate at the various levels of national, city and local neighborhood administration, with all sorts of bureaucratic demands for federal oversight encumbering local politics with insurmountable obstacles. Ironically, in a program intended to maximize citizen participation, federal and city staff ended up in the dominant roles; centralized 'planning-as-usual' had merely been wrapped in the banners of local community participation (Hall, P.: p. 284), and after a decade of haphazard initiatives, the program was judged, in a masterpiece of understatement, not to have achieved 'its own high-flown promises' (Haar, 1975: p. 194).

Despite this catalogue of failure, individual success stories blossomed, such as the community activism in the poor suburb of Roxbury in Boston, MA. Within one of the poorest areas of a wealthy city, only two miles south of Boston's downtown, residents of the Dudley Street neighborhood became increasingly tired and angry at living in an area characterized by arson, physical deterioration, vacant land, illegal dumping, crime and financial disinvestment. After years of being ignored by city authorities, they took charge of their own future and formed a neighborhood association to clean up vacant properties and stop the illegal dumping of rubbish by individuals and commercial contractors. Encouraged by their success in these efforts, residents produced the Dudley Street Comprehensive Revitalization Plan in 1987 which was adopted by the city authorities, and in a highly unusual move the neighborhood association was granted the power of eminent domain (compulsory purchase in the UK) over vacant land in the immediate Dudley Street area. Since then, commuter rail service has been restored, in excess of 200 new affordable homes constructed, more than 300 houses rehabilitated, and over 300 of the original 1300 vacant lots transformed by new buildings, playgrounds, gardens and other community facilities (see Figure 4.9). By purchasing vacant land for development through a low interest loan from the Ford Foundation, and creating community education programs, homebuyer classes and scholarship funds, residents have radically improved the morale and appearance of the neighborhood, and its perception by outsiders. Banks are once again lending money for home improvements and purchases, and the federal Fannie Mae Foundation honored the Dudley Street neighborhood as one of the top 10 neighborhoods in the country for affordable home ownership (www.dsni.org/Community%20Information/time line.htm).

These are inspiring tales, but the reactions to the failures of modernist city planning were not limited to young anti-establishment professionals and citizen activists. Other attempts were made to reform city

Figure 4.9 Affordable housing in the Dudley Street neighborhood, Roxbury, Boston, MA. Providing decent, affordable housing is one important strategy for revitalizing run-down urban areas. *(Photo by Adrian Walters)*

redevelopment processes and priorities from within the various power structures, and one brilliant project stands head and shoulders above all others: Ralph Erskine's Byker redevelopment in Newcastle-upon-Tyne, in northeast England.

BUILDING COMMUNITY TRUST: RALPH ERSKINE AT BYKER

In the late 1960s, British-born Erskine was an architect with an established reputation, largely in his adopted homeland of Sweden, for well-designed housing schemes that were sensitively adapted to site, climate and community. He had been associated with Team 10, the polemic group of younger, post-World War II architects who mounted opposition during the late 1940s and 1950s to the large-scale, technical and abstract generalizations of their modernist elders, Le Corbusier, Walter Gropius and other major figures of the architectural establishment. Team 10 proposed an urbanism that valued 'the personal, the particular and the precise' (Banham, 1963), and in the words of Aldo van Eyck, one of Team 10's founders, 'Whatever space and time mean, place and occasion mean more' (van Eyck, 1962: p. 27).

In his work, Erskine sought to enrich modernism with a sense of social realism that it lacked, and to pay special attention to the particulars of human behavior and community dynamics. This approach provided a dramatic counterpoint to the general set of values,

Figure 4.10 Architects' office, Byker, Newcastle-upon-Tyne, UK, 1971. This converted funeral parlor was the setting for much community activity during the lengthy redevelopment process (See Table 4.1).

assumptions and procedures that pertained to most British and American urban renewal programs, where homes were 'housing units,' residents were regarded as passive consumers and quantified merely as numbers to be rehoused, and paternalistic city architects and planners could not understand why people were not grateful for their efforts to provide them with newer, better accommodation.

Erskine stood the standard process on its head, involving the residents as partners and forging a strong bond between the community and the designers. Erskine's partner, Vernon Gracie, lived on site for many years during the rebuilding process in a flat above the drawing office set up in an old corner store, previously a funeral parlor, which became as much a community resource space as a professional drawing office (see Figure 4.10). The architects kept a daybook of visitors, complaints and solutions, and a page from this is excerpted in Table 4.1 (Ravetz: p. 741).

Table 4.1 Extracts from daybook record complied over several days in the offices of Ralph Erskine, Architects, Byker, Newcastle-upon-Tyne, May, 1974. Reproduced with permission of *The Architects' Journal*.

Time	Name or description	Reason for visit	Action	Comment
8.50	Mrs Smith	asked for sand from sandbox for grandchildren to play with	got some	
11.30	Mrs Spraggon	reported gas leak at Mrs Smith's Carville Road	phoned Gas Board	
12.45	Billy Bucket	came for matches	got them	
5.30	Thomas Something	playing 'hide and seek,' wanted to hide here	hid under table	difficult to throw out
11.20	man from first handover	wanted his fence altering as rubbish blows under it	said we'd think about it	
2.45	Mrs Smith	lady had fallen in Gordon Road, broken wrist and shock	called ambulance, came after 5 minutes	
3.00	Mrs Rogerson and friend	she wanted some grass seed	got some in a very nice paper bag	will come back with bag later
6.10	Eddie	to wash	washed	
7.10	Mrs Wann	upset – kids broke window – news of move too much, broke down	sherry and a chat	
9.15	two men (from North East Electricity Board?)	said they had a cooker to fix in Shipley Place	told them Shipley Place not yet built	they left in a confused state
10.00	Ian Muckle, Action Centre	to call meeting about Shipley Rise play area	Roger, Caroline discussed	arranged for another tenants' meeting
10.10	tenant, Gordon Road	collected key from Action Centre		very happy man

As this daybook record shows, this connection between architects and residents was not one derived from the public policy manuals of questionnaires and scripted meetings for public participation, but one built around the concepts of mutual trust, respect and open, transparent communication. In this program of urban redevelopment that lasted for 14 years, Erskine and his team showed what could be done when urban designers took community values seriously. Suddenly there was a real alternative to the standard urban renewal procedures that had devastated so many communities. Erskine's design team evolved a new process and they also derived an architecture that was contemporary in its details, but which grew from an understanding of the traditional pedestrian scale of urban space (see Figure 4.11). As a young architect working for the local practice doing the detail design and preparing the construction drawings for the famous Byker Wall, the author was privileged to be associated with Erskine's office in the early 1970s, an experience that invigorated a lifelong pursuit of democratic urban design.

The accomplishments and disappointments of Byker have been discussed in more detail elsewhere (Ravetz, 1976; Malpass, 1979; Walters and Brown, 2004), but every account confirms the role the architects' office played in the community. The old corner shop became an informal community resource centre and a focal place in the life of the neighborhood, where residents could obtain information and see the designers of their community at work. This level of mutual respect allowed the architects a relatively high level of freedom to interpret the community's needs into three-dimensional forms and spaces. They developed an original architectural language for the new buildings, having more to do with Erskine's personal aesthetic than local precedent, and created an intimate 'jumble' of urban spaces instead of the long bleak streets. Erskine's first response was to keep as many of the old rows of houses as possible and renovate them, but technical issues and an important survey that revealed that 80 percent of the local residents wanted the old, steep terraces demolished forced the team to change their approach (Ravetz: p. 739) (see Figure 4.12).

Erskine's approach vividly demonstrated that meaningful public participation was not necessarily a process whereby residents were intimately involved in the detail design of their dwellings; there was only one relatively small and early pilot project that focused on resident preferences for detail house design. The issue was much more a matter of establishing strong bonds of trust between professional designers and residents, where the architects first and foremost were good listeners and good communicators.

This tale of public participation in planning and design is inevitably truncated, and many important works and efforts are omitted from detailed mention. Examples include: the important work of English

Figure 4.11 Byker redevelopment, Newcastle-upon-Tyne, 1968–1982. The architecture bears the idiosyncratic stamp of Ralph Erskine's personal aesthetics, but the pedestrian-scaled urban spaces create a robust armature for new community life.

Figure 4.12 Typical 19th century street on Byker Hill, 1969; now demolished. While valuing the community life and the neighborliness of this working class environment, residents held no sentimental attachment to their bleak old terrace houses, and asked the architects to demolish them instead of the designers' original plans to retain substantial areas and modernize the buildings with new facilities.

anarchist architect John Turner in South America during the 1950s and 1960s and his tireless campaigning for the housing rights of disempowered populations in the developing world (Turner, 1965, 1976; Turner and Fichter, 1972); the insightful practical research by Sherry Arnstein about participation in American urban neighborhoods culminating in her 'Ladder of Citizen Participation' (Arnstein, 1969); the attempts to marry citizen participation with sophisticated prefabrication at the PSSHAK (Primary Structural Supports Housing Assembly Kit) housing experiment in London derived by Naabs Hamdi and Nick Wilkinson from the research of Dutch architect Nicolas Habraken (AJ, 1974, 1975); and the very clever approach to rationalized lightweight building technology developed by Walter Segal for self-build sites in almost any location (McKean, 1976a, 1976b). All these are worthy of detailed discussion in their own right.

However, one major figure who cannot be left out is Christopher Alexander, whose 1977 book *A Pattern Language* bridges between urban and community design and self-build construction. Alexander explains the design language expressed in his extensive series of interrelated 'patterns' is 'extremely practical' (in contrast to the esoteric theorizing about ideal societies and contexts for building set out in his companion volume *A Timeless Way of Building*). Alexander writes:

> You can use it to work with your neighbors, to improve your town and neighborhood. You can use it to design a house for yourself, with your family; or to work with other people to design an office or a workshop or a public building like a school. And you can use it to guide you in the actual construction. (Alexander *et al.*, 1977: p. x)

COMMUNITY PLANNING AND DESIGN: CHRISTOPHER ALEXANDER'S PATTERN LANGUAGE

Alexander's collection of 253 patterns is organized 'beginning with the very largest, for regions and towns, then working down through neighborhoods, clusters of buildings, buildings, rooms and alcoves, ending finally with the details of construction' (Alexander *et al.*, 1977: p. xii). In a cleverly organized system, the patterns are interrelated to others at larger and smaller scales, so that each particular issue is embedded in an expansive context of connections with other conditions and phenomena, and embraces more detailed concerns at reduced scales and sizes.

An example will serve to illustrate this set of interrelationships. Pattern 44 is entitled 'Local Town Hall' and the problem statement explains: 'Local government of communities and local control by the inhabitants will only happen if each community has its own physical town hall which forms the nucleus of its political activity.' Alexander's format immediately relates this pattern to several larger-scale ones – 'Mosaic of Subcultures,' 'Community of 7000' and 'Identifiable Neighborhood' (Alexander *et al.*, 1977: p. 237). There is a clearly recognizably anarchist strand of thinking behind these patterns for self-governing communities as the building blocks of society in a direct lineage from Kropotkin and Reclus, but Alexander's concept also relates to American precedent. In Pattern 12, 'Community of 7000,' Alexander states the proposition that:

> Individuals have no effective voice in any community of more than 5000–10 000 persons. People can only have a genuine effect on local government when the units of local government are autonomous, self-governing, self-budgeting communities, which are small enough to create the possibility of a link between the man in the street and his local officials and elected representatives. This is an old idea … it was Jefferson's plan for American democracy … Jefferson wanted to spread out the power not because 'the people' were so bright and clever, but precisely because they were prone to error, and it was therefore dangerous to vest power in the hands of a few who would inevitably make big mistakes. (Alexander *et al.*, 1977: p. 71)

This sentiment relates directly back to the discussion concerning the intentionally fragmented construction of American government, and it also provides perspective on the ambitions of large-scale comprehensive planning. This author's experience of working with communities to reform and rewrite their zoning ordinances around design-based principles has always been that smaller communities are most amenable to this difficult change of direction and concept. In these smaller communities, elected officials are known to a wider section of the population, and are more directly accountable. Gathering public interest in matters of community governance and future planning is easier in smaller towns and participation is more effective. In particular, working with three contiguous towns in north Mecklenburg County, north of Charlotte, NC, who made common purpose by completely rewriting their zoning ordinances around form-based New

Urbanist and Smart Growth principles in the mid-1990s was exemplary in this regard. These towns took the lead in planning reform, leaving larger cities like Charlotte behind, and visibly embodied the advantages set out by Alexander's pattern of smaller autonomous communities.

This philosophy of localized control for communities of limited size has other clear historical overtones from 14th century Siena and other Tuscan cities where, as noted by Kropotkin, separate parishes, or *contrade*, provided some local government services. Today, each Sienese neighborhood has clearly defined boundaries and its own local churches and *piazze* for community activities, and the *contrade* still manage many local rhythms of life, rites of passage and communal responsibilities (see Figure 4.1). This kind of connective resonance, whereby anarchist philosophy and Jeffersonian democracy combine with Italian urbanism and politics is characteristic of Alexander's methodology: it provides clear guidance on design and social issues, but in ways that leave plenty of room for individual interpretation. Alexander stands unique in his achievement in bridging so many precedents, issues and scales of operation, and relating urban and building design to both social and aesthetic considerations. He reveals how almost everything can be connected to everything else, and succeeds in making what could become an impossible intellectual task into something that falls within the grasp of lay people, enabling them to design any part of the environment for themselves.

COMMUNITY POWER AND URBAN DESIGN

Providing individuals and communities with ways to understand the physical implications of policies and ideas – what they might look like on the ground – is crucial to citizen empowerment in the process of planning the postmodern, post-industrial city. Contrary to some critics, who have maintained that an emphasis on urban design is 'deadly for the future of planning' (Kunzmann: p. 594), it is precisely the ability for ordinary people to be able to see what their ideas look like in three dimensions that is so important and refreshing in the urban planning process. The case against urban design as a central component of planning seeks to defend planning as a wide-ranging academic discipline against its takeover by architects who, so the argument goes, inevitably narrow the focus of planning concerns to the arrangement of form and space

in the physical world, neglecting parallel social cultural dimensions in the community and the academic context. The arguments and case studies in this book are specifically intended to counter that contention, to show that making master plans, when properly combined with communicative planning techniques, can bring relevant issues from all parties to the forefront of public discussion rather than hide them beneath a mantle of professional mystique.

But this is not just an academic argument. The importance of physical space in the city is witnessed by social movements such as 'Reclaim the Streets,' an anarchist and activist troupe in Britain that has staged several spectacular actions in British cites since its inception in the early 1990s to protest the increasing dominance of cars in public space, and the consequent loss of attractive, safe spaces for pedestrians and other road users. This spontaneous direct action has since spread to radical ecological groups in Europe, Australia and America where, chillingly, Reclaim the Streets was declared a 'terrorist organization' by the FBI in May 2001 for its anti-capitalist politics. Direct action movements such as Reclaim the Streets remind us of the cultural and political importance of shared pedestrian space in the city; we have only to recall the huge street demonstrations during the 'velvet revolutions' in the eastern European countries as they shook off the yoke of communist rule to comprehend the importance of public space for a democratic society.

The importance of physical space as an agent of social policy is also evident in the British government's grand push for improved urban design, not as a city beautification project, but as the key to urban regeneration and the creation of a new civil society. This principle, that 'people make cities, but cities make citizens,' was articulated by architect-peer Richard Rogers and elaborated by him as follows:

> Active citizenship and vibrant urban life are essential components of a good city and civic identity. To restore these where they are lacking, citizens must be involved in the evolution of their cities. They must feel that public space is in their communal ownership and responsibility. From the modest back street to the grand civic square these spaces belong to the citizen and make up the totality of the public domain, a public institution in its own right which like any other can enhance or frustrate our urban existence. The public domain is the theatre of an urban culture. It is where citizenship is enacted, it is the glue that can bind an urban society. (Rogers, 1997: p. 16)

Rogers' attitude to urban space, city life and citizenship became embedded in British government policy through his chairmanship of the government committee, the Urban Task Force, which produced the influential report *Towards an Urban Renaissance* in 1999. The work of the Task Force was enshrined in a government White Paper, *Our Towns and Cities: the Future: Delivering an Urban Renaissance*, published in the following year, 2000. Since then, this concept has expanded in British policy to become the mantra of 'creating sustainable communities,' which appeared on all documents emanating from the Office of the Deputy Prime Minister, John Prescott, the minister in charge of planning and the environment before the government reorganization of 2006.

The public domain Rogers describes, and about which this book is most concerned, is conceived in terms of traditional public spaces – streets and squares, alleys and parks – and this new invigorated public realm has been politicized by Britain's Labour government in part 'to sweep away the dark days of Thatcherite individualism, and usher in a new age where community emerges as the primary mode of citizenship' (Holden and Iveson: p. 58). In this context, urban design concepts have a major role to play in forging this urban rebirth, not only their embodiment in three-dimensional master plans, but also in the strategies designed for the plans' implementation over periods of several years. A community needs assurance that the plan they worked so hard to develop will be carried forward in accordance with the design's principles and in close approximation to its details. Some aspects may change over a long period of implementation, but they should do so in relation to clear guidelines so that the integrity of the original community vision is not compromised. The most important implementation strategy in this regard is the set of regulations that controls the build-out of the development, and the most efficient and effective types of regulation for this purpose are American form-based zoning codes as developed by the New Urbanists and the British design codes created, in part, by adapting American precedent to British conditions. These codes, their history, legal justification, theory and practical application are discussed in the next chapter.

Theory

Codes and guidelines

SYNOPSIS

Despite several similarities of objectives and techniques, the differences between the planning systems in Britain and America make easy transfer of concepts and methodologies from one country to the other problematic. There has been much discussion in Britain about the role of design coding for new development and what level of detail is required for codes to work effectively, and to reduce the potential for misapplying lessons from differing contexts this chapter provides a brief history of design regulation in various locations. Because some of the models examined by British government agencies are American New Urbanist precedents, the history, objectives and methodologies of New Urbanist codes are examined in some detail, including an explanation of the major differences between American form-based zoning ordinances, design guidelines and pattern books. This analysis itself requires a synopsis of the legal foundations for design regulation in the USA, and the legal constraints and permissions placed upon that process.

The necessity in America to reform zoning nationwide, and the need to achieve this objective quickly in the face of expanding suburban sprawl, has led to the integrated development of the universal principles of the Transect and the Smart Code developed by Duany Plater-Zyberk and others. These regulations and other more place-specific examples of American regulations are then compared with the philosophy and content of typical British design codes with a view to clarifying, particularly for the British reader, the most appropriate format and content of codes to meet recent government expectations of reliably delivered, high quality urban design. This is particularly pertinent as current research in the UK indicates only a partial understanding of

American practice (CABE, 2005b). The chapter concludes with a summary of recent British examples of design codes to suggest some potential and valuable lessons for American readers. A summary of the essential attributes of form-based codes is included as Appendix I at the end of the book.

PRECEDENTS FOR DESIGN REGULATION

Design regulation has been an issue in city development for 2000 years. In Roman times, urban developments often incorporated common standards for streets, and Vitruvius' famous *Ten Books of Architecture* contained information on the layout of cities and their constituent public and private buildings (Southworth and Ben Joseph, 1997; Rowland and Howe, 1999). Another example, stemming from immediate post-Roman times in the Middle East, is Julian of Ascalon's treatise of construction and design rules for change and growth in expanding urban areas in Palestine, which was part of the Byzantine Empire during the sixth century. Julian's code dealt predominantly with five urban categories: land use, views, relationships between different types of housing, drainage and planting. His code was prescriptive in nature, and laid down authoritative rules about what must be done and what not to do. Despite criticisms today of this type of code (rigid, unresponsive to change, not place specific, etc.), Julian's code maintained its influence for almost 1400 years in Byzantine and Mediterranean countries (Hakim, 2001).

In medieval London, a destructive fire in 1189 resulted in a new code that specified the use of incombustible materials such as tile roofs and masonry party walls to prevent the spread of flame (Lai, 1988: p. 22). Similar measures were enacted for public safety in subsequent centuries, especially after London's Great Fire in 1666, which destroyed the old medieval core of the city. The 1667 Act for the Rebuilding of the City of London set out a definitive typology of streets and matching buildings. Along with provisions for building materials and structural requirements, these regulations promoted straighter, paved streets and buildings with uniform cornice lines, and became the system of building control that regulated London's major urban expansions through the 19th century. The Act created four new classes of housing and sets of regulations for each class. Sometimes uniform rooflines were mandated, and houses fronting on major streets were required to include balconies of specific dimensions and construction (Bosselman, Callies and Banta: p. 68, in Lai, 1988: p. 32).

Taller buildings were permitted along major, and therefore wider streets, with lower structures fronting narrower streets so as not to block daylight, and although prescriptive in some aspects, the new code generally struck a balance between strict rules to protect community safety and welfare, and the rights of property owners to control their own land and buildings (Lai, 1988: p. 33). Importantly for this study is the fact that the codes contained within the Act were based on the construction of a new urban morphology or pattern of growth for the city of London. They were 'contemporary rather than backward looking' and proved 'pragmatic and robust over time' (CABE, 2005b). These points are important; the writers of the codes for rebuilding London in the 17th century were looking forward, and utilizing the best available technologies of masonry construction to establish new and better standards.

This balance between public responsibilities and private rights was further exemplified by urban developments in London during the 18th and 19th centuries, when aristocratic landowners developed portions of their estates west of the medieval city in what are now Bloomsbury and Belgravia. The standard typology was the residential square lined with town houses, and codes in the form of restrictive covenants covered many of the details of building scale and external appearance, enforcing relative uniformity of design and urban character. By contrast, the interiors of the dwellings were often individually customized to owners' requirements, and these internal spaces have seen many generations of changes of use and a myriad of different plan arrangements, but with almost no changes to the public front façades of the buildings that frame the public spaces of the streets and squares (see Figure 5.1).

Figure 5.1 Bedford Square, London, built c. 1780. Many London squares were developed with private leasehold agreements rather than simple freehold land sales. These lease agreements often stipulated conditions for the design of building façades and shared outdoor spaces. These covenants controlled subsequent redevelopment, thus allowing an urban unity to be maintained.

Another significant piece of design regulation dates from much earlier, in 1262, when the city government in Siena, Italy, enacted an ordinance governing the design of the urban palaces facing the city's main square, the *Piazza del Campo* (Lai, 1988: p. 22). This code was very different in concept from previous examples: it was not based on concerns for public health and safety, but on concepts of architectural and urban design. The Sienese sought to preserve the unique radial design and scale of the city's central public space and did so by controlling the design of the buildings that framed the piazza (see Figure 5.2). Thirty-five years later in 1297, the city further codified the civic heart of their city by stipulating that windows in new *palazze* fronting the Campo should match those in the *Palazzo Publico* (City Hall), the main block of which was being constructed along the southern edge of the *Campo* (Broadbent: p. 31). These Sienese codes established the same important principle visible in London's squares and still relevant today: the best way to orchestrate the design of public space is to control the design of the private buildings that line the space and create the 'walls' of an 'urban room.'

Many major European cities enacted codes of one sort or another, especially during the 18th and 19th centuries, and Paris was no exception. During the reign of Louis XIV, building regulations in 18th century Paris required that all new buildings respect the street

Figure 5.2 *Piazza del Campo*, Siena, Italy, 1262 onwards. The design of the *palazze* surrounding the main public square demonstrates the unifying themes imposed by medieval design codes. *(Photo by Adrian Walters)*

Figure 5.3 Boulevards in Paris, 1860s. This renowned model of urbanity was achieved by centralized government regulations and the draconian displacement of working class residents.

alignment, and specified details such as the solid-to-void ratio of building façades, the continuity of eaves lines from one building to the next and the depth of courtyards in the building plans (Ellin: p. 46). Similar codifications pertained to the massive urban surgery performed on the city between 1855 and 1869 by Baron Georges-Eugène Haussmann and his royal patron Napoleon III. Based in part on Napoleon's desire to eradicate the rabbit warren of medieval Parisian streets that provided a protective urban haven for rioters during the 1848 revolution, Haussmann's great new, radiating boulevards were lined by apartment blocks built by private developers to standards established as a condition for obtaining government funding. This urban consistency conferred the additional benefit of faster implementation for this comprehensive city redevelopment, but there was little recompense for the thousands of poor Parisians whose lives and property were trampled beneath this *grand projet* that redefined Paris as we know it today (see Figure 5.3).

In America, the most significant historical urban codes were contained in the Spanish Laws of the Indies, codified in 1573 by King Phillip II of Castille to regulate the founding and master planning of new settlements in the New World. These Laws were a landmark in the history of urban development on the new continent, but in fact they codified earlier Spanish practices based on Royal Ordinances sent to the Americas from Seville as early as 1513. The Laws specified that new towns be built with a standardized urban structure – a grid plan of square blocks around a large central plaza that contained civic buildings (Broadbent: p. 43). In the same way that Roman imperial urbanization stamped symbolic geometric plans on virgin soil across Europe, North Africa and the Middle East nearly two millennia ago, so did the Spanish over four centuries ago in what are now the states of California, Arizona, New Mexico, Texas and Florida. However, the Spanish master planning concept and town planning codes did more than set out a grid of streets around a plaza. As a useful precedent for our studies on design-based coding, these early codes specified sizes of spaces and buildings, and orientations to take advantage of climatic factors such as sun, shade and wind direction. They established street hierarchies and promoted urban devices such as arcades (Broadbent: p. 45).

In a more contemporary setting, local governments in America began experimenting with controlling land use and building arrangement in the late 19th century, drawing on precedents from Europe, particularly Germany. As early as 1888, a court in New York approved height limitations on residential structures. Baltimore followed in 1904 with another height limit

Figure 5.4 Queens Road West, Myers Park, Charlotte, NC, 1911; John Nolen and Earl Draper. Nolen wrote landscape design requirements for semi-public spaces into all deeds for houses in this seminal streetcar suburb that mandated open lawns and specific tree planting and spacing.

on new buildings to 'maintain the character of its neighborhoods and commercial areas.' This regulation was upheld in 1908 by the State of Maryland's highest court on the grounds it was designed to lessen fire hazards in addition to advancing aesthetic goals (*Cochran v. Preston*, 70 A.113 [Md. 1908]) (Duerksen and Goebel: p. 6).

More directly pertinent to the current situation in the USA and Britain are the various codes developed and employed in the 19th century expansion of American suburbs, such as the one used by Frederick Law Olmsted in his Chicago suburb of Riverside (1869). Much as contemporary practice intends, Olmsted used codes to enforce the precepts of his master plan, and, specifically at Riverside, to maintain the desired garden suburb aesthetic recently imported from England. Like its English precedents (and many successors on both sides of the Atlantic), the plan of Riverside set houses back a uniform distance from the street, with a specific tree planting placement enforced in the 'semi-public' spaces of private front yards, as well as in the public realm of the street right-of-way, to create an enfolding green canopy so typical of these suburbs. One of Olmsted's great successors, John Nolen, used similar devices in his work, a particularly fine example of which is the great, green boulevard of Queens Road West, in Nolen's streetcar suburb of Myers Park (1911) in Charlotte, NC (see Figure 5.4).

Codes such as the one for Myers Park were generally formulated as private restrictive covenants, binding on

all homeowners in a development, and covering a wide range of matters, including provisions that were shamefully racist. Myers Park, and its adjacent suburb of Eastover, laid out in the 1920s by Nolen's former assistant Earl Draper, were 'restricted residential districts' with racial covenants and minimum cost clauses that guaranteed no one but affluent whites could own property or live in the neighborhood (Hanchett: p. 221). There is no evidence that Nolen or Draper actively promulgated these racist provisions; in the early decades of the 20th century, this institutionalized exclusion was simply taken for granted and was standard procedure in all suburban developments in Charlotte and in other cities across the American South. While such egregious examples of discrimination are long gone, zoning codes can still institutionalize racism by requiring large minimum size house lots in residential subdivisions, thus ensuring that only wealthy individuals can afford to live there. As the social fabric of America in 2007 is commonly divided into more prosperous white and poorer black and Hispanic ethnic groupings, the stipulation of large lot sizes can be synonymous with the exclusion of blacks and Hispanics by affluent whites.

On the positive side, the generalist scope and intent of Olmsted's and Nolen's codes enabled the regulations to influence the overall environment by specifying design elements that contributed to the character of the public space. This level of urban design was not equaled in British codes until recent decades; any similar breadth of scope was sadly lacking from regulations contained in later 19th century British building legislation. The Public Health Act of 1875 and subsequent laws, for example, did create building standards that improved working class housing design, but they were applied simplistically and literally by speculative builders with no correlation to a cohesive master plan; they were technical documents only, and contained no design content other than the most basic arrangement of buildings and public streets. This resulted in what became the typical environment of working class areas in British cities – a collection of monotonous straight streets constructed with no higher ambitions of civic design (see Figure 5.5). There were no parks and few trees; these were regarded as unnecessary embellishments that reduced the developer's profits.

This downward trend in 19th century Britain from codes that contained clear design thinking to mere technical documents based on generic formulas was unfortunately followed in America during the 20th century. Olmsted and Nolen had used codes to deliver the design qualities inherent in their master plans, but rather than building on this home-grown precedent,

Figure 5.5 Back lane in Benwell, Newcastle-upon-Tyne, UK, 1970. Working class housing in Britain's 19th century industrial cities was uniformly drab and monotonous with streets laid out in tight blocks for maximum profit, unrelieved by any parks or amenities.

Figure 5.6 Seagram Plaza, New York, 1958, Ludwig Mies van der Rohe and Philip Johnson. The empty spaces of modernist urbanism had little regard for human scale or enclosure.

American practice in the 1930s regrettably followed the more prosaic British examples. When the Federal Housing Administration (FHA) created technical standards for subdivisions as requirements for federal insurance and mortgages, these regulations merely increased the widths of streets, enlarged the sizes of blocks by minimizing cross streets and encouraged cul-de-sacs (Dutton: p. 72). Since the 1930s, the holistic design intent of the earlier American codes for projects like Riverside and Myers Park was smothered by a plethora of specific requirements from an increasing range of professional specialisms, each concerned with its own rules and not worrying about relationships to any larger picture. For example, regulations that now govern much subdivision design include separate requirements from planners, transportation engineers, fire departments, lending institutions, utility providers of gas, water and electricity, and public works departments for storm water and sewers. This fragmentation of different regulations is one of the biggest hurdles American New Urbanist architects and planners face in their efforts to establish new codes that refocus development control around design standards that embody a holistic vision.

Twentieth century urban design in American cities has not been uniformly devoid of cohesive content, however. One of the earliest examples of physical design affecting zoning ordinances dates from 1916 in New York. These regulations followed German models in constraining the bulk of skyscrapers rising directly from the line of the street by limiting their height and mandating setbacks at specific levels above ground level, in order to ease the overshadowing of public streets and adjacent buildings. The architectural illustrator Hugh Ferris rendered these ordinances into three-dimensional forms in his famous series of drawings, 'Zoning Envelopes: First through Fourth Stages,' first published in the *New York Times* in 1922 (Ferris, 1922). This zoning law was not replaced until 1961, when new ordinances were enacted based on different design ideas.

The 1961 New York ordinance was based on new modernist design concepts of a tower set back from the street and surrounded by open space. Models for this new ordinance – buildings like the Seagram Building by Mies van der Rohe and Philip Johnson (1958) – were simple vertical boxes positioned well away from the sidewalk with an intervening plaza (see Figure 5.6). Residential ordinances in the city followed the same pattern, and these regulations became a prototype for similar codes in cities across the USA.

These codes virtually eliminated the traditional idea of the street as a linear public space defined by the walls of buildings, and it was not until the late 1970s and early 1980s that cities like New York, Pittsburgh and San Francisco led a revisionist trend in urban design, bringing back requirements for streets and plazas defined by continuous 'street walls' of building façades. One of the stimuli for this movement was Jonathan

Barnett's book *Urban Design as Public Policy* (1974) that argued a powerful (and prescient) case for urban design criteria being embedded within zoning controls. Typical of these new zoning codes has been a proliferation of urban design guidelines attached to, or parallel with zoning categories. Such guidelines spell out criteria for developers and their architects to follow in developing their designs, and include: street width and building height; volumetric massing; percentages and arrangements of glazed areas in building façades; entrances and storefronts at sidewalk level; and landscaping provisions to streets and sidewalks. These guidelines are generally the subject of detailed negotiation on a site-by-site basis between planners and developers regarding approval of projects, and tend to be affected by the vagaries of political pressure for stricter or looser interpretation. They are most useful when a planner has some leverage to cause a developer or designer to adhere to them, such as a commitment by elected officials not to approve developments that ignore the good design practice specified in the guidelines.

Some cities, especially places such as San Francisco and New York, operate very specific and complex systems of architectural control and design review that extend aesthetic zoning into detailed architectural matters (the San Francisco provisions are detailed in Punter: pp. 107–143), but these ambitious, comprehensive and prescriptive regulations comprise a minority of American practice, and would not be legal in several states. Punter notes in passing that the San Francisco design controls have created a very complex system that 'only a handful of professionals (and highly skilled lawyers) understand' (Punter: p. 141). This raises obvious and difficult issues regarding the comprehensibility of this information by members of the public, citizens' groups and the larger democratic audience. The level of specialist expertise necessary to understand and work with very sophisticated regulations such as the San Francisco ordinance illustrates some of the difficulties that accrue to attempts at controlling matters of detailed design, and this opaque complexity of regulations is one specific problem form-based zoning codes set out to avoid.

Unless these design concepts are truly embedded in the text of a zoning ordinance, it is important to be clear on their legal limitations. Guidelines are essentially codes without teeth; as their name suggests, they 'guide' rather than 'require'; they are recommendations and suggestions rather than legal obligations. Guidelines employ the advisory language of 'should' rather than the legal lingo of 'must.' Their purpose is to educate planners, design consultants and developers about good design principles and any specific design objectives for an area or a project. Despite these relative weaknesses, design guidelines can play a useful role in articulating good practice when a municipality baulks at revising its zoning ordinance to conform to form-based principles or when a project extends over several different jurisdictions and a uniform zoning ordinance is not legally feasible. An excerpt from a set of guidelines typical of this latter condition can be seen in Table 5.1.

One condition that unites municipalities in America and Britain is the search for economic advantage in the global economy, and increasingly success is tied to the preservation or creation of a specific sense of place and identity. As Punter notes in his book *Design Guidelines in American Cities*, communities increasingly seek ways to retain local character through regulations that protect existing assets and strive to harmonize new development with the existing built fabric. Local governments in Britain and America, and the national government in the UK, are recognizing what urban designers have known for many years: a well-designed 'sense of place' can foster economic regeneration and community identity (Punter: p. 1).

This desire to enhance the specific urban and architectural attributes of particular places is both highlighted and threatened by the tendency of globalized capital and culture to produce the sameness of 'themed' environments everywhere. Punter points out that many of the current, conventional systems of planning regulation in America that seek to resist this tendency are 'ineffective, unfair, exclusionary, undemocratic and visually illiterate' (Punter: p. 1), and attempts to solve these problems have catalyzed the development of form-based ordinances in many communities across the USA. In almost all cases, these codes have been products of New Urbanist theory and practice, and have sought from the outset to respect and enhance the characteristics of the particular places where they are used. Most form-based codes are much more respectful of the natural environment than conventional, use-based ordinances, and this environmental impetus has increased over the years of their use. As issues of sustainability become more widely recognized, the emphasis placed on the longevity of the form of buildings and spaces in form-based codes, as opposed to the transience of use, becomes a positive factor in sustainable design: when buildings are more durable, there is a longer period of time over which the environmental impact of the buildings and the energy used in their construction can be spread (Symes and Pauwells: p. 104).

Table 5.1 Page from *Design Guidelines*

5·3   STREET LEVEL ACTIVITY

SITE & BUILDING DESIGN

The sidewalks remain the principal place of pedestrian movement and casual social interaction. Designs and uses should be complementary of that function.

Sidewalks should encourage casual social interaction

Porches and stoops create a semi-public outdoor space that encourages pedestrian activity

Small sidewalk displays help bring the indoors outside and add pedestrian interest

Guidelines

1. The ground floors of buildings in Mixed-Use Activity Centers should be encouraged to contain public or semi-public uses such as retail or entertainment uses with direct entry from the street. In residential areas, the predominate architectural feature of the home should be porches and stoops. These features encourage pedestrian activity by providing an attractive destination and an interesting journey.

2. Retail activities within buildings should be oriented towards the street and have direct access from sidewalks through storefront entries.

3. Buildings should have at least one primary entrance facing a pedestrian-oriented street. Alternatively, a primary entrance may be directly accessed by a sidewalk or plaza within 20 feet of the entrance (except single family detached homes).

4. Street level windows should be transparent to permit views to the interior and to provide exterior security through "eyes on the street."

5. Open-air pedestrian passageways (with or without overhead cover) are generally more visible and more inviting than interior hallways. This can be an attractive, successful location for store entries, window displays, and/or restaurant/café seating.

6. Take the "indoors" outdoors by spilling interior space (e.g. dining areas, small merchandise displays) onto walkways and plazas and bring the "outdoors" into the building by opening interior spaces (e.g. atriums) to views and sunshine.

39

THE DEVELOPMENT OF CONTEMPORARY FORM-BASED CODES

The recent history of form-based codes in America has been documented by Peter Katz in an article in the November 2004 issue of the American *Planning* magazine. In this article he gives well-earned praise to Andres Duany and Elizabeth Plater-Zyberk for their pioneering work on the building code for the small private development (80 acres or 32 hectares) of Seaside, FL, in 1981–1982:

> Duany and his wife, Elizabeth Plater-Zyberk, initially set out to design all the town's buildings themselves. But once the true scale of the project became evident, they realized that such a high level of design control would not be possible, or even desirable. Instead, they handed off the design responsibility to the lot purchasers, or their architects. That decision led to a new challenge – finding a way to impart a distinctive character to specific areas within the development.
>
> On study trips to historic Southern communities, the design team saw that certain building types tended to dominate in certain parts of a town: shopfronts on the main square, rowhouses on side streets and mansions flanking Main Street just beyond the edges of the downtown. The team also noted that, while building types were fairly consistent in a given area, there was always enough variety within the design of each building to avoid a cookie-cutter look.
>
> The first Seaside code established a hierarchy of seven (later expanded to eight) 'classes' of buildings for use in the new community. Each class was based on a traditional Southern vernacular building type. The code specified the rudimentary physical characteristics of each class, controlling siting on the lot, building height, location of porches and outbuildings, how parking should be handled, etc.
>
> After the firm's experience at Seaside, Duany Plater-Zyberk adapted form-based codes to work within the legal framework of a planned-unit development. The Kentlands in Gaithersburg, MD, is one early example of that application. Since 1989, when its plan and code were created in a highly publicized charrette, Duany Plater-Zyberk has crafted similar documents to regulate the build-out of over 200 new and existing communities (Katz, 2004: p. 20).

Katz continues:

> Other urban designers have since used form-based codes in a wide variety of projects and locations.

> In 1999, Dover, Kohl & Partners of South Miami, working in collaboration with DPZ, prepared a master plan and form-based development ordinance for a new downtown for Kendall, an edge city just south of Miami. The 240-acre project site is adjacent to two commuter rail stations and a state highway. (Katz, 2004: p. 20)

This account is accurate, but omits the important transit-oriented code developed for San Diego, CA, by nationally regarded New Urbanist pioneer Peter Calthorpe in 1992, and misses out several significant accomplishments by other architect-planners outside the mainstream of big-name national firms. A case in point is the work the author and others carried out in north Mecklenburg County, NC, several miles north of Charlotte, between 1994 and 1996, and a brief review of this work helps clarify the scope, content and operation of form-based codes in America. Three contiguous towns in Mecklenburg County, Davidson, Cornelius and Huntersville, worked sequentially with the author as planning consultant to craft new town master plans and new form-based zoning ordinances to replace existing conventional documents. Unlike the Seaside code, which operates as a controlling mechanism for 80 acres (32 hectares) of private development, the new town codes for the three north Mecklenburg towns comprehensively regulate all manner of private and municipal development in an area covering more than 80 square miles. These codes specifically emphasize the preservation of rural areas and promote transit-supportive development along a planned commuter rail line.

Several key points were learned from this process of code creation, especially the relationship between urban morphology (the sense of overall grain and character of an area) and building typology (a lexicon of different types of buildings based on their formal characteristics). The author's familiarity with European morphological urban analysis, and the work of M.R.G. Conzen on historical urban transect studies at the University of Newcastle-upon-Tyne in the 1960s, suggested a way of coding based on hierarchical geographic zones of urban or rural character rather than separated uses, and these 'character zones' dictated the overall scale and arrangement of building types within their areas (Town of Davidson, 1995: pp. 8–14). This same logic forms the basis of the more sophisticated 'Transect' classification developed separately by Duany Plater-Zyberk (described below), and within this morphological urban categorization new development was regulated by building types (with flexible patterns

Figure 5.7 Site layout for development in Cornelius, NC, 1995; David Walters. This hypothetical design illustrated the ability for new development to integrate different commercial and residential uses, and achieve high densities while preserving important landscapes on a complex site traversed by utility easements.

of use), design standards for streets, parking areas and public open spaces, and by provisions covering landscape and signage.

A second and essential strategy was for the code to be developed around design concepts relevant for particular locations. In the mid-1990s there were few contemporary developments to use as precedents, so as part of this multi-year public process, the author, working with community groups in all three towns, developed alternative designs for contentious tracts of land as a focus for discussion and public education. Many of these designs combined into a large hand-drawn map depicting a build-out scenario for the whole area covered by the contiguous jurisdictions of the three towns (see Figures 5.7 and 5.8). This map established a comprehensive vision of collaborative growth management and featured extensive interconnected street and open space networks with transit village centers along a proposed commuter rail line to and from Charlotte (now scheduled to start operation in 2012). Most importantly, the vision embodied in the plan was backed by form-based zoning that was compatible across all three jurisdictions.

The work in Mecklenburg County was unusual in its geographic scope, but otherwise typical of new coding initiatives elsewhere during the mid to late 1990s when form-based ordinances began to spread to various communities across the USA. To name just

a few, Hillsboro, OR, created transit-supportive regulations based around design standards in 1997; the same year Calvert County, MD, developed their comprehensive plan with design-based guidelines promoting compact, mixed-use town centers; in 2000, Sonoma, CA, adopted a fully-form-based development code; and Fort Collins, CO, adopted a similar form-based land use code in 2001 (Steuteville and Langdon: pp. 10–8). More recently, other communities have begun experimenting with versions of the new Smart Code, developed by Duany Plater-Zyberk as a standardized form-based zoning ordinance based on Transect principles and formatted for widespread use across the USA.

In Britain, the primary example of design coding, apart from Gordon Cullen's advanced but not widely used 'Notation' system developed in the mid-1960s (Cullen, 1967), was the *Design Guide for Residential Areas*, a groundbreaking code developed in the early 1970s to improve the standards of new housing design in the towns and villages within the County of Essex, northeast of London (County Council of Essex, 1973). Well illustrated and full of sensible advice about urban spaces and contextual architecture, the *Design Guide* was generally regarded as an excellent publication despite initial controversy (see Figure 3.7). Developed from Cullen's 'townscape' principles, and before that Raymond Unwin, the *Design Guide* attacked the purely

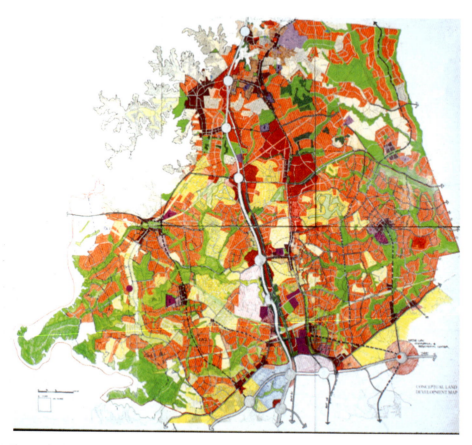

Figure 5.8 Composite development 'build-out' map of north Mecklenburg County, NC, 1995–1996; David Walters. This map, covering approximately 80 square miles and three separate jurisdictions, was compiled from design studies over a period of 18 months, and tried to balance development opportunities with the preservation of landscape corridors for environmental protection and alternative transportation. The area drawn in Figure 5.7, located immediately below and to the left of the third freeway interchange down from the top of the map, shows how individual projects could be woven together into a larger pattern of development.

quantitative approach to residential and highway design that was common across the whole country, and which had produced dull and characterless suburbs in every town. The *Guide*'s success spurred similar codes in many planning departments far beyond the County of Essex, and after a few years, developers dropped their opposition to the new standards and began to translate the sensible design guidance into development formulas by which they arranged their proposed new developments. Even when manipulated by mediocre developers and their architects to comply with the letter but not the spirit of the regulations, and administered by planners with little design sensitivity, the *Design Guide* produced developments that were discernibly better than the previous cookie-cutter suburban dross.

With lessons learned from the Essex *Design Guide*, the overall objective of the British government's planning policy initiatives since the mid-1990s has been to re-embed good urban design within the planning system to ensure high quality and predictability without falling prey to codes that suggest a 'laundry list' or design by 'checking the box.' Instead, urban design guidelines and codes have been reconceptualized as the generative 'DNA' of new projects, establishing consistent design principles across a wide range of different projects. Within the British plan-led system, design codes become the mechanism for development control, fulfilling a role in the British system akin in many ways to American form-based zoning ordinances.

As a means to this end, the Office of the Deputy Prime Minister, along with its coterie of advisory bodies

Figure 5.9 Hulme, Manchester, UK, 1990s. A troubled 1960s modernist housing estate on the edge of Manchester city center was demolished and replaced with new housing laid out in traditional urban street patterns and controlled by a design code to maintain good quality throughout the development. *(Photo by Ben Williams)*

and partnership organizations such as CABE (the Commission for Architecture and the Built Environment), English Partnerships and the Housing Corporation, promoted studies and pilot projects to determine appropriate levels of design coding, and the best methods and techniques for creating and administering codes once they were created. Among the projects examined in that research were major new developments at Hulme, an inner city community in Manchester, and two new greenfield 'town extension' projects: Newhall, in Harlow, Essex, and Upton, in Northampton (see Figures 5.9, 5.10 and 5.11). Other projects ongoing at the time of writing include new developments on reused surplus military sites in Aldershot and Ashford, two towns in southern England, and an ambitious urban regeneration project in Walker, a 19th century working class area in Newcastle-upon-Tyne, next to Erskine's Byker redevelopment (CABE, 2005b: pp. 48–49).

Codes such as the Essex *Design Guide* did spawn great hostility from architects, not so much from the standpoint of urban design, but from the detailed prescriptions for building façades, roof pitches and materials. The predominantly neo-vernacular, contextual aesthetic set out in the *Design Guide* stuck in the craw of modernist-minded architects; ironically this same neo-vernacular style garnered great popularity in the market place, illustrating the considerable gap that still exists on both sides of the Atlantic between 'highbrow' professional tastes and 'middle-brow' popular preferences for residential design. This raises the issue of which audience is primarily served by design

Figure 5.10 Abode, Newhall, Harlow, UK, 2002; Proctor Matthews, Architects. This attractive new development indicates how design codes can be interpreted to provide traditional urbanism combined with contemporary architectural style to avoid any vestige of historical pastiche.

codes – and is the code an esoteric document for the design specialist or is it a compendium of the popular taste of the community? Other questions of content, scope and coverage also abound.

ISSUES WITH FORM-BASED DESIGN CODES

This question of codes, their content and their audience is complicated by the fact that architects tend to think in terms of the design of individual buildings, but urban designers think more broadly about the design of whole communities and the spaces that people inhabit. This inevitably widens the debate on codes to include the opinions of people other than architects – the citizens, residents and workers who use the urban spaces and buildings on a daily basis. Ultimately, design codes, whether they are the detailed British versions or

Figure 5.11 Upton, Northampton, UK, 2006. Northampton Borough Council, English Partnerships and The Prince's Foundation commissioned a master plan and development code from a design team led by EDAW and Alan Baxter and Associates for a town extension to the southwest of Northampton. (See also Figures 5.28, 5.30, 5.31 and 5.34.) The Prince's Foundation's preference for traditional architecture partly accounts for the historicist building aesthetics.

the more restrained form-based zoning ordinances of progressive American practice, must reflect community taste and standards as well as those of design professionals. 'Middle England' and 'middle America' may demonstrate considerable cultural differences in many ways, but they are alike in their general preference for traditional, somewhat conservative building aesthetics. The 'high' taste of architects, although valid and important, is only one component of the range of factors that drive the content of codes.

The process of drafting codes around form-based principles opens up many other important questions about what should and should not be coded. Should a code concentrate on the creation of the urban infrastructure and the public realm by focusing only on the

layout of urban space and building massing? Or should architectural aesthetics specific to a place be included, because the building façades act as the walls to the urban rooms of streets and squares? Or should historic details be replicated because a community possesses a valuable but fragile historic architectural heritage? How can a code establish the basic rhythms of urbanity and scale of a neighborhood and promote contemporary design that is respectful of its context without enshrining a nostalgic image of the past into new development? How can codes control poor design without restricting appropriate innovation? The fear is always that codes will become overly prescriptive, but experience shows that if codes back away from the levels of prescription necessary to achieve urban order and clarity in spatial layout, they run the real danger of becoming too flexible and allowing bad design to flourish alongside more creative interpretations.

Sadly, the author has found over the years that many outspoken critics of codes calling loudly for looser standards and 'creative freedom' are architects with limited talent, to whom the rhetoric of 'freedom' and 'flexibility' is merely a mechanism to conceal bad, or at best mediocre, design under a smokescreen of 'creativity.' In these cases, codes play a vital role in elevating standards of design to an acceptable minimum level. In other contrasting instances, where architects find their design intentions compromised by unsympathetic developer clients, codes can perform the useful function of supplying 'backbone' to the designer's argument. A developer may not want to follow his or her architect's recommendations for good design, but if the architect can state that the design code requires certain standards, then these necessary qualities in a project can survive the depredations of philistine developers.

Form-based codes inevitably include some basic presumptions about what constitutes good urban design. These have to do largely with the creation of a connected framework of well-defined urban spaces, ones that are framed by coherently placed buildings whose façades respond to the scale of the pedestrian environment, particularly in their arrangement of entrances and fenestration of the lower storeys. While the definition of public space and the attractive and informative placement of windows and doors into a building might seem to be a matter of common sense for architects, these basic rules of urban design have been actively dismantled by modernist and postmodern buildings that demonstrate hubristic concern for their own aesthetic form and little regard for the neighbors and surrounding context. Indeed this object fixation and disdain for context was a central tenet of modernist architecture in its quest to build a brave new world that owed little to past eras and their eclectic, historicist aesthetics. Although contextual approaches to architectural design became more prevalent during the postmodern period of the 1980s and 1990s, the coherence of the urban fabric is once again challenged in the early years of the 21st century by the emergence of free-form 'blob' architecture enabled by new computer design and construction software. Buildings characterized by exaggerated formal gestures and complex curves are now in fashion, and the pursuit of form for form's sake often takes precedence over the creation of coherent, attractive urban space between buildings (see Figure 5.12).

Such buildings raise difficult issues concerning design freedom and innovation versus urban clarity

Figure 5.12 Selfridges department store, Birmingham, UK, 2004; Future Systems, Architects. The mannered curves of this windowless building do little to enhance safety or the attractiveness of the street level pedestrian experience of this much-vaunted addition to Birmingham's redeveloped Bull Ring area. (*Photo by Joe Holyoak*)

Figure 5.13 Guggenheim Museum, Bilbao, Spain, 1997; Frank Gehry, Architect. Individual free-form buildings set within well-defined urban areas can provide a wonderful counterpoint to regular urban texture, but a collection of self-regarding, object buildings can ruin the pedestrian scale and grain of a city. (*Photo by Charles C. Hight*)

and coherence of the public realm. While an occasional individualistic 'blob' building in an area of consistent urban texture can create a wonderful highlight – the Bilbao Guggenheim being an obvious example (see Figure 5.13) – cities need many more handsome background buildings than foregrounded monumental structures, especially those that care more for their own aesthetic shock value than for the qualities of the urban place they inhabit. Creating this connective tissue of city space and form means seeking continuity with context and history and necessarily limits the number of formalist buildings based primarily on contrast with their setting. This may not be a popular message to architects, especially in the UK, where many seem stuck in a modernist and disturbingly anti-urban mindset. However, the need for better contextual design is increasingly evident, and design codes can provide that dose of architectural discipline so indispensable for coherent urban areas, including the creation of urban texture in sufficient quantity (and quality) to allow significant civic or institutional buildings to stand apart as architectural landmarks.

But many architects still espouse an extreme dislike of design codes. One especially harsh attack was articulated by Australian architect and academic, Ian McDougall, at a conference in Melbourne in 2000. McDougall expressed his antagonism against 'so-called New Urbanism,' by arguing that he was utterly sick of the urbanism of 'the café and the perimeter block.' He raged against what he saw as 'nostalgic' rules for urban design derived from 'outmoded models of the city.' This rhetoric was ratcheted up several notches by McDougall's assertion that it was important for architects to debunk the sanctity of context, history and memory (McDougall: p. 30).

This sounds like the worst of modernist rhetoric retooled for a new and unsuspecting audience. All too often, the modernist city was a place of demolition and reconstitution by unrelated and isolated object buildings in reduced and hostile landscapes devoid of human scale. Only modernist doctrine considered it cool or appropriate to revel in the destruction of the past; all other periods of architecture established some relationship with history other than destroying it, and the restoration of traditional urbanism through design coding marks a return to respect for people and the public spaces they inhabit. Paying attention to history and context does not necessarily mean copying it. Instead it enables us to return to an urbanism centered on people rather than abstract ideas, and a world of urban spaces rather than architectural objects. Using form-based codes is not historicizing the city. It is implementing good urban manners and putting people first. How many loud, boorish buildings from bombastic architectural egos do our cities need?

The work of the Catalan architect Antonio Gaudi provides a dramatic illustration of how architects can create individually compelling and idiosyncratic

Figure 5.14 Casa Mila, Barcelona, 1906–1910; Antonio Gaudi, Architect. The building plan follows the urban design regulations for massing and building placement, but the building façades and roofscape provide a myriad of opportunities for architectural invention.

buildings without breaking the rules of established urban typologies and urban design guidelines. Two of Gaudi's buildings in central Barcelona, the Casa Mila apartment building (1906–1910) and the nearby Casa Battlo (1904–1906), demonstrate conformity with the urban design code established in 1859 by Ildefonso Cerda in the Eixample, the city's massive 19th century expansion. The surfaces of both buildings are rich in forms and details, expressing in some cases profound metaphysical ideas about Catalonian nationalism, yet the ground plans of the buildings are modest and subservient to the city context. Instead of breaking the urban rules to express his own vision or to make some kind of contrasting statement to the urban pattern, Gaudi celebrated his personal architecture through the design, materials and detailing of the building façades and roofscapes (see Figure 5.14). This mixture of reticence and flamboyance is compelling and a model for all contemporary architects working in urban settings.

Just as Barcelona's magnificent spatial organization creates a setting for many different kinds of architecture, so good urban design requires the spaces between buildings to have priority over the formal ambitions of most individual structures. In pursuit of high design standards for the public realm that can be shared by all citizens, urban design criteria require that special attention be given to the lower stories, or base, of the building. The building's plan shape, materials, location and proportion of windows and doors, and general signification of meanings to the pedestrian all combine to support the patterns of activity in the street, on the square and around the block. As in the Gaudi examples, buildings can enhance the quality of the public space which they themselves help shape, but the self-absorbed aesthetics and object fixation common to many modernist, deconstructionist, and 'blob' buildings are antithetical to these urban design and public policy objectives. Form-based zoning does not preclude the use of eccentric styles in the urban environment; indeed an *occasional* burst of idiosyncratic architecture in an otherwise well-ordered urban setting can impart distinction and excitement (see Figure 5.13). For this reason, most form-based codes exclude civic and institutional buildings from regulation on principle, but special care needs to be taken to ensure that such 'iconic' architecture does not impair the functionality, cohesion and visual attractiveness of the pedestrian realm.

These questions indicate many topics that should be considered in any attempt to construct form-based or design codes that carry legal and mandatory significance, but most issues devolve ultimately onto questions of prescription versus flexibility. In this context, it is important to distinguish between the three main categories of urban and aesthetic coding that are used in current practice, each with different levels of detail, prescription and flexibility. These are: form-based zoning ordinances, pattern books and design codes. While not mutually exclusive in their definitions, these different types of design guidance and design control do serve clear and distinct purposes. The kind of design guidelines discussed earlier can be considered a fourth category, but they differ fundamentally by being advisory documents rather than mandatory.

Form-based zoning ordinances and pattern books are two models drawn predominantly from American practice. Design guidelines are prevalent in both cultures, while design codes as discussed here are chiefly a British device constructed from the other types of design controls to suit the specific and detailed demands placed on the planning system by the British government. Apart from the British/American distinctions, codes are also split between their use in public and private contexts. American zoning ordinances and British design codes are (usually) public documents with some legal mandate behind them and both are embedded in their respective planning systems; design guidelines can be part of public or private regulatory systems; and pattern books, with their greater level of detail regarding architectural style, are generally restricted to the domain of private development – certainly in America.

British planning practice in 2006 incorporates urban design guidance at many levels. However, contemporary research and pilot projects on design codes in Britain have focused extensively on American form-based zoning ordinances and pattern books, and accordingly, we now turn our attention to these two very different kinds of documents.

AMERICAN FORM-BASED ZONING ORDINANCES

American form-based zoning ordinances are different from conventional zoning because of their primary focus on urban and architectural form and their relative de-emphasis of use, although that remains a consideration. These documents control the three-dimensional forms of buildings as they relate to the public spaces of streets, squares, parks, greenways, playgrounds and other urban places, and they include holistic design requirements for all types of public space. These codes focus less on the uses *in* buildings, which often change rapidly, and more on the forms *of* buildings, which are more long-lasting and determine the character of public space by their massing, overall character, and placement on the site. These considerations are often summarized and categorized as 'types' of buildings (such as row house, apartment building, storefront/mixed-use, etc.), or spatial types such as urban square, village green, playground and different classifications of streets (e.g. Main Street, urban boulevard, neighborhood street, etc.). Because of their emphasis on building and spatial types, these codes are often referred to as typological; or where their primary concern is with urban pattern and spatial infrastructure, they are sometimes called urban or morphological codes. In practice 'typology' and 'morphology' tend to be used loosely and synonymously, although that is not accurate, and the terms should be kept separate according to their meanings.

Form-based ordinances fall into three main types: those that deal with a specific locale and are tied to a master plan; those that comprise 'floating zones' that are generic and can be overlaid onto particular areas according to the request of the property owner or the mandate of the local authority; and those that are comprehensive and cover all the territory and all aspects of development control in a municipality. Examples of the first and third category are illustrated in this chapter. The more detailed case study in Chapter 9 provides an example of the 'floating' or 'overlay' zoning district (see Table 9.1). In general terms, codes that apply to a

Figure 5.15 Wake Forest, NC, downtown Master Plan, 2003–2004; The Lawrence Group, Town Planners & Architects. The master plan seeks to revive and reinforce the simple urban structure of the traditional town center to provide maximum development opportunities compatible with the historical scale of the area. *(Reproduction courtesy of the Town of Wake Forest, NC)*

restricted area tend to be more detailed and typological, whereas ordinances that cover an entire municipality are by necessity coarser grained and morphological in content and scope, with less building detail.

Form-based zoning codes comprise written and diagrammatic regulations governing matters of urban layout and typologies of buildings and urban spaces, and are keyed either to a regulating plan for a specific area or to the municipality's official zoning map. Regulating plans are almost always site specific and derived from the master plan created for a particular development or redevelopment opportunity. Following the best practice described in this book, such a master plan would be produced from a community charrette and be accompanied by a detailed implementation schedule of actions by various parties, one of which would be a new zoning code that is typically prepared within 6–8 weeks of the charrette's conclusion. The 'Renaissance Plan' for the town of Wake Forest, NC, provides an example of a form-based zoning code and associated regulating plan for the urban core of a small town struggling to retain and enhance its historic character. The whole project comprised a master plan for the central area and a series of implementation strategies, including a form-based code that superceded conventional regulations (see Figures 5.15 and 5.16).

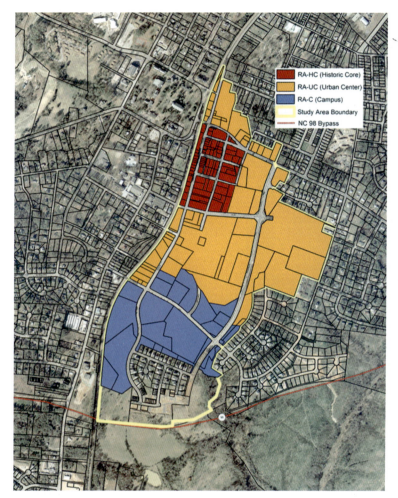

Figure 5.16 Wake Forest, NC, downtown Regulating Plan, 2003–2004; The Lawrence Groups, Town Planners & Architects. The urban design detail of the master plan is translated into a simple hierarchy of form-based zoning categories to regulate future development. *(Reproduction courtesy of the Town of Wake Forest, NC)*

The project report for the Renaissance Plan noted the following provisions:

Renaissance Area Urban Code serves to replace the existing H-CBD (Historic Central Business District) and CBD districts in the Zoning Ordinance and on the Zoning Map … This Urban Code has been ordered in a manner that first addresses the standards for the public realm, the street, and then the private realm, the building …

The guiding principle of this Urban Code is that the use of the property, while important, is subordinated to the design of the building within which uses are contained. This permits a greater [degree] of visual compatibility while encouraging mixed uses to be in close proximity of one another.

The Urban Code reclassifies the town center into three morphologically distinct urban areas, the Historic Core, the Urban Center and a more loosely organized 'Campus' quarter. The Historic Core permits the sensitive continuation of the 'Main Street' environment along primary and secondary streets. The ground floor of buildings on primary streets should comprise active uses including retail or restaurants with office and residential located on second stories. Side (secondary) streets may have a greater variety of ground floor uses.

As with the Historic Core, the Urban Center accommodates an active, pedestrian-friendly area of commercial, residential, office and civic uses in vertically mixed-use buildings, as well as freestanding structures. Retail should be placed at street

TABLE 5.2 Renaissance plan: summary table of urban provisions

	Historic Core	Urban Center	Campus
Lot dimensions			
Front setback (min)	0 feet	0 feet	10 feet
Front setback (max)	5 feet	15 feet	n/a
Side setback	0 feet	0 feet	6 feet
Rear setback (no alley)	0 feet	20 feet	20 feet
Rear setback (measured from centerline of alley)	0 feet from edge of alley pavement	15 feet	15 feet
Encroachments	Balconies, stoops, stairs, chimneys, open porches, bay windows and raised doorways are permitted to encroach into the front setback. Upper story balconies may encroach into the right-of-way up to 3 feet with permission from the Village.		
Height			
Minimum	16 feet	n/a	n/a
Maximum	4 stories (3 stories along White Street from Elm to Roosevelt)	3 stories	3 stories
Parking requirements (minimum)			
Residential	None	1 space per unit	1 space per unit
Lodging	None	1 space per room	1 space per room
All other uses	None	1 per 300 square feet	1 per 300 square feet

Reproduced courtesy of the Town of Wake Forest, NC.

level, with residential uses in the rear or on upper stories. Larger buildings are more easily accommodated in this area due to the presence of larger parcels of land.

The Campus area, while predominately comprised of civic, assembly and institutional buildings, is encouraged to be mixed-use in overall composition while maintaining a close integration with the natural surroundings. Streets in this area should be planted with a regular spacing of canopy trees and parking lots should be screened from the pedestrian realm. (The Lawrence Group, 2003)

Two tables extracted from the form-based code illustrate the relationship between coding the form of buildings and their uses. Table 5.2 deals first with the form and placement of buildings on site to ensure the appropriate urban enclosure of public space, and Table 5.3 follows with the permitted uses, phrased to encourage mixed uses wherever possible.

Because this plan and its site-specific zoning code are part of an historic district, the building design provisions are more detailed and extensive than usual. Another excerpt from the code illustrates a balance between prescriptive design guidance and flexibility by

giving designers a choice of which (style-neutral) design elements they can use in any given condition. If some of these requirements and choices seem obvious to readers, it has to be remembered just how bad and banal much residential and retail design can be! (See Table 5.4.)

The Wake Forest example illustrates a small-scale project with a defined urban area and localized character. The alternative formulation of form-based zoning ordinances comprises the policy and development control document covering the whole municipality and which is subject to the full rigors and challenges of constitutional law. A good example is provided by the municipal code for the town of Huntersville, NC, co-written in its original form in 1995–1996 by the author and Ann Hammond, at that time the Huntersville Planning Director. This ordinance has been in use for 10 years and is still noted as a national model (Steuteville and Langdon: pp. 10–18; Miller: p. 6; Greenberg: pp. 56–59; Tracy: p. 18): the design content of the code is rendered succinctly in diagrams, photographs and clear text, but the document also includes much lengthier sections on legal and procedural details (see Tables 5.5–5.7).

This kind of comprehensive ordinance is constrained by American law regarding the amount of

TABLE 5.3 Renaissance plan: summary table of permitted uses

	Historic Core	Urban Center	Campus
Residential	Multi-family homes	Single-family homes Multi-family homes	Single-family homes Multi-family homes
Lodging	Bed & breakfast inns, Hotels	Bed & breakfast inns, Hotels	Bed & breakfast inns
Retail	Retail uses Convenience store Shopping centers Recreation centers/amusements Food sales and service Self-storage facility Day care centers	Retail uses Shopping centers Recreation centers/amusements Food sales and service Convenience store	Retail uses Shopping centers Recreation centers/ amusements Food sales and service Convenience store Gas station Self-storage facility Day care centers
Office/service	Professional office Home occupations Self-storage facility Personal services Professional/business services Repair services	Professional office Home occupations	Professional office Home occupations Personal services Repair services Professional/business services
Manufacturing	None permitted	None permitted	None permitted
Civic/assembly	Civic/assembly uses Public facilities	Civic/assembly uses Public facilities	Civic/assembly uses Public facilities
Other	Accessory use/building Essential services Wholesale trade Warehousing	Accessory use/building	Accessory use/building Essential services Wholesale trade Warehousing

Reproduced courtesy of the Town of Wake Forest, NC.

architectural detail that can be controlled (this varies from state to state), and it thus concentrates primarily on issues of public spatial infrastructure, e.g. the design of good streets, and regulates buildings to the extent that they must play their roles in creating these spaces, acting as human-scaled walls to urban rooms. Zoning codes can control what one might call 'the public aspects of private buildings' in a similar way that private covenants controlled the development of many London squares in the 18th and 19th centuries (see Figure 5.1). For example, the zoning ordinance can specify a 'build-to' line that creates a uniform street wall of house fronts and it can dictate the placement of the garage to the rear of the lot, or at least recessed several feet behind the house façade so that the garage doors do not dominate the street view. Beyond this level of detail, its powers are often limited. The code can allow and encourage design features such as porches and

balconies, but not require them, as did the London ordinance of 1667. It can also recommend that the ground floors of dwellings be raised off the ground for better proportions, but it cannot stop builders building slab-on-grade as a cheaper but meaner-looking alternative. The extent to which the Huntersville planners and their elected officials feel comfortable, legally and professionally, in regulating 'design' can be gauged from the planning staff's identification of those 'design features mandated by Huntersville's ordinance' as set out on the town's website (www.huntersville.org/planning_1.asp zoning%20ordinance%20highlights).

These 'design features' comprise the following '10 commandments':

1. *Delineate town and country*. Regulations work in concert with the zoning map to strengthen the identity of Huntersville by delineating clear edges

TABLE 5.4 Renaissance plan: ground floor treatment

The first floor of all buildings should be designed to encourage and complement pedestrian-style interest and activity by incorporating the following elements:

1. The ground level of the building must offer pedestrian interest along sidewalks and paths. This includes windows, entrances, and architectural details. Incidental signage on buildings, awnings, and ornamentation is encouraged. Blank walls at the street level are not permitted.

Visually reduce large expanses of wall with windows and/or doors. (Ref. 8.2.1)

2. In non-residential buildings, windows, entryways, awnings, and arcades shall total at least sixty percent (60%) of the facade length abutting a public street. Windows and glass doors shall be clear, transparent glass. No window or door shall be horizontally separated by more than fifteen (15) feet from the nearest other window or door in the same facade visible from any public street.

3. Differentiate the entrance to commercial use of the ground floor from the secondary entrance, if any, to the upper levels.

4. Ventilation grates or emergency exit doors located at the first floor level in the building facade, which are oriented to any public street, shall be decorative.

The ground floor should be interesting and inviting to the pedestrian with clear windows and easily accessible doorways.

Building Entrances

A primary entrance facade shall be oriented toward the street, be designed for the pedestrian, and be distinguishable from the rest of the building. Such entrances shall be designed to convey their prominence on the fronting façade. Use building massing, special architectural features, and changes in the roof line to emphasize building entrances. Additional entrances may be oriented toward side or rear parking lots. Service entrances for shipping and receiving shall be oriented away from the public street.

Residential Building Entrances

Residential building entrances should be raised above the sidewalk a minimum of 1½ feet to reinforce a privacy zone and distinguish them from the commercial entrances.

Raise residential building entries above street level to create privacy.

Reproduced courtesy of the Town of Wake Forest, NC.

TABLE 5.5 Urban district regulations

ARTICLE 3 NEIGHBORHOOD RESIDENTIAL DISTRICT

3.2.4 NEIGHBORHOOD RESIDENTIAL DISTRICT (NR)

Intent: The Neighborhood Residential District provides for residential **infill** development surrounding the traditional town center and its logical extensions. This district also provides for town-scaled residential development within walking distance (generally ½ mile) of satellite village centers, identified on the Land Development Plan. Streets in the Neighborhood Residential District must be interconnected, according to Article 5, Streets, and Urban Open Space provided according to Article 7. A range of housing types is encouraged. Low-intensity business activity is permitted in mixed-use buildings at residential scale, according to locational criteria. The intensity to which permitted uses may be built is regulated by the building type which corresponds to the use.

"towns offer an important lesson in both architecture and citizenship: buildings, like citizens, warrant their idiosyncrasies so long as they behave civilly toward their neighbors..."

Alex Krieger
PLACES
Winter, 1996 (67)

a) Permitted Uses

Uses permitted by right
- bed and breakfast inns
- boarding or rooming houses for up to four roomers
- congregate housing designed within the "civic" building type
- multi-family homes
- single family homes

Uses permitted with conditions
- cemeteries, (9.7)
- religious institutions, (9.8)
- commercial use, including office, in a mixed use building, located on an arterial or at the intersection of a neighborhood street and a larger capacity street
- essential services 1 and 2, (9.14)
- government buildings up to 5000 square feet of gross floor area
- neighborhood and outdoor recreation, (9.21)
- parks, (9.29)
- retirement communities (9.50)
- schools, (9.35)
- transit-oriented parking lots as a principal use, (9.49)
- transit shelters, (9.39)

b) Permitted Building and Lot Types
- apartment
- attached house
- civic building
- detached house
- mixed use[1], up to 3,000 SF of first floor area

c) Permitted Accessory Uses
- accessory dwelling, (9.1)
- day care home (small), (9.11)
- home occupation, (9.19)
- marinas, (9.42)
- accessory uses permitted in all districts (8.11)

[1] The mixed use building duplicates the shopfront building type and has at least two occupiable stories; at least 50% of the habitable area of the building shall be in residential use, the remainder shall be in commercial use. However, when an existing residential building is redeveloped to a mixed-use, at least 40% of the habitable area shall be in residential use.

Reproduced courtesy of the Town of Huntersville, NC.

TABLE 5.6 Building type regulations – I

ARTICLE 4	BUILDING AND LOT TYPES

Lot Type / Apartment Building

Building Placement/Parking/Vehicle Access	Encroachment/Pedestrian Access

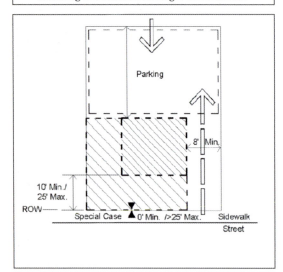

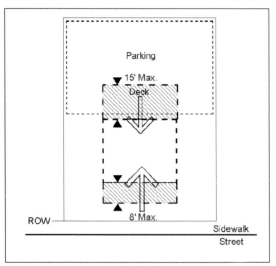

Building Placement/Parking/Vehicle Access

1. Buildings shall be placed on the lot within the zone represented within the hatched area.
2. In most cases, the build to line will be 15' behind street ROW. Special site conditions such as topography, pattern of lot widths, or setbacks of existing buildings permit a larger setback. In urban conditions, apartments may be set up to the property line at the sidewalk, including corner conditions.
3. Building facades shall be generally parallel to front property lines. All buildings shall front onto a public street. All ground floor residential units with exterior access shall front a public street, unless specifically exempted by one of the provisions of Section 8.1.
4. Parking shall be located to the rear of the building.
5. Points of permitted access to the parking indicated by arrows.
6. Hedges, garden walls, or fences may be built on property lines or as the continuation of building walls. A garden wall, fence, or hedge (min. 3' in height) shall be installed along any street frontage adjacent to parking areas.
7. Trash containers shall be located in the rear parking area (see Parking Regulations).
8. Mechanical equipment at ground level shall be placed on the parking lot side of building away from buildings on adjacent sites and shall be screened from view by an opaque screen.

Encroachment/Pedestrian Access

1. For buildings set back from sidewalk, balconies, stoops, stairs, open porches, bay windows, and awnings are permitted to encroach into setback area up to 8'.
2. Attached decks are permitted to encroach into the rear setback up to 15 feet.
3. For buildings set up to the sidewalk, upper level balconies, bay windows and their supports at ground level may encroach a maximum of 5'0" over the sidewalk.
4. Main pedestrian access to the building and to individual units is from the street (indicated by larger arrow), unless specifically exempted by one of the provisions of Section 8.1. Secondary access may be from parking areas (indicated by smaller arrow).

Description:
The apartment building is a residential building accommodating several households. In traditional towns, this building type coexists with a variety of other building types. A successful contemporary design permits its integration with other residential types through the coordination of site and building design (see Architectural Regulations). Apartment complexes should be one or more separated buildings similar in their scale on the public street to large detached housing. Where possible, structures shall be designed to terminate vistas or serve as key focal points in the neighborhood.

Special Conditions:
1. The intention of buildings in all locations must be to relate the principal facade to the sidewalk and public space of the street.
2. Corners: Setback at street corners will generally replicate frontage conditions. However, side setbacks on a minor street may be less than the front dimension.
3. Within the limits described, front and side setbacks will vary depending upon site conditions. Setbacks should be used in a manner which encourages pedestrian activity. Squares or spatially defined plazas within building setback areas can act as focal points for pedestrians.

Reproduced courtesy of the Town of Huntersville, NC.

TABLE 5.7 Building type regulations – II

ARTICLE 4	BUILDING AND LOT TYPES

Building Type / Apartment Building

<table>
<tr><th>Permitted Height and Uses</th><th>Architectural Standards</th></tr>
<tr><td>

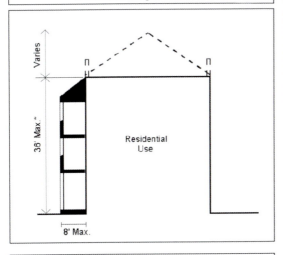

Varies

36' Max.*

Residential Use

8' Max.

1. Building height shall be measured as the vertical distance from the highest finished grade relative to the street frontage, up to the eaves or the highest level of a flat roof.
2. The height of parapet walls may vary depending upon the need to screen mechanical equipment.
3. Building height to the ridge may vary depending on the roof pitch.
4. Permitted uses are indicated above.

</td><td>

Principles

4. To perpetuate the unique building character of the town and its environs, and to re-establish its local identity, development shall generally employ building types that are sympathetic to the historic architectural vocabulary of the area in their massing and external materials.
5. The front elevations facing the street, and the overall massing shall communicate an emphasis on the human scale and the pedestrian environment.
6. Each building should be designed to form part of a larger composition of the area in which it is situated. Adjacent buildings should thus be of similar scale, height, and configuration.
7. Building silhouettes should be generally consistent. The scale and pitch of roof lines should thus be similar across groups of buildings.
8. Porches should form a predominant motif of house designs, and be located on the front or to the side of the dwelling. When attached to the front, they should extend over at least 15% of the front facade. All porches should be constructed of materials in keeping with those of the main building.
9. Front loaded garages, if provided, shall meet the standards of Section 8.16.
10. At a minimum, the Americans with Disabilities Act standards for accessibility shall be met.

Configurations

A. Main roofs on residential buildings shall be symmetrical gables or hips with a pitch of between 4:12 and 12:12. Monopitch (shed) roofs are allowed only if they are attached to the wall of the main building. No monopitch shall be less than 4:12. All accessory buildings shall have roof pitches that conform to those of the main building.
B. Balconies should generally be simply supported by posts and beams. The support of cantilevered balconies should be assisted by visible brackets.
C. Two wall materials may be combined horizontally on one facade. The "heavier" material should be below.
D. Exterior chimneys should be finished in brick or stucco.

Techniques

A. Overhanging eaves may expose rafters.
B. Flush eaves should be finished by profiled molding or gutters.

</td></tr>
</table>

Reproduced courtesy of the Town of Huntersville, NC.

to town development while providing for a more rural-appearing landscape punctuated by pockets of development.

2. *Build a public realm.* A consciously conceived public realm must be provided to strengthen and enliven the public life of the town. Town streets in combination with squares, greens, parks or plazas should be designed into each project.

3. *Connect pedestrian-friendly streets.* Town streets are characterized by slow-speed geometry and the presence of sidewalks and street trees. Space for parallel parking is provided where on-street parking will meet the day-to-day needs of adjoining development. Town streets are fully connected in a system of blocks, creating a fine-grained network to disperse traffic and meet the mobility needs of vehicles, pedestrians and bicyclists. Street design should incorporate traffic calming intersections to forestall high-speed traffic opportunities in neighborhoods.

4. *Enclose streets with buildings to create the public space of the street.* Buildings should have consistent setbacks and be aligned along the street. In urban, village and hamlet settings, buildings will be close to the street. In less urban settings, a larger setback is permitted as long as regular rows of large maturing street trees are provided to form the vertical edge of the street. Parking is placed behind buildings.

5. *Maintain compatible building relationships along streets.* Buildings of similar scale are placed alongside and across the street from one another. Changes in building scale should be negotiated at mid-block (i.e. at back property lines). This technique reduces dependency on wide buffers to separate variously sized buildings and differing uses.

6. *Screen unattractive uses thoroughly.* Dense screening of parking lots and other unsightly areas of projects provides good visual separation without space-consuming buffers.

7. *Mix housing types.* Infrastructure cost is offset and affordable housing is encouraged by allowing a broad mixture of lot sizes and housing types in the residential districts.

8. *Design buildings to respect human scale.* Rigorous attention must be paid to the scale and massing of buildings and the character of pedestrian entrances along streets. Appearance standards [architectural standards noted under each building type and general provisions for compatibility in each zoning district] are provided to allow for a mixture of uses and housing types while maintaining compatible relationships between buildings.

9. *In the Rural District preserve natural features which reflect the rural heritage of the community.* … Rural heritage features should be excluded from buildable areas at the outset of project design. Development should be clustered on the remaining land. To protect the lot yield, residential lot sizes are unrestricted and single-family houses may be attached or detached.

10. *Thoroughly buffer uses that disregard the human scale.* Most non-residential land uses can be integrated into the townscape by regulating building placement, massing and scale. However, rigorous conditions and large buffers apply to uses that cannot respect human scale or may detract from neighborhood livability. These include big-box retail, quarries, commercial communication towers, various waste-handling facilities, junk yards, outdoor storage and the like.

These provisions are drafted to ensure that basic urban design standards are met. They are amplified by the architectural standards under each building type noted under the eighth commandment. These standards are also limited in scope, restricting themselves to some general principles and configurations of three-dimensional composition as noted in the architectural standards for the Apartment Building Type in Table 5.7. Some of the regulations refer to fairly generic issues and use the definitive and mandatory 'shall' form of instruction, such as: 'The front elevation facing the street, and the overall massing shall communicate an emphasis on human scale and the pedestrian environment.' But as matters get more detailed, the tone changes from requirements to expectations, and the wording uses the conditional 'should,' e.g. 'Balconies should generally be simply supported by posts and beams. The support of cantilevered balconies should be assisted by visible brackets' (Town of Huntersville: sect. 4–9).

The Huntersville code manages to avoid specifying historicist architectural aesthetics, settling for a modest instruction that 'development *shall* generally employ building types that are sympathetic to the historic architectural vocabulary of the area,' thus leaving open the possibility for contemporary interpretation of traditional forms (Town of Huntersville: sect. 4–9). However, most new developments utilize some kind of historical or generic neo-classical references in their façade design without any prompting by the code. This architectural conservatism is bred largely from market forces responding to consumer preferences in the American South (and elsewhere) for cozy traditionalist aesthetics, and to meet this perceived demand architects design in historicist styles to suit their clients' dictates. While architects might consider a wide range of aesthetic choices in developing their designs, the public, the elected officials and, it must be said, planners too, are much more comfortable with the quasi-vernacular historicism that is prevalent in most American suburban development (see Figure 5.17).

In writing the Huntersville code, Ann Hammond and this author focused their ambitions at the level of urban structure rather than engage architectural aesthetics. Street connectivity was a cardinal principle, as were the mandates that all buildings front onto a public street and that main building entrances open off the sidewalk. These apparently innocuous and common-sense requirements were perceived as very radical back in the mid-1990s; they effectively outlawed conventional strip shopping centers with buildings set well back from the street behind large areas of parking. With the code in force, such shopping centers had to be configured to include pedestrian-oriented shopping streets with on street parking, street trees and wide

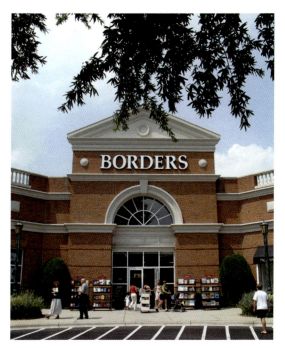

Figure 5.17 Borders book store, Morrocroft shopping center, Charlotte, NC. Neo-classicism is the style of choice for most American suburban shopping centers built since the 1990s.

sidewalks, and wherever possible, be part of a mixed or multi-use development (see Figures 8.1 and 8.7).

The Huntersville example was an early test case for form-based zoning and was thus fashioned conservatively to resist challenges under North Carolina law. Accordingly, the level of design control is modest, in contrast to the level of detail incorporated into privately administered pattern books described later in this chapter. The scope of American form-based ordinances that cover a whole community is also far more constrained than British pilot design codes, and part of the reason for this American caution and conservatism comes directly from that nation's legal system itself, and its evolving history of legalizing design and aesthetic control.

The Legal Basis for Form-based Codes in the USA

Form-based zoning obtains its validity through American law and precedent regarding 'aesthetic' zoning and 'design review,' whereby communities seek to control how buildings are designed, usually to help ensure a fit between new buildings and the preferred or established urban character of an area. American courts have demonstrated frustration with vague wording and criteria regarding concepts like 'community character,' and accordingly, design standards in form-based zoning should be tied to measurable outcomes, such as increasing pedestrian activity and safety. Extra legal strength is achieved by linking the provisions of form-based zoning to other, tangible, public policy goals such as avoiding congestion, or economic development. While aesthetic-based regulations have been subjected to many legal challenges, American courts have, for the most part, supported such regulations as long as they are grounded in enabling authority and are based on clear, objective standards (Duerksen and Goebel: p. 5). A 2004 California law provides a strong and specific platform for form-based zoning, but at the moment it stands alone in its clarity, with no companion legislation in other states, although Florida is considering similar directives. The California law is simply worded:

> The text and diagrams ... [of the general plan] that address the location and extent of land uses, and the zoning ordinances that implement these provisions, may also express community intentions regarding urban form and design. These expressions may differentiate neighborhoods, districts, and corridors, provide for a mixture of land uses

and housing types within each, and provide specific measures for regulating relationships between buildings and outdoor public areas, including streets. (Katz, 2004: p. 21)

This is directly written to facilitate New Urbanist form-based zoning, but outside California the legal landscape is less clear. The increasing prevalence of design review legislation in American towns and cities is a function of the lack of design concepts and content in conventional zoning ordinances; clearly such quantitative zoning regulations do not satisfy communities' desire to have some say over the appearance and 'fit' of new development. However, as Katz notes, there is a continuing legal concern about overly prescriptive design guidelines that try to tie up every detail of a building's appearance, often using historical models as their base criteria. These design guidelines, essentially 'Band-aids' to support weak conventional zoning, are often mistaken for form-based codes, but they are very different in their formulation, and their degree of specificity leaves them open to legal challenge when municipalities attempt to use their detailed provisions as mandatory controls over development.

When design regulations have some legal force in the USA, they have historically been 'add-on' provisions to conventional 'Euclidian,' zoning – so-called because of the landmark Supreme Court decision of 1926 in the case of *The Village of Euclid (Ohio) et al. v. Ambler Realty* that established the legality of local government regulation of uses of private property on the grounds of 'public welfare.' This was typical of the attitudes of courts in America during the first half of the 20th century; regulations intended to uphold visual and aesthetic matters would be supported only if they were inextricably linked to other considerations of public safety or economics – the so-called 'aesthetics-plus' doctrine. Not until the 1950s did the US Supreme Court validate laws dealing with aesthetic regulations without the covering support of other, functional criteria. In *Berman v. Parker*, 348 US 26 (1954) the court gave strong support for government action based on aesthetic considerations, stating that the definition of 'public welfare' included physical and aesthetic values (Duerksen and Goebel: p. 7). This legal precedent was strengthened quickly in subsequent years, and in the case of *People v. Stover*, 191 NE 2d 272, 275 (NY 1963) the court held that once aesthetics had been deemed a valid subject of legislative concern, 'reasonable legislation' for that purpose was 'a valid and permissible exercise of the police power' (Garvin and LeRoy: p. 5).

Following these judgments, courts began upholding regulations on aesthetic grounds alone. By 1978, matters had evolved so quickly that in a famous case concerning laws protecting a local landmark building, the US Supreme Court emphasized that it was no longer a matter of dispute that cities had the power to enact land-use regulations aimed at enhancing their quality of life by preserving their character and aesthetic features (*Penn Central Transportation Co. v. New York City*, 438 US 104 (1978) at 129, in Duerksen and Goebel: p. 7).

This opinion has an important impact on the validity of form-based zoning. Although form-based zoning is often equated with aesthetic zoning as a means of establishing its legal authority, it usually deliberately sidesteps matters of aesthetic detail, e.g. in its determination to be 'style neutral,' and focuses instead on more basic issues of urban character. As aesthetics in architecture are usually equated with questions of style, this creates something of a logical conundrum: form-based zoning disavows aesthetics as its main concern yet is historically enabled under law by invoking aesthetic considerations. Fortunately this potential problem can be resolved in the wording of the *Penn Central* legal opinion that regards the 'character ... of a city' (the urban substance of most form-based codes) and its 'aesthetic features' as equivalent under the law.

The ability to validate form-based zoning legally under the rubric of urban character is an important foundation of contemporary planning and urban design practice in America. The law provides legal security especially if regulations focus on questions of basic urban design, not stylistic or aesthetic appearance; codes written in this way can avoid any challenge on the grounds that for a government agency to require a specific aesthetic appearance for new development infringes on a landowner's individual property rights. However, despite this security, it is always good practice to connect form-based zoning codes to clearly stated public purposes. Clearly argued rationales for a particular urban character, based on matters such as street width and connectivity, building height, contextual relationships of building massing, relationship of buildings to streets at the pedestrian level, positioning of building entrances, clear visibility through glazed openings and so forth, are all items that can be fairly and legally controlled through form-based zoning codes. These provisions are bolstered by the standard of 'reasonableness' established by clear public policy objectives for safe and attractive urban areas. Such regulations are able to withstand legal challenge because they are based on more objective principles of architectural typology and urban morphology rather than on subjective aesthetic taste concerning a building's appearance. They are also more clearly understandable to the general public, and as in the case of the 1667 London urban regulations, are likely to remain 'robust over time.' In this regard, the Huntersville code, as one of the first of its kind in the USA, has been in operation for 10 years at this time of writing in 2006. It is appropriate, therefore to examine the operation of the code in practice during that time, and to this end the author sought the frank opinions of the current Huntersville town staff regarding the code's efficacy, its strengths and its weaknesses.

Form-based Zoning in Operation

Even after 10 years, Huntersville planners still find some developers resistant to many ideas contained in the code. Having good examples on the ground helps a lot, both for developers and elected officials, who often lack knowledge about urban issues that are well understood by the specialist staff (see Figures 8.1 and 8.7). Planners engage in a constant process of educating elected officials and the general public about the concepts and requirements contained in the code, and at the time of writing in 2006 are developing a picture book of urban design concepts specifically for elected officials and planning board members. This educational process will continue as new elected officials take office, planning staff come and go, and new residents enter the community. The author's experience in Huntersville has shown this continuing educational mission to be extremely important: without such a commitment, it is likely that the code would have been overturned at one point by politically motivated opponents. This need for education also applies to architects, a number of whom demonstrate a surprising lack of knowledge about urban design concepts in the projects submitted for approval.

Modifications to the code should be expected over time, and these must also be explained to everybody involved. All municipalities operating a form-based code must have professional design expertise on staff in the person of an urban designer, architect or landscape architect, or else a design consultant retained to work with elected officials, developers and builders to help implement the code's objectives. This requirement was born out in Huntersville when, about 5 years after the code was adopted, key members of the town staff who had been involved in writing the document left for other employment. Without this institutional memory,

or a planner with design qualifications, there was a very steep learning curve for new staff. These difficulties were overcome, and the normative operation of the planning department in 2006 has evolved to the point where an interdisciplinary team of town employees, comprising generalist planners, an urban designer, a transportation planner, a traffic engineer and a civil engineer, meet weekly for several hours to discuss the design ramifications of new projects submitted for approval.

Having a fully qualified urban designer on staff is considered by the planning director to be essential. The Huntersville team keeps a definitive 'interpretation file' from their weekly discussions, whereby any interpretations of the code by town staff concerning innovative design or previously unmet planning conditions are recorded and filed. This establishes precedents and a reference source for future discussions and seeks to avoid conflicting interpretations of similar matters. Even with a tightly drafted code such as the Huntersville example, there is always interpretation involved, and this takes time. Review of major schemes that seek a conditional rezoning approval is never as simple as staff 'checking the box' and issuing a quick permit. (This submission is similar in its level of detail to approval of reserved matters or a full planning application in the UK.) Projects with several buildings and an urban layout generally require about 6–8 months for approval of planning and design matters, and another 3–4 months for approval of civil engineering permits. Building permits issued by the county (similar to UK Building Regulation approval) can then take a further 2–3 months depending on the project's complexity. This is not appreciably faster than conventional zoning approval processes. On smaller developments where the development is 'by right,' and no rezoning of land is required, for example, a small apartment building in a Neighborhood Residential zone (see Tables 5.5–5.7), the process is naturally quicker, with plan approval in about 3–4 months. This speedier process is partly because 'by right' developments involve only staff administrative approval rather than submission of the project to the appointed planning commission and discussion in the political arena of the full town council.

The lengthier, political, process applies to all projects that involve rezoning of land, major new subdivisions and other special permissions. This scheduling of sequential public meetings accounts for a large percentage of the time required for project approval, along with coordination between town planning staff and county officials who check engineering issues.

The experience of the town staff indicates one other main reason for extended approval times: the lack of good design quality in many original submissions. Planning staff, particularly the urban designer, often have to lead the client's architect or engineer through the basic principles of urban design enshrined in the code in what is essentially a series of private tutorials. In some instances, the town's urban designer will redesign a project to improve the standard sufficiently to meet the code requirements.

The experience of Huntersville staff, and other planners in the Charlotte area working with form-based codes, does not bear out the oft-quoted claim that form-based codes expedite permitting and provide incentives for developers with a quick and less expensive approval process. In theory, because the code establishes a clear physical vision and standards for new development, projects that meet those standards can be quickly approved. This may happen in some jurisdictions, but in Huntersville, a town well equipped to deal with these matters with an expert staff sympathetic to the principles of form-based coding, the design basis of the regulations injects a greater degree of subjectivity into the approval process. However carefully worded and illustrated the code might be, this subjectivity needs careful handling, politically and legally. The approval process was 'streamlined' and effective, but not necessarily any faster than conventional zoning practices. However, the town staff was unanimous in stating that the design content of the code had brought about a big improvement in the quality of new development in the town during the 10 years of its operation since its inception in 1996.

While quicker permitting may not be realistic, Huntersville has benefited unexpectedly from form-based coding. The town has been consistently mentioned in the American professional press as a national leader in progressive zoning reform, and this forward thinking image has transcended the planning world into the realms of economic development. The town is now home to companies that would not normally consider a community of 30 000 people for their corporate headquarters and has been included in lists of the best places to live in America.

Typical pages from the Huntersville ordinance are illustrated in Tables 5.5–5.7, and the whole code is keyed back to the town's zoning map, constructed with relatively few zoning categories based morphologically on the type of urban area classified by its intensity (town center, neighborhood center, neighborhood residential, rural area, etc.) instead of the multitude of individual use-based zoning categories mandated by conventional zoning (see Figure 5.18). This morphological classification of urban areas along a scale of intensity from rural to dense urban has been formalized by Andres Duany and Elizabeth Plater-Zyberk as the 'Transect,' a conceptual section through a typical settlement, following the precedent of Patrick Geddes' famous Valley Section of 1905, whereby places within each geographic region were evaluated and described according to their location on a scale from mountain to sea. This new Transect has become a central planning tool of the recently introduced Smart Code, again a Duany Plater-Zyberk development over a 20-year period of incubation.

The Transect

Geddes and other users of a similar concept, such as M.R.G. Conzen's transect studies of historical town plans and places built during various periods since the Industrial Revolution (Conzen, 1968) or Coleman's analysis of the central city, older and newer suburbs, and rural areas (Coleman, R., 1978), utilized the technique to describe existing situations. By contrast, Duany Plater-Zyberk and other New Urbanists use the Transect to describe the way things *ought to be* (Brower, 2002: p. 314). This use of urban design concepts and categories of urban or rural character to define and manage the future is characteristic of most form-based zoning codes, and is especially evident in *A Pattern Image*, a parallel and separate Dutch version of the Transect (Urhahn and Bobic, 1994). However, the key to the Duany Plater-Zyberk Transect lies in giving legal weight to concepts of morphological urban analysis.

The Transect draws a cross section through an imaginary landscape, identifying six types of environmental zones, each defined by its morphological character and moving from T1 (Rural Preserve) through ascending scales of suburban and urban areas leading to the densest area T6 (Urban Core) (Duany and Plater-Zyberk, 2002: A.4.1) (see Figure 5.19). A seventh classification, an 'Assigned' or 'Specialized District,' similar to conventional planning's 'special use districts,' exists for non-urban uses such as hospital complexes, airports, landfills and the like that do not fit easily into urban or suburban zones, or which, because of noxious by-products such as dust and noise, need to be kept at a distance from residential areas. This hierarchical scale enables designers, planners and the public to see the various kinds of rural and urban landscape as a continuum that relates urban uses to

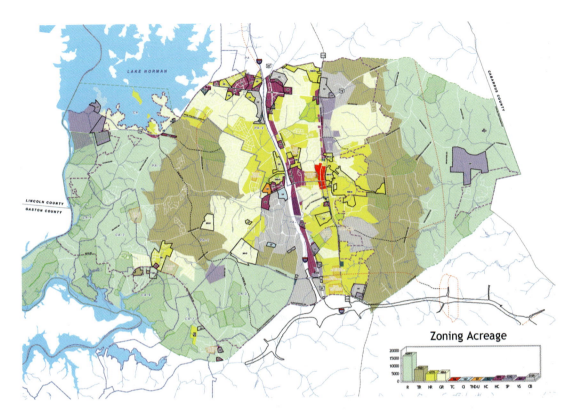

Figure 5.18 Town of Huntersville Zoning Map (Rev. January 2006). This indicates the hierarchy from rural areas (light green) through low- and medium-density housing (varying tans and yellows) to more intense development paralleling main north–south highways. Light gray indicates large office and institutional campus development while crimson indicates commercial and mixed-use development. The historic town center is indicated in red. *(Reproduction courtesy of the Town of Huntersville, NC)*

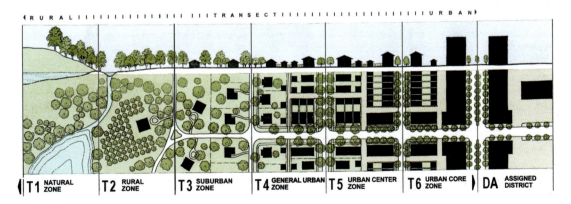

Figure 5.19 Transect diagram. The Transect has become the main tool used in American form-based coding. Its hierarchy of urban conditions incorporates a wide variety of uses within patterns of traditional urbanism. *(Diagram courtesy of Duany Plater-Zyberk & Co.)*

111

Figure 5.20 Haynie-Sirrine neighborhood, Greenville, SC, Regulating Plan, 2001; The Lawrence Group, Town Planners & Architects. The detailed urban design plan is split into a hierarchy of urban zones based on character and scale, not use.
(Reproduction courtesy of the City of Greenville, SC)

the ecological factors of particular zones. This simplified spectrum enables planners and designers to work out where different types of buildings and different uses fit best.

Because the Transect relies on urban form as the primary organizer of towns and cities, it has been criticized as not taking sufficient account of social factors in the makeup of community. In a series of studies regarding neighborhood satisfaction, Brower (1996) suggested that places tend to be valued less for their physical elements than for their social opportunities and connections. Brower argued in a later paper that any transect methodology used as an instrument of public policy should accordingly take social elements into consideration as well as physical ones (Brower, 2002: pp. 314–315).

Questions regarding the relationships between built form and social context are at the heart of several criticisms regarding the universality of the Transect methodology. For example, Michael Southworth complains the Transect presents a false and singular vision of a

mononuclear city, at odds with contemporary realities (Southworth, 2003: p. 215). Southworth correctly states that American cities are evolving in polycentric patterns, with multiple centers, but fails to acknowledge that the Transect model, because it is a generic section without a specific scale, can be applied to a planning problem as large and complex as a polycentric region, or as defined as a single community (Duany and Talen: p. 258). The methodology can be adapted to each new site condition and can be used as a regulating mechanism for growth management in any location.

Neither does the Transect have to exist in its entirety. A project in Greenville, SC, in which the author was involved, used a Transect model to describe a limited hierarchy of urban conditions in a compact inner city neighborhood. These zones ascended from Neighborhood Edge to Neighborhood General to Neighborhood Core to Village Center, where each zone encapsulated both its geographical location and potential for development and rehabilitation within the new community master plan (see Figures 5.20 and 5.21). A planning

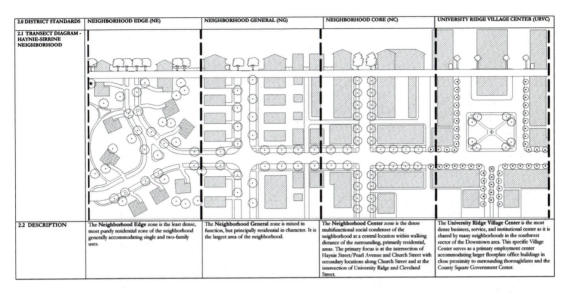

2.0 DISTRICT STANDARDS	NEIGHBORHOOD EDGE (NE)	NEIGHBORHOOD GENERAL (NG)	NEIGHBORHOOD CORE (NC)	UNIVERSITY RIDGE VILLAGE CENTER (URVC)
2.1 TRANSECT DIAGRAM - HAYNIE-SIRRINE NEIGHBORHOOD				
2.2 DESCRIPTION	The **Neighborhood Edge** zone is the least dense, most purely residential zone of the neighborhood generally accommodating single and two-family uses.	The **Neighborhood General** zone is mixed in function, but principally residential in character. It is the largest area of the neighborhood.	The **Neighborhood Center** zone is the dense multifunctional social condenser of the neighborhood at a central location within walking distance of the surrounding, primarily residential, areas. The primary focus is at the intersection of Haynie Street/Pearl Avenue and Church Street with secondary locations along Church Street and at the intersection of University Ridge and Cleveland Street.	The **University Ridge Village Center** is the most dense business, service, and institutional center as it is shared by many neighborhoods in the southwest sector of the Downtown area. This specific Village Center serves as a primary employment center accommodating larger floorplate office buildings in close proximity to surrounding thoroughfares and the County Square Government Center.

Figure 5.21 Haynie-Sirrine neighborhood, Greenville, SC, Transect, 2001; The Lawrence Group, Town Planners & Architects. The Transect is tailored to the particular characteristics of each urban zone in the Regulating Plan. *(Reproduction courtesy of the City of Greenville, SC)*

project in an adjacent neighborhood would utilize its own version of the Transect's hierarchy to fit its particular parameters, establishing edges and centers of its own. In this way adjacent projects can match their edge conditions together while creating the kind of polycentric arrangement advocated by Southworth.

Southworth also criticizes the Transect for freezing the city into 'a static spatial entity, where suburbs are always suburbs and centers always centers' (Southworth, 2003: p. 216). This may indicate a basic misunderstanding about form-based zoning. One of the major points of such codes is to manage the different timescales of urban development: the uses of buildings which change the fastest; the building types that can absorb several changes of use with only relatively minor changes to the building fabric; and the urban neighborhood or district, which, with its network of streets, squares, parks and other public spaces, changes most slowly of all. The examples of London squares, where two centuries of changes have taken place within the same urban fabric, shaped by the same architectural façades (see Figure 5.1), or the streets of Boston's Back Bay where extensive rows of what were once terrace houses are now shops, offices, restaurants and apartments, illustrate how urban forms and building types can absorb dramatic alterations in use without major urban surgery (see Figure 5.22). Social, commercial and cultural changes have all taken place

Figure 5.22 Newbury Street, Back Bay, Boston, MA. The form of this 19th century residential architecture has remained constant while the uses have changed dramatically. *(Photo by Adrian Walters)*

within areas of stable urban form, and this interchange between change and stability has leant a patina of interest and sophistication to each urban area.

Form-based codes specifically provide for this short-term flexibility of use, medium-term adaptability of buildings, and long-term urban order established by building types and spatial patterns. Cities are living agglomerations of form, space and human activity, and zoning codes need to provide tools to manage this process of continual adaptation. In the same way that the urban density and cultural profile of Boston's Back Bay has changed over the decades without major changes in urban form, it is quite possible to imagine a gradual densification of a 'General Urban' Transect zone into an 'Urban Center,' or a neighborhood 'Urban Center' into an 'Urban Core' without substantial changes in building fabric. Use-based zoning changes every time a significant shift in use occurs with no thought for design, but form-based zoning changes more slowly because each urban zone and set of building types absorb change and provide inherent flexibility within their own parameters.

Comparing the American transect model of urban classification to a 2006 proposal by MacCormac Jamieson Pritchard for a generic high-density low-rise city development illustrates an interesting convergence of Anglo-American practice. Richard MacCormac has been interested in the urban form of high-density housing for several decades: he developed an urban layout in 1973 which demonstrated that densities of 250 persons per hectare (approximately 38 dwellings per acre) could be achieved by interlocking courts of terraced houses (MacCormac: pp. 549–551). All the homes had private gardens and the density targets were achieved without recourse to the publicly despised high-rise flats. Built projects using MacCormac's approach, such as Pollards Hill, in Merton, South London (1977), by the Borough of Merton Architects' Department, bear a strong resemblance to the influential plan of Radburn New Town, NJ, of 50 years earlier by Clarence Stein and Henry Wright. In both cases, cul-de-sac vehicle courts bring cars to one side of the houses which open up to parkland and pedestrian greenways on the other, all organized within a large 'superblock' of major roads. In his latest development MacCormac has reverted to traditional urban hierarchies of interconnected streets and alleys, illustrated with isometric drawings of a generic set of progressively urbanizing conditions – from a rural, landscaped edge, through lower-density low-rise housing, then medium-density low-rise development, and ultimately to high-density, medium-rise buildings. This follows very closely the physical hierarchy of the Duany Plater-Zyberk Transect, and MacCormac's intention was to counter the prevalence of small urban apartments as the dominant housing type in inner-city development by providing a mixture of housing types (including accommodation for larger families) and a high degree of spatial richness that allows both for social interaction and individual privacy within the neighborhood (Kucharek: p. 66).

In the system devised by Duany Plater-Zyberk, the Transect is linked directly to the Smart Code – an urban code and a unified land development ordinance that integrates planning and urban design (www.dpz.com and www.placemakers.com/info/workshop.html). The Smart Code attempts to do in generic form for all municipalities in America what the Huntersville zoning ordinance achieved for that one community and is a far cry from Duany Plater-Zyberk's large single sheet of diagrams that regulated Seaside in 1982. (Version 7.0 of the Smart Code runs to 74 pages, which is still relatively brief for an American zoning ordinance.) There is no equivalent in the UK to this comprehensive effort to reform how America builds its towns and cities, and it represents two decades of research, experimentation and debate.

Like the Huntersville example, the Smart Code includes design standards for urban space, streets and parking, and for building massing, type and placement (all according to the Transect) together with the administrative provisions necessary for the adoption and management of a complete municipal ordinance. Whereas Huntersville's code was tailor-made and crafted for that municipality, the Smart Code is designed to be adapted to any community, large or small. Because of its intentional generic applicability, the Smart Code does not include regulating plans – these site-specific constructs, such as the Wake Forest, NC, and Greenville, SC, examples (see Figures 5.16 and 5.20), are the responsibility of individual municipalities – but the Transect formula provides the practical framework for creating such plans. For a small fee ($156 or £83) a town or individual planner can obtain a copy of the code and begin to learn it, but using the code is more expensive as a municipality must pay a licensing fee to adopt the code into law. In addition, that community will need expert guidance to administer the code on a continuing basis (Steuteville and Langdon: pp. 10–17). Petaluma, CA, was one of the first municipalities to adopt a version of the Smart Code in July 2003 (Katz: p. 21), and in the wake of the 2005 hurricane disasters along the American Gulf Coast, the Smart Code has proved a valuable tool in establishing the rebuilding priorities of storm-ravaged communities. In the early months of 2006, for example, the Louisiana city of Lake Charles endorsed the Smart Code as the basis for its rebuilding and other municipalities are following suit (Langdon: pp. 1, 5).

The Smart Code is perhaps the most significant effort to reform American land use regulations since the introduction of zoning in its conventional form in the early 20th century. Its logic and provisions attempt to reverse more than 50 years of development control based on separated single use districts with no urban design content and to replace these outdated methods with a single, comprehensive instrument based primarily on urban design concepts but formulated in ways that make it usable by planners and other municipal officials who do not have design training. In this regard it is an experiment worthy of careful study over time. The Huntersville experience of administering a detailed design-based ordinance over a 10-year period demonstrated the need for planning staff trained in urban design, and for continued education programs about design concepts for planning commissioners and elected officials. The Smart Code is intended for use not only in well-prepared communities such as Huntersville, but also in places where that expertise does not exist. To this end, the Smart Code is intentionally prescriptive to limit the amount of subjective interpretation required. This lends clarity to the code, but renders it susceptible to criticisms on the grounds that it imposes a ready-made planning vision on a community from above rather than growing one organically from the grass roots.

For municipalities intending to use the Smart Code, the key to success lies in the process of tailoring its generic provisions to particular locations and community conditions. The urban design provisions are sensible and straightforward, based on concepts of traditional urban spaces and hierarchies overlaid with environmental standards for the protection and conservation of open space and natural habitats. These provisions are applicable in many different locations, and the process of tailoring the Smart Code to a particular community may consist less of adapting the technical standards as ensuring a full process of public participation and education, so that the community feels it owns the code, rather than having it thrust upon them. Similar to the Essex *Design Guide* in England, where improvement in the design and layout of new developments resulted from the code's requirements even when implemented by planners and architects with limited design sensibilities, the Smart Code is likely to enhance the environment of American towns because it is based on good design principles. America has suffered for 50 years at the hands of zoning ordinances that have no urban design standards administered by planners with no training in design; the Smart Code can only improve matters.

The design content of municipal form-based ordinances such as the Smart Code and the Huntersville example is intentionally limited mainly to matters of urban form and spatial infrastructure, partly because of legal constraints on the regulation of private property

by government. When codes are privately developed and administered, much more architectural detail can be included, creating 'pattern books' as design guides and methods of development control by private developers over large projects involving other builders.

AMERICAN PATTERN BOOKS

Pattern books in America are used almost exclusively by private developers to mandate consistency of architectural style and detail across a range of house types constructed by different builders. They are legal documents between private consenting parties only. Having no public government role, they become very specific, even draconian in what they will and will not allow. In general, pattern books are highly detailed and conservative in outlook, based on analyses of local and regional architectural styles and precedents. The normal intent is to connect large new developments to the traditions and mythology of the region or locality, partly for environmental and architectural reasons and partly as a marketing strategy that confers instant credibility and distinction on a development in a very competitive market. The introduction to one such pattern book, for the large and multi-phase Baxter development in Fort Mill, in the 'Upcountry' region of South Carolina, just a few miles south of Charlotte, NC, states:

The design of each village is based on the treasured legacy of Upcountry towns and villages that developed during the 19th century and into the early part of the 20th century. These places are admired today for their character and quality of architecture. The pattern of development is an expression of the democratic ideals of civic responsibility and participation. Each neighborhood, street, park, or public space is designed using the regional palette of landscape and architecture ensuring a continuation of the best traditions and sense of identity that is unmistakably Upcountry. (Urban Design Associates, 1999: A-1)

The text and graphics, prepared by Urban Design Associates (UDA) (with LandDesign Inc.) in 1999, extols the predominance of neo-classical historical styles in these older communities, particularly Adams/Federal and Greek Revival. Colonial Revival houses play a major part in the historical legacy, while Victorian styles 'add spice to the neighborhood fabric.' The pattern book explains that houses built in Baxter 'will be

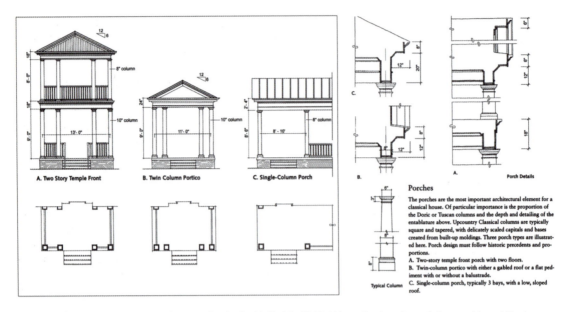

Figure 5.23 Page from Baxter Pattern Book, Fort Mill, SC, 1999; Urban Design Associates and Land Design. American pattern books instruct builders on the correct proportions and details of historical architectural styles. *(Reproduction courtesy of Urban Design Associates and Land Design)*

designed in one of these three architectural vocabularies [Neo-classical, Colonial or Victorian]. While there are pre-approved house plans available to builders and homeowners, this *Pattern Book*™ contains a series of design guidelines for architects to use when designing individual houses in one of the three styles' (Urban Design Associates: A-3). Diagrams illustrate the required placement of buildings on their individual lots so that they form coherent 'walls' to the urban room of the street, while detailed block layout plans enforce the desired urban consistency with street sections and perspective drawings of the streetscape aesthetic (see Figure 5.36). These urban requirements are expanded in detail to the aesthetics and constructional details of the houses themselves, with a series of approved alternative arrangements for each of the three styles: these standards become progressively more detailed, from massing and three-dimensional composition, to fenestration rhythms and proportions, window and door styles, and dimensions and construction details of porches and façade elements (see Figures 5.23 and 5.24). Finally, landscape details are covered in terms of different styles of walls, fences and planting schemes.

This particular pattern book, like all UDA's work, is beautifully produced, and as an instrument of private regulation – agreed to by individual homeowners and builders as part of their land transaction

Figure 5.24 Baxter, Fort Mill, SC, 1999–2006; Urban Design Associates and Land Design. Urban design and architectural details are rendered faithfully by a variety of different builders to create a commercially successful housing product.

agreements – it has performed well both as a marketing tool for the developer and as a means of maintaining consistently high standards of design and construction across the whole development amongst a varied set of different homebuilders. Documents in the USA like *The Baxter Pattern Book* tend towards historicist architecture, largely because these styles best fit the

American public's taste in mass-produced suburban housing. Stylistic preferences apart, it is clear that developments produced under private pattern book regulations administered by a master developer can create higher standards of design and construction than developments controlled only by public form-based zoning ordinances. Pattern books can literally outlaw what is considered bad design by insisting on specific design features and qualities; as such they mirror some of the British government's ambitions for delivering guaranteed high standards of development, but within the American legal framework, despite the legal grounding of aesthetic zoning, it is not possible to legislate such great specificity of detail in a public form-based zoning ordinance. Nor would many urban designers wish to do so when working in the fully public world of zoning regulation or development control; most would see regulating style, even if legal, as too prescriptive. The amount of detailed aesthetic control contained in pattern books is therefore almost always reserved for private sector work.

Several experimental British codes represent a hybrid condition relative to American precedent, ranging across the spectrum of form-based zoning ordinances, design guidelines and pattern books. These codes are one layer of an integrated approach to planning and urban design guidance, involving urban design frameworks, design or development briefs, master plans and the codes themselves. For American readers in particular, it is important to clarify these various components and to describe how they fit into the overall planning system in the UK in 2006.

BRITISH URBAN DESIGN GUIDANCE

British government policy on cities and urban revitalization became clear and focused around the turning of the millennium, following the report of the Urban Task Force noted earlier. In essence this policy places good urban design at the center of the national effort to improve British cities. At the heart of this endeavor are 'spatial master plans,' defined as three-dimensional frameworks of buildings and public spaces. These are 'the fundamental building blocks' of this new 'design-led regeneration' (Rouse, 2002: p. 7).

Contained within the torrent of urban design guidance that issued forth from British government sources and their consultants since 2000, is a simple statement that sums up the present conundrum facing architects, urban designers and planners alike in that country.

Robert Cowan, primary author of *Urban Design Guidance*, a review of urban design practice and procedures in the planning system, stated in 2002:

> There is at last a general understanding that making places socially, economically and environmentally successful depends on high standards of urban design. What is less understood is how good design can be delivered. *The challenge is to influence the development process, not only on high-profile sites but wherever urban change is reshaping places.* (Cowan: p. 4) (Author's italics added).

The key to delivering good quality urban design, especially when mediocre developers and professional consultants are involved, relies heavily on design guidance, and the hierarchy of tools – urban design frameworks, development briefs, master plans and design codes – has emerged through a process of experimentation to become the dominant process administered by local governments in Britain.

The first level of urban design guidance is the urban design framework, usually a two-dimensional map that describes how planning and design policies should be implemented in areas where local government sees a need to control, guide or promote change, or where coordinated action is required by several different parties. This framework usually includes future infrastructure requirements, comprising new roads, public spaces, transit or other public works such as schools and health care facilities, and the sites of special heritage features or protected buildings. The framework can examine urban quarters or districts, urban corridors, town centers, or urban extensions into previously undeveloped land (see Figure 5.25). Sometimes an urban design framework may be more ambitious and three-dimensional, such as one prepared by Birmingham City Council in 1996 for the Digbeth Millennium Quarter (see Figure 5.26), which contains detailed guidance more akin to development briefs, described below.

Development briefs provide the next level of guidance and are site specific and more detailed in terms of an illustrative design. They usually contain 'some indicative, but flexible, vision of future development form' (Cowan: p. 12) (see Figure 5.27). Development briefs are prepared for sites where more specific and specialized guidance is required for major new developments due to particular circumstances such as significant historic, environmental or conservation issues.

Urban design frameworks and development briefs are generally produced by local government, or some

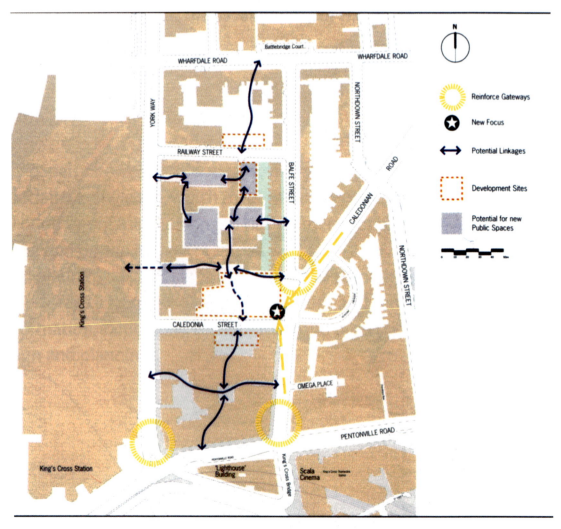

Figure 5.25 Typical British urban design framework, from *Urban Design Guidance* (Cowan, 2002). Diagrams such as these set out the basic urban design constraints and opportunities to guide design development. *(Reproduction courtesy of Thomas Telford Publishing)*

quasi-public regeneration agency such as English Partnerships, and the documents establish the criteria within which private developers are expected to operate. Master plans, the next step in this process, can be produced by either public or private sectors, or both in partnership; most often they are products of consultants working for private development consortia or for organizations that own particular sites or control the development process. As with all design guidance:

… the purpose of a master plan is to set out principles on matters of importance, not to prescribe in detail how development should be designed. But a master plan should show in some detail how the principles are to be implemented. If the master plan shows an area designated for mixed-use development, for example, it should show a layout that will support such uses … ensuring that the footprints of the buildings are appropriate to the envisaged uses. (Cowan: p. 13)

Typical master plans 'set out proposals for buildings, spaces, movement and land use in three dimensions and match these aspirations with an implementation

Park Street/Moor Street

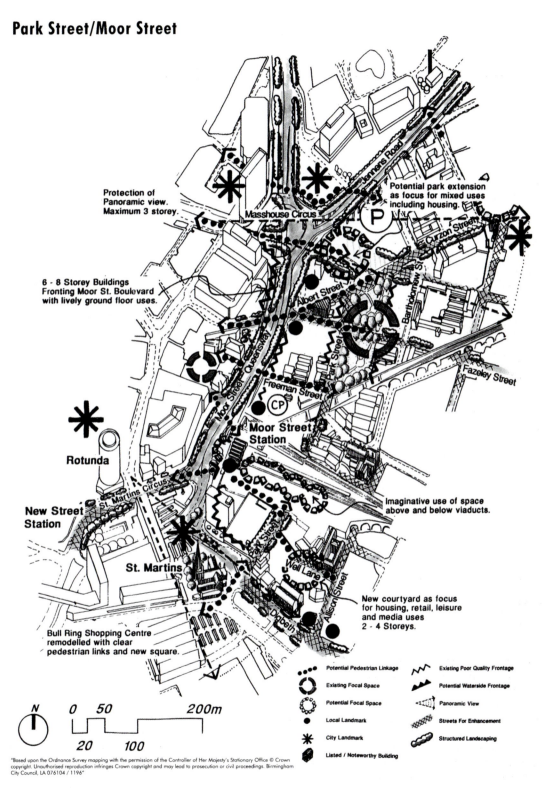

Protection of
Panoramic view.
Maximum 3 storey.

Potential park extension
as focus for mixed uses
including housing.

6 - 8 Storey Buildings
Fronting Moor St. Boulevard
with lively ground floor uses.

Rotunda

New Street
Station

Imaginative use of space
above and below viaducts.

St. Martins

New courtyard as focus
for housing, retail, leisure
and media uses
2 - 4 Storeys.

Bull Ring Shopping Centre
remodelled with clear
pedestrian links and new square.

Masshouse Circus

Moor Street
Station

St. Martins Circus

Jennens Road

Curzon Street

Albert Street

Bartholomew St

Fazeley Street

Freeman Street

Well Lane

Allison Street

Digbeth

•••• Potential Pedestrian Linkage	∿∿ Existing Poor Quality Frontage
◌ Existing Focal Space	▲▲ Potential Waterside Frontage
◯ Potential Focal Space	◁ Panoramic View
● Local Landmark	▨ Streets For Enhancement
✳ City Landmark	▨▨ Structured Landscaping
◆ Listed / Noteworthy Building	

N   0   50   200m
    20   100

"Based upon the Ordnance Survey mapping with the permission of the Controller of Her Majesty's Stationary Office © Crown
copyright. Unauthorised reproduction infringes Crown copyright and may lead to prosecution or civil proceedings. Birmingham
City Council, LA 076104 / 1196"

Figure 5.26 Urban design framework for Digbeth Millennium Quarter, Birmingham, UK, 1996. Prepared by
architecture and planning staff at Birmingham City Council, this urban design framework provides extensive
three-dimensional detail to communicate the design vision for the area to developers and architects.
(Reproduction courtesy of the City of Birmingham)

Figure 5.27 Typical British development brief, from *Urban Design Guidance* (Cowan, 2002). Development briefs can become very design specific. While not master plans in themselves, they illustrate preferred urban design solutions in schematic terms. *(Reproduction courtesy of Thomas Telford Publishing)*

strategy' (CABE, 2004b: unpaginated). Specifically, master plans illustrate and define the following issues:

- The layout and connections of the streets, squares and open spaces in a neighborhood.
- The height, bulk and massing of buildings.
- The relationships between buildings and public spaces.
- The activities and uses in the area.
- The movement patterns for pedestrians, cyclists, cars, public transit, service and refuse vehicles.
- The provision of utilities and other elements of infrastructure.
- The relationship of physical form to the social, economic and cultural context.
- The integration of new development into existing communities, and the built and natural environments. (CABE, 2004a: p. 13)

This scope and content for master plans is very similar on both sides of the Atlantic, and Figures 5.28 and 5.29 illustrate typical examples from each nation, from Upton, Northampton, in the UK and Concord, NC, in America.

The most detailed element in the hierarchy of design guidance comprising urban design frameworks, development briefs, master plans and design codes are the codes themselves. These are detailed documents with drawings, photographs and diagrams that precisely describe how the design and planning principles established in the urban design framework, development brief or master plan should be applied to a particular site. They operate to ensure that the good design qualities established in the various types of design guidance are delivered in the final built project. Recent British practice, such as the urban expansion at Upton, Northampton, has derived codes directly from a master plan: the master plan sets out the vision and the design code provides instructions for realizing that vision and maintaining design standards (see Figure 5.30).

Improving design standards is particularly critical in Britain in the context of the government's stated plan to create over a million new homes around London and the South East region of the country by 2016. This is especially urgent as a national audit of housing design quality in 2004 by CABE revealed significant shortcomings in the standards of suburban housing constructed by volume house builders. Particular points of concern were poor site design; unresolved relationships between vehicles and pedestrians, particularly in parking areas; and a reliance on superficial historical pastiche architectural motifs stuck on to the building envelope to provide architectural character. Overall, less than a fifth of the designs (17%) were judged to be 'good' or 'very good'; most (61%) were 'average', while over a fifth (22%) were rated as 'poor.' Despite the plethora of government sponsored design guidance, the audit concluded that 'good urban and architectural design is not the norm, and this suggests that the way policy and practice interact may need to be reviewed.' The audit specifically identified the need for 'the planning regulatory regime to intervene and improve submitted proposals' (CABE, 2004c: p. 7).

These findings explain in part the desire by British government and planners to include a greater level of detail in design codes than is normal in American form-based zoning ordinances: the need to improve design standards is seen by the government as an essential corrective action if they are to deliver their election promises and ambitious building plans for the nation's housing. Key items in the British government's Sustainable Communities Plan include building 'successful, thriving and inclusive communities in which people want to live,' and delivering 'high quality homes and more affordable housing' (Thorpe, 2004). Design codes are thus regarded as central, both politically and technically, to solving the inconsistent design quality exposed by the CABE *Housing Audit.*

Some British developers, like developers everywhere, are averse to design regulation simply because of the codes' ability to hold them to higher standards and reduce wriggle room to cut corners. Others realize that design codes have advantages, particularly the documents' ability to create consensus rather than conflict and their 'potential to deliver a faster and more certain planning approval process, particularly by reducing inconsistencies in advice from local planning authorities' (CABE, 2005b: p. 30). Design codes also possess advantages for those developers acting as master developers for a large site or series of sites involving multiple smaller developers and builders. In much the same way as American pattern books, such as the one for Baxter, SC, allow the main developer to control the quality of individual buildings by means of very detailed advice and private legal agreements, so British developers can use the delivery of high design quality throughout their developments as a major marketing tool.

As part of the effort to improve British design standards, the publication *By Design: Urban Design in the Planning System* identifies eight aspects of development form: urban structure, urban grain, landscape, density and mix, height, massing, details and materials (DETR and CABE, 2000: p. 16). These eight factors can be grouped into three main sets of concerns: *urban layout* deals with issues of urban structure, urban grain, landscape, density and mix; *urban scale* covers height and massing; and *building appearance* is a function of details and materials. This three-part analysis allows us to distinguish clearly those matters that can most easily and appropriately be coded in all public and private applications, i.e. *layout* and *massing*, and those covering *appearance* where greater restraint from covering architectural details is evident in American public sector codes compared to their fledgling British counterparts. American form-based codes administered by public authorities (outside specific historic districts where a higher degree of aesthetic regulation is permissible) have generally restricted regulation to those factors pertaining to urban layout and urban scale, and provided only schematic regulation of architectural issues regarding appearance for the reasons of legal constraints on municipal power.

American reluctance to embrace detailed architectural aesthetics within form-based coding has not stopped British efforts to prescribe architectural detail in the government-backed push to improve the quality of new development in the UK. Ironically, in its report on pilot coding projects in Britain, CABE refers extensively to American New Urbanist precedents, but has tended to learn the wrong lessons from its research. The Congress for the New Urbanism (this author is a signatory of the founding Charter dating from 1996) is an organization that has been split since its founding by a divergence of opinion between a traditionalist, neo-classical wing, based largely in the American South and east coast, and a 'modernist,' more innovative and environmentally conscious wing most usually associated with America's west coast. British research, unfortunately, focuses only on the historicist and neo-classical end of the New Urbanist spectrum as manifested in such unique and unrepresentative places as Seaside, FL (CABE, 2005b), and neither this famous 80-acre (32-hectare) tract, nor other privately coded developments like Disney's Celebration, or more modest examples such as Baxter, SC, characterizes American practice in public, municipal form-based zoning. Limiting attention and analysis to these sorts of developments while ignoring more progressive projects with advanced, contemporary architecture evident in other parts of the USA, paints a false picture of New Urbanist practice and of the ends to which codes can be put.

The CABE report also fails to distinguish between the various types of design coding in the USA – zoning ordinances, design guidelines and pattern books – a failing evident in a previous CABE publication entitled *Building Sustainable Communities: The Use of Urban Design Codes.* This document sets out the pros

Figures 5.28 and 5.29 Master plan, Upton, Northampton, UK, 2001; The Prince's Foundation and EDAW, Master Planners (left) and Master Plan, Concord, NC, 2004; The Lawrence Group, Town Planners & Architects (right). These two master plans, although produced under different planning regimes in different countries, demonstrate significant similarities in their urban design concepts and layouts based on concepts of traditional urbanism. *(Reproduction courtesy of English Partnerships and the City of Concord, NC)*

Figure 7.2 Central Courtyard block-plan

7.3 BLOCK PRINCIPLES

- The block layout set out in Figure 7.1 establishes the urban form of Upton and must be followed.
- The perimeter block form must be respected. There is some room for flexibility with respect to their precise dimensions and boundaries.
- Blocks cannot be combined to create larger blocks.
- The street hierarchy as set out in Chapter 6 must be respected. Street types cannot be changed.

Central Courtyard Perimeter Blocks
Figure 7.3 illustrates the character of a central courtyard perimeter block, with annotations referred below:

① Increased height to mark corner
② Access to central courtyard

Figure 7.4 Central Courtyard Block-Elevation

Figure 7.3 Central Courtyard block-axonmetric

Figure 5.30 Typical page from *Upton Design Code, Version 2*, 2005; EDAW *et al.* The urban design principles of the master plan are explained in detail for developers and their architects to follow. *(Reproduction courtesy of English Partnerships)*

and cons for design codes in a generally clear manner, but contains the statement 'In the most prescriptive plans, such as those favored by the Congress of the New Urbanism in the US ... the code will probably provide a pattern book, detailing clearly and exactly the limitations on the design of buildings, the choice of streetscape materials, private landscaping options, ornamentation restrictions, etc., in different locations within the plan area' (CABE, 2003c: sect. 2, unpaginated). Contrary to this assertion, the bulk of New Urbanist practice in local government coding does *not* deal with the level of architectural detail envisioned by British design codes.

British research as documented in the CABE publications has only scratched the surface of New Urbanism. It is accurate that *some* codes for New Urbanist developments – those produced by the traditionalist wing – do provide such a pattern book of regulations; however,

others do not, and it is not correct to ascribe this traditionalist approach to the New Urbanist movement as a whole. CABE's failure to make crucial distinctions between different types of American codes, and to ignore the urban-based public codes in favor of aesthetics-based private pattern books presents a skewed and incomplete analysis of American practice.

Experimental British practice involving design codes has thus embraced the idea of regulating architectural detail with few qualms. The Office of the Deputy Prime Minister, CABE and English Partnerships jointly developed a working definition of a design code as follows:

A design code is a set of specific rules or requirements to guide the physical development of a site or place. The aim of design coding is to provide clarity as to what constitutes acceptable design quality and thereby a level of certainty for developers and the local community alike that can help accelerate the delivery of good quality new development … [The design codes] can extend from urban design principles aimed at delivering better quality places and include requirements for streets, blocks, massing and so on, or may be focused more on architectural or building performance, for example aiming to increase energy efficiency. (CABE, 2005b: p. 16)

British design codes tend to set down hard and fast rules, rather than guidelines, and thus provide a definitive set of instructions rather than advice. British codes are almost always place-specific products of master plans for major developments. As part of this process, public participation is important but limited. The CABE document *Design Coding* continues: '[T]he code should always be drawn up in consultation with a range of local stakeholders … e.g. the developer, the local planning authority, highways department, local councillors and landowners' (CABE, 2005b: pp. 16, 17). The role of the general public is limited to community planning events (such as charrettes) that establish the broad physical vision encapsulated in the master plan. This is similar to the author's American experience, where the development of public, form-based zoning codes following the approval of a particular development master plan (or Small Area Plan in American parlance, such as the Wake Forest, NC, and Greenville, SC, examples) remains a purely technical task, without direct citizen input. Few difficulties arise if the codes remain true to the plan's content. However, in more expansive cases where form-based zoning codes are written to cover whole towns, such as the Huntersville zoning ordinance, numerous and regular public meetings are essential for citizens to understand the objectives, principles and mechanisms of the code, both before its adoption and afterwards to deal with amendments and additions.

In the process of development and adoption of the Huntersville code, the author carried out design exercises for many parts of town to examine the potential impact of the new zoning rules, and these illustrative designs were debated by a large steering committee of citizens, developers and elected officials over a 12-month period. During this time the town declared a moratorium on new development in order to restrict further development under the old rules and to release planning staff from day-to-day operations of development control so that they could concentrate on the detailed task of rewriting the complete ordinance in its full legal complexity. By contrast, writing form-based

codes for limited areas such as those in the Wake Forest and Greenville projects took only four to six weeks. The approval process for the code, once written, varies according to local politics: the Wake Forest code was approved within 3 months after technical completion, while the Greenville code took nearly 9 months before being adopted, delayed because of revisions being made to a larger city ordinance.

Research and analysis of pilot coding projects in the UK has shown that the process of writing a design code to meet British expectations takes between 3 and 5 months, due perhaps to the wider range of architectural issues covered than in most American counterparts. The research also shows that once the code is in place, applications for planning permission for large or complex projects are processed faster and more smoothly than usual (CABE, 2005b: p. 42). The comparison between the scope and content of British design codes and American form-based ordinances is instructive. Similarities exist where both systems see the codes as primarily technical instruments. They are not vision-making documents, but mechanisms for delivering appropriate standards of development, either in the context of all-embracing visions for a whole community (such as the Smart Code or the Huntersville example), or more geographically limited developments set out in a master plan as part of a Small Area Plan (USA) or a Local Development Framework (UK).

It is in the content and scope of design-based codes that substantial differences between British and American practice are revealed. British research into coding methods and content has established seven specific topics to be covered by design codes, and these create a useful means of cross-cultural comparison. Most similarities occur at the urban level, while considerable disparities emerge at the level of architectural design. The seven topics are: Built form and townscape, Streets and enclosure, Parking, Open space and landscape, Land use mix, Architectural design, and Sustainability (CABE, 2005b: p. 35).

Built Form and Townscape

This category comprises the form and layout of urban blocks, and is coded in considerable detail in both British and American systems, although some details vary. Common issues are block size, building height and massing, building lines, building frontage and building edge/street wall details. Controls on building line and height can become quite detailed, especially in British codes, in respect to porches, balconies, arcades, etc., what UK practice identifies as 'boundary conditions.'

Also common to both systems are regulation by building type, e.g. terrace house (attached single-family or row house in the USA), semi-detached house (duplex), apartment building and so forth. The Upton code, for example, relates the prevalence of particular building types to certain 'character areas' – 'Urban Boulevard,' 'Neighbourhood Spine,' 'Neighbourhood General' and 'Neighbourhood Edge' – and notes the range of uses in each condition (see Figure 5.31). This method of cross-classification between urban character, building type and permitted use is directly analogous to American practice, to which the equivalent pages in the Greenville, SC, code bear witness (see Figures 5.20, 5.21 and 5.32).

British practice specifically identifies urban forms such as the perimeter block and related density figures. American form-based codes often avoid specific density numbers as being too redolent of conventional ordinances where the debates are always about numbers and rarely about design, preferring instead for density to be implied by building type and urban character zone, i.e. a matter of design within specified parameters rather than numerical prejudgment. Exceptions to this are found in codes specifically for transit-oriented development, where *minimum* residential densities and commercial floor-area ratios are established in order to ensure the required development intensity – to boost population around train stations and ridership figures for light rail systems.

Streets and Enclosure

Streets are generally coded in both systems as a series of hierarchical types, specifying dimensions, radii, sightlines, curb details, bicycle lanes, street trees, and traffic calming measures for streets and sidewalks. Some of the UK dimensions for vehicle parking and circulation are smaller and dimensions for pedestrian spaces bigger than their American counterparts, but otherwise the similarities outweigh differences except for one important issue, Sustainable Urban Drainage Systems (SUDS). The Upton code contains extensive guidance on how street design can play an important role in enhancing rainwater storage on site and infiltration functions to convey runoff to shallow storage wetlands around community playing fields. This aspect of the sustainability agenda, increasingly common in British practice, has few counterparts in America as part of urban design or stormwater engineering practice – although some progressive town codes (e.g. Huntersville) have added requirements for Low Impact Development (LID) that have detail similarities to

European sustainable urban drainage systems. This author, with a University of North Carolina colleague, Professor Chris Grech have utilized innovative work using similar sustainable techniques from Vancouver, Canada, by landscape architect Patrick Condon (see www.sustainable-communities.agsci.ubc.ca) in a sustainable community design studio project at the University of North Carolina at Charlotte College of Architecture for a real-life client, the Culture and Heritage Commission of York County, SC. This project, in conjunction with Clemson University in South Carolina, established master plan alternatives and a sustainable site design guidelines for a residential and mixed-use development on a 400-acre (160-hectare) riverside site adjacent to a new ecological museum building to be designed by one of America's leading 'green' architects, William McDonough (see Figure 5.33). The sustainable site design guidelines produced by the studio have been included in the client/developer agreement and if the development is constructed in accordance with these codes, this development will become one of the most advanced examples of sustainable site design in the USA. The end result of the sustainable drainage design would look similar to the details at Upton, in the UK, as illustrated in Figures 5.11 and 5.34.

Parking

Off-street parking in American codes is usually handled by its own section of the code in terms of its location (behind buildings) and controlling dimensions. On-street parking is always encouraged and often counted towards the overall parking requirement for the development. In the Upton code, dealing with mainly residential development, parking is handled as part of the urban block structure rather than a separate provision, and includes two requirements uncommon in American practice, both relating to a more advanced sustainability agenda: permeable surfaces for parking areas as part of the SUDS system and exterior electrical sockets metered to each home for charging electrical vehicles.

Open Space and Landscape

This issue receives considerable attention under regulations in both nations. Many American form-based codes have a specific section for urban open space (excluding streets, which have their own section), classifying it into various types such squares, parks, playgrounds, greenways and in some instances larger greenbelts at the edges of neighborhoods (see Figure 5.35). British

	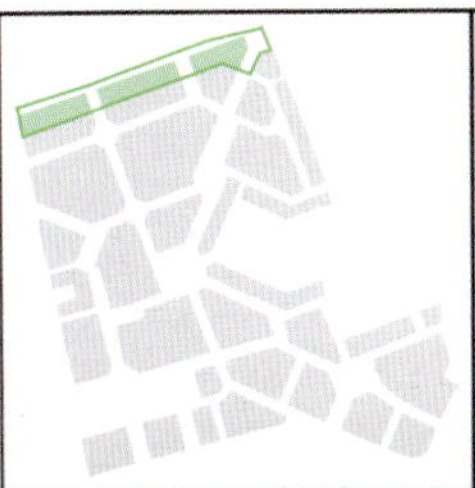 URBAN BOULEVARD (WEEDON ROAD)	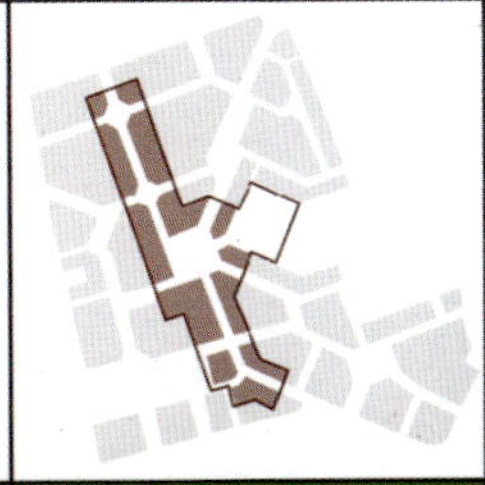 NEIGHBOURHOOD SPINE	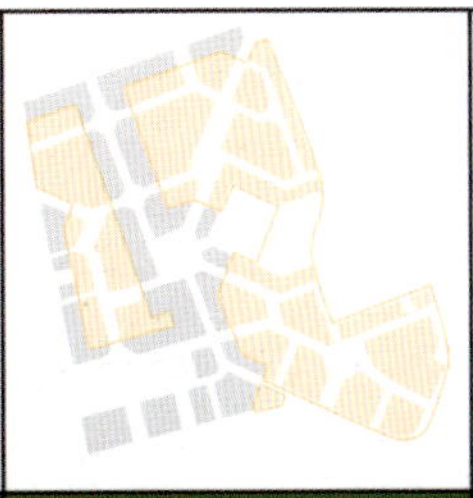 NEIGHBOURHOOD GENERAL	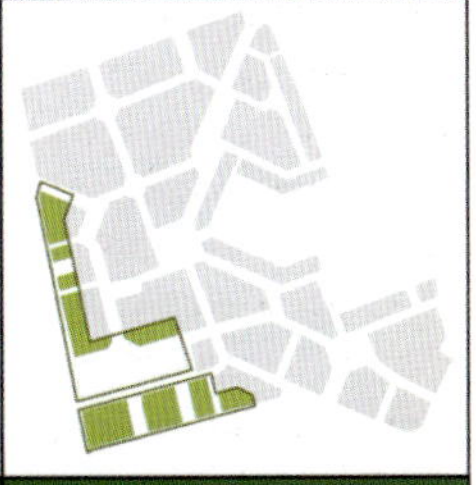 NEIGHBOURHOOD EDGE
Street Type	Urban Boulevard	Main Street Street Mews	Main Street Street Lane Mews	Main Street Street Lane
Land Use	Offices, Live work, Shops Restaurants/Pub Housing Community Facilities	Housing Local Shops Community Facilities School	Housing	Housing
Building Type	Mixed Use	Apartments Townhouses Mixed Use, Mews, School	Townhouses Apartments Mews Semi-detached	Townhouses Detached Semi-detached
Height	Minimum 4 Storeys	Varies	Varies	Varies
Boundary Treatment		Varies	Varies	Varies
Parks and Open Space		Upton Square	Neighbourhood Square SUDS Upton Country Park	Ashby Wood SUDS Upton Country Park

	NEIGHBORHOOD EDGE (NE)	NEIGHBORHOOD GENERAL (NG)	NEIGHBORHOOD CENTER (NC)	UNIVERSITY RIDGE VILLAGE CENTER (URVC)
2.3 MIXED USE PROVISIONS	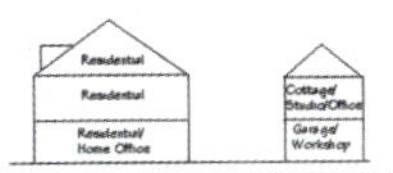	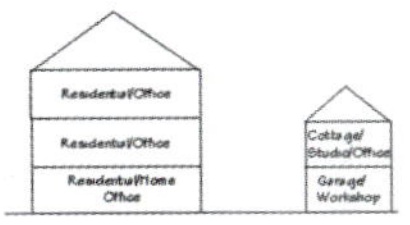	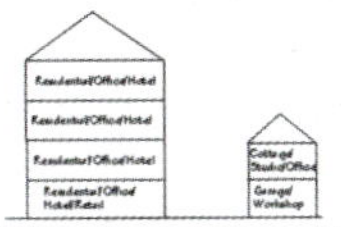	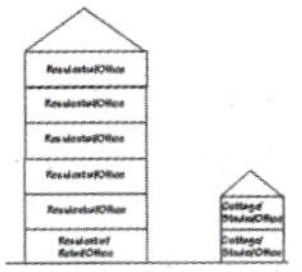
2.4 SPECIFIC BUILDING TYPES PERMITTED Except where topographic conditions prohibit, all buildings shall enfront on public streets or parks.	Detached House – Street Lot Detached House – Alley Lot Civic Building	Detached House – Street Lot Detached House – Alley Lot Townhouse Apartment Building Civic Building	Detached House – Alley Lot Townhouse Apartment Building Shopfront Building Civic Building	Detached House – Alley Lot Townhouse Apartment Building Shopfront Building Workplace Building Civic Building
2.5 PERMITTED OPEN SPACE TYPES	Greenway Meadow Park Sportsfield	Greenway Park Sportsfield Green Square Plaza Community Garden Close Playground	Greenway Square Plaza Community Garden Close Playground	Greenway Square Plaza Community Garden Close Playground
2.6 MAX. HEIGHT	2 ½ Stories	3 Stories	4 Stories (exception-6 stories for Hotels)	6 Stories
2.7 SIGNAGE	Arm Sign Only (Monument Signs for Civic Buildings only)	Arm Sign Only (Monument Signs for Civic Buildings only)	All Permitted Signage	

Figures 5.31 and 5.32 Page from the *Upton Design Code, Version 2*, 2005; EDAW *et al.* (top) and page from the zoning ordinance for the Haynie-Sirrine neighborhood, Greenville, SC, 2001; The Lawrence Group, Town Planners & Architects (bottom). In both these examples, building type and uses are keyed back to the hierarchical zones of urban character as the framework of development control (see also Figures 5.20 and 5.21). *(Reproductions courtesy of English Partnerships and the City of Greenville, SC)*

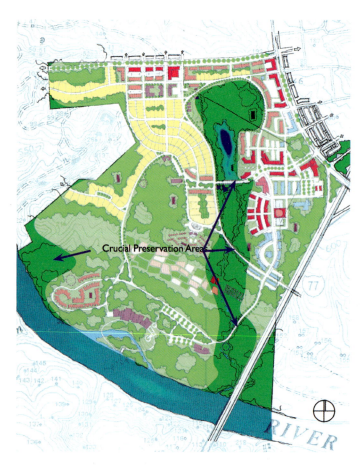

Crucial Preservation Area

Figure 5.33 Site plan for sustainable development, Fort Mill, SC, 2004: College of Architecture students, University of North Carolina at Charlotte. Instructors David Walters, RIBA and Chris Grech, RIBA. Design concepts for sustainable development have been incorporated into developer's legal agreements to ensure good design quality in this project due to commence in 2007. *(Reproduction courtesy of the Culture and Heritage Museums of York County, SC)*

Figure 5.34 Sustainable Urban Drainage System (SUDS) at Upton, Northampton, UK. Landscaping devices to retain water for on-site filtration are incorporated into the urban design detailing for public spaces. See also Figure 5.11.

practice extends this design focus on public space into front and rear gardens of housing development as part of the concentration on 'boundary treatments,' the zones of transition between public and private realms. The overall tendency for publicly sponsored British codes to be more site specific than their municipal American counterparts is especially clear in dealing with this area of concern; the amount of site-specific detail in British codes is more like American pattern books than local government form-based zoning ordinances (see Figures 5.36 and 5.37).

Land Use Mix

British design codes rarely regulate this factor, as the mix of uses is usually established at the master plan stage, although the Upton code, for example, does specifically relate a range of uses to particular character zones and

Forecourt

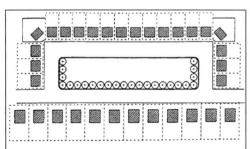

Forecourts are open space areas which act as buffers between residential buildings and non-residential buildings or streets. Forecourts are entirely bounded by streets. It is recommended that forecourts be planted parallel to all street ROW's with one tree species. Such plantings shall be a minimum of 10 ft. on center and a maximum of 30 ft. on center.

Plaza

A plaza is an open area adjacent to a civic or commercial building. Plazas function as gathering places and may incorporate a variety of non permanent activities, such as vendors and display stands. Limited parking is also permitted. Plazas are always paved in brick or another type of paver, or crushed stone. Plazas shall be level, stepped, or gently sloping (less than 5% grade).

The following sizes are recommended but may be smaller or larger depending on the building or facility design. At no time shall a plaza's horizontal length or width be greater than 3 times the height of surrounding buildings.

Minimum size: 2,000 sq. ft.
Maximum size: 30,000 sq. ft.

Plazas may be left unplanted. If planted, trees should form the geometric frame of the plaza space or for the structure the plaza services. Spacing shall be a minimum of 10 ft. on center and a maximum of 30 ft. on center.

Parkways

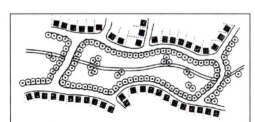

Parkways are open spaces designed to incorporate natural settings such as creeks and significant stands of trees within a neighborhood. Parkways are to be entirely bounded by streets or pedestrian ROW's within developed areas. Parkways differ from parks and squares in that their detailing is natural (i.e. informally planted). Parkways are used for walking, jogging, or bicycling. In addition, small scale recreational features such as a playground area or soccer field are appropriate in parkways. Streets bordering the parkway shall match the Neighborhood Parkway street standards in Article 5.

Greenbelts

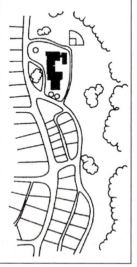

Greenbelts run along the perimeter of a neighborhood or town and serve to buffer a neighborhood from surrounding non-compatible uses such as a highway corridor, industrial district, or a town from agricultural areas or adjacent towns.

Greenbelts are left natural but may include walking trails. In addition, schools located adjacent to Greenbelts can provide all recreational and athletic fields within the greenbelt. Streets bordering greenbelts shall match the Neighborhood Parkway street standards in Article 5.

Figure 5.35 Open space diagrams, Zoning Ordinance, Huntersville, NC. The design of public spaces is a primary concern of American form-based zoning codes. (*Reproduction courtesy of the Town of Huntersville, NC*)

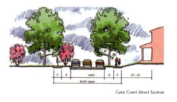

View of park at Cara Court

Cara Court, Julia Street and Glen Walk Plan

Cara Court Street Section

Figure 5.36 Typical page from Baxter Pattern Book, Fort Mill, SC, 1999: Urban Design Associates and Land Design. These diagrams control the placement of buildings relative to the street and the character of the public and semi-public spaces. *(Reproduction courtesy of Urban Design Associates and Land Design)*

building types in a way that is very similar to American practice. Site specific form-based zoning ordinances, such as the Greenville, SC, example (see Figure 5.32) operate in almost the same, tight way as the Upton code, while municipal zoning codes covering a whole community, such as the Huntersville document, extend this principle across the entire jurisdiction. Each zoning classification, e.g. character areas such as Neighborhood Residential, establishes the range of permitted building types, and through these typologies, permitted uses are defined (see Figure 5.18 and Tables 5.5, 5.6 and 5.7).

Architectural Design and Sustainability

These last topics are the two areas where American and British practices diverge to the greatest degree. The CABE analysis (from which much of this British information is drawn) notes that 'aspirations for the coding of architectural design are typically extensive … All the well-developed codes have detailed aesthetic principles based on analysis of local architectural context' (CABE, 2005b: p. 35). For example, the Upton code requires certain types of brick bonding patterns and specifies hand-made bricks rather than the cheaper wire-cut varieties, and that 'window reveals should be a minimum of 75 mm [3 inches] where a subcill is used and a minimum of 50 mm [2 inches] where there is no subcill.'

Advancing the sustainability agenda, the code states that 'photovoltaic cells must be incorporated into the overall roof design' (English Partnerships, 2005: p. 84). This level of detail equates or exceeds American pattern books, and extends considerably beyond even the most ambitious municipal form-based code. There is no doubt that there is a traditional slant to the aesthetics at Upton, perhaps as a result of the involvement of The Prince's Foundation, well-known for its preference for traditional architecture. When combined with earlier high-profile developments such as Poundbury, in Dorset (again, overseen by The Prince's Foundation) this neo-traditional emphasis has become uppermost in many people's minds when discussing the issue of design codes. This view has been compounded by the prevalent equation in the UK between neo-classicism and American New Urbanism, once more partly a function of American New Urbanist influence within the leadership of the Prince's Foundation, through Chief Executive Hank Dittmar, who also chairs the US-based Congress for the New Urbanism.

This warped perception of New Urbanism creates unnecessary barriers to the development and acceptance of coding in the UK; other successfully coded projects in Britain, especially Hulme, in Manchester, Greenwich Millennium Village in London, and Newhall, in Harlow, Essex, exemplify projects that use traditional

CHARACTER AREAS	BOUNDARY CODING	MAIN STREET	STREET	SUDS STREET	LANE	MEWS
	PRIVACY STRIP					
	Dimension	1m at junctions 2.5m otherwise	2m	N/A	N/A	0.6-1m
	Materials	Hard landscape; paving materials should be complementary to public realm	Hard or soft landscape; materials should be complementary to public realm	N/A	N/A	Granite setts
NEIGHBOURHOOD SPINE	**ENCROACHMENT**					
	At Junctions	N/A	Max. 1m	N/A	N/A	N/A
	Otherwise	Max. 1.5m	Max. 1m	N/A	N/A	N/A
	BOUNDARY TREATMENT					
	Height	0.9m - 1.1m	0.9m - 1.1m	N/A	N/A	N/A
	Materials	Wrought iron railing (stone or rendered upstand is permitted)	Wrought iron railing (stone or rendered upstand is permitted)	N/A	N/A	N/A

Figure 8.3 Front Boundary - Main Street

Figure 8.4 Front Boundary - Street

Figure 8.5 Front Boundary - Lane

Figure 8.6 Front Boundary - Mews

Front boundary Main Street

Front Boundary Street

Front Boundary Lane

Front boundary Mews

Figure 5.37 Typical page from the *Upton Design Code, Version 2*, 2005; EDAW *et al.* The Upton code regulates similar issues to the American example at Baxter, but in a more urban setting. *(Reproduction courtesy of English Partnerships)*

Figure 5.38 Greenwich Millennium Village, London. 2001–2006; Erskine Tovatt, Architects. Master plan design code by Ralph Erskine. Erskine's office designed Phase I of this large development and the design codes prepared for later stages ensured that the overall master plan vision was realized.

urbanism with contemporary architecture (see Figures 5.9, 5.10 and 5.38). Despite these examples, the prevalent professional opinion in the UK in 2006 continues to equate design codes with New Urbanist pattern books such as the Baxter example, rather than form-based codes such as the Huntersville document. The official RIBA response in March 2006 to the British government's draft Planning Policy Statement 3 (PPS3) that promoted further use of codes in new housing developments stated that codes should be developed only in accordance with a comprehensive master plan for a specific site and should concern themselves only with 'objective' urban issues such as form and public realm, rather than 'subjective' architectural issues. The RIBA regarded codes as 'dangerous' in that they will cause 'formulaic and pattern-book housing' (RIBA, 2006).

From his extensive experience creating and working with form-based codes in the USA, this author agrees with the RIBA position that design codes are most effective and appropriate when they deal with urban form, building massing and the public realm. With the proviso that the ground floor of buildings need to be firmly coded as they create the public realm for the pedestrian, most codes (in the author's opinion) do not need to venture much further into building aesthetics. However, it has to be said that pattern books are not the evil mandates the RIBA and others make them out to be. Many architects are guilty of knee-jerk reactions to design standards, preferring the 'freedom' to produce poor buildings rather than be required to improve standards of design to meet mandated criteria. Much suburban development in the UK, as in America, is built to very low aesthetic standards. Either architects are not involved, or if they are, they apparently represent the lowest rungs of the profession in terms of design ability. In either case, well-formulated pattern books are likely to improve the end products by raising design standards several notches. Interestingly, the contemporary architecture at Newhall in Harlow resulted from a detailed code set out by the master developer in much the same way that the overall development company at Baxter created a code that required historicist architecture (see Figures 5.10 and 5.24). This ability for codes to produce very different types of architecture dependant on particular development factors was noted in December 2005 by a government circular entitled *The Future for Design Codes*, which confirmed that the delivery of improved design quality was the major benefit of design codes. Perhaps anticipating the RIBA's response, the document went on to specify that codes could deliver high quality *contemporary* architectural solutions as well as traditional results (ODPM, 2005b: p. 8; this author's italics added).

Much more substantive than issues of architectural style are those of sustainability, and it is here that the biggest difference emerges between codes in Britain and the USA. Even the most highly detailed American codes and pattern books rarely discuss or recommend much action in this regard. Beyond common sense issues such as relating development to public transport, mixing uses to reduce travel trips by car and standards for storm water retention to protect water quality, sustainability is not an item that figures very largely on the agenda of American government at federal, state or local levels despite the fact that America comprises less than 5 percent of the world's population while consuming 25 percent of global resources. There are some welcome initiatives that relieve this bleak picture: new buildings on some land sold or leased by the government are required to meet the energy-saving LEED criteria noted below and new federal buildings have similar mandates. Modest but

worthwhile programmes for sustainable design exist under the auspices of the Environmental Protection Agency and some useful tax credits for energy efficient design are offered under the 2005 Energy Policy Act along with similar state initiatives in Maryland, New York, Nevada and Oregon; and in a bold political move, Mayor Richard Daley in Chicago declared in 2004 that all city buildings would meet LEED Standards. However, American public policy has tended to leave it up to the non-profit and private sectors to advance a green agenda, such as the efforts sponsored by US Green Building Council's LEED (Leadership in Energy and Environmental Design) programs, and in the development industry an increasing number of innovative design and planning projects have begun to move beyond upscale niche markets for green design (Urban Land Institute, 2006). There are, thankfully, exceptions to pervasive public sector indifference; all new federal buildings have to meet criteria for LEED certification, a few states and individual local governments are moving in that same direction, and other governmental organizations, such as the Triangle J Council of Governments in central North Carolina, publish *High Performance Guidelines* for public buildings that cover resource efficiency and environmental impacts in similar fashion to the LEED standards (www.tjcog.dst.nc.us/hpgtrpf.htm).

There are other indicators that the public mood in America is slowly shifting to embrace more issues of sustainability, but the concerted opposition to phenomena such as climate change and global warming by influential sectors of political opinion which equate proposals to combat these problems as 'un-American' and 'socialistic,' and who go so far as to deny that the phenomenon of global warming even exists, means that progress is slow. Accordingly, the USA is far behind even Britain's incomplete agenda in its thinking about sustainability issues and even further adrift in respect of policies to reduce environmental problems.

New urbanism and neighborhoods

SYNOPSIS

This chapter focuses mainly on urbanism in America in the early years of the 21st century and examines aspects of New Urbanism in detail, specifically with regard to the movement's internal dialectic between its radical town planning principles and its antithetical tendency to be commodified by the marketplace into a conservative aesthetic style. These principles focus on the concept and design of the neighborhood as an essential building block for towns and cities, but the role of 'neighborhood unit theory' has been hotly debated for the last 80 years since American sociologist Clarence Perry first introduced it into modern urban discourse. Accordingly, this chapter also provides a critical analysis of the arguments surrounding neighborhood theory and its continued relevance to contemporary urban designers and planners in Britain and America.

The chapter also includes a brief discussion of 'Everyday Urbanism' – a celebration by some American critics of low-key, small-scale acts of urban placemaking by ethnic minority groups in their adopted American cities. Everyday Urbanism comprises things or events such as temporary markets that spring up at street intersections, *ad hoc* festivals that take over a deserted parking lot or urban murals – usually unauthorized – that enliven otherwise ugly surroundings. This American phenomenon is a counterculture version of the street markets still fairly common in British towns and cities, and quite normal in mainland Europe (see Figure 6.1), but the dearth of public life in many American cities transforms these modest appropriations of urban space into cultural spectacles that garner much critical attention.

Figure 6.1 Street market, Bucine, Tuscany. Weekly markets are still a regular feature of urban life in Europe.

NEW URBANISM IN CONTEXT

New Urbanism forms the most visible bridge between British and American urban thinking, the latest example of the two-way transatlantic transfer of urban ideas that has been going on at least since the mid-19th century. The latest upsurge of New Urbanism in the UK is partly due to the influence of Prince Charles and his architectural advisors, who have included several international figures active in the world of traditional urbanism, but also because of the clear message contained in the 1999 report by the Urban Task Force in the UK, under the chairmanship of architect-peer Lord (Richard) Rogers. In this report, Rogers and his team cited American Smart Growth and New Urbanist ideas in their argument for meeting a large proportion of Britain's demand for new housing, schools, workplaces, recreation and retail development on existing brownfield and greyfield sites, rather than extending new building into green belt sites around the edges of British cities. Writing in the Introduction to one of the series of 'Michigan Debates on Urbanism,' Douglas Kelbaugh, one of New Urbanism's west coast founders and the original convenor of the debates, noted this confluence of ideas with measured irony: 'What [a] strange, unexpected architectural bedfellow Rogers is with a New Urbanist like Andres Duany' (Kelbaugh, 2005, Vol. III: p. 8). There could be no clearer example of the distinctions made below between New Urbanism as a set of urban design principles versus a nostalgic aesthetic style; clearly Lord Rogers would have no truck with cute picket fences and classical porches as part of his committee's strategy for Britain's urban renaissance; it is ideas of efficient, economical, sustainable and attractive urban structure that draw one of Britain's leading high-tech architects to New Urbanist concepts.

The baseline for these discussions is the uncoordinated *laissez-faire* urbanism of American cities, characterized by three main conditions: reinvigorated downtown cores, sprawling new, far-flung suburbs and decaying 1950s 'inner-ring' suburban zones. Center cities are revitalizing themselves (at least in several American regions) by transforming from business hubs to central districts packed with a mixture of uses: new office towers, sports arenas, convention centers, theaters and museums, shopping and entertainment complexes, and new high-density housing rise side by side with warehouses converted to loft apartments and older office buildings rehabilitated as hotels or housing (see Figure 6.2). The author's adopted home city of Charlotte, NC, has all of the above and is planning more at a frenetic pace. As impressive as this development is, it is dwarfed in quantity by new growth around the urban periphery of most cities. This new rash of suburban building is still largely separated into large 'pods' of single-use development and spreads over what were previously green fields, eroding natural resources and adding to air pollution by requiring increased driving times and distances. In contrast, the older suburbs from the 1950s languish; their modest homes and mediocre infrastructure (no sidewalks, no convenient access to shops or community facilities) have fallen out of favor with an American home-buying public that now demands bigger homes and more amenities. These three components of market-driven urbanism rarely form coherent patterns and their quality varies widely. Some new developments are good; many, mostly in the outer suburbs, are poor.

Figure 6.2 Office building converted to housing, Charlotte, NC, 2006. Demand for city center living is so great in several American cities that old (1960s) office blocks are being recycled into up-market condominiums.

In addition to general market forces, new development at the urban edge is shaped also by conventional use-based zoning ordinances. A study of land use regulation in the State of Illinois (Talen and Knapp, 2000) … verified the extent to which planning is a victim of its own devices. An analysis of the regulations of 168 cities and counties found that mixed-use zoning was limited, Smart Growth tools were almost non-existent, and the prescriptive requirements for lot sizes, setbacks road widths and parking decidedly favored low-density sprawl and urban fragmentation. (Talen and Duany: p. 246).

In contrast to this predominantly *laissez-faire* regime of urban growth and decline, New Urbanism was forged in the early 1990s as a reformist and utopian movement, pursuing agendas of social and environmental improvement and armed with typologies of urbanism authenticated by several centuries of human use. Now, the most important development in American urbanism for 50 years is caught in a dichotomy between the promise of its radical founding principles and its potential commodification as a conservative aesthetic style for wealthy consumers. On the positive side, it is the only type of urbanism in America that evinces any interest in issues of sustainability, so important to British and other European audiences. This is highlighted by New Urbanism's common sense urban design principles that support compact development and choices of transportation and lifestyle – making it possible and attractive for people to live, work, play and shop more economically in terms of space, time, energy and resources. On the other side of the ledger, the zealous historicism of some New Urbanist architects diminishes the movement's contemporary relevance and panders to the fuzzy nostalgia of popular taste.

DILEMMAS OF NEW URBANISM

American New Urbanism is central to many questions regarding new development in Britain, not least of which is the question of design coding. However, particularly in Britain, New Urbanism tends to be misunderstood as historicist or nostalgic architecture. The author attended a conference in London early in 2006 on the new English planning procedures stemming from the 2004 Planning and Compulsory Purchase Act, and while most of the discussion and the design examples illustrated in the various presentation fell well within any reasonable definition of New Urbanism, the British architects and planners who were creating work based on ideas indistinguishable from New Urbanism took pains to distance themselves from the term. The conference participants demonstrated a surprising misunderstanding and ignorance of the work of many progressive American New Urbanist architect-planners, following instead American academic criticism of the movement as retrogressive and nostalgic.

Similar misconceptions also exist in America, and many practitioners and critics (including this author) are 'exasperated by the stylistic foregrounding of its East Coast versions' (Baird: p. 4). Peter Calthorpe, another of the west coast founders of New Urbanism, has offered a trenchant critique of the movement's achievements and failings. Calthorpe was particularly critical of the tendency for New Urbanism to be misrepresented as a style of traditional aesthetics rather than a radical and challenging set of urban design and planning principles. To counter critics from within the movement and without, Calthorpe argued that:

New Urbanism struggles between two identities, one a lofty set of principles that many criticize as utopian and the other a style which is stereotyped as retro and simplistic. In fact, it is many other things as well; a coalition meant to unify a broad range of disciplines and interest groups; a rebirth of urban design over planning; and a powerful counterpoint to the norm of sprawl … Unfortunately every movement or set of ideas becomes identified as a style that somehow soon becomes independent of its core principles. But … in its principles … it finds its greatest strength and as a style it finds its most debilitating limits.

Unfortunately even within New Urbanism there is debate as to whether the movement is guided by a set of open-ended principles or a design canon with specific forms and norms. The Charter of New Urbanism is a clear articulation of the principles and steers clear of prescribing a specific set of urban design forms or architecture. The Transect, a more recent outcome of the Congress for New Urbanism, is more formal and creates a more definitive urban design taxonomy (although it does not declare a style). (Calthorpe, 2005: p. 16)

In contrast to viewing New Urbanism as a style, Calthorpe argued that strategic design thinking about issues of resources and social equity is most fundamental to New Urbanism, as is extending urban design thinking into regional scales and ecosystems. Calthorpe shares this sense of urgency with Andres Duany, although the two differ widely on the issues of style and traditionalism. Duany's Transect planning method is directly applicable to regional scale problems, following the principle embedded in the Charter of New Urbanism that the New Urbanist problem-solving design approach is applicable from the scale of a region down to the scale of an individual urban block (Walters and Brown: pp. 153–226).

Britons and Americans now live at a metropolitan scale, accessing different fragments of our daily routines in locations considerably distant from each other, and certainly the air we breathe, the water we drink and the spaces we inhabit are all influenced by factors that are part of a regional network. The dubious air quality in Charlotte, for example, is only partly the result of increasing congestion and quantities of noxious gases and particles from automobile exhausts within the city's own boundaries; it is also due to contaminated air bequeathed by upwind power stations in Tennessee that lack stringent pollution controls.

Our cultural opportunities and economic development strategies are also regional, yet despite all these interconnected strands, American planning is in the hands not of regional authorities but of fractured and competitive local governments. Opportunities for regional intervention are rare, although both Calthorpe and Duany Plater-Zyberk have been actively involved in regional planning exercises in California and Florida, respectively, and sub-regional projects by the author are noted in this volume and a previous publication (Walters and Brown: pp. 157–172).

Apart from regional planning opportunities, working to infuse communities with social equity and opportunity is also an avowed aim of many New Urbanist practitioners. A negative misnomer that rankles particularly with those urban designers and planners active in this endeavor is that New Urbanism is about making pretty little communities and isolated enclaves of privilege, as parodied in the movie *The Truman Show*, using Seaside to star alongside Jim Carey. New Urbanism is much more than stand-alone Traditional Neighborhoods: this author's work in depressed African-American neighborhoods such as Haynie-Sirrine in Greenville, SC (Walters and Brown: pp. 201–217) and similar work by other New Urbanist practitioners bears witness to this undertaking. At a national scale, New Urbanism's achievement also includes well-designed low-income housing, with some spectacular successes under the ill-fated HOPE VI program before it was defunded by the ideologically driven administration of George W. Bush.

The HOPE VI program stood almost alone in federal government policies with its integration of urban design concepts into legislation, policy and guidance notes. Indeed, it has been the only American urban regeneration policy in recent decades that can be compared directly with British government attitudes on the value of urban design. Since the mid-1990s, when federal Housing and Urban Development (HUD) Secretary Henry Cisneros signed the Charter of New Urbanism, until the demise of HOPE VI in 2006, New Urbanist design principles and theories of mixed-use neighborhoods were briefly at the heart of American government policy. Cisneros' successor as HUD Secretary, Andrew Cuomo, stated:

All of us at the department are committed … to the goal of livable, mixed-use neighborhoods built to a human scale. This is consistent with the principles of New Urbanism – and yes, we strongly support

this approach because we've seen that it works. (HUD, 1997, in Bohl, 2000: p. 765)

With active New Urbanist involvement, the HOPE VI program grew 'from nine demonstration projects funded in 1993 to 300 grants involving some 53 000 units of public housing and $3.5 billion [US] in appropriations by 1999' (Bohl, 2000: p. 765). The urban design concepts are married with management improvements, and initiatives to reduce crime, increase employment opportunities, and provide social, community and educational services to residents – all with the aim of creating more economically sustainable and visually attractive communities for lower-income citizens.

The HOPE VI program has not been without influential critics, however, who have branded it as urban revitalization through gentrification, whereby homeowners continually displace lower-income renters because the concept of homeownership itself is seen as the primary solution to neighborhood revitalization. From this perspective, 'those *without* property stand in the way of progress, and since they are much cheaper to move … some must be displaced to create healthier communities' (Pyatok: p. 807). Instead of New Urbanism's emphasis on design as a way of improving communities, architect-activists such as Michael Pyatok suggest spending less on physical improvements and more on 'serious job training, educational trust funds for residents, [and] microloans for small businesses.' Pyatok criticizes both public and private developers, and their architects, for seeing the world from a middle-class perspective, where a well-designed environment is 'a higher priority that intensive people-oriented solutions' (Pyatok: p. 807). Critics like Pyatok point out that not all low-income residents of public housing are equitably rehoused. In Charlotte's HOPE VI project in the First Ward area of the central city, residents who did not qualify for educational programs of self-improvement because of criminal records or other negative factors, or who did not attempt to register for these programs, were not included in the rehousing program and were forced to find other accommodation elsewhere, usually with government-financed 'Section 8' rental vouchers that cover part of the cost of market-rate housing. Only those people, who in a different age the Victorians would have classified as 'the deserving poor,' found opportunities in the HOPE VI program.

This Charlotte example is interesting, and not simply because it contains those contradictions noted by Pyatok. The HOPE VI development did transform a part of Charlotte that was once very dangerous (one did not stop at red traffic lights when driving through the original public housing area) into a thriving residential community. This has provided new opportunities for selected residents of the previous decrepit and barrack-like public housing to live in what is now an indistinguishable mix of approximately one-third market-rate housing, one-third affordable housing and one-third public housing, arranged in much more urban and street-oriented configurations. This urban revitalization had 'knock-on' effects and opened up extensive opportunities for private sector development on land near downtown that had been vacant for more than two decades. New housing sprang up all around, followed by civic buildings, including two new schools, a community center, elderly housing and soon a major new university building for the University of North Carolina at Charlotte (see Figure 6.3). Proponents of HOPE VI who see market opportunity as a means of self-improvement for low-income citizens and civic

improvement for the neighborhood can point to Charlotte's First Ward as a very successful example. Critics, conversely, regard it as a clear manifestation of how government policy, gentrification and market economics continue to oppress the very poorest and most disadvantaged sections of American society. This is a valid and important debate. Far less valid are the complaints by ill-informed critics of New Urbanism in general who, by equating New Urbanism only with luxury housing at Seaside, and in apparent ignorance of HOPE VI initiatives, baldly state that New Urbanism offers scant help to poor people in American society (Forgey, 1999; Kolson, 2001: p. 119).

The HOPE VI example in Charlotte, and its adjacent private development, provides decent, low-key urban architecture, but in more generic situations of infill and redevelopment the result has often been respectable urbanism but mediocre architecture (see Figure 6.4). Perhaps (Calthorpe suggests, and this

Figure 6.3 First Ward Place and Garden District, Charlotte, NC, 2006. While other sites await the arrival of light rail transit and future development, the HOPE VI project (center foreground) has stimulated extensive private development on adjacent blocks in a part of town once considered a 'no-go area' due to gang violence.

Figure 6.4 City center housing, Charlotte, NC, 2005. At a large scale, this urban housing block demonstrates decent urban design in terms of placement and massing, but the architecture fails through its lack of attention to street-level detail. The omission of porches, stoops or visible entrances diminishes the pedestrian environment, and the low placement of windows to private rooms severely compromises the visual privacy of those spaces. The useless strip of grass and a few bushes against the building are a feeble attempt to provide a privacy screen, but they simply create an unwanted suburban feel completely at odds with the building's context.

author agrees) this is because not enough architecture students experience the realities of budget-driven urban development in their education. If they did, they would understand better the economics of construction and the factors about marketing a housing product that affect the building's design, including the purchasers' or renters' preferences and tastes. The students would come to terms with many things that constrain individual 'artistic expression,' still too often the ultimate goal of architects in thrall to the outdated 'Fountainhead syndrome.' Here, as in Ayn Rand's eponymous novel the genius architect stands alone as a beacon of supposed honor and artistic integrity against constraints created by the alleged venal idiocy of other architects, urban designers, planners, clients, developers and the public- at-large.

This cult of the individual is the antithesis of community design, or design within the larger context of the urban and social milieu of the city, and from these contextual factors talented designers can construe significant architecture, as demonstrated by the work of such architects as Michael Pyatok in the USA and Edward Cullinan and Proctor Matthews in the UK (see Figure 6.5). But sadly, many talented architects

do not gravitate to this sector of the profession; they do not like being 'constrained' by context and community, and prefer instead to design exclusively high-style, high-profile buildings. A welcome counterpoint to this elitism in architecture and architectural education was a project completed in 2006 by a graduate student working under the direction of the author and other faculty from the College of Architecture and the real estate program in the College of Business at the University of North Carolina at Charlotte. This student, Richard Boswell, specifically sought to identify where the points of tension existed between good design and development economics by constantly costing out his design proposals for an infill development along a busy arterial street in Charlotte. Correlating land cost, urban form, density, building complexity and detail, car parking provision, and construction costs, Boswell was able to establish a level of urban and architectural quality that made a positive contribution to the neighborhood without descending into pastiche historicism. Importantly, the development was also economically feasible in terms of development returns and profit margins (see Figure 6.6).

This 'pastiche historicism,' the application of 'cut-out' classicist motifs to buildings, is largely a function of the marketplace and how consumer preferences for nostalgic images are interpreted by mediocre designers. Often lampooned by cultural critics, these consumer preferences are real and should be taken seriously; they could be rephrased more positively as a desire for 'a sense of history, scale and uniqueness' (Calthorpe, 2005: p. 17). This issue of public taste is important, as it brings into focus the central quandary for New Urbanism and its practitioners – the dialectic between design principles and aesthetic style. If popular taste can be satisfied by the cartoon versions of traditional architecture presented by many developers and their architects, just think how much greater fulfillment of these desires could be achieved by talented designers moving beyond flimsy imitations of past styles into contemporary architecture that took context and history seriously (see Figure 6.7).

New Urbanism was conceived as a set of high-minded principles, but founding members understood very well that if the movement was to change the face of American cities and suburbs it had to engage and transform, at least in part, the real estate and construction industries. This meant leaving behind academia or the realms of boutique design and entering the hurly-burly world of everyday practice at a populist level. It meant giving up the luxury of commentating and critiquing

Figure 6.5 Millennium Village, Greenwich, London, 2005. Working within a master plan and code by Ralph Erskine, Proctor Matthews (housing, left and right foreground), Ted Cullinan (primary school, left middle ground) and Erskine Tovatt with EPR (housing right middle ground) have created attractive buildings that are respectful of their context but also full of architectural expression. This British example embodies design principles identical with those of American New Urbanism.

Figure 6.6 Urban development student project, Charlotte, NC, 2006; Richard Boswell. This student thesis studied the relationships between good urban design, effective urban architecture and development economics. *(Reproduction courtesy of Richard Boswell)*

from the sidelines, and instead plunging directly into the fray where the realities of the real estate and construction industries in America are driven by two main motives: a worship of profit and a sensitivity to consumer preferences. Neither has been valued highly in academia, and this bias accounts for some levels of criticism aimed at New Urbanism from ivory towers. At one architecture faculty meeting at which

Figure 6.7 Donnybrook Quarter, Bow, London, 2005; Peter Barber, Architects. This urban infill housing creates a memorable residential character unsullied by pastiche details. It marries the traditional and contextual urbanism of terrace, street, square and alley with aesthetics evoking the spirit of modernist pioneers such as Le Corbusier or J.J.P Oud, London's white stucco architecture from the 19th century and Mediterranean towns (it is known locally as the 'Costa del Bow').

New Urbanism came up, a colleague of the author at the University of North Carolina at Charlotte disparaged the concepts on the grounds that 'people like you deal with developers!' This sentiment reflects a common attitude in architectural academia: if an idea works in the marketplace it must be dirty or sullied in some way.

Some academics like to argue that New Urbanist ideas have become co-opted and transformed into shallow concepts by developers to maximize profit. Indeed, history teaches an uncomfortable lesson in this regard. When the ideas and concepts of the modern movement in architecture were imported to America from Europe before and after World War II they were introduced, significantly, as the International *Style*, so named despite the fervent desire of modernist pioneers to avoid the whole concept of style. Within a few years, the deeply embedded social agenda of European

modernism had been eviscerated as the new building techniques and aesthetics became embraced by the real estate and construction industries in America for shallower ideas of newness and convenience. The same danger lurks for New Urbanism; it will be a hard task (as Calthorpe implies) to retain a firm grip on design and planning principles while working directly in the commercial marketplace that much prefers style, curb appeal and nostalgia to intellectual rigor and contemporary substance. American architect Michael Pyatok is not optimistic in this regard. He sounds a word of warning when he writes:

The price paid by [New Urbanists] is going to bed with the centers of power that embrace the logic and ideology of the free market ... When used in this manner, our work as architects and planners becomes a kind of cultural legitimization for the inordinate preoccupation with property values held by elements of the larger society ... While [New Urbanists] will help many in the years ahead, we can only hope that [they] will make the effort to minimize the pain they will be causing others. If not, the next generation will soon be after them, pointing to their contradictions and failings and noting how capitalism compromised their charter and co-opted their membership into simply creating a more seductive form of business as usual. (Pyatok: pp. 808–814)

As urban development in America is almost exclusively market-driven with little or no government direction of the kind now more visible in Britain, compromises will inevitably take place in order to get projects built, but only through built projects will the shape of urban America gradually be transformed into more sustainable patterns of development. Economic logic dictates that the marketplace naturally embraces first and foremost consumers with money – the middle class and above – and developers compete to provide the kind of products most desired by those more affluent customers. This means that many New Urbanist projects initially cater to Americans who are reasonably wealthy, leading to charges of exclusivity from critics in academia. This charge is combined with accusations of avoiding the 'realities' of the contemporary city, and constructing a rose-tinted imagined past, even a falsification of history where traditional urban forms are used to promote a fantasy world of small town America and memories of unpleasant facts like racial segregation are expunged from the historical record (Ellis, 2002). Indeed, these charges that New Urbanists want to impose a sanitized, simplified representation of reality on the complex pluralism that is the contemporary city appear in many critiques of traditional urbanism (Ingersoll, 1989; Sudjic, 1992; Rybczynski, 1995; Landecker, 1996; Huxtable, 1997; Safdie, 1997; Southworth, 1997, 2003; Chase, Crawford and Kaliski, 1999).

Many of these commentators themselves enjoy a critical distance from the 'realities' of urban development that they so readily critique, as opposed to most New Urbanists who are first and foremost practitioners, immersed in the realities of everyday practice and trying to reform the juggernaut of America's real estate industry from within the capitalist system. But the risks of commodification, between architectural and urban ideals on the one hand, and market preferences on the other, are well illustrated by plans for a bizarre

new town in Florida, named Ave Maria, developed by Ave Maria Catholic University with a contribution to the tune of $250 million (£133 million) by Domino's Pizza founder Tom Monaghan. News reports in late 2005 announced that the university, its new town, and its residents 'would hew to traditional values: no pornography, no contraceptives' (Jacobs, K., 2006). The homebuilder's publicity exclaims:

The emergence of old European world charm and modern American ingenuity awaits you! Ave Maria is an approximately 5000-acre master planned community nestled in the heart of Southwest Florida. Reflecting the traditional European town centers, you will be delighted to discover a new life inspiring every lifestyle, every family, every dream. (http://www.metropolismag.com/cda/story.php?artid=1946)

A critique in *Metropolis* magazine by reporter Karrie Jacobs sought

... to pin this one on Duany Plater-Zyberk (DPZ) ... Ave Maria ... is configured like Seaside – only instead of a town green full of frolicking children and macramé vendors, there is a 1100-seat church and a 65-foot cross. It is like Celebration, but in lieu of Mickey Mouse ears turning up as car-antenna ornaments and on colorful front-porch banners, there will likely be crosses ... the town plan itself, with streets radiating from a central church is drawn directly from the Middle Ages ... But we can't pin this one on DPZ because ... Ave Maria is stranger than that. (http://www.metropolismag.com/cda/story.php?artid=1946)

Once Jacobs gets past trying to bash Duany Plater-Zyberk, she makes a valid point that should concern all New Urbanists who promote historicist architecture to the detriment of the movement's more substantive social and environment aims.

The ... eagerness of [New Urbanism] ... to reclaim values from the past – cherry-picking the style but not necessarily the mores that were embedded in it – has inevitably led us here. Ave Maria is arguably the ultimate New Urbanist place: it combines the hallmarks of neo-traditionalism – mixed-use town center, the alleys, the pedestrian-friendly layout – with a heavy dose of plain old traditionalism. If you spend enough time using traditionalism as a sales tool for a package of restrictive building codes at which developers might otherwise balk, you also wind up selling traditionalism. (http://www.metropolismag.com/cda/story.php?artid=1946)

While the gross bastardization of New Urbanist concepts on this scale is relatively rare, the social and environmental agendas of the movement need to be promoted with utmost vigor to contrast with and overcome this kind of consumerist shambles. New Urbanists' desires for affordability and social equity will not become integral to new development in America's market-driven economy unless public policy and government leadership mandates it – an attitude currently conspicuous by its absence except in individually progressive cities (such as Berkeley, CA) and in some New Urbanist codes (such as Davidson, NC) that mandate, for example, a certain provision of affordable housing in all new developments. New Urbanists can make the greatest contributions towards social equity and justice in America's communities by writing new zoning codes that incorporate policies towards these ends, e.g. by requiring affordable housing and outlawing exclusionary large lot zoning that bars people earning lower incomes from living in certain communities because they cannot afford large plots of land. Leadership for social equity in America is not going to come from the private marketplace; concepts of profit and social justice do not sit easily with each other.

The problem of social equity and sustainable urban infrastructure in American towns and cities is so urgent, that many New Urbanists would, frankly, compromise on aesthetics in order to ensure the presence in new development of more substantive elements, such as good urban structure, increased social equity and affordability, and safe and attractive public space. In the long run, good urbanism always trumps bad architecture. Peter Calthorpe has been equally blunt. Critiquing a new but architecturally mediocre infill building in Berkeley, Calthorpe stated:

> But do I care [about the aesthetics]? Not really. What I care about is that 20 percent of the housing is affordable; what I care about is that the ground floor is retail and active; what I care about is that there are windows overlooking University Avenue and the drug dealings and the muggings are going down. (Calthorpe, 2005: p. 25)

Making improvements to America's suburban infrastructure, reducing the environmental damage of suburban sprawl and increasing the attractiveness of urban space are important, urgent objectives. The town planning principles enshrined in New Urbanism, although based on traditional models of street and square, are still radical and strange to many municipalities and developers in the USA, and sometimes the only way to gain municipal approval or developer buy-in for improved urbanism is to avoid imposing architectural high taste about building design on communities and clients, and instead work with their aesthetic preferences. Many critics are disingenuous about this; they regard engaging public consumer attitudes towards design as selling out to the marketplace. It is as if they never read *Learning from Las Vegas*.

The New Urbanist strategy for reforms and improvements in American towns and cities accepts that reform will come in large part through the actions of the private sector, unlike Britain, where government policy now lays out an agenda almost indistinguishable from New Urbanist principles as set out in the Charter. However, the private sector in America can (and must) be guided by the public sector at the local level by means of new form-based zoning codes. These should mandate, at the very least, efficient and attractive design of the public infrastructure of streets and public spaces to accommodate pedestrians and alternative modes of transportation, mixed uses, the protection of environmental attributes such as water quality and key landscape elements, and the promotion of affordable housing as an integral element of new development. At the heart of this New Urbanist agenda, and the Sustainable Communities initiative in Britain, is the belief that well-designed neighborhoods are the essential foundations not only of good urban form but also of thriving communities.

Part of this belief derives from the influence of the European urbanist, Leon Krier. Krier was a leading advocate of the Movement for the Reconstruction of the European City during the 1970s, an organization whose major themes included: the preservation of historic centers; the neighborhood (or *quartier* in Krier's lexicon) as the basis for new city development; the use of historic urban types and patterns such as the perimeter block, the street, the square, etc., as the basic urban language of new development and redevelopment; and the reconstruction of single-use residential 'bedroom suburbs' into articulate mixed-use neighborhoods. While the specific European urban patterns and types were transformed by their travel across the Atlantic during the following decade, these underlying theoretical principles became founding concepts for Traditional Neighborhood Development in the 1980s and made their way into New Urbanist theory in the 1990s. However, the whole concept of neighborhood theory has been intensely debated in design, planning and social science circles in Britain and America for several decades, and it is important to examine the arguments for and against this urban and social typology.

NEIGHBORHOOD UNIT THEORY

Krier's focus on the European urban quarter was matched by Duany Platter-Zyberk's revived interest in the American concept of the neighborhood unit – first articulated by social planner Clarence Perry in the early 1920s and more fully developed in Volume 7 of the *1929 Regional Survey of New York and its Environs.* These principles were:

- *Size.* The population of a residential neighborhood should be no greater than can be accommodated by one elementary school.
- *Boundaries.* Arterial streets designed to carry all through traffic should form the boundaries of each neighborhood.
- *Internal street system.* The street system should be designed specifically to facilitate circulation within the neighborhood and to discourage through traffic.
- *Open spaces.* Each neighborhood should have an integrated network of small parks and playgrounds, planned for its needs.
- *Institutional sites.* Schools and other institutions serving the neighborhood should be grouped together.
- *Local shops.* One or more shopping areas sized to serve the neighborhood's population should be sited along the main streets at the edges of the neighborhood. (Perry: pp. 34–35, in Garvin, 1996: p. 273)

Perry's training as a sociologist had taught him the importance of cohesive neighborhoods as political, social and even moral units of a city. Moreover, Perry lived in the New York railroad suburb of Forest Hills Gardens and this experience stimulated his concept of the neighborhood unit as the fundamental unit of city planning. In his 1929 monograph for the Regional Plan of New York, Perry wrote from first-hand experience about the value of high quality urban design in fostering the good spirit and character of a neighborhood, and created a plan diagram of a typical neighborhood layout (Perry: pp. 90–93, in Hall, P.: p. 132).

This diagram illustrated a hypothetical area by major roads with community facilities, including a school and a park, at the center (see Figure 6.8).

Perry was active in the American Regional Planning Association with Lewis Mumford and with Clarence Stein and Henry Wright, the architect-planners of Radburn, the innovative and influential suburb in New Jersey, dating from 1928. (Originally Radburn was planned as a new town on the model of Letchworth and Welwyn Garden City in England, but these plans crumbled in the Great Depression of 1929, and only one small part of the plan was ever built.)

Central to Perry's concept was the ability of all residents to walk to those facilities they needed on a daily basis, such as shops, schools and playgrounds. The size of the neighborhood was thus determined by a 5-minute walking distance (approximately a quarter of a mile) from center to edge where shopping was located at the intersections of the main roads. These dimensions created a population of about 5000 people at the normal densities of the time, large enough to support local shops but small enough to generate a sense of community (Broadbent: p. 126). The street pattern was a mixture of radial avenues interspersed with irregular straight and curving grids with small parks and playgrounds liberally scattered throughout as befitted Perry's emphasis on the safety and welfare of children.

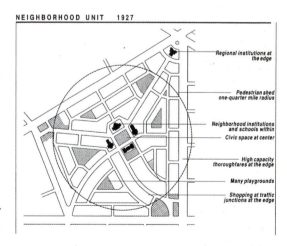

NEIGHBORHOOD UNIT   1927

Regional institutions at the edge

Pedestrian shed one-quarter mile radius

Neighborhood institutions and schools within

Civic space at center

High capacity thoroughfares at the edge

Many playgrounds

Shopping at traffic junctions at the edge

Figure 6.8 Clarence Perry's Neighborhood Unit, 1929. The circle illustrates a five-minute walk (approximately a quarter of a mile) from center to edge. *(Diagram (2002 version) courtesy of Duany Plater-Zyberk & Co.)*

ed this same concept
ban conditions at the
their *Lexicon of New*
illustrated a similar sized
hways and scaled to the
k. In this contemporary
mmercial development is
locat___ f the bounding highways,
and a street of ___ e buildings leads from one
corner into the central public park, where community institutions and some local shops are located.
The school has moved to the edge, due to much
larger space requirements for playing fields and parking, and this educational facility is now shared
between neighborhoods. Duany Plater-Zyberk's
street grid is tighter and more organized than Perry's,
but similar in concept to the original (see Figure 6.9).

This synergy creates a powerful and seemingly
commonsense argument in favor of neighborhood
design and the neighborhood's role as the basic building block of community; indeed much current planning and urban design in Britain and America
operates on this principle. By the early years of this
new century, urban theory has seemingly rejected the
once-powerful theses developed in the 1960s by
American planner Melvin Webber to the effect that
traditional urban forms are irrelevant and that place
does not matter any more; these have gone the same
way as the more recent predictions of techno-futurists
that 'geography is dead' (Walters and Brown: p. 23).
In his influential essays entitled *Order in Diversity:
Community without Propinquity* and *The Urban Place*

and the Nonplace Urban Realm, Webber rejected models of the city based on traditional spatial patterns, but
contemporary research increasingly demonstrates the
opposite: place itself is fast becoming the main organizing feature of economic activity. Given the flexible
and unpredictable work schedules typical of a globalized work force, people are increasingly requiring
access to recreational and entertainment opportunities
at a moment's notice. They are beginning to act 'like
tourists in their own city' (Lloyd and Clark, 2001, in
Florida: p. 225) and require amenities close at hand,
within walking distance if possible. There is only one
kind of urbanism that can meet these economic and
social needs: the concept of the mixed-use neighborhood or urban village, and the traditional public spaces
of street and square, park and boulevard.

American New Urbanism, with its twin typologies of
Calthorpe's Transit-Oriented Development and Duany
Plater-Zyberk's Traditional Neighborhood Development, have been paralleled in Britain by the urban
villages promoted by the Urban Villages Group, subsequently renamed the Urban Villages Forum (Aldous,
1992; 1995). In America explicit connections were
drawn to traditional urban types of the small town and
streetcar suburb, as well as to Ebenezer Howard's
Garden City and the Anglo-American Garden Suburb.
In the UK, British market towns and their architecture
substituted for American models, but the other sources
were the same. One of the key reasons for the promotion of the urban village, mixed-use development typology in Britain has been the search for an urban form
that is more environmentally sustainable than conventional suburbia, and a key study in this quest came from
Australia in 1989, where two planners, Peter Newman
and Jeffrey Kenworthy, compared the use of energy by
urban Australians, Americans and Europeans (Newman
and Kenworthy, 1989). Not surprisingly, Americans
used most energy, the Australians came in second and
the Europeans were the most frugal of the three study
groups. The researchers related this energy use to the
spatial character of cities and the availability of public
transport, and concluded that the compactness of
European cities combined with the high standard
of public transport accounted for the lower figures of
energy consumption. From this conclusion came the
oft-repeated wisdom that the most sustainable form of
urban development was one that restricted the geographical spread to a defined area and then served this
area with good public transportation. The corollary to
this was that cities and neighborhoods should be
denser and have a mixture of uses within walking distance. Bingo! The urban village was born.

TRADITIONAL NEIGHBORHOOD DEVELOPMENT 1997

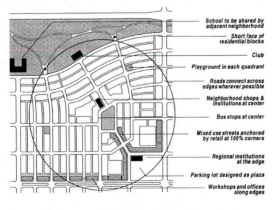

School to be shared by
adjacent neighborhood

Short face of
residential blocks

Club

Playground in each quadrant

Roads connect across
edges wherever possible

Neighborhood shops &
institutions at center

Bus stops at center

Mixed use streets anchored
by retail at 100% corners

Regional institutions
at the edge

Parking lot designed as plaza

Workshops and offices
along edges

Figure 6.9 Duany Plater-Zyberk's traditional
neighborhood, 1997. Perry's concept updated. As
before, the radius of the circle is a quarter of a mile.
(Diagram courtesy of Duany Plater-Zyberk & Co.)

British thinking on urban villages closely matched the equivalent concepts of traditional neighborhoods and transit-oriented neighborhoods in the USA. In the context of increasing concern about the mediocre quality of contemporary development in and around British towns and cities, especially when compared to older, traditional areas, remedial design concepts coalesced around 'well-designed, mixed-use and sustainable urban areas, with a sense of place and community involvement' (Biddulph *et al.*: p. 167). These concepts were based on the view that 'good urban design would create more interesting and stimulating forms of development suitable to the context, that adoption of neo-traditional design principles would allow residents to choose more sustainable lifestyles, and that a well-designed scheme would create a community focus and allow social integration' (Biddulph *et al.*: p. 180). The concept also suggested that higher densities within a local, walkable area would provide sufficient people to sustain neighborhood shops and community services in the face of competition from distant supermarkets, and mixing uses together would create greater urban vitality for longer periods during the day. Having a range of uses close at hand was also seen as a means of reducing the need to travel out of the neighborhood, thus potentially fostering greater attachment to a particular place and a sense of community identity (Biddulph *et al.*: p. 185).

During the 1990s the Urban Villages Forum lobbied the British government hard, promoting the urban village concept as the preferred form of development and seeking for it to be enshrined in national planning policy. This was an effective campaign, and by 1997 government guidance stated clearly:

> The planning system can be used to deliver high quality, mixed-use developments, such as 'urban villages' ... [These] are characterized by compactness, a mixture of uses and dwelling types, including affordable housing, a range of employment, leisure and community facilities, appropriate infrastructure and services, high standards of urban design, access to public open space and green spaces, and ready access to public transport. (DoE, 1997: pp. 3–4, in Biddulph *et al.*: p. 169)

Despite the apparent contradiction of the words 'urban' and 'village' (up to this point they were generally defined in opposition to one another, with 'village' being part of a *rural* environment) the phrase had an attractive resonance with several constituencies

and it soon became synonymous with the European concept of the urban quarter. In America, with that society's long cultural history of distaste for cities and urbanism, the appellation of 'village' softened the hard image of urbanity and made the idea palatable to an otherwise suburban-oriented public. In Britain, the thinking behind the urban village concept was well illustrated by David Rudlin and Nicholas Falk, who, in their book *Building the 21st Century Home: The Sustainable Urban Neighbourhood*, cleverly updated Ebenezer Howard's famous diagram of the Three Magnets. Instead of Howard's 19th and early 20th century combination of 'Town,' 'Country' and 'Town-Country,' Rudlin and Falk 'changed the polarity' of the magnets to suit the altered times and demographics of the 21st century. 'Suburban Sprawl' vies with the 'Inner City' in terms of their inbuilt contradictions, and this dilemma is resolved by 'The Urban Neighbourhood' taking the place of Howard's third 'Town-Country' magnet representing the Garden City (Rudlin and Falk: p. 5. See Figure 6.10).

Newman and Kenworthy's studies about the sustainability of urban village development have not gone unchallenged (Gordon and Richardson, 1989; Gómez-Ibáñez, 1991), but in America the technical debates concerning density, land use and vehicle miles traveled were quickly subsumed within larger ideological controversies regarding the permissible amount of government intervention into the 'free' market that might be necessary to bring about more concentrated urban forms. However, the balance of professional opinion in Europe and America, and sustained efforts by government policy in Britain have continued to support the idea of denser, mixed-use neighborhoods well served by public transit as one very important technique in the struggle to create more sustainable cities.

In this context, two other important articles from the 1960s about urban form have shared Webber's fate and lost traction in current urban design theory: British sociologist Maurice Broady's critique from 1966 of the neighborhood concept itself as falsely and naively deterministic (Broady, 1966); and Christopher Alexander's theory about city/neighborhood relations so elegantly stated that same year in 'A City is Not a Tree' (Alexander, 1966). Despite their reduced influence today, both articles raise important points that should not be overlooked in our rush to embrace the walkable neighborhood or urban village as a panacea for our transatlantic urban ills.

In his introduction to Broady's essay in his later compilation of articles on environmental relationships

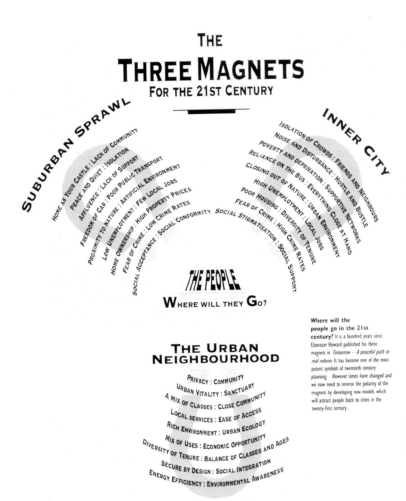

THE
THREE MAGNETS
FOR THE 21ST CENTURY

SUBURBAN SPRAWL

INNER CITY

THE PEOPLE
WHERE WILL THEY **G**O?

THE URBAN NEIGHBOURHOOD

PRIVACY : COMMUNITY
URBAN VITALITY : SANCTUARY
A MIX OF CLASSES : CLOSE COMMUNITY
LOCAL SERVICES : EASE OF ACCESS
RICH ENVIRONMENT : URBAN ECOLOGY
MIX OF USES : ECONOMIC OPPORTUNITY
DIVERSITY OF TENURE : BALANCE OF CLASSES AND AGES
SECURE BY DESIGN : SOCIAL INTEGRATION
ENERGY EFFICIENCY : ENVIRONMENTAL AWARENESS

AFTER EBENEZER HOWARD'S THREE MAGNETS FROM - TOMORROW: A PEACEFUL PATH TO REAL REFORM

Where will the people go in the 21st century? It is a hundred years since Ebenezer Howard published his three magnets in *Tomorrow – A peaceful path to real reform*. It has become one of the most potent symbols of twentieth century planning. However times have changed and we now need to reverse the polarity of the magnets by developing new models which will attract people back to cities in the twenty-first century.

Figure 6.10 Amended 'Three Magnets' diagram, Rudlin and Falk, 1999. Ebenezer Howard's original compelling diagram has been cleverly updated to account for modern circumstances and aspirations. (Reproduced from *Building the 21st Century Home* with permission from Elsevier)

between buildings and people, Robert Gutman expressed the conundrum succinctly:

Despite the findings of behavioral science research, which indicates that design factors by themselves do not determine patterns of social interaction or provide social cohesion, many architects and planners continue to … believe instead in the doctrine of architectural determinism … [that is] the architect's decision about the placement of buildings determines the social relationships of the occupants … Because architects *hope* that certain social outcomes will result from their designs they tend to expect that these outcomes will happen. (Gutman: p. 170)

Unfortunately for urban designers, the classic case of contemporary architectural determinism is the

Neighborhood Unit theory, and when Clarence Perry first promulgated the idea in its modern form during the 1920s he was inspired by at least four sources. The first of these comprised the garden suburb: the English version, such as Hampstead Garden Suburb in north London by Raymond Unwin and Barry Parker, begun in 1907 (see Figure 6.11); and the American rendition of similar ideas in railroad suburbs like Forest Hills Gardens, in Queens, New York (1906–1911) laid out by Frederick Law Olmsted, Jr with buildings by Grosvenor Atterbury, and where Perry himself lived. The second source was the neighborhood center movement begun in St Louis in 1907 (and derived from the pioneering work of Jane Addams in Chicago during the late 19th century) as a way of 'socializing immigrants' by means of schools and community centers

Figure 6.11 Hampstead Garden Suburb, London, 1907; Raymond Unwin and Barry Parker, Architects and Town Planners. The planning success of Hampstead was not lost on American sociologist Clarence Perry, who later developed his famous neighborhood unit as the basis of city design.

Figure 6.12 Radburn, NJ, 1928; Clarence Stein and Henry Wright. In projects from the 1950s onwards, developers and planners devalued the concept of this model development by omitting its central pedestrian landscape, leaving only the bare bones of disconnected dead end roads. Such minimal designs then became the norm for decades of dull and dreary Anglo-American suburban layouts.

interspersed throughout the city. In a similar regard, Perry was influenced by a third source, the writings of American sociologist Charles Horton Cooley, who had stressed the importance of 'primary groups' characterized by 'intimate face-to-face association and cooperation' (Cooley: pp. 23, 408–409, in Hall, P.: p. 129) and which were 'especially important in the dense, fragmented life of the modern city' (Hall, P.: p. 129). This same sentiment, of creating a specific local world for citizens faced with the growing complexity of the modern city, was evident in Perry's fourth inspiration, which came once again from Raymond Unwin, whose article in 1920–21 entitled 'Distribution,' argued for 'the adequate localization of the life of … citizens,' in the face of ever enlarging and diffuse metropolitan areas (Unwin, 1920/21: p. 37, in Biddulph: p. 69).

Through his first-hand experience of living in the well-designed suburb of Forest Hills, Perry came to understand that good design could contribute to community spirit, but he always made clear his main reason for promoting the neighborhood unit concept was to relate physical amenities to population in a systematic way. Within this objective Perry placed specific focus on the safety of pedestrians and children (Broady: p. 174). Perry regarded the automobile as a 'menace' but a 'blessing in disguise' that made the definition of protective neighborhood units imperative. He argued that the 'virtues of the village' would flourish in such neighborhoods by means of their scale and definition as places distinct from the metropolis (Biddulph: p. 69). This separation was symbolized and actualized in Perry's famous diagram by keeping through traffic to

the edges of the neighborhood, while internal streets provided for local traffic only.

The ultimate definition of this idea was provided by Clarence Stein and Henry Wright in their design for Radburn, whereby a 'superblock' was defined by arterial roads around the edges, allowing all through traffic to be eliminated and local vehicle access provided instead by a series of cul-de-sacs interlocking with a network of pedestrian-only green spaces leading to a main landscaped park, shared by all residents. A typical 30- to 50-acre (12- to 20-hectare) superblock was planned as a neighborhood for 7500–10 000 residents fitted within a half-mile radius centered around an elementary school and its playgrounds. Shopping was located on the edges, accessible by walking or driving (Garvin: p. 273). Pedestrian circulation was internalized along an extensive network of car-free green spaces that were planned to link to adjacent neighborhoods and community centers by means of footpaths that went under the boundary arterial roads (see Figure 6.12). But even more than creating pedestrian safety and refuge from the fast-moving automobile, Perry argued strongly that a healthy, balanced society needed a locally-based counterpoint to the overwhelming scale and complexity of modern city life, and this became the essence of neighborhood unit theory in subsequent decades.

The ideas of the neighborhood unit and the superblock were conflated in modernist town planning theory as prescribed by the Congrès International de l'Architecture Moderne, the most influential organization governing architectural and urban thinking before and several years after World War II. Under this doctrine, which guided most British urban design in the 1950s to the 1970s, the neighborhood unit became a superblock with a small district center and pedestrian precinct at the heart of the area, and everything turned its back on the arterial roads at the periphery. No frontage development was allowed on these highways to ensure free flow of traffic as highway engineering gained ascendancy over other urban values. This was a dramatically different urban form than Perry's original conception, where shopping was at the junctions of the major roads dividing the neighborhoods, and although busy, these highways retained their character as traditional streets (Rudlin and Falk: p. 42). Moreover, whereas Perry envisaged the neighborhood comprising a network of small local streets, modernist doctrine swept away all vestiges of streets lined with buildings and replaced this traditional urban form with a series of separated buildings with open areas often dominated by parking and service requirements (see Figure 6.13).

These modernist neighborhoods have not stood the test of time, and their manifest failings account to some degree for the substantial critique of neighborhood unity theory that developed from the 1960s onwards. By contrast, many of the older neighborhoods noted as precedents for New Urbanism and some of those newly designed under the impetus of contemporary neighborhood theory provide very pleasant and economically successful environments (see Figure 6.14). However, sociologists and some planners have continued to criticize the concept: empirical research has consistently failed to demonstrate that physical design can determine social behavior to the extent that architects and planners have desired (Broady: p. 180). In his influential article, 'Social Theory and Architectural Design' from 1966, Broady went so far as to call neighborhood unit theory 'a dubious social theory … grafted onto a reasonable technical solution' (Broady: p. 174).

Broady was specifically referring to British practice in post-World War II Britain, when aspects of American theory and practice from the 1920s and 1930s were very influential. The physical layout of Radburn was imitated in many aspects of British new town design during the 1950s: Radburn-style housing layouts with extensive cul-de-sacs and separation of cars and pedestrians to different sides of the dwelling were common in many British public housing schemes, even as late as the 1980s. Ironically, despite this initial popularity, a 2005 government-sponsored report on failing housing areas noted that

Figure 6.13 Housing at Lyon, France, 1977. Modernist urban design swept away traditional multi-purpose spaces of streets and squares, replacing them with single function walkways and parking areas amidst widely spaced, large buildings.

Figure 6.14 Street in Dilworth, Charlotte, NC. Designed as part of a streetcar suburb in the first decade of the 20th century when car ownership was almost non-existent, this neighborhood street's pedestrian-friendly design enables it to function well in 2006 when car ownership averaged two to three cars per household.

Radburn-style housing 'is deeply unpopular in many cases and demolition is considered to be the most desirable option' (CABE, 2005c: p. 15). This unpopularity was related to the confusion between fronts and backs to the housing generated by the segregated layout of cars and pedestrians. Vehicle access led to parking areas at the backs of the houses, and thus visitors who come by car entered the houses through back doors and kitchens, trespassing on private domains. At the same time, front doors open out onto undefined pedestrian public space that was rarely used. However, design studies have shown that where the unsatisfactory cul-de-sac layout can be transformed into a traditional connected street system with clearly delineated fronts and backs to the houses, established by traditional front gardens and back yards, and where the streets can be recreated as meaningful elements of a wider neighborhood, many problems with these houses can be overcome (CABE, 2005c: p. 17).

While some American design precedents were influential in post-World War II Britain, the social thinking contained within neighborhood unit theory also found its way into official British government policy, and whereas design concepts like Radburn have fallen out of favor, the related social ideas have retained much of their influence despite a series of powerful critiques over the last 40 years. During the years of combat in World War II, the British government was making plans for rebuilding the nation after the anticipated victory over Hitler's Third Reich, and two documents in particular, the Dudley Report in 1944 and *The Size and Social Structure of a Town*, dating from 1943, laid the groundwork for ideas about neighborhood design that are recognizably similar to those espoused by contemporary British government policies.

These two wartime reports argued '[t]hough physical planning and administrative measures cannot by themselves change social relationships, they can, if wisely and positively conceived, encourage and facilitate the growth of that spirit of fellowship without which true community life is impossible' (quoted in Broady: p. 174). However, within a few years overly optimistic architects and planners transformed this guarded conclusion into the simplistic proposition that the way a neighborhood was designed *would* create a sense of community among the residents. The neighborhood unit principle was perhaps most famously encapsulated in Sir Patrick Abercrombie's plan for Greater London in 1943–1944, where surveys using methods derived from Geddes teased out the community structure of the capital as a metropolis

of distinct villages. This finding was then allied with Perry's neighborhood unit theory, and a plan was created for the urban rebuilding and expansion of Britain's capital city that reinforced the existing neighborhood structure and extended the same idea into new urban areas. In the words of the official plan document, '[t]he communities themselves consist of a series of sub-units, generally with their own shops and schools, corresponding to neighborhood units' (Forshaw and Abercrombie, 1943; Abercrombie, 1945, in Alexander, 1966: p. 49–50). Prescribing the form, function and character of neighborhoods became planning doctrine to the extent that the great American urban critic Lewis Mumford could proclaim in 1954 that neighborhoods were 'a fact of nature' (Mumford, 1954: p. 257, in Biddulph: p. 72).

Broady's insightful article demonstrates how and why this transformation took place in the UK, and similar reasoning can be implied to American professionals. Mass-produced British suburbs from the 1930s and early post-war housing estates in the new towns around London were widely criticized shortly after their construction, not only because they appeared visually unattractive and lacked social amenities, but because their residents complained strongly of missing the friendliness and community feeling they had experienced in their older, run-down inner city neighborhoods. The question facing architects and planners was therefore how to combine the community friendliness of the older slum areas with the advantages of better-designed housing in new towns and suburbs, and the assumptions of architectural determinism stand out clearly in the answers they found. It is interesting to quote Broady's explanation at length as it exposes the good intentions and tendencies towards superficial analysis common among architects and planners in the 1950s, and still prevalent today:

What was it about the slum street that made it so friendly? Obviously, they said, its amenities: its pubs and church halls and above all, the dear little corner shop where Ma could get 'tick' [credit] to bide her over till wage night and meet her friends for a chat. The answer for the new towns, then, was to provide the same kind of amenities (especially the little corner shops) and, *eureka!* people would be as friendly and neighborly in their new surroundings as they had been in the old. Of course, people do meet each other and chat in pubs and corner shops. But not all pubs and corner shops engender the neighborliness of the slum street. For what is much more important in explaining that neighborliness are the *social* facts, first, that the people who lived in the slums had often lived in the same street for several generations and thus had longstanding contacts with their neighbors and kin; and second, that people who suffer economic hardship are prone to band together for mutual help and protection. It is true that neighborliness is induced by environmental factors. Of these, however, the most relevant are social and economic rather than physical. But it can readily be understood why planners (and [architects] who wished to do something to make life better for their fellow-men) should have been so ready to suppose that the prime factor in the growth of 'community spirit' was the design of the *physical* environment which it was uniquely in their power to modify. (Broady: pp. 175–176)

At the most, Broady suggested, architecture and urban design can *influence* social behavior, but they cannot *determine* it. The distinction that designers must make is between what sociologists define as 'potential' and 'effective' environments. Herbert Gans argued that the physical form of a neighborhood is only a 'potential' environment because it simply provides possibilities or clues for social behavior. The 'effective' – or total – environment is more complex; it is the product of those physical patterns *plus* the behavior of the people who use them, and this behavior will vary according to each person's social background and his or her way of life (Gans, 1962, in Broady: p. 181). In the same year as Gans' study, research in one of the British new towns found that the boundaries of neighborhoods were 'of no special significance in terms of informal social relationships' developed by their residents (Willmott: p. 125). This same research did however give rise to the conclusion that while neighborhoods did not play a major social role in the lives of their inhabitants, they did perform well in several functional ways, particularly in terms of using neighborhood shops for day-to-day needs (Biddulph: p. 74).

Another sharp challenge to the mainstream theory of neighborhood units was provided by Christopher Alexander's 1966 essay 'A City is Not a Tree.' In this seminal work, Alexander drew on his mathematical sensibilities to demolish what he regarded as the cozy but limiting assumptions of neighborhood unit theory (which he categorized as a 'tree') and proposed instead a freer, more diverse view of city relationships (the 'semi-lattice'). Alexander's 'tree' was a simplified structure where small units were grouped into a larger one, and a series of these larger units related to entities

of yet greater magnitude. Under this topology, a small unit, say a family or household, was gathered into a neighborhood of similar households and then this neighborhood related to the city along with many other similar yet separate neighborhood units. In this abstract, hierarchical model each household could only relate to the city by means of the neighborhood and direct contact with households in other neighborhoods was difficult due to the topological boundaries and defined structure of the group. Alexander illustrated this arrangement by specific negative reference to Abercrombie's London plan, particularly the initial 1943 neighborhood mapping and analysis. (In fairness to Abercrombie, however, Londoners today still conceptualize and administer their city as a collection of 'urban villages,' with this physical identity approximated by the municipal structure of the city's partially self-governing boroughs.)

The semi-lattice, Alexander's preferred structure, was by contrast a flexible, more complex configuration where individual units, such as households, could make direct connections across a range of neighborhoods without being limited to their own spatial boundaries, and the largest of these units, the city, was made up from many diverse and overlapping layers of interaction rather than simply a series of discrete neighborhoods. Alexander argued the semi-lattice most clearly mirrored the way we lived our lives in Britain and America during the 1960s. This is arguably even more apposite today, with each of us creating a spatial network of travel and destinations, and a social network of friends, work and recreation, none of which are necessarily prescribed by the boundaries of the particular neighborhood where we live. Sometimes the relationships are bounded and supported by our locality; other times they are not.

These conclusions were presaged in America as early as 1948 by Harvard planner Reginald Isaacs, who noted that:

[w]e live in a highly complex society which, to a great extent, has loosened the individual citizen from traditional controls – a society in which the individual has greater freedom to choose many alternative schemes of behavior, leads a highly segmentalized life, belongs to numerous groups whose members are scattered throughout the city, is characterized by extreme mobility, and seldom forms attachments to specific localities. (Isaacs: p. 22, in Biddulph: p. 74)

A similar conclusion was stated by the great American urbanist Kevin Lynch, who, while giving value to the concept of a small 'neighborhood of proximity' (up to 100 households where people know each other) argued that the concept of a 'large, autonomous, sharply defined, and rigid neighborhood units of a standard size, to which all physical and social relations are keyed … seems inappropriate for our society' (Lynch: p. 250). Lynch stated that to plan a city 'as a series of neighborhoods is futile, or may support social segregation. Any good city has a continuous fabric, rather than a cellular one. Then it is possible for people to choose their own friends and services, and to move their residences freely, by small or large increments, as they choose' (Lynch: p. 401). Even Jane Jacobs, the doyen of American New Urbanists, and who is often too simplistically read as a supporter of neighborhoods, was explicitly critical of the neighborhood unit concept. 'It is fashionable to suppose,' she wrote, 'that certain touchstones of the good life will create good neighborhoods – schools, parks, clean housing, and the like. How easy life would be if this were so! … In real life, cause and effect are not so simple' (Jacobs: p. 122). Jacobs went on to contrast a small town community of between 5000 and 10 000 people with a city 'neighborhood' of the same size:

> If you go to Main Street (analogous to the consolidated commercial facilities or community center for a planned neighborhood), you run into people who you also know at work, or went to school with, or see at church, or people who are your children's teachers, or who have sold or given you professional or artisan's services, or whom you know to be friends of your casual acquaintances, or whom you know by reputation. Within the limits of a town or village, the connections among its people keep crossing and recrossing and this can make workable and essentially cohesive communities … But a population of five or ten thousand residents in a big city has no such innate degree of natural cross-connections within itself, except under the most extraordinary circumstances. Nor can city neighborhood planning, no matter how cozy in intent, change this fact. (Jacobs: p. 125)

However, much urban design and planning theory continues to be predicated on the supposition that close-knit, well-defined and supportive neighborhoods are the basic building blocks of cities. Mike Biddulph, a British critic of the traditional neighborhood concept and its British counterpart, the urban village, has criticized the 'exclusive promotion of neighborhoods,' and particularly New Urbanist claims that:

> … if we design this way we will get the communities we want; we will overcome auto-dependent forms of development by adopting a deformed grid, mixing uses, developing to appropriate densities and having utilities and services within walking distance from all houses; we will encourage a great mixing of socio-economic groups and mask the socio-economic distinctions between residents if we design houses that look similar in status, and if we adopt 'polite' and neo-vernacular architectural expression; we will promote community and improved community relations. (Biddulph: p. 73)

American academic planner Michael Southworth makes similar criticisms, arguing that the environmental determinism he detects in much New Urbanist writing 'runs counter to most environmental behavior research over the past 40 years' (Southworth, 2003: p. 214). Since Broady's articulate dissection of architectural determinism in post-war neighborhood unity theory, several other social scientists and planners have noted this same problem with specific reference to New Urbanism (Audirac and Sheryen, 1994; Harvey, 1997; Audirac, 1999; Talen, 1999). In the light of this research, Southworth concludes, the 'conception of how people live today seems based on a naïve, idealistic interpretation of social structure in the traditional neighborhood … Indeed, the concept of the socio-spatial neighborhood may be archaic … We … cannot count on built form to generate sociability.' However, Southworth immediately qualifies this conclusion by stating 'This does not mean that neighborhood design cannot stimulate and support social interaction (Southworth, 2003: p. 214). This qualifier is similar to one that Biddulph adds to his conclusions by admitting that New Urbanists are 'careful to state that physical solutions will not solve social, economic or even environmental problems' (Biddulph: p. 73). Indeed, the Charter of New Urbanism states clearly in the third paragraph of its Preamble: 'We recognize that physical solutions by themselves will not solve social and economic problems, but neither can economic vitality, community stability, and environmental health be sustained without a coherent and supportive physical framework' (Congress of the New Urbanism, 2000: p. v).

The assertion that good outcomes cannot be created by good design, but that good design is one necessary component for good outcomes draws a fine line, and it is easy to imagine how the qualifiers to this position may easily become blurred and indistinct. Design attributes and objectives that are, at most, only *supportive* of social goals can become, as with British thinking after World War II, preferred mechanisms for *achieving* social improvements in society.

There is another piece to this critical puzzle that needs to be examined. Despite the cogency of his earlier arguments in 1966, Christopher Alexander reversed himself quite dramatically a decade later in his subsequent major work, *A Pattern Language* (Alexander *et al.*, 1977). As noted in Chapter 4 of this volume when discussing the principle of self-governing and participatory communities, certain of Alexander's patterns specify in fairly prescriptive ways the best size and relationships for self-governing communities, specifications that sound an awful lot like neighborhood units. Government is focused around communities of 7000 people for viable face-to-face contact and political accountability, and this figure is broken down into smaller neighborhoods containing 500 persons within clearly identifiable boundaries. For comparison, Perry's neighborhood unit suggested about 5000 people, hence Jacobs' analogy with small towns of that size. New Urbanist Traditional Neighborhoods average about 2500 residents [1000 homes on 125 acres (50 hectares) at typical densities of eight dwellings per acre (50 persons per hectare)] and British urban villages envisage a population of 3000–5000 residents living at a range of densities on 250 acres (100 hectares). Lynch's smaller 'neighborhood of proximity,' at up to 100 households, or between 250 and 300 people, is not too dissimilar in size to Alexander's smaller group. Each neighborhood in Alexander's patterns should have 'a mix of uses, a mix of household types and a central place around which community facilities and shops should be located. These nodes should be about 300 yards apart and [Alexander] suggests that the boundaries to these neighborhoods should be defined by gateways' (Biddulph: p. 72). Like Perry and the designers of Radburn, Alexander keeps major highways to the periphery of the neighborhood unit (Alexander *et al.*, 1977: p. 84). Like British post-war planners and contemporary New Urbanists, he decreed that each neighborhood would benefit from local cafés, pubs and corner shops (Alexander *et al.*, 1977: pp. 439, 442).

Within Alexander's later logic regarding neighborhood structure, the physical size of the unit and its definition through urban design become necessary factors for setting up political and social governance.

Further aspects of life, such as work, recreation and shopping can take place outside the neighborhood and collections of Alexander's other patterns such as 'scattered workplaces,' 'work communities,' 'networks for learning' and 'webs of shopping' support this connectivity between neighborhoods (Alexander *et al.*, 1977: p. 51–57, 222–226, 99–109).

While Alexander's change of perspective regarding neighborhood structure provided unexpected support for New Urbanist ideas, there are more critics than supporters of neighborhood unit theory. In the light of so much criticism, often by people such as Lynch and Jacobs, who in other ways are regarded as precursors to much New Urbanist thinking, why do New Urbanists, like British proponents of urban villages, place so much faith in the mixed-use, walkable, neighborhood formula? First, there is a common sense dimension of usefulness to the concept. Social research has found that neighborhoods can usefully provide some functions such as local shops and other facilities that are used on a daily basis, and empirical evidence provides many examples of neighborhoods that are recognizable physical entities, provide some local services, and are well liked by residents. This is particularly true in older parts of British and American cities, such as Chorlton in Manchester, Moseley in Birmingham, the Castro in San Francisco or the North End in Boston (see Figures 4.5 and 6.15). Although their boundaries may be imprecise and sometimes changing, areas like these 'may reflect physical appearance, social composition, cultural values, political interests, history or any combination of

Figure 6.15 Street in the Castro district, San Francisco. Gay and lesbian lifestyles have come to define the Castro district as much as its architecture and urbanism.

these factors' (Garvin: p. 230). Despite volumes of planning theory that have decried the concept over the past four decades, some definition of 'neighborhood' thus remains a useful way for professionals and lay people alike to understand a city's spatial and social structure, and is thus an effective means of communicating ideas about urban design and planning issues. This is exemplified in British planning policies for the renewal and revitalization of old and outworn housing areas: the Commission for Architecture and the Built Environment's report *Creating Successful Neighbourhoods* was specifically aimed at this problem, and stated the need 'for a continued commitment to the long-term objective of transforming neighbourhoods through good design, sustainable development and valuing heritage' (CABE, 2005c: p. 2).

In the American case, and perhaps in the British context too, there is a second answer that is very strategic. Neighborhood theory and design has been promoted specifically in recent decades as a device to intervene effectively in the real estate development system that builds cities as a series of disconnected, mass-produced subdivisions, yet markets them under the false but appealing soubriquet of 'communities'. The traditional neighborhood is an alternative development model that fits the scale of contemporary subdivision production, connects directly to the marketing mythology of community, and thus can gradually supplant conventional sprawl with a more efficient and environmentally sustainable product. It is a strategy to transform conservative and entrenched real estate practices by infiltration rather than direct conflict and frontal assault.

As part of this effort to engage private developers and homebuilders, New Urbanism enters into a discourse with popular taste, as Venturi, Scott-Brown and Isenour advocated architecture should. As a first move in a skeptical marketplace, New Urbanist design repackages consumer preferences for new suburban developments into more coherent and environmentally sustainable forms, with more efficient and economic infrastructure of connected streets and public space. Once this generic level of development has been improved, the next step is to integrate a mixture of housing types and uses into the suburbs in ways that provide alternatives to driving and are more supportive of present or future transit, and these two pragmatic steps taken together lead to the development of something very close to the neighborhood unit as originally conceptualized. This provides a strategy for gradually restructuring suburban development in a form that is successful in the marketplace, true to

design principles, and which validates (at least in part and pragmatically) the neighborhood unit as a planning and design concept. As Broady states, the neighborhood is indeed a 'reasonable technical solution' to problems of urban structure (Broady: p. 174). This is particularly apt in the context of an increasingly atomistic society, where communal bonds are fading and being replaced by rampant individualism, and where architects and planners still seek some design rationale that underpins the idea of community as a stabilizing force for local interests in a globalized world. The ability to identify with one's home neighborhood, satisfy several daily needs within that defined area and have transportation alternatives to other destinations that form part of daily life is a perfectly reasonable and defensible construct so long as no other more ambitious social claims are made for it. Neighborhood design should not be made to carry the weight of deterministic and simplistic theory thrust upon it over many decades by architects and planners.

In current British practice, neighborhood design forms an increasingly important strategy in urban design and planning. British government design guidance in the late 1990s and early 2000s was focused on contextual design and the concept of 'place,' but more recent programs such as the Sustainable Communities initiative have brought social aspects of neighborhood design more to the fore in urban design thinking (ODPM, 2005c). In marked contrast to several years of planning doctrine that premiated low-density single-use housing estates and business parks, and which located schools and health facilities in locations that paid little attention to local accessibility, the landmark *Planning Policy Guidance Note 13* published in 1994 promoted the concept of mixed-use development ... suggesting that ... planning for a variety of uses – shops and restaurants – on the ground floor of developments will help keep streets lively. Attention to preserving or enhancing continuous pavement [sidewalk in the USA] level streetscapes and the avoidance of blank frontages ... can be a major contribution to retaining pedestrian activity, retaining the commercial life of the area and to crime prevention. (Rudlin and Falk: p. 127). This mirror image of New Urbanist concepts set the scene for subsequent British policy documents that now encourage sustainable communities and neighborhoods. The new policies for the desired 'urban renaissance' focus on

... the huge potential for neighborhood sustainability strategies that encompass housing, local facilities,

155

rewarding livelihoods, green spaces, community development, food, energy, water and biodiversity. Such strategies can invigorate local communities while simultaneously playing a part in reducing the threat of global climate change and other pressing environmental and social concerns. All this is exactly in line with [British] government aspirations; here in the UK, national policies for health, regeneration, transport energy and town planning all emphasize the importance of getting things right at the neighborhood level. (Porritt: p. ix)

In contrast to the more activist and utopian aspirations of New Urbanism in America regarding 'authentic communities,' British design policies intended to foster similar physical outcomes tend to have more pragmatic justifications. The definition of a neighborhood, for example, is low-key and pragmatic:

Neighborhoods are the localities in which people live. They imply a sense of belonging and community, grounding our lives in a specific place. Aspirations for neighborhoods are surprisingly consistent amongst people with very different lifestyles. We want neighborhoods that are attractive, safe, healthy and unpolluted, with high-quality local facilities, access to green spaces, and excellent connections to other areas. We would like the opportunity for convivial social activity and friendship. There is a recognition that for some people – particularly the old and the young, and those who are home-based throughout the day – the neighborhood is vitally important for health and well-being. (Barton et al.: p. 1)

This line of practical reasoning is followed in the government publication *By Design: Better Places to Live* (DTLR and CABE, 2001: p. 34), which argues the case for mixed communities on the grounds of several factors, including: a wider range and better balanced demand for community services and facilities; the opportunity for people to 'age in place' (to use the American term) whereby people can move to accommodation suitable for various stages of life without having to leave the community or neighborhood; and the fact that differing household types and sizes give rise to different living and working routines, encouraging activity on the street throughout the day and evening and thus adding to community safety through greater surveillance (Tiesdell: p. 361, 364).

The core beliefs within these policies articulate the view that 'planning, design and management of the

physical environment can enhance quality of life, promote social inclusion and husband natural resources' (Barton et al.: p. x). Within this founding principle, the neighborhood becomes the medium through which a sustainable and convivial living environment can be created and subsequently managed by the various public and private stakeholders within the community. The neighborhoods of the future, be they reinvigorated existing communities or newly constructed developments, 'need to reflect cultural shifts and new technology. We cannot return to the (supposedly) localism of the past. Rather, neighborhoods will be open, varied, egalitarian and connected places – providing more choice, opportunity and beauty but without undesirable impacts on health and ecology' (Barton et al.: p. 3). The main difference between British and American motivations has been the more idealistic social agenda in New Urbanist theory, leading to the various accusations of environmental determinism noted earlier.

Critics of that ilk have tended to overstate their case. As Tiesdell has pointed out, 'In essence, [the New Urbanists'] argument is that "design matters", that behavior is situational and that by configuring the situation in certain ways the probability of certain behaviors can be increased' (Tiesdell: p. 373). However, New Urbanists (this author included) do themselves no favors when they claim certain design strategies *will* create a sense of community and when they exaggerate the social importance of the neighborhood in allegedly transforming behavior in American society (Talen, 1999, 2000).

Architectural and urban design are *complementary* to human activity but, contrary to Winston Churchill's famous quote 'We shape our buildings; then they shape us,' *design does not mold behavior*. Urban design does not possess some magic quality or concept by which society can be reformed. But it does have an influence on the lives of residents in urban areas. Urban design's main purpose, paraphrasing Broady, is to make people's lives pleasant, safe and more convenient as they go about their daily business (Broady: p. 183). Because human behavior is changeable, and since urban designers cannot predict what these changes might be, they have to provide for such changes to take place without major demolition and replacement of whole sections of the city. This flexibility of use and stability of urban structure is exactly what can be provided by development control through form-based codes, so this offshoot of social theory illustrates how well such codes can serve the community in many scenarios.

For all its flaws, no other activist approach to city design in America can match New Urbanism in terms of projects built over the past decade, nor in the number of new form-based zoning codes adopted by local governments. New Urbanism has emerged during that time as the dominant body of reformative theory and practice, and this is echoed in British urbanism over the same period, for despite many protestations to the contrary by British architects, almost all the recent good development in British towns and cities illustrates the principles of New Urbanism set out in its Charter. The Charter is not an American invention exported to the UK as an act of cultural imperialism, as some British critics and architects seem to think. It is merely the latest manifestation of centuries of transatlantic transference of urban ideas between the two continents, and many founding concepts of American New Urbanism are European in origin.

There is, however, another theoretical position in America, 'Everyday Urbanism,' that has not had much impact on British thinking, and which provides an interesting and alternative appreciation of urbanity, particularly in the USA. It is valuable therefore to review briefly the main tenets of this alternative critical perspective on the city.

EVERYDAY URBANISM

John Chase, Margaret Crawford and John Kaliski popularized the term Everyday Urbanism in the USA through their eponymous book (Chase *et al.*, 1999). The spaces of Everyday Urbanism are an amalgam of 'wide boulevards and trash-strewn alleys, luxurious stores and street vendors, manicured lawns and dilapidated public parks; they are the products of the intricate social, political, economic and aesthetic forces at work in the contemporary urban environment' (Chase *et al.*: jacket notes) (see Figure 6.16). In essence, however, this view of urbanism spends very little time on manicured lawns and the spaces of the bourgeoisie. The spaces most beloved by the critics who have coined this phrase are in the poorer parts of the city; these are everyday spaces, defined by Crawford as a diffuse landscape of banal, repetitive and 'non-designed' locations (Crawford: pp. 19–20), essentially the opposite of the well-designed network of public spaces sought by New Urbanists.

Everyday Urbanism 'celebrates and builds on the richness and vitality of daily life and ordinary reality. It has little pretense about the perfectibility of the built environment ... [b]ut it is idealistic about social

Figure 6.16 Taco truck, Charlotte, NC, 2005. Hispanic street vendors create instant pockets of urban activity when they set up shop on urban sites that are often otherwise unused. *(Photo by Catherine Cervantes)*

equity and citizen participation, especially for disadvantaged populations. It is grass-roots and populist' (Kelbaugh, 2005, Vol. I: p. 8). This view of urbanism delights in the spontaneous and indigenous; it rejoices in the ways that migrant groups, for instance, appropriate and adapt the marginal spaces of their environment, and it champions vernacular architecture in vibrant ethnic neighborhoods like the *barrios* of Los Angeles. Everyday Urbanism is *ad hoc* and not driven by aesthetics; it is not so concerned about physical beauty or coherence but is egalitarian and focuses on street life (Kelbaugh, 2005, Vol. I: p. 8). It is inherently small-scale, and in the best scenarios it is a process of accretion, where little actions accumulate to make larger changes in urban environments.

At a more theoretical level, the critical view of Everyday Urbanism is based in part on the ideas of Henri Lefebvre (1970, 1979, 1991), i.e. that space is inherently a social and political construct, the repository of all kinds of meanings and significance derived from everyday life and its materiality. From this viewpoint, elaborated by geographers such as David Harvey (1989) and Edward Soja (1989), extraordinary things can be found within the banality of ordinary or even lost and discarded spaces. Community life can burst forth in such locations through murals, *ad hoc* street fairs, individual food vendors or small marketing opportunities created out of almost nothing, where rugs are hung over metal railings, disguising them, softening the environment and displaying goods for sale all at the same time. Such actions can temporarily transform barren spaces of empty lots, driveways or petrol station forecourts into social places. Local communities and entrepreneurs reclaim leftover spaces of the capitalist city for their own use, spaces that have been ignored or forgotten by mainstream urban design. Understanding this improvement by appropriation is one of the most important insights provided by Everyday Urbanist theory.

True to its roots in theories of postmodern geography and postmodern planning theory, Everyday Urbanism is mostly interested in reading the city like a text, interpreting space and activities to generate meaning; it is not primarily concerned with the actual activities of urban design and planning (Speaks: p. 35). Like so much architectural theory of the 1980s that borrowed heavily from linguistic theory and other branches of non-architectural discourse, Everyday Urbanism is less concerned with design as a practice; it is more interested in trying to hypothesize a range of meanings contained within an urban condition. It is a theory of explanation, not a theory of action. 'Everyday urbanism is a commentator on the city, an interpreter rather than a force for transformation' (Speaks: p. 36). As Crawford states:

> ... it is 'situational and specific, responding to very particular circumstances ... [It] is not an over-arching design philosophy. It does not seek to transform the world through totalizing master-planning, large-scale operations or 'best practices ... [It] retrofits existing situations ... [and] ... works in the nooks and crannies of existing urban environments ... [A]s a design approach, it is elusive and hard to characterize. (Crawford: p. 20)

Indeed, if the main question for New Urbanism is how to avoid being caught in a trap of commodification, the equivalent challenge for Everyday Urbanism is whether it can move beyond clever descriptions of urbanism to become any kind of strategy for urban design (Mehrotra: p. 13) (see Figure 6.17).

The ideas contained within Everyday Urbanism have several adherents in American academia, and the

Figure 6.17 Hypothetical redevelopment of Eastland Mall, Charlotte, NC, 2006; Catherine Cervantes. This student thesis examined hybrid conditions between New Urbanism and Everyday Urbanism. Urban surgery has been proposed for a failing shopping mall to provide community facilities, affordable housing and a transit center. Parking areas have been scaled back to provide sports fields and areas for community markets. The student concluded that Everyday Urbanism was an ineffective tool for dealing with large urban sites. *(Reproduction courtesy of Cathy Cervantes)*

urban events that comprise Everyday Urbanism are easily recognizable to critics and designers from developing nations, where local street markets are the norm, and small-scale enterprises that set up shop unofficially in every available corner of outdoor space are far more common. Current critical fascination in America with this kind of unofficial and organic urban intervention has to do with its potential to humanize the lost or surplus interstitial spaces of modern, low-density cities where so much of the 'public' realm is dead space (Mehrotra: p. 12). As such it provides urban designers and planners with useful material about the social use of space – if they will follow Jane Jacobs' injunction to use their eyes to study the city and look at places with open minds.

PART

IV

Practice

Urban design, public participation and planning in practice

SYNOPSIS

This chapter discusses the role of design in assisting public education and participation in the planning process, and how this public input can, in turn, inform and enrich urban design proposals for community development. It outlines the principles and processes for conducting successful charrettes, explains how to assemble an effective charrette team, how to develop a budget for the process, and how to create the most effective and engaging products from the event. The two case studies in the following chapters illustrate the final products from successful charrettes.

DESIGN AND COMMUNITY

In the Introduction, a quote from British Prime Minister Tony Blair provided a brief definition of community, and an expanded view of this notion is at the heart of current British urban politics and policy. This social concept is specifically intended to create a marked contrast with the earlier, Thatcherite view of society that placed all emphasis on individuals and none whatsoever on community. From this more recent national perspective, people whose conduct is to be governed are not seen as isolated individuals, 'but neither are they understood as members of a national collective … They are understood as citizens of communities, of associations, of networks' (Rose, 1999: p. 475, in Holden and Iveson: p. 62). In the fast-changing globalized world of shifting demographics, the British state proposes nothing less than a new relationship between 'ethical citizenship' and 'responsible community' as the most effective means of linking national and local government.

The principle that people who use public spaces and buildings should have a say in designing them is central to this enhanced notion of community. This belief is enshrined in British government policy and in America it represents a fundamental tenet of New Urbanism. British government documents such as *By Design: Urban Design in the Planning System: Towards Better Practice* make this point forcefully:

> It is not enough to consult people about decisions that will impact on their lives: they must be fully engaged from the start. (DETR, 2000: p. 32)

Hand-in-hand with this focus on public participation is a belief in the transformative power of design to improve communities in Britain and America. The main difference between the two nations is that American initiatives tend to be very localized, the result of individual towns and cities trying to establish a sophisticated framework for growth management with little coordinated help from federal or state government, while in Britain, three design disciplines – urban design, transportation design and environmental design – are now specifically incorporated in the British government's policy of sustainable communities. As the Commission for Architecture and the Built Environment (CABE), notes: 'In CABE's experience [of neighborhood revitalization], high quality design is an essential attribute of physical environments, be they homes, streets, schools, health centres or open spaces' (CABE, 2005c: p. 1). Urban, transportation and environmental design comprise three of eight criteria deemed necessary for sustainable urban neighborhoods in the UK, the others being safety, good governance, a flourishing local economy, good community services (including schools and health care) and social fairness

(ODPM, 2005c: pp. 56–59). This mix of factors promises a better balance between physical design and social and economic criteria, one that can avoid the pitfalls of architectural or environmental determinism and avoid the failure of earlier utopian but naïve urban regeneration schemes.

This kind of comprehensive approach to urban revitalization can only come from coordinated government policy in partnership with the private sector, and at the time of writing this degree of government action at federal or state levels is not common in the USA. The renewed appreciation for urban design has remained localized in some towns and cities and not spread to others, and this has spawned various public and private initiatives to educate elected officials across the nation about the importance of urban design as a tool for economic and environmental regeneration. Chief among these educational and outreach programs are the national and regional versions of the Mayors' Institute on City Design, run jointly by the National Endowment for the Arts, the American Architectural Foundation and the US Conference of Mayors. This format involves an intensive 2- or 3-day workshop built around the participation of half-a-dozen mayors, who bring issues from their communities to a panel comprised of urban designers, architects, landscape architects, planners, transportation planners, economic development experts and the like. Issues and potential solutions for each problem are discussed and sketched, and in almost all cases in which this author has been involved, urban design ideas have been the catalysts for new or renewed economic development opportunities, actions to increase social equity and important changes in municipal policies.

The success of the Mayors' Institute has given rise to similar events such as the Urban Open Space Leadership Institute, developed by the College of Architecture at the University of North Carolina at Charlotte with funding from the John S. and James L. Knight Foundation and the Urban Land Institute. This particular variant is based on educating elected officials and other community leaders about the importance of urban open space in the city. Citizens in many American communities appreciate the significance of preserving open space in the landscape of farms and countryside around the urban periphery (although policies to achieve this are very inconsistent) but far fewer understand the role urban open space – in the form of town greens, squares and plazas, parks, greenways, playgrounds, and above all, well-designed streets – can play in enhancing the quality of life in a community. From this original design focus on urban open space, this Institute has been able to extend its influence into various environmental and economic issues affecting communities in the Carolinas. Clearly explained and illustrated urban design ideas can be an effective key to unlock people's understanding of the potential that resides within their communities, and proposed changes to the physical environment can act as mechanisms to build public understanding of the range of issues involved with urban regeneration and growth management.

The power of design-based educational events such as these can be illustrated by an example expanded from the strategic SWOT analysis noted in Chapter 2 and which was a direct offshoot of these Urban Open Space design forums. Graduate architecture and planning students in a Community Planning class at the University of North Carolina at Charlotte followed up discussions that took place in two Institute workshops regarding different problems from the same small rural community of Mineral Springs, just south of Charlotte. Citizens were very concerned to retain as much of this countryside character as possible in the face of fast-spreading suburban sprawl all around them (see Figure 2.6).

The interdisciplinary team of architects and planners under the guidance of the author and Ken Chilton, a planning colleague from the University of North Carolina at Charlotte, undertook various analyses, and organized extensive public participation events, including a community visual survey where residents identified their priorities in relation to an extensive menu of illustrated options. The team then examined various housing layout and design typologies together with alternative designs for an improved town center, and constructed a managed growth scenario with implementation tools for the community. One of the main drivers in this public process that integrated planning analyses with design proposals was a detailed geographic information system (GIS) land capacity analysis, which determined the degrees of suitability for development of land within the town. A variety of objective physical factors and conditions – such as soil type, permeability, topography and stream buffers for water quality protection – were mapped to reveal the 'hidden' factors in the landscape that should be allowed to influence the type and location of new development. These objective criteria were then combined with subjective visual analyses of existing landscape quality and local heritage features, and from these integrated studies student teams created illustrative housing design layouts and a housing strategy map to provide the future vision and regulatory framework for future growth (see Figure 7.1).

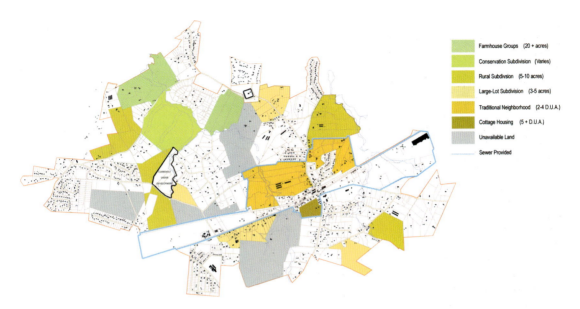

Farmhouse Groups (20 + acres)

Conservation Subdivision (Varies)

Rural Subdivision (5-10 acres)

Large-Lot Subdivision (3-5 acres)

Traditional Neighborhood (2-4 D.U.A.)

Cottage Housing (5 + D.U.A.)

Unavailable Land

Sewer Provided

Figure 7.1 Housing strategy map, Mineral Springs, NC, 2006; Community Planning Workshop, University of North Carolina at Charlotte. Combining planning concepts of low-density, conservation-based housing layouts on outlying parcels of land with denser development closer to the fledgling town center will need determined political resolve by elected officials in order to be implemented. The town council will need to downzone land over the objections of landowners who, while saying they desire to preserve the low-density, rural character of the community, want to be able to sell their own property for higher-density suburban subdivisions. (*Reproduction courtesy of the Town of Mineral Springs, NC*)

In concert with citizens, the team established a 'build-out' population over a 25-year period consistent with the carrying capacity of the land and the preservation of the rural heritage. Limits on growth were established to avoid the town having to make major investments in new infrastructure that would, in turn, necessitate large increases in local property taxes. Within this population limit, the team then worked hard to wean the citizens away from their desires for exclusively large-lot single-family zoning that would prohibit the possibility of affordable housing for people with a range of incomes becoming part of the community. This effort evolved into the simple concept of densifying around the center of the town, utilizing smaller, more affordable homes, while promoting a variety of low-density options in the outlying areas that allowed for the protection of streams and other important environmental features.

The housing typologies and strategy map specifically provide housing options ranging from small, in-town 'urban cottages' and live-work units on small lots to 20-acre (8-hectare) horse farms. The smaller affordable units promote the density needed to support a new small-scale town center and create a walkable in-town

neighborhood to facilitate 'aging in place' and other demographic trends (see Figure 7.2). At the time of writing this book, these design-based recommendations had been presented to the town and were being taken forward into a new town plan and improved zoning provisions.

The leaps in understanding made by citizens and elected officials in this design-based process were quite remarkable in terms of leading the town away from generic planning concepts and mistaken beliefs, e.g. that 1-acre lot zoning is the best way to preserve a rural landscape, and towards the acceptance of a more diverse and less exclusive population base. This educational process took two forms: (1) the intensive workshops with individual elected officials during the Urban Open Space Leadership Institute and (2) a series of conventional public meetings spaced out over a 3-month period. In this instance a concentrated charrette format was not workable because of logistic limits imposed by the academic schedules of the individual student team members, but there is little doubt that a more intensive charrette process involving more members of the community as active participants could have both shortened the process and

Figure 7.2 Proposed town center, Mineral Springs, NC, 2006; Community Planning Workshop, University of North Carolina at Charlotte. Quick three-dimensional modeling in programs such as Sketch-Up provide useful illustrations of design concepts to enrich community discussions. (*Reproduction courtesy of the Town of Mineral Springs, NC*)

perhaps inspired more innovative proposals. The power of charrettes to stimulate community learning is one of their most important and valuable attributes, but to achieve these aims, it is very important to organize the charrette process effectively. Therefore, the following sections of this chapter outline the principles and processes for conducting successful charrettes, how to assemble an effective charrette team, how to develop a budget for the process, and how to create the most effective and engaging products from the event.

CHARRETTE PRINCIPLES AND PROCESSES

In their proper form, charrettes are intensive workshops that last between 4 and 7 consecutive days; the author has found from extensive experience that this is the shortest amount of time to produce a feasible yet visionary plan that motivates community action. The event is an open forum that includes all interested parties in a collaborative process involving a wide range of disciplines. It adopts a generalist, holistic approach to solving the problems under discussion and sets out to produce a plan that is, above all else,

practicable. Charrettes increase the likelihood of getting projects built by gaining broad support from citizens, professionals, staff and elected officials. Plans are improved through diverse input and involvement, a key attribute of communicative planning. By fostering a shared community vision, charrettes can turn opposition into support.

A charrette is *not* simply a 1-day workshop. It is definitely not a plan authored by a select few that will affect many as in the old days of comprehensive master plans! Nor is it a 'visioning session' that stops short of implementation. Short workshops and visioning exercises are useful techniques that have their place within the gamut of public participation procedures, but they are not charrettes, nor in the author's opinion are they as effective. People unused to the charrette format sometimes think that charrettes are onerous, marathon talk-fests involving everyone all the time. This is not true, and although all sessions are open to the public, careful scheduling is needed to involve key stakeholder groups at the most effective times and in the most effective ways. What looks like a spontaneous, free-wheeling affair from the outside is always carefully orchestrated, so that when unforeseen developments occur (they always do) and team members dive off at odd tangents (they can be relied on to do that), the charrette leader has an organizational framework in place to compensate for these unexpected bursts of initiative.

There are five guiding principles for every charrette:

1. Involve everyone from the start to foster a shared community vision.
2. Manage the process effectively to build trust between the team and the public.
3. Work across disciplines to maximize group learning and productivity.
4. Work in short feedback loops to test ideas and stimulate public participation.
5. Work in detail to test the feasibility of alternative concepts.

First, it is important to get all points of view into the open for vigorous discussion so that elected officials, planning and design professionals, and concerned citizens can understand the full scope of the problem. Anyone who might have an opinion or be affected by the plan should be involved from the very beginning. Specific consultation times should be arranged with various stakeholder groups, while design activity is running constantly in the background, accessible to all on the other side of the room. By getting local people involved with the design team, the process gains mutual authorship and benefits from a shared vision.

Second, the management of the charrette is vital, and not all architecture and planning firms are skilled at conducting charrettes. The charrette manager, usually a principal in the lead firm, has the responsibility to set the democratic and communicative tone for the event: if this is not done effectively, the charrette, however 'good' the design may be, is likely to be a failure as an exercise in communicative planning. The charrette manager has to ensure that the team members work with the public in an approachable manner; the professionals need to engage participants in open dialogue to draw out their ideas and attitudes, genuinely seeking local knowledge and priorities rather than leading members of the public round to a designer's predetermined position by smooth talking and clever graphics. Through this open dialogue the design team can comprehend the community's culture and avoid imposing their own values. This multi-faceted discourse between the public, the individual stakeholders and the design team is at the heart of communicative planning theory and practice.

Building trust between participants cannot be left to chance, and the process generally starts long before the charrette begins by identifying and meeting key players and constituency groups. This sets the stage for maximum public involvement. Ideally an advisory committee of stakeholders should be established in advance of the actual event; this committee should include local decision makers and also people who can spread the word in the community to bring as many citizens into the process as possible. It is also important to include those who are skeptical of the project's objectives and the process. One or two of these should be included in the advisory group, and others invited to the public sessions. It is often inconvenient to have these people participate as they can be obstructionist and sometimes disruptive, but their voices deserve to be heard; it is important not to edit public opinion for the team. In an open forum, continued intransigence often isolates opponents from majority opinion to the extent that they lose credibility, but ethically it is important to be able to say that people with opposing views were given a fair hearing.

Third, the best charrette teams consist of individuals who have expertise in the following areas: urban design, planning, architecture, landscape architecture, transportation planning, market analysis, development economics and form-based coding. In addition to this range of skills, the presence of an illustrator, someone who can produce renderings of design ideas in three dimensions quickly and vividly, is essential. Other environmental and marketing specialists should be added if the task demands it, and local artists often contribute useful and unique perspectives. During the charrette all these specialists become generalists, assimilating each other's expertise and working across professional boundaries on problems and opportunities that arise as the charrette progresses.

There are two primary considerations in assembling an effective charrette team: the sets of professional skills necessary for the project and the personalities of the individuals involved. No matter how skilled someone might be, if he or she is not a hard-working team player, then that person has no place in the group. Charrette teams are not venues for prima donnas. Team members must be secure in their own professional knowledge and take the lead where necessary, but also willing to cross boundaries and to take advice and direction from other team members in their turn. In this context, someone with decent skills, a hard work ethic and easy-going personality is infinitely preferable to a prickly or temperamental genius. Every charrette team needs at least one, preferably two members who are good verbal presenters, with lively and engaging styles of public speaking. It is very

167

important to connect credibly with the public, both in terms of communicating information in a clear manner and for the important task of building trust.

Fourth, the pace of work is fast; tentative solutions to problems get pinned up on the wall for discussion as soon as possible, often after only a few hours. Members of the public need to be able to propose ideas and see them designed briskly for review and comment. Pin-up sessions are held every evening to gather public input on the preferred direction(s) for development based upon what the team heard during the day. The end product of a charrette is almost always a detailed master plan, but for master plans to have validity in our post-modern culture, and to avoid the problems of the well-intentioned but stifling paternalism that bedevilled master plans of a previous era, these drawings must be produced through a process that satisfies criteria for diversity and inclusiveness. In this regard, communicative planning is a vital form of information gathering and sharing, and of community education. Design plays a fundamentally important role in this process; it enables alternatives to be evaluated and decisions taken.

Professionals still tend to think that 'education' means them educating the public; however, some of the most useful and important facets of the charrette process are the ways in which the public can teach the professionals while educating themselves. Most often this occurs through local knowledge about the history of the area, or understanding the prevailing mood of the residents; at other times this form of communicative planning reveals important reasoning and expectations at the public level that do not match the 'official' statements of priorities. All of this is vital information to the designers, but information in this last category is especially valuable. This connection between professionals and residents was at the heart of Ralph Erskine's success in Byker, Newcastle, and enabled the architects to embrace local people as clients above and beyond the official channels of communication with elected officials and planning staff. Only when trust between residents and professionals is established in this way can a community come to own its plan, and thus allow it to be 'implemented' rather than 'imposed.'

Fifth, working in detail has many advantages. Opportunities can be revealed and flaws quickly reduced or eliminated by designing to a level of detail that includes building types, urban blocks and public spaces as well as the big picture issues such as circulation, transportation, land use, and landscape preservation. Many drawings are done to a large scale, designing over an aerial photograph with printed topography

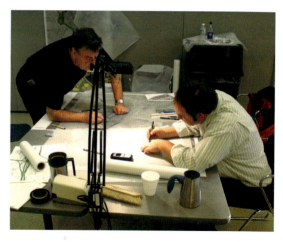

Figure 7.3 Designing in detail. The author (left) and Lawrence Group colleague Chad Hall design alternative layouts for neighborhoods. While on charrette, design ideas are produced quickly but in detail and tested in open discussion later that same day.

and property lines as a base. The high level of detail is achievable in the compressed timeframe partly because of sophisticated base mapping, but also because of the typological framework favored by New Urbanists. This brings to the process typologies of building form and spatial arrangement that retain wide applicability at different times and places, and this kind of information enables the team to move quickly into site-specific detail (see Figure 7.3).

Charrettes are fun and attract the interest of a broad range of people; the 'all day and into the night' studio atmosphere provides many opportunities for the public to participate, and creates an ambience that many find unusual and exciting. The intensive atmosphere of charrettes makes them convenient marketing events that can be used to raise public interest for the issues under discussion – and they provide good news stories for the media with plenty of photo opportunities and quotable material (see Figure 7.4). Through this process of collaborative design and public input occurring over several consecutive days, everyone – from city planner to local business owner to local resident – becomes aware of the complexities of development and design issues, and this knowledge helps participants work together to arrive at the best possible solution.

Despite the French origins of the term, the direct forerunner of this participatory design forum comes from the USA, specifically the American Institute of Architects' (AIA) Regional/Urban Design Assistance

Figure 7.4 Newspaper coverage of a charrette. This publicity is worth its weight in gold for spreading the word amongst politicians and the public.

Teams (R/UDAT) established in 1967. The 137th R/UDAT charrette was completed in January 2006, an average of 3.5 charrettes a year since the inception of the program. During these years, the R/UDAT format has changed relatively little and relies on three simple principles that are integral to any charrette process: the quality and experience of the team members; objectivity derived from team members' lack of vested interest in the community; and the keystone element of public participation by all sectors of the community. The R/UDAT program is comprehensively explained in the 2004 AIA publication *R/UDAT – Planning Your Community's Future: A Guide to the Regional/Urban Assistance Team Program*, including the detailed organization of charrettes, their required lead time for preparation, the processes and products of the event itself, and the follow-up stages of implementation and monitoring. There are certain important variations (mainly regarding the implementation of charrette recommendations) between the AIA R/UDAT format and the one developed by the author and his colleagues in practice, but the similarities outweigh the differences, and the R/UDAT format has been influential both in America and in Britain, where it formed the basis of the Action Planning movement beginning in the mid-1980s. Today, the format promulgated in the USA by the National Charrette Institute (www.charretteinstitute.com/charrette.html) is most comparable to the 'Enquiry by Design' process in Britain structured by the Prince's Foundation (www.princes-foundation.org/projects.html).

All these various formats operate from the premise that conventional approaches for public participation fail to produce either the best design products or the most inclusive process.

Conventional methods have been based for decades on the practice of consultants designing and crafting policies in isolation and then presenting the results to the public for 'comment'; this kind of design, carried out behind closed doors by experts who were happy in their conviction that they knew best, proved a recipe for much bad urbanism in the modernist period. Historic European cities, of course, do provide many examples of successful urban places that were created with no public input, brought into being by order of a king, duke, Pope or some other autocratic ruler, but we admire these boulevards and squares across the luxurious landscape of history (see Figure 5.3). We did not have to bear the brunt of dispossession or experience the forcible relocation of powerless peasants, tenant farmers or working class urban residents. We did not hear their cries of anguish and complaint. Creating good design in a democracy is much harder, not least because while all opinions are valued, not everybody may be equally informed, or fully understand the true circumstances concerning a community's problems and opportunities. The open forum of the charrette, with all its discussions, drawings and plans, provides one of the most effective learning opportunities for citizens about important issues affecting their community.

Even when fully committed to public participation, it is easy to overly romanticize the positive role of the public in these processes. As Holden and Iveson pointedly suggest, why should we always assume that local people know what is best for their community? Designers and planners would certainly be wary of granting this privilege to wealthy homeowners who try to privatize the community by keeping the public out of gated and guarded developments (Holden and Iveson: p. 68). There can be a lot of negativity in some communities, and often people come to charrettes to complain and in a few extreme cases to stop the process from even taking place. These folk rise from the ranks of the NIMBYs (Not In My Back Yard) and the BANANAs (Build Absolutely Nothing Anywhere Near Anything); they come to talk, not to listen, and least of all to hear. Many have made up their mind about issues usually on the basis of half-truths, myths and downright falsehoods circulating about the particular project in question. Often public opinion is in direct opposition to good planning and urban design, and a charrette team has to work hard to overcome these obstacles of ignorance. Quite often, in an echo of equity planning, one of the roles required of team members is to introduce ideas of environmental sustainability and social equity into group discussions when these are not forthcoming from stakeholders.

Several principles enshrined in American initiatives for Smart Growth and British plans for Sustainable Communities are almost guaranteed to generate opposition from community groups and neighborhood associations on both sides of the Atlantic. These concepts usually involve higher-density, mixed-use and infill developments that introduce new buildings, new residents, and visitors into existing neighborhoods. Citizen groups often pay lip service to such ideas in general, but maintain steadfastly that they're not right for *their* particular area. It is a well-known paradox in American social attitudes that citizens complain loudly against sprawl and the loss of open space, and equally loudly about the higher-density development that is the most effective solution to the problem. While the numbers in the British density equations are traditionally higher than American examples, the same sentiments exist in both nations.

Nevertheless, a good professional must strive to garner public input, and a lot of this work involves public education. The best way to educate the public is in public – to allow them to see the design process in action, to see how variables are balanced against each other and on what criteria priorities are assessed. The charrette method allows the public to watch professionals at work, to interject and to give daily, even hourly feedback on the ideas taking shape – a process that actively helps the design team. At its best, the floodlight of public design dialogue can illuminate many murky corners of private prejudice, and thus provide opportunities for more honest and productive debate. Usually some accord can be reached, but it is rarely possible to please all participants. However, by working out the most awkward and hotly debated problems in design detail it is possible to get close to common agreement about contentious issues.

But not everyone is going to be happy. The aim is not necessarily consensus (although that is an excellent outcome if possible); it is a fact of life that in almost every development scenario there are going to be winners and losers. Bearing in mind Michael Pyatok's concerns and critique of what he perceives to be New Urbanist priorities, one of the charrette team's main objectives should always be to minimize the disadvantages to individuals and groups within the community while capitalizing on the potential for overall community improvement. For concepts of social sustainability to work at the community level, public

participation is an absolute necessity: if residents and users can participate in decisions affecting their area, they will get a 'sense of psychological ownership.' In this way, urban places can be created within which 'harmonious, lively, sustainable communities can flourish' (Symes and Pauwels: p. 104, noting Rudlin and Falk, 1995). Therefore one of the primary features of the charrette process is the cyclical process of debate, design and demonstration; in this way issues of social equity always remain in view.

This exercise in building trust and the isolation of intransigent naysayers was well illustrated in the charrette for the Haynie-Sirrine neighborhood in Greenville, SC. This historically African-American community just south of downtown Greenville had been ravaged by neglect (see Figure 7.5) and the construction of a six-lane highway that bore through the middle of the neighborhood at an angle, damaging not only its frontage properties but much of the existing street grid network as well. In this instance, the neighborhood plan was the brainchild of a developer seeking to redevelop the site of a failing motel in the middle of the neighborhood. He convinced the city and other key landowners to pool their resources and create a redevelopment plan for the entire neighborhood that both capitalized on the redevelopment potential of key sites (the area was close to downtown and adjacent to a spectacular river gorge) while creating new and improved affordable housing for existing residents.

Using the motel banqueting room as a public studio, hundreds of citizens, property owners and city officials worked with the design team to craft the master plan during a 6-day planning and design charrette. All parties embraced the final plan, comprising a combination of redevelopment opportunities, protection of historic neighborhood resources, and the refurbishment and creation of new affordable housing. During the closing presentation on the last night of the charrette, a standing-room only crowd packed the temporary design studio. Team leaders began their digital presentation of dozens of plans, drawings, and strategies that had matured throughout the week. Suddenly, a man stood up and harangued the speakers. The fact that this individual was white instantly differentiated him from the rest of the predominately African-American crowd. What followed was both surprising and liberating. In a belligerent tone the speaker chided the designers for what he perceived as another attempt by government to move the 'black residents out.' Boos emanated from the audience and another person stood up, this time a resident.

Figure 7.5 Decayed house and public street in Greenville, SC, 2001. Shocking conditions can still be found in parts of the American South. Many New Urbanists are spurred by a sense of social justice to try and improve the living conditions of residents in neighborhoods such as these.

Without hesitation she said, 'If you were here all week you would know that what they are presenting is what we want.' Applause erupted from the meeting. This lady knew that the plan called for public investment in the substandard rental housing and new affordable housing that would allow existing residents to stay in the neighborhood. When members of the public defend the plan, the professionals know they have done a good job.

The planning and design process must be truly collaborative, and harness the talents and energies of all interested parties if the plan is to be both feasible and transformative in terms of bringing about change in a community. This is a hard task in a 4- or 5-day charrette, even over 7 days, but it is doable if the team listens attentively and, importantly, is *seen* to listen and take people seriously. The biggest compliment designers and planners can pay to members of the public is to take their ideas seriously and test them out quickly and vividly on paper or computer screen. The rhythm of a typical 4-day charrette is illustrated on the Charrette Process graphic (see Figure 7.6). In this graphic representation, Day 1 comprises Phase 1; Day 2 includes Phases 2 and 3; Day 3 equals Phases 4 and 5; and the final Day 4 wraps up with Phases 6 and 7. In a 7-day charrette, each phase corresponds to a working day.

A TYPICAL CHARRETTE

On Day 1, the design team sets up its workspace at an easily accessible venue within the study area and typically conducts a team meeting over lunch when the market analysts present their findings. Planning staff, elected officials and members of the public are welcome to attend, and often do, but the main purpose of this presentation is to make the design team aware of the economic parameters that surround the project in terms of absorption rates for different types of development, market rent structures, land costs, and local and regional trends. This analysis and its capacity to guide the design development of the project are key elements of any future plan's feasibility. This presentation is usually followed by a tour of the site and the first of a series of scheduled meetings with key stakeholders. The early evening is filled by dinner in the workspace with elected officials and local leaders, and prior to this some members of the design team may have put first thoughts on paper, relating site information and context to the main market opportunities or stated social objectives of the project. The main event of the first evening is a public presentation, at which the team leader explains the process and purposes of the charrette in order to create a clear understanding for everybody involved, followed by a structured work session designed to solicit the public's

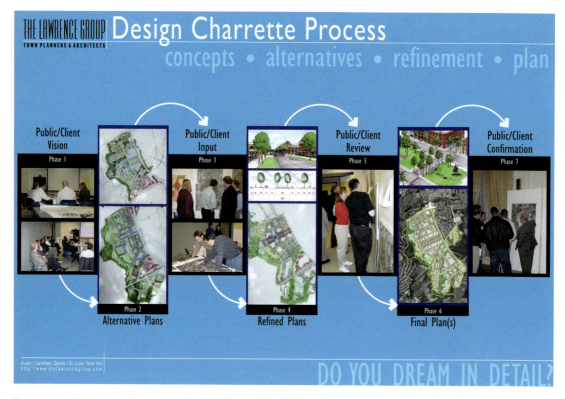

Figure 7.6 The Charrette Process. Illustration adapted by The Lawrence Group from the original on the National Charrette Institute's website: http://www.charretteinstitute.com/charrette.html

initial thoughts about the project. At this time, and throughout the charrette, particular attention should be paid to members of the local media, offering interviews and answering their questions carefully. Press support for and coverage of charrette events is very important (see Figure 7.4).

Day 2 begins with a working breakfast where the team runs over its plans for the day. Some members of the design team create the first of a series of alternative plans based on information gathered to date, including the public vision, while other team members participate in more scheduled meetings with stakeholder groups, gathering new information and relaying it back to designers working on various scenarios at the drawing boards and computers. Throughout the day one team member is allotted the task of greeting members of the public who wander in, and explaining to them what is happening and inviting their comments. At 5.30 (after work but before dinner) there is a public pin-up session of all the work produced that day where the team, members of the public and

various stakeholders critique the ideas and potential solutions. The drawings produced at this time are preliminary but detailed, usually in plan form but with the first of a series of three-dimensional sketches that may eventually be developed into final renderings during the course of the event (see Figure 7.7).

A high level of detail is required at all stages of the project. Loose 'bubble diagrams' of concepts are very rarely used; when a concept needs to be tested, it is done through scaled layouts of buildings and infrastructure, not abstract diagrams. This commitment to urban design detail allows much greater speed and accuracy of investigation, with the result that concepts are tested far more thoroughly than can be achieved using conventional planning graphics of signs, symbols and colors. To this end, three-dimensional illustrations play a vital role in the communication and presentation of ideas, and the team's illustrator begins to set up sketches during this second day, both to contribute to the ongoing discussion and development of ideas and also as the basis for the final presentation

Figure 7.7 Charrette Day 2; early evening pin-up. Drawings are preliminary but detailed so the audience can see plans of buildings and spaces highlighted with three-dimensional sketches of important concepts. Planner Craig Lewis from The Lawrence Group answers audience questions.

drawings. Accordingly, by late on the second day, the team tries to fix those locations that will play a major role in the plan and a team member is dispatched to take digital photographs for subsequent overdrawing by hand or computer. The final event of the second day is an open evening session where more public input is gathered from citizens who could not make earlier meetings and where the design team clarifies the major directions for the following day's work. Digitized images of each day's work can be posted on the sponsor's website to inform members of the public who may not be able to attend the event. E-mailed comments from citizens can also be received and fed into the team discussions.

The third day follows broadly the pattern of the previous sessions, where part of the design team develops a selected range of alternative scenarios to a more detailed level while others meet with additional individuals and groups. This input is used to improve the alternatives and create more detailed plans that are once more reviewed and critiqued by the public during sessions before and after dinner. That evening, the design team prioritizes all the feedback and refines the design concepts into a draft final plan ready for redrawing into presentation format; this redrawing process begins late that third evening and often continues long into the night, usually as a Photoshop collage of hand-drawn detailed plans for key areas laid into an aerial photograph (see Figure 7.8).

This last day differs in organization from the preceding ones. While the public are still allowed to wander in and observe, the time has passed for major public discussion; most team members are involved in presentation work – either finalizing drawings, figuring out development economics, public expenditures and tax revenues or modeling traffic flows. However, one person from the team is always on the look out for members of the public with interesting things to say, both for the content of the comments and to maintain the lines of open communication so important to the process. At least two team members are involved in preparing the evening's PowerPoint presentation, scanning and photographing images as soon as they become available.

The detailed presentation of all the material on the final evening comprises a well-produced PowerPoint summary of digitized plans and three-dimensional images, economic calculations, and implementation proposals. This is followed by detailed discussions; the original drawings line the walls of the room for further individual study by the public and one-on-one conversations with design team members. Additionally, at the closing presentation, team spokespersons should provide interviews to the local media to explain the proposals and invite the maximum public commentary about their contents. The PowerPoint can immediately be uploaded onto the sponsor's website for further public input.

It is important to note that the project does not start with the charrette nor is it complete when the charrette ends. Except in very low budget versions, the on-site charrette is normally preceded by several weeks of preparation, gathering and collating background material for analysis before the event begins, preparing site plans, taking photographs, undertaking market analyses, meeting with the key stakeholders, getting to grips with local politics, and generating news stories on local radio, TV and in the newspapers. After the charrette comes refinement of the documentation, particularly the development of detailed and prioritized implementation strategies that include form-based codes or revisions to existing ordinances. This period usually takes 4–6 weeks, and is followed by another major public meeting where the provisions of the new code can be fully explained and further feedback obtained. This meeting allows all participants to check the refined plan and provides one final feedback loop, although subsequent meetings are likely to be required on code issues prior to its adoption. These pre- and post-charrette activities point out the importance of charrette planning that goes beyond the on-site event itself, especially how to budget for the whole process and how to maintain quality control on the final products.

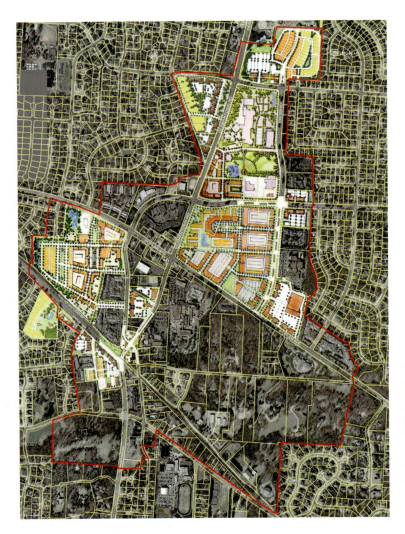

Figure 7.8 Photoshop collage; The Lawrence Group, Town Planners & Architects. Master plans are most easily produced by scanning or photographing detailed hand drawings and collaging them into an aerial photograph of the project area using Adobe Photoshop. This eliminates the previously arduous task of redrawing the whole area by hand.

CHARRETTE BUDGETS

One of the most important skills in preparing for a charrette is creating a workable budget that covers all necessary costs, provides company profit but still remains competitive enough to win the contract. Charrette teams usually come in two formats – either all the relevant professional skills are provided in-house by one large firm or, more usually, a lead firm with several but not all of the required skills assembles a team from a variety of other consultants who round out the professional expertise and perhaps provide important local knowledge and connections. In practice, even large in-house firms, especially if working far from their home base, usually have one or two local consultants to provide specific design and planning expertise and/or

economic information about market conditions in the area.

Charrettes are economical because they utilize highly productive work sessions that reach shared conclusions and thus avoid costly reworking of plans by consultants over the long periods of conventional processes. The concentrated focus and definitive end product of a true charrette is invaluable, and provides a much better method than the slow drip feed of community meetings once a month for several months. These lengthy enterprises, though worthy, drag the process out, lose momentum and end up being a burden on all involved. By contrast, an eight-person design team, working 12–14 hours a day for 4 days, can rack up the equivalent man-hours for one planner laboring on the problem all day, every day for nearly 3 months. To match the output of a 12-person team working for 7 days a single planner would have to work every weekday for half a year! And the brainpower increases exponentially because of the interaction between team members and the public!

Typical skill sets for charrette teams have already been noted: architecture, planning, urban design, landscape architecture, code writing, transportation planning, market analysis, economic development and graphic illustration form the core disciplines, and there may be some overlap in the personal skills of team members that can help reduce the size and cost of the team. For example, an architect may also be the illustrator. Another architect may also be a planner and/or urban designer. The planner may also understand economic development or code writing, or both, and so forth. At the same time it is very important to have sufficient personnel to handle both the design activities and the public participation functions effectively and seamlessly. It is also important to have someone on the team who is an excellent facilitator. This person must possess an active professional understanding of the issues involved in the project, either from a discipline base or local knowledge, and it is usually advantageous if this facilitation skill can be provided in-house rather than by means of a specialist brought in from outside. In the case study examples in this volume, the size of the charrette teams for each project numbered from nine to eleven people: the core unit comprised two planners, who also handled code writing and meeting facilitation; four architects, who contained within their number various skills in urban design, code writing, illustration, facilitation and planning; one transportation planner, a landscape architect with urban design skills and a market analyst. For the project illustrated in Chapter 8, two professionals with expertise in marketing, product branding and graphic design were added to the team because of the scope of that particular plan.

In practice, the budget usually controls the number of participants, although a team of eight to 10 people is normal for a project of any real size and complexity, and the project budget is a function of three basic elements:

1. The size and composition of the team necessary to conduct the charrette.
2. The length of the charrette.
3. The expected deliverables following the charrette.

The first two factors are a function of the size of the area to be studied, the detail required for realistic

implementation and the complexity of the problems. Only a seasoned charrette team leader can adequately determine these but there are some basic guidelines. First, if no planning has been done in the area or in the community, then some pre-design work will be necessary to assess the community's values and expectations. Often, because of lack of awareness of other possibilities elsewhere in the county, state or region, communities have low or modest expectations, and imagine something only slightly better than the last project built in that community, thus selling themselves short. The author has worked in several communities whose members were unaware of the power of the charrette process and three-dimensional design; accordingly, planners and elected officials anticipated merely updated versions of their old maps and policies. In such cases, it is valuable (if possible) to pack the planners, elected officials and advisory committee members in a bus, and give them a tour of other communities which have good examples of urban design and where circumstances of land area, growth pressures and demographics are similar. Too often, local boards and commissions comprise individuals who have limited exposure to other areas and ideas. Certainly the initial package sent by the charrette team to the potential client in response to a Request for Qualifications or Request for Proposals needs to illustrate very clearly the scope of work that is possible and normal within a well-run charrette; this is a very important step in client and public education as well as the best marketing and competitive strategy for winning the job.

Sometimes the client will specify a budget; in this case the charrette team skills have to be assembled in a way that fits within this figure. More usually it is up to the lead firm to estimate the likely costs and assemble a competitive bid. There is a difficult balance between covering the professional skills needed and keeping the costs within reasonable bounds. In practice 4-day charrettes, with their pre-charrette analysis work and post-charrette deliverables can cost anything between $80 000 and $180 000, dependent on the project scope and deliverables (approximately between £42 500 and £96 000). Of this amount, $40 000–60 000 (£21 250–32 000) is likely to be the cost of the basic charrette team members turning up on site for the event, producing a master plan in hard copy and digital format and presenting the plan in PowerPoint format at the closing. It is possible in some circumstances for a charrette to be conducted on a total budget in this lower cost bracket, but this low cost is predicated on all the site analysis, material collection and collation being provided in advance by the client or local authority; it represents simply the cost of the team members' time, meals and accommodation at a local hotel plus materials used during the event. No post-charrette production work is included in this low budget figure, and the charrette team members are likely to be limited to the smallest number who can provide basic planning, urban design, architecture, traffic planning and presentation skills. By comparison, the typical budget for an AIA R/UDAT is in the range of $40 000 (£21 250), of which nearly $26 000 (£13 800) covers the cost of the charrette itself (AIA: p. 41). The deliverables from the typical R/UDAT are generally less specific and focused when compared to the type of charrette described here, and this is reflected in the smaller budget.

Costs begin to rise from these lower figures according to the more comprehensive range of services and products envisaged by the client. Pre-charrette costs comprise travel, time spent meeting with key individuals prior to the event, perhaps holding a major public kick-off meeting a couple weeks ahead of the event in order to raise the project profile and public interest, undertaking detailed site analysis work, with site plan and aerial photograph preparation and printing, and market research studies. Extensive analysis and preparation work to set up the charrette can cost as much as the charrette event itself, particularly if extensive travel for the team members is involved. The costs of the charrette itself will increase if there is the need for a wider range of skills on the team, such as project marketing and 'rebranding' an area to improve its image, detailed computer modeling of traffic flows, civil engineering or specific expertise in sustainable landscape design. Branding exercises can appear superficial at first glance, and somewhat antithetical to the more substantive changes regarding social equity and environmental improvement that may be at the heart of charrette objectives, but experience has shown that given the image-driven proclivities that dominate British and American culture in the early 21st century, this kind of exercise in reframing public perception is often a very important precursor to public acceptance of other, more profound concepts.

Costs for post-charrette services and deliverables can also be extensive. A fully documented report, with implementation recommendations and strategies can add $10 000–15 000 (£5500–8000); a detailed form-based code developed from the charrette master plan, another $25 000 to as much as $70 000 (£13 300–37 200). Publicity materials such as posters that illustrate the plan and summarize its recommendations, detailed traffic analyses and calculations, the creation

of physical presentation models or high quality three-dimensional computer simulations all add to the cost of post-charrette activities, and a 'deluxe' charrette with all the above refinements can easily top $150 000 (£80 000). Prominent national and international firms in America have been known to charge as much as $250 000 (£133 000) for extensive 7- to 10-day charrettes.

Budgets for the charrette team can thus vary widely from *pro bono* efforts to expensive fees for internationally known firms. With the exception of AIA R/UDAT teams, low budget or *pro bono* volunteer efforts, although sometimes valuable, tend to lack the necessary breadth of disciplines to ensure full implementation; nor do they provide much in the way of project deliverables. These efforts often are valuable for creating a vision, but lack the essential detail to ensure accurate implementation. One notable exception was the Mississippi Forum led by the Congress for the New Urbanism in 2005 following the devastating Gulf coast hurricanes Katrina and Rita. Press coverage in the USA has preferred to highlight the political problems surrounding the charrette recommendations in the biggest community, Biloxi, MS, and to pass over the enthusiastic acceptance of proposed plans in other coastal communities such as Ocean Springs and Pass Christian (Lewis, J.: p. 103).

Firms who use conventional planning techniques often claim the charrette process is more expensive, but in fact charrette costs are very competitive with the conventional process. When the team is involved in the charrette, 100 percent of the professionals' focus is on the community. They work long hours to complete the work and have a number of disciplines working together to ensure that the plan is realistic and implementable. The team works and draws in the public eye to ensure that each version is consistent with the evolving public opinions that are generated through active engagement with the designers.

This focused professional effort remains competitive with the conventional process because although the latter has less time-intensive contact with the public, its 'drip feed' method of occasional and spaced out meetings mandates more revisions to plans and documents, and the time required to make changes between each public meeting adds considerably to project costs. Because the conventional process only uses brief public meetings to gather input, the planners and designers must rely upon a substantial set of untested assumptions back in their office when they begin to generate the plan. When they return to the public forum, they often bring back a plan that is production quality rather than a working draft because this provides a more effective visual presentation. To make changes in these plans can be expensive, yet in this conventional process the planners will go through similar exercises perhaps several times before the public agrees with the contents of the plan. How many times can the public attend meetings each month before they lose interest? Or remember what was in the plan the last time they saw it? With lengthy conventional processes, it sometimes seems as if the public 'gives in' rather than buys into the final outcome.

The key for success in winning charrette contracts is simple to state but not easy to achieve. One has to produce excellent design plans and illustrations that: (1) combine future vision with practicable feasibility; (2) meet goals for environmental sustainability and social equity (even if these are not specifically stated in the client's charrette objectives, they should be inherent in all design team judgments and decisions); (3) are produced with extensive public participation and community buy-in to the finished plan; and (4) identify actions for implementation that are clearly defined, costed and prioritized. Presentations at interview should illustrate and stress the comprehensiveness of the service and products, with specific emphasis on detailed implementation strategies and costs to enhance the feasibility of the planning and design solutions.

Charrette clients usually award contracts on the basis of a firm's or a team's reputation related to the projected costs. The temptation exists to cut costs to win the project, but in this context, reduced budgets directly affect the outcome and quality of the final products, and a firm's reputation can easily suffer as a result of undertaking projects too cheaply and not leaving themselves the ability to produce excellent work on time and in the quantity required at the end of the process.

CHARRETTE PRODUCTS

At the time of writing, most charrettes are relatively low-tech affairs, partly because sophisticated media and technology, despite their advantages, can introduce barriers of unfamiliarity in the public's mind that inhibit the direct, personal communication so vital to a successful process. Anyone can scribble a thought on a 'Post-it' note and place it on a map. Not everybody feels confident when presented with a computer interface at the charrette table. Technology can provide

considerable benefits to team members in their analysis and synthesis of complex factors, but this same technology can unwittingly reinforce an unwanted feeling of distance between the charrette team member who has the expertise to handle the digital interface and the member of the public who feels inhibited by his or her lack of skill. Despite these problems, digital media are increasingly having a useful impact on charrette methodology and products, and will quickly become more prevalent. There are two main forums where these changes are occurring: in the charrette studio itself and through 'distance learning' technologies whereby participants at remote locations can make useful contributions, either as design team consultants or simply as members of the public who are not able to be present at the charrette site.

In the most immediate sense, change is happening in the charrette studio itself, where some firms now offer completely digitized working methods and presentations, utilizing new software such as the INDEX Planning Support System, 'a suite of interactive GIS planning tools that measure existing conditions, evaluate alternatives, and support implementation of adopted plans' (www.crit.com/index/index.html). In addition to these sophisticated packages, more simple technologies such as 'keypad polling' during public sessions can increase the amount of public input. Handheld polling devices provide extensive and immediate feedback on various scenarios and options. Preferences are registered anonymously, no one group or individual can dominate the proceedings, and everyone's opinion counts.

At a basic level, particularly in relation to urban infill projects, three-dimensional graphics software, such as Sketch-Up, in combination with simple digital cameras, offer the design team convenient options for quickly representing alternative urban design and architectural possibilities. Increasingly, charrette teams utilize digital models of the site area, or portions thereof, in the design and presentation process, but these still need a lot of time to create the initial graphic information base. Ideally, a digital model of existing conditions should be prepared before the charrette begins, but this increases the time and expense for the firm or firms involved. Trying to build a digital model during the charrette usually takes one team member out of the interactive discourse with the public and is not recommended, but if the model is built beforehand and the work during the charrette involves only inserting different proposals either for static representations, or more dynamic 'fly-by' demonstrations, the time and money spent can pay handsome dividends. Another

177

promising software development is the link between Sketch-Up with Google Earth, so that when the aerial photograph is tilted, Sketch-Up can provide quick and very realistic three-dimensional axonometric projections. The author's charrette team has experimented with this technique, with only partial success, but the potential is enormous.

Something of a paradox exists regarding digital presentations in charrettes. While most sectors of British and American society are computer literate, or are fast becoming so, and computers are accepted and (usually) welcomed as facts of life, there is anecdotal evidence that the public at large still places higher value on beautifully handcrafted perspectives or carefully rendered plans from the pens and pencils of the designers. There remains a degree of skepticism about computer renderings and plans; they appear too 'easy,' too glib and therefore less trustworthy than traditionally rendered drawings. The author and many other professionals accordingly work in charrette teams that are digitally supported, not digitally driven, but this is certain to change over the next decade as computer graphics become the norm. The pace of change is as much a matter of public acceptance of the media as the charrette team's technical capacities. However, the value of hand drawing will remain a valuable communication tool and, equally importantly, a medium of conceptual design that can handle multiple concepts quickly and efficiently. The architect-illustrator on the author's charrette team can still produce a rendered perspective more efficiently and effectively by overdrawing a digital photograph by hand despite the ease of application offered by three-dimensional graphics programs (see Figure 8.21).

Computer installations and wireless technologies are now regularly part of any charrette setup, and are able to offer increased opportunities to connect with people and information distant from the charrette site. Charrette products are regularly uploaded onto websites for dissemination to the public throughout the event and can be updated as necessary after the charrette has finished to continue to receive public commentary. However, while real-time streaming and distance learning technologies are beginning to make an impact on charrette methodology, the main emphasis presently remains on direct face-to-face communication as the most important and vital form of communicative planning during the charrette. This immediacy of personal contact and interaction is likely to continue to frame charrette events for several years to come in the same way that the hand drawn sketch and perspective continues to hold sway over

computer rendering. The real promise that technology offers is the extensive democratization of community planning, where a public meeting meets a 'Sim City virtual world where everyone can role play as mayor, developer, ecologist or town planner. Ideas would rush from the bottom up to meet those coming from the top down' (Snyder: p. 24).

Whatever media are involved in the charrette process and product creation, the deliverables following a charrette usually include the following elements:

- Master plan map.
- Three-dimensional renderings.
- Project report.
- Detailed presentation (usually in PowerPoint).
- Digital files of all major drawings and recommendations ready for uploading to the client's website.

Beyond this package, the final product may vary widely by design team and project type. Other deliverables often include:

- Marketing posters/brochures.
- Supplementary PowerPoint presentations for technical or economic details.
- Form-based codes/design guidelines.
- Market feasibility analyses.
- Traffic impact analysis/modeling.
- Physical site models or computer simulations.

Master plans and their associated supplementary drawings of details and three-dimensional views, most usefully in the form of street-level perspectives, form the heart of the final charrette presentation. The cynically simplistic cliché about urban design – give the client a big colored drawing – holds good here. A large, finely rendered master plan is the primary product, and one that communicates all the essential points concerning the future vision for the project (see Figures 7.8, 8.6 and 9.13). This is most effective when the public sees the drawing literally taking shape before their eyes from the pens and pencils of the designers, where they can see ideas that were discussed earlier in the charrette crystalizing in the final plan. In developing the graphics, all master plans must strike a balance between two different objectives. On the one hand, they must provide clear vision and directions about future developments and their form on the landscape; on the other, they must not become rigid blueprints that could stifle future design as circumstances change. To achieve these sometimes contradictory aims, master plans should illustrate 'best-case scenarios,' depicting well-considered solutions to problems of urban infrastructure, environmental and social sustainability, economic development opportunities, building massing and spatial layout, and transportation and parking. They can do this best by realistic depictions of proposed buildings, streets, parks and parking areas. These are not diagrammatic drawings; they conform to the basic charrette principle of designing in detail.

However, for all their apparent specificity, master plans produced through charrettes are illustrative rather than definitive. Good master plans will be based on deep structural understandings of site characteristics, potentials and limitations, along with relevant social, economic and political circumstances, and they will be produced by extensive collaboration with the community. Because of these intertwined factors, the provisions illustrated in the final drawings will be robust and stand the test of time in terms of their continued relevance as times change. One of the basic precepts of form-based coding is that buildings can be adapted over time to host numerous and diverse uses, so buildings and spaces given one kind of life in the master plan may take on different uses in the future with perhaps substantial interior renovations but limited changes to the external fabric of urban form and space. The form-based or design code derived from the master plan is the instrument that most accurately manages the future build-out for the development, perhaps over several years: this code guides the design of new buildings and urban spaces so they fit with the spirit and intentions of the plan until such time as the plan is complete or some radical changes in circumstances necessitate a revision to the original documents.

The purpose of the charrette master plan drawing is to communicate the main concepts that will guide new development quickly and effectively to a lay audience. This is best achieved by illustrating likely outcomes in terms of new buildings, landscapes and urban infrastructure. Some presentation methods simply show the building footprints rendered in color according to the uses of the buildings, but this undercuts the basic premise of form-based codes – that the use of buildings changes over time while the form remains relatively unaltered – and single-function colors deny the mixed-use content of many urban buildings. Various attempts to show mixed uses in a single building footprint, such as mixing the different use colors within the plan footprint, diagonally, or lining the shape with the color of the ground floor use and filling in the remainder with colors representing the primary

uses of the upper floors, tend to be hard to read, and at worst can obscure, like camouflage, the figure-ground quality of the master plan, where the buildings and spaces read as symbiotic elements (see Figure 7.9). Another alternative is to use a single color that means 'mixed use,' but the easiest graphic for a lay audience to understand is a master plan rendered as a 'rooftop' plan or aerial view that depicts the buildings in a representational or 'naturalistic' manner. In this technique, buildings are drawn with realistic pitched or flat roofs and with the spaces between the buildings fully rendered in terms of streetscape and landscape detail. This level of detail is akin to an aerial photograph, which is a medium understood by most people. To collage the plan for the project area into an aerial photograph of the surrounding context is a very useful presentation device for a lay audience; in this way it is possible to draw details such as green roofs or extensive solar panel/photovoltaic systems which can bring to the fore issues of sustainability (see Figure 9.19).

By drawing accurately in detail (*not* impressionistically), the building types with their roof plans, detailed road layouts, parking areas, parks and playgrounds can be rendered in ways that are easy for members of the public to understand: they can generally recognize

Figure 7.9 Plan detail with stripes; The Lawrence Group, Town Planners & Architects. Attempting to pinpoint uses in this way undercuts the central concept of form-based zoning that uses may change over time while building forms remain largely unaltered. This plan remains a functional diagram rather than a means of communicating the urban design qualities of buildings and spaces.

houses, or apartment buildings, or offices, or grocery stores and other building types by the size and shape of the building footprints and their surrounding landscape detail without the need for a detailed color code. Building roofs are best colored brown (if grey is used to represent asphalt on flat roofs, the plan can easily become graphically dominated by that color); pitched roofs should be differentiated by heavier shading on one side of the pitch. If flat roofs are planted green roofs, some small-scale landscape detail can usefully be drawn. Roads and parking areas are best colored with a light beige rather than representational grey, as extensive areas of grey tend to dominate the drawing and reduce its ability to communicate the holistic nature of the building to space relationships. Different colors of green can usefully distinguish private open space (lightest) from public open space (darker) with tree mass depicted by the darkest green of all. The use of heavier line weights to outline portions of the building plan or consistent shadow casts from the buildings and trees to emphasize the three-dimensionality of the forms are also useful presentation techniques as they aid the naturalistic quality of the drawing (see Figure 7.10; compare with Figure 7.9). In charrettes and other situations where public involvement is

important, drawings should always be as realistic as possible. The kinds of slick, abstracted graphics aimed at impressing (or confusing) fellow professionals that are common in other varieties of architectural presentations have no place in this context. Straightforward plan graphics and convincing three-dimensional renderings are the stock-in-trade of successful charrette teams.

While the detailed master plan is the single most important artifact to come from a charrette itself, the principal post-charrette product is a final, polished project report. This document includes an executive summary of the main plan proposals, backed by the full panoply of project drawings and elaborated by a detailed implementation strategy defining and prioritizing the tasks to be accomplished and identifying the responsible parties for each action. Related to this implementation strategy are economic calculations of development yield forecasts (the amount and approximate value of new developments) and estimates of the increased tax revenues that will accrue over time to the municipality from new development. These figures provide valuable information to elected officials and staff charged with executing the plan; council members in particular need to be convinced of the plan's economic benefits to both public and private sectors if they are to champion its proposals. It is thus important to demonstrate that the costs of major new public investments proposed in the master plan can be recouped in whole or substantial part within (preferably) a 10-year time frame. This reassures elected officials, staff and public alike that new expenditures are not reckless gambles with public money. Examples of implementation strategies and analyses of development costs and revenues are illustrated in Chapter 8.

A form-based code keyed from the master plan comprises the last component of the full charrette package of services. Without this code, the master plan is reduced to a vision document without appropriate mechanisms for control of development type and quality. An experienced New Urbanist code writer can normally produce a suitably detailed form-based code in 4–6 weeks after the completion of the charrette master plan. Increasingly in American practice the provisions of the Transect methodology are used to define appropriate areas and their hierarchical relationships and these classifications by urban form and scale are overlaid on the relevant sectors of the master plan. It is not normal for the code to be produced within the charrette time frame or format, although the availability of the Transect concept and graphics

Figure 7.10 Plan detail with shadow; The Lawrence Group, Town Planners & Architects. This master plan excerpt depicts all buildings with one 'naturalistic' roof color. The uses of the buildings can be inferred from the sizes and shapes of the building footprints and roofscapes: this example shows town homes with rear garages, detached houses and commercial buildings. The buildings and urban spaces can be easily understood in a manner akin to an aerial photograph, and lining the buildings, trees and cars with shadows provides extra three-dimensional emphasis.

allows the main form-based principles to be set out and explained in the final public presentation. Once this principle has been understood and accepted, the detail code writing can take place over subsequent weeks with separate presentations made to staff and elected officials to check progress and move towards formal adoption in due course. Complying with various and varying state laws governing the adoption of new planning legislation in the USA means this period of code writing, public presentation, public comment, revision and final adoption can take anywhere from 6 months to over a year for new, fully fledged form-based zoning ordinances. If the code provisions are amendments to existing ordinances this period can be considerably reduced. Examples of all these charrette processes and products are illustrated in the final two case study chapters.

Preamble to case studies

Democratic debate is vital in all types of design processes about making urban places, and the following two case studies illustrate what is achievable by using design charrettes to stimulate public involvement in the creation of new master plans. In both charrettes, all the work illustrated was created during the public process. The only work not carried out in public were those tasks required as preparation for most charrettes, such as economic analyses of existing development and statistical projections about future growth, public opinion surveys, traffic data collection, environmental analyses, and the collation of demographic data. Each charrette team also worked with both municipalities before the charrettes to produce full and accurate mapping of the area to a large scale, showing all roads, streets and structures, topography, tree mass, floodplains and property boundaries. Other meetings were arranged with the sponsoring groups to identify and meet key stakeholders. After the charrettes were completed, team members prepared the detailed project reports, including zoning code recommendations and other implementation strategies.

The master plans deal with very different situations. The Huntersville, NC, study examines how to redevelop approximately 710 acres (287 hectares) of a fading downtown core within a community only 12 miles north of the major city of Charlotte, NC, that has grown dramatically from a small farming village into a prosperous suburban town of over 30 000 people (see Figure 8.6). The plan for Concord, NC, a former mill town 25 miles northeast of Charlotte, illustrates the potential for a major urban extension, located on 780 acres (315 hectares) of greenfield land circumscribed by sporadic and uncoordinated low-density suburban development (see Figure 9.13).

The Huntersville master plan is intended to guide development in the short and medium term, stimulating action to revive the downtown as an urgent matter of civic improvement and economic development. Each project in the master plan is specifically tailored to market and site conditions. The Concord plan has different objectives: to trigger an awareness in the minds of local officials, developers and citizens about more sustainable and environmentally sensitive forms of growth than the generic suburban subdivisions and strip centers that dominate that community's townscape. Although this plan is designed and drawn in detail to communicate these design principles and development potential, the projects illustrated are more conceptual than definitive.

Apart from these physical and programmatic differences, the legal context of development control regulations also varies. Huntersville, as discussed earlier, has operated a sophisticated form-based zoning ordinance since 1996; the recommendations of the master plan fitted directly within the existing regulatory scheme with only minor amendments. Concord, by contrast, has worked with conventional zoning regulations for many years, but recently added 'traditional neighborhood' and 'transit-oriented neighborhood' classifications to permit and encourage more compact 'urban village' types of development. As part of the implementation strategies for the master plan described in Chapter 9, the charrette team developed a form-based code for mixed-use districts that was added to the town's existing ordinance. The limited and partial success of this process illustrates the limitations of 'grafting on' form-based regulations to a conventional zoning ordinance, even one that is generally well organized.

The on-site charrettes and associated work on both case study projects were undertaken by a team led by the North Carolina office of The Lawrence Group, Town Planners and Architects, headquartered in St Louis, under the leadership of Craig Lewis, AICP, with the assistance of several other professionals from a variety of firms and design disciplines in the Charlotte region. The author, in addition to his position as Professor of Urban Design at the University of North Carolina at Charlotte, is a Senior Urban Designer with The Lawrence Group and led the urban design effort on the two projects. The Huntersville master plan was honored by the North Carolina Chapter of the American Planning Association in 2006 with its Smart Growth Award.

Case Study I: Downtown Redevelopment, Huntersville, NC

EXISTING CONDITIONS

The town of Huntersville is located in northern Mecklenburg County in the state of North Carolina. Incorporated in 1873, the town's early history was tied to farming and its location on a once busy but now rarely used rail corridor connecting the town of Statesville to the north, to the city of Charlotte to the south. Huntersville's first century was marked by very slow growth and development, with a 1990 US Census population of approximately 3000. Fueled by improved accessibility to Charlotte (via new interchanges on adjacent Interstate-77) and the draw of Lake Norman, a large man-made lake created by Duke Energy Company to serve their nearby nuclear power station, development during the 1990s rapidly increased the town's population to 29 387 in 2003 (NC State Data Center, 2003 Certified Municipal Population Estimates).

To cope with this high growth rate, and to avoid being inundated by the waves of generic suburban development moving north from Charlotte, Huntersville enacted a comprehensive form-based zoning ordinance in 1996, one of the first communities in America to do so (Walters and Brown: pp. 220–221). The intention of the new ordinance was to increase the standards of urban and environmental design in new development, an objective that has been largely successful over the last 10 years. However, even with sophisticated urban design controls at its disposal, the legal limitations of the American planning system prevent Huntersville from undertaking the kind of pro-active spatial planning that is normal in the UK. This puts the town in the position of responding to market-driven development rather than directing it to preferred locations. Thus most recent developments, although better designed than typical examples

elsewhere, have taken place in suburban locations, driven by the accessibility and availability of land adjacent to freeway interchanges on Interstate-77. This kind of development is exemplified by the well-known Birkdale Village, a mixed-use, walkable 'urban village' some 3 miles from Huntersville's old downtown core (see Figure 8.1).

This suburban expansion has left the small downtown area to stagnate, despite public investment in a new town hall and police station along with the town's main fire station and a small farmers' market (see Figure 8.2). The town center developed originally along the rail line adjacent to the intersection of Highway 115 running north–south and Gilead Road/Huntersville–Concord Road running east–west. The prosperity of this central area faded with the loss of regular train service and the construction of an interstate freeway three-quarters of a mile to the west, which drew new commercial and residential development to greenfield land around its interchanges, one of which (Exit 23) provides a link to the downtown area. In recent years the Charlotte Area Transit System (CATS) has developed plans to upgrade this old rail line to operate a new commuter passenger service linking Huntersville and its adjacent towns of Cornelius and Davidson to the north with the city of Charlotte to the south. The first trains are planned to run sometime in 2012, and in expectation of this new public transit service Huntersville and its neighboring communities have tried to stimulate a series of transit-oriented developments around the proposed train stations, one of which would be in downtown Huntersville. These transit plans are the catalyst for efforts to redevelop the old town center into a mixed-use core worthy of a community of Huntersville's new size and stature. The Huntersville downtown

Figure 8.1 Birkdale Village, Huntersville, NC, 2003; Shook Kelley, Architects. The mixed-use core of Birkdale Village links to adjacent developments through a connected network of streets. The urban form of this development is directly attributable to the town's form-based zoning ordinance. *(Photograph by Aerial Dimensions. Reproduced courtesy of the Town of Huntersville)*

master plan, completed in autumn 2004, was the culmination of an intensive community input process, and was designed to provide the foundation for revitalization and redevelopment efforts around the historic downtown core and surrounding areas.

The downtown Huntersville planning area encompasses approximately 710 acres (287 hectares), and includes a number of retail, service, office, governmental and residential uses. A local park fills much of the northwest portion of the study area adjacent to the downtown core. A variety of undeveloped properties and vacant lots are scattered throughout the planning area, and a general air of decay and lack of investment permeates the northeastern part of the site, dominated by the derelict Anchor textile mill located on a disused

30-acre (12.14-hectare) site adjacent to the railroad track (see Figure 8.3). Although Huntersville's general demographics are well above the national American average [the median household income is over $70 000 (£37 300) compared to a figure of $44 684 (£23 831) nationally], figures for the area around downtown are considerably lower, with much of the housing stock comprising mobile homes or small houses of generally medium or poor quality (see Figure 8.4). Most of this substandard housing comprises the remnants of a small mill village east of the rail line that served the textile plant.

East of downtown is Vermillion, one of the first 'traditional neighborhood developments' in the southeastern USA. Designed by Duany Plater-Zyberk during

Figure 8.2 Downtown Huntersville, NC, 2004. As Huntersville grew from a struggling small town into a prosperous bedroom community for the adjacent city of Charlotte, most growth occurred around the adjacent freeway interchanges (see Figures 8.1 and 8.7) leaving the old town center underdeveloped.

Figure 8.4 Existing housing, Huntersville, NC. In older parts of town, housing is unpretentious but affordable for lower income residents, with several mobile homes.

Figure 8.3 Anchor Mill, Huntersville, NC. Apart from agriculture, textile mills historically formed the backbone of the local and regional economy. By the 1990s, cheaper foreign imports killed off the remnants of the Carolina textile industry, leaving a legacy of empty, decaying buildings.

the mid-1990s, this high-quality housing development was well conceived but not easily connected to the downtown area (see Figure 8.5). An attempt by Duany Plater-Zyberk to remedy this situation in 1999 by extending the Vermillion planning area to include a new high-density transit-oriented development on the nearby Anchor Mill site failed to come to fruition.

The majority of the Downtown Huntersville Planning Area is within the Town Center (TC) and Neighborhood Residential (NR) zoning districts.

A Traditional Neighborhood Development (TND) Overlay fits on the eastern edge of the study area incorporating the Vermillion neighborhood. All these zoning districts are controlled by form-based zoning principles.

EXECUTIVE SUMMARY

The downtown master plan was intended to establish a clear framework for the revitalization of downtown Huntersville through a series of incremental private and public development decisions, and within this overall purpose, there were three specific objectives. First, the plan sought to provide policy, programmatic and capital investment recommendations for public buildings and transportation infrastructure in the downtown area. Second, it proposed a number of realistic private development opportunities specifically designed to create a more vibrant location for all who visit, work and live in the area. Third, to help with the creation of a sense of place in the minds of residents and visitors alike, the plan recommended a series of marketing and branding strategies for the promotion of Huntersville, and the downtown area in particular, around a 'green' theme that capitalized on the community's agricultural roots and strong horticultural emphasis in the make-up of current businesses.

Overall, new development in the master plan comprised:

- 72 single-family detached homes
- 94 duplex homes (semi-detached)

Figure 8.5 Aerial view of Huntersville, NC, with the Vermillion neighborhood (right). The traditional neighborhood of Vermillion, designed by Duany Plater-Zyberk in the mid-1990s, provides a structured counterpoint to the diffuse and scattered patterns of development in and around the downtown area.

- 173 town homes
- 465 apartments or condominiums
- 100 units of senior housing or assisted living accommodation
- 292 925 square feet (27 214 square meters) of office space
- 205 300 square feet (19 073 square meters) of retail space
- 59 000 square feet (5481 square meters) of civic space
- 13 000 square foot (1208 square meter) Growers' Hall (expanded farmers' market)
- 27 600 square foot (2564 square meter) Civic Plaza
- 400-space car parking deck in the civic core area
- Road improvements to upgrade Main Street parallel to the railroad track.

The project report noted that patience would be necessary as components of this plan might take 15–20 years to reach fruition. The downtown master plan was both definitive and conceptual in its illustration of development within the area; it expected that individual project plans might vary but specified that the delineated framework of urban spaces, streets, development intensity, mixture of uses and urban form should be consistent with the plan (see Figures 8.6 and 8.28).

DESIGN PROCESS – ANALYSIS

Feedback from civic leaders, government representatives and residents suggested that the community

Figure 8.6 Huntersville Downtown Master Plan, 2004; The Lawrence Group, Town Planners & Architects. The master plan capitalizes on the proposed commuter rail service to Charlotte as one catalyst of future development, together with a boosted civic and institutional presence downtown, providing the facilities missing from the faux town center at Birkdale Village (see Figure 8.1).

continues to embrace its historical rural roots and small-town character despite its extensive suburbanization and the relative lack (from a British perspective) of substantial built heritage. Some older structures have remained, scattered throughout the planning area, and these should be preserved and adapted to new uses as necessary. The challenge facing the design team was to turn this sense of heritage into something more concrete, to re-establish the town's identity and to use new development to create a 'sense of place' within the downtown area.

Birkdale Village, 3 miles from downtown at Exit 25 off Interstate-77 (see Figure 8.1) operates as a *de facto* town center, even though it includes no civic functions. One specific opportunity for downtown was to position itself as a counterpoint to Birkdale Village by capitalizing on its active civic facilities, and expanding these functions along with commercial, recreational and residential opportunities linked to the proposed new passenger train service to and from Charlotte. Pre-charrette analysis suggested that rebranding and marketing the downtown area through new graphics, signage and publicity campaigns would be an important companion to the normal disciplines of urban design and traffic planning, and the charrette team was enlarged accordingly to include that expertise.

As part of the analysis undertaken prior to the charrette, team members prepared a detailed market analysis to ascertain prevailing conditions and anticipated absorption rates for new development along with future prospects, especially looking for potential 'niche market' businesses and local opportunities that could distinguish the downtown area from the generic national retailers at Birkdale Village.

Market Analysis

The market analysis evaluated the physical, legal and economic feasibility for future development throughout downtown Huntersville. The town as a whole has enjoyed sustained affluence and growth over the past decade, benefiting from its inclusion in the booming Charlotte Metropolitan Statistical Area (MSA) where the economy is primarily based on banking, healthcare, energy and retail. (Charlotte is the headquarters city for two of America's biggest banks, Bank of America and Wachovia, and a major energy corporation, Duke

Energy; it is also a hub airport for US Airways.) Huntersville's population and job growth in non-manufacturing sectors has increased substantially as a part of this prosperity, demonstrating the town's potential as a diverse, service-oriented local economy. These factors, coupled with a quality of life that has attracted young families and professionals, have stimulated demand for a variety of housing types and commercial buildings for offices, service occupations and shopping. The specialists on the charrette team examined trends in the major market sectors of office, retail and residential development, and presented several conclusions that impacted the initial design directions and the final outcome.

The town has a large, high-quality office park adjacent to Exit 23 on Interstate-77 with room for expansion, and in 2005 a new hospital was completed within this development about 1 mile west of downtown. Opposite the hospital at the same freeway exit is a well-established multi-use development of retail, offices and housing known as Rosedale, which together with other commercial and retail buildings around the interchange, provides for many of the downtown population's everyday needs (see Figure 8.7).

Figure 8.7 Rosedale development and Presbyterian hospital, Huntersville, NC. In the late 1990s, the author helped resolve the plans of two competing developers on the Rosedale site. The end result was a cohesive plan for shops, offices and housing organized around a connected street pattern instead of separate parking lots. Less ambitious than the mixed-use Birkdale Village (see Figure 8.1), Rosedale has become a model for 'multi-use developments' where uses are horizontally adjacent but not mixed vertically within buildings. Like Birkdale, the urban form of this development was created through the town's form-based zoning regulations. (*Photograph by Aerial Dimensions; reproduced courtesy of Town of Huntersville*)

Shopping venues in Huntersville along Interstate-77 host an array of local, regional, and national retailers and restaurants. Combined, these centers total approximately 1 284 000 square feet (119 287 square meters) including 286 000 square feet (26 570 square meters) at Birkdale Village. Huntersville is evolving from a suburban bedroom community, whose primary employment once resided in the Charlotte area, to one that is establishing its own economic base in the professional service sector. Along with these commercial sectors, the residential apartment submarket has enjoyed fairly stable vacancy and rental rates compared to the remainder of the regional housing scene.

The analysis concluded that future employment growth within the community would be primarily service related jobs in various professional and medical fields, and this would create demand for additional office space. The 'multiplier effect' of this growth would in turn lead to a demand for additional housing and retail, and the charrette team was guided by the following programmatic factors in developing the master plan.

Office and Retail

The study suggested that the most appropriate additions should comprise a mix of office and retail uses in mixed-use buildings wherever possible throughout the area. These should generally consist of smaller, residential-scaled buildings along the east–west Gilead Road corridor leading from the Interstate to downtown to fit in with the existing pattern, transitioning into higher density and larger structures in the downtown core.

Residential

The study indicated most new housing should comprise apartments, condominiums and town homes to meet the density expectations for downtown and transit-oriented development. These densities should range between 10 and 25 units per acre (25 and 62.5 dwellings per hectare): a smaller number of single-family dwellings should be reserved for locations adjacent to existing detached homes to minimize conflicts with settled neighborhoods. All market segments should be covered, from affordable to luxury in both rental and housing for sale. Careful attention should be given to integrating new housing with existing developments and creating pedestrian and vehicular

connections to the adjacent civic and commercial uses throughout downtown.

Public Space

Although not normally a category of market research, the analysis also pinpointed the importance of attractive public space as a supporting factor in promoting economic activity. In particular the analysis highlighted the potential for creating a focal public space in the downtown core for social gatherings which residents and people from adjacent neighborhoods could enjoy. This space would include an outdoor venue to accommodate larger events and the farmers' market. In the same vein, the study noted that careful attention should be given to creating an attractive streetscape leading from the Interstate to the downtown area, including sidewalks, street trees and lighting as critical design elements. Distinctive signage could also help create an identity for the downtown area.

The overall goal would be to provide a destination for a more unique, intimate urban experience – an inviting and interesting place to draw residents, train commuters, families, shoppers, and workers from the hospital and other places of employment. In this way, the downtown area would become the main sub-regional focus of economic activity for the northern part of Mecklenburg County east of Interstate-77.

Physical Analysis

In addition to the market studies, and prior to any design work, a physical 'ripe and firm' analysis was completed for all of the properties in the Downtown Planning Area. 'Firm' properties were those that were generally in good condition with stable uses; little change was recommended in these cases. Properties that were determined to be 'ripe' for development included those that were undeveloped, under-developed (where additional development opportunities existed on the property including expansion of existing buildings and new construction) or that could be redeveloped (such as an old, vacant shopping center). In essence, this analysis identified those properties that should be left alone and those that presented development opportunities (see Figure 8.8). Any buildings and sites with historic value were identified as prime candidates for conservation (see Figure 8.9).

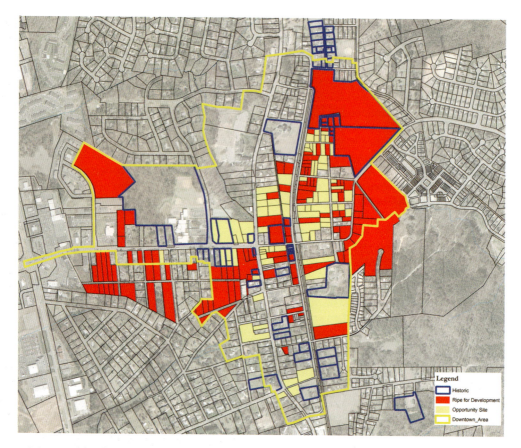

Figure 8.8 Ripe and Firm analysis, Huntersville Master Plan, 2004; The Lawrence Group, Town Planners & Architects. This analysis identifies sites for development and preservation based on physical character, condition and market availability.

Figure 8.9 Main Street, Huntersville, NC. The remnants of a classic American one-sided Main Street along the railroad provide most of the remaining historic buildings in the downtown area.

DESIGN PROCESS – PUBLIC INPUT

The master planning effort was presaged by a kick-off meeting 1 month prior to the charrette consisting of an opening presentation and an interactive workshop to gain initial feedback from citizens. Once this information had been evaluated, the charrette was held over 5 days in late September 2004 at the Huntersville town hall in the downtown, where a temporary design studio was set up, complete with drawing tables, meeting areas, computer equipment and a presentation space.

Public input was an integral part of the planning process in developing a realistic revitalization plan. Throughout the charrette, residents, business owners, property owners, developers, economic development officials, government agencies and community groups shared their thoughts and visions about various topics related to the area's future, including: transportation, retailing, parking, cultural development, new buildings, urban spaces and signage. The schedule included numerous opportunities for public participation through small group meetings, individual conferences and a questionnaire prepared by the charrette team (see Figure 8.10). The charrette concluded with a digital presentation of the plan's recommendations and an exhibition of the drawings.

Charrette participants identified a number of important issues relevant to the planning process that were carefully reviewed by the planning team and served as a foundation for the master plan. In many respects citizen comments closely mirrored the recommendations from the market analysis and the physical survey of the study area. Downtown Huntersville was described as being devoid of identity and lacking a significant attraction. Many commented that the business district lacked basic services such as a grocery store, a coffee shop and nightlife, and suggested it would be improved by direct connections to a gathering place, such as an amphitheatre or green, parks and a cultural facility. Others said they did not patronize the downtown as much as they would like due to limited parking and congested traffic. The main intersection of north–south and east–west routes at the town center handled 20 000 vehicles a day, and performed poorly at peak times causing considerable delays. This condition was exacerbated by the fact there was very little room within existing rights-of-way for street widening or extra turn lanes.

During the charrette, discussion evolved within two distinct sets of criteria – what the charrette team described as 'structural' and 'non-structural' deficiencies that needed to be remedied. Structural deficiencies included those tangible items requiring direct physical attention such as new buildings for businesses and housing, signage, streetscapes, traffic management and parking. Non-structural deficiencies

	Monday 9/27/2004	PLANNING & DESIGN	Tuesday 9/28/2004	PLANNING & DESIGN	Wednesday 9/29/2004	PLANNING & DESIGN	Thursday 9/30/2004	PLANNING & DESIGN	Friday 10/1/2004	Tuesday 10/5/2004
8:00	Breakfast		Breakfast		Breakfast		Breakfast		Breakfast	
9:00	9:00 Design Studio Setup and Tour of Study Area		8:00 Business Owners		9:00 Area Developers		PLANNING & DESIGN		PLANNING & DESIGN	
	11:00 Utilities		10:00 Major Property Owners		11:00 Streetscaping & Signage					
12:00	DDA/Econ. Dev. Lunch and Market Study Overview		Lunch		Lunch		Lunch		Lunch	
1:00			1:00 Arts & Recreation		1:00 Design Standards & Codes		PLANNING & DESIGN		Close-Up Studio and Prepare Final Presentation	
	2:00 Transportation & Parking		3:00 Public Safety		Hold for Additional Meetings					
5:00	5:00 Dinner with Committee & Elected/Appt'd Officials		5:30 Pin-Up Session and Project Update		5:30 Pin-Up Session and Project Update		5:30 Pin-Up Session and Project Update		5:30 Pin-Up Session and Project Update	
6:00			Dinner		Dinner		Dinner			
7:00	Opening Presentation and Facilitated Design Session		7:00 Interested Residents and Citizens		7:00 Interested Residents & Citizens		7:00 Interested Residents & Citizens			7:00 Closing Presentation

Figure 8.10 Charrette schedule, Huntersville Master Plan, 2004; The Lawrence Group, Town Planners & Architects. All design work was completed by the end of Friday. Over the weekend the team created a more sophisticated digital presentation for a town council meeting the following Tuesday.

included marketing and other non-tangible consider-ations that make up the 'culture' of a community; in other words, how the community leaders, business owners and residents perceive and communicate what Huntersville is about.

With 'structural' changes, the continued renovation and new construction of additional space could com-bine with other improvements in access, circulation and parking to provide incentives and increased oppor-tunities for people to come downtown to buy goods and services. The other main objective in reviving downtown was to attract citizens to come downtown to participate in public gatherings and events. These are 'non-structural' changes, and include recruitment and retention efforts to bring retailers and people together via programmed events. These would include coop-erative marketing plans with downtown businesses and civic leaders, and the creation of a new image and sense of expectation through a place-specific advertis-ing campaign.

New marketing strategies would allow the down-town to 'brand' itself with an identity and purpose, which then could be communicated effectively to Huntersville residents, workers and visitors. When a spatial structure is created with buildings, streetscapes, signage and parking to support commercial and resi-dential activities, and combined with a mix of public and cultural events, the results bring people together and create a sense of 'destination.' This concept has evolved into what industry analysts in the USA call 'lifestyle communities' with a sense of place that draws people to visit and to stay. Indeed, the incorpo-ration of a range of housing types, including housing specifically for senior citizens, makes such places attrac-tive for people to 'age in place,' i.e. to be able to grow old within the same community without having to sell property and move away to specific retirement communities. This is an important public health issue being studied in many American communities.

DESIGN PROCESS – DEVELOPMENT STRATEGIES AND PROJECTS

Development opportunities that capitalized on the community's history and the potential to fill market 'niches' gave rise to several design, planning and mar-keting strategies for the downtown area which were elaborated by site-specific design proposals. These were grouped under five categories: Transportation,

Circulation and Parking; Civic Infrastructure; Private Development Opportunities; Marketing and Branding Strategies; and Environmental Protection.

Transportation, Circulation and Parking

The main recommendations in this category were highlighted as follows.

(1) Computer simulations showed that the best way to mitigate traffic congestion in downtown would be to upgrade an existing local street (Main Street) parallel to Highway 115 and adjacent to the rail line to implement a 'two-way pair' system of streets for north-south traffic movement. This would require widening Main Street to 24 feet (7.3 meters) and adding dedicated left-turn lanes, synchronized traffic signals, and new connections with Highway 115 north and south of the downtown area (see Figure 8.11). Motorists would be given options for through move-ment or local access and pedestrians would be protected by keeping vehicle speeds low with narrow street widths. The improvements to Main Street would be compatible with the designs of the commuter train sta-tion and Growers' Market at Garden Hall (see Civic Infrastructure below). The costs of these street improve-ments would need to be negotiated on a shared basis with the North Carolina Department of Transportation (NC DOT) and added to the regional Transportation Improvement Program within a 5-year time frame.

(2) Site the commuter rail station in downtown on the north side of Huntersville–Concord Road. This would provide easier access and enable the station to connect with other public components of the plan such as the Growers' Market and the new town square (see Figures 8.13 and 8.17). The plan recommended that all urban elements such as lighting, railings, benches, drinking fountains and trash receptacles pro-duced by the CATS Public Art-in-Transit program be consistent with the detailing around the Garden Hall facility to tie the two together visually and establish a community identity for the station.

(3) Construct a shared-use parking deck with a minimum of 400 spaces in the downtown area to sup-port the commuter rail station, the proposed Growers' Market and new cultural facilities as well as downtown merchants (see Figures 8.13 and 8.17). Three-story, mixed-use buildings should mask the deck and create attractive frontages along public streets. These buildings would provide private development opportunities to

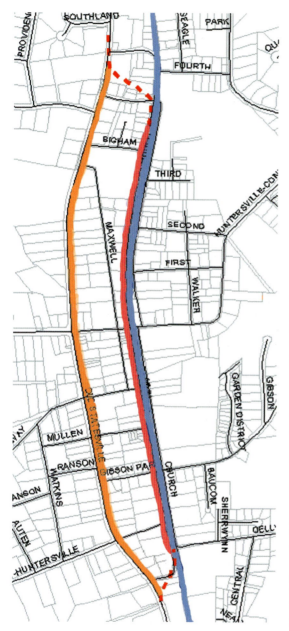

Figure 8.11 Transportation strategy, Huntersville Master Plan, 2004; The Lawrence Group, Town Planners & Architects. The proposed commuter rail line is shown in blue, the existing Highway 115 in orange and the upgraded Main Street in red. New street connections at north and south extremities (dotted red) create a 'two-way pair' of two-lane streets with enough capacity to handle increased traffic without excessive widening and disruption of properties in the downtown area.

help offset land and construction costs. The parking deck should be supplemented by on-street parking on all existing streets.

(4) Several other recommendations were included regarding traffic and parking management especially improving the block structure in the downtown area with new streets and enhanced connectivity between Highway 115 and the improved Main Street (see Figure 8.12). Most of these improvements would be made as part of private redevelopment projects, but a few would need to be paid for by the town.

Civic Infrastructure

There were six main recommendations under this heading.

(1) Construct a new town square between the Town Hall and the historic Holbrook house, currently a popular restaurant. The town has no civic gathering space and this would provide a focal point for public activities; like many great European plazas, this location would permit the space to be utilized for parking during business hours and then cleared for special activities during the evenings and on weekends (see Figure 8.13).

(2) Develop a cultural center as an integral part of the town square. The plan suggests a two-storey building of 20 000 square feet (1858 square meters) with interactive classrooms and other spaces that could be used for a variety of community events including exhibitions and performances coordinated with regional theaters and museums. In addition, the plan recommended the insertion of one or two storefronts for retail operations such as an ice cream store or a sandwich shop; the combination of these civic and retail uses would help activate the plaza.

The design of this building should set a precedent for environmental sustainability. This was a consistent theme throughout the master plan and reinforces the 'green' theme for the downtown area. Given its prominence and potential as a learning laboratory for arts and culture, this building should set the standard by incorporating sustainable design elements such as a planted roof system and passive solar shading on the façade (see Figure 8.13).

As an alternative to the proposed cultural center, a multi-story mixed-use building with continuous retail storefronts or restaurants at ground level would also be an appropriate anchor for the north side of the plaza, with outdoor seating spilling into the square.

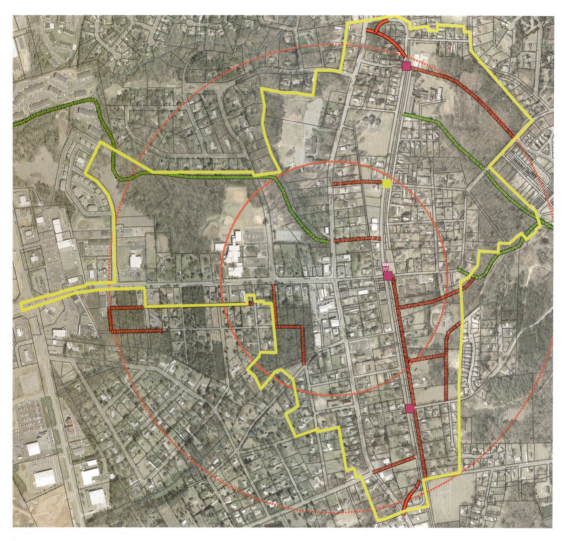

Figure 8.12 New streets and connections, Huntersville Master Plan, 2004; The Lawrence Group, Town Planners & Architects. To complement the main transportation improvements shown in Figure 8.11, a network of smaller cross-streets and connections (shown in red) could radically improve traffic circulation and parking management in the downtown area.

Regardless of whether the building is a civic building or a more traditional mixed-use structure, it should be a minimum of two stories in height. This height not only helps to enclose the plaza visually, making it more useable and people friendly, but would also screen the proposed parking deck to the rear.

(3) Redevelop the existing farmers' market into the Growers' Market at Garden Hall (see Figure 8.14). The current farmers' market is an under-utilized structure in a key location between the proposed

commuter rail platform and the civic plaza. Apart from its twice-weekly use for produce sales, the structure is utilized only for occasional events such as the Hispanic Halloween Party and some neighborhood celebrations. But even such minimal use underscores its potential value as a gathering place.

Because the building is small, obscured from view, lacks signage and any urban landscaping that could dignify the space, the plan proposed replacing the existing structure with a new 13 000 square foot (1208

Figure 8.13 Town Hall Plaza, Huntersville Master Plan, 2004; The Lawrence Group, Town Planners & Architects. A new civic space links the town hall, a new children's environmental museum (Discovery Place Kids) and a local restaurant (in yellow) with the enlarged Growers' Market and the commuter train station (behind the Market Hall; see also Figure 8.17). Although this particular design did not materialize, this compelling image catalyzed development of various components of the plan in different formats.

square meter) open-air pavilion approximately twice the size of the current facility. Included within this structure would be 1000 square feet (93 square meters) of space for a train ticket kiosk, security area, staff office and public restrooms. During the peak morning and evening times, the new Garden Hall would shelter 'kiss and ride' commuters (transit riders who are dropped off by a friend or family member) during inclement weather.

The conceptual design of the Garden Hall uses an authentic farm vernacular with exposed rafters and eaves and a standing seam metal roof. Additionally, to disperse heat as well as add height to the structure, the design incorporates a clerestory along its entire length. The post, beam and truss construction would be painted white to make the structure feel light and airy. A children's 'sprayground' could be incorporated nearby to serve the surrounding neighborhoods with an interactive water feature that is safe, clean and low maintenance. Spraygrounds, like other water features,

also help to provide background noise, which make public environments more inviting for private or semi-private conversations.

(4) Encourage the improvement of the nearby American Legion building and construct a Veterans' Memorial between it and the Garden Hall (see Figures 8.15 and 8.16). The existing building serves a useful function as a meeting facility for the community but its utilitarian design leaves much to be desired. To address this problem and improve the overall aesthetics of the area adjacent to the train station, the plan suggested some strategic upgrades to the building entrances and landscaping that could help to soften its box-like appearance. The erection of a town War Memorial between the American Legion building and the expanded Garden Hall would add another appropriate civic focus to the public space.

(5) Meet the expansion needs of the Town Hall and Police Department buildings in their current locations by purchasing extra land as necessary (see

Figure 8.14 Growers' Market at Garden Hall, Huntersville Master Plan, 2004; The Lawrence Group, Town Planners & Architects. This enlarged facility establishes a clear identity for the downtown area.

Figure 8.15 American Legion building, downtown Huntersville, 2004. Retired American servicemen and women meet for social and cultural activities in this windowless brick box. (Compare with Figure 8.16).

Figures 8.17 and 8.18, respectively). As part of this expansion, the town should install 'green' roofs on all new civic buildings and encourage their use for all new non-residential construction. Such roofing systems reduce energy costs, and can also capture and filter rainwater. This reduces the buildings' environmental footprints and promotes sustainable development.

(6) Develop a system of greenways and 'green streets' traversing the planning area using stream corridors wherever possible. This could provide recreational

Figure 8.16 American Legion building, proposed refurbishment, Huntersville Master Plan, 2004; The Lawrence Group, Town Planners & Architects. The building receives an improved civic presence and is related to the adjacent Garden Hall. A small war memorial (with three flagpoles) adds dignity and communal memories to the new public space.

opportunities, access to the existing park, and link existing and new developments with an alternative and sustainable transportation option (see Figure 8.19).

Private Development Opportunities

It was very important to encourage sensitive infill and redevelopment that enhanced the fledgling urbanism of downtown while encouraging contemporary architecture. Of many opportunities, the following three projects were regarded as the most important.

(1) A key site diagonally opposite the town hall and facing the police station was ideal for a small specialty grocer or pharmacy as part of a mixed-use development. This area, currently including a used-car lot, a consignment shop and a small office building, comprised one of the ripest opportunities for redevelopment in the downtown; there was a good combination of under-utilized parcels and willing property owners that would permit redevelopment in the near-term (see Figures 8.20 and 8.21).

The plan considered a number of alternatives for this area, including a specialty grocer or pharmacy, and various urban storefronts. The market study discouraged the placement of a full-service grocery store in this location, given the number of large stores clustered around the Interstate within 1.5 miles of downtown. Therefore, the plan recommended that the maximum building size for any single use generally not exceed 20 000 square feet (1858 square meters), which could accommodate a smaller, specialty grocer or a typical pharmacy. Either format could be adapted to create a pedestrian-friendly building which fronted onto the street and recreated the missing urban edge at the intersection (see Figure 8.21).

As an alternative, the report suggested that the cultural facility could be placed at this corner if the preferred site next to the town hall did not materialize. In this case, a small pedestrian plaza at the corner would serve as a public focal point. Regardless of the particulars, the conceptual images in this plan strongly suggested that the architecture at this corner should fit well into the urban context but at the same time be contemporary and differentiated from the municipal buildings. More importantly than style, buildings at this intersection should be a minimum of two stories in height to establish the visual prominence of this location. This massing and intensity of use should extend at least two blocks (approximately 800 feet or 244 meters) from the intersection in order to create a visual and economic focus at the heart of downtown.

(2) Utilize the Anchor Mill site for a continuing care retirement community (CCRC). This would fulfill

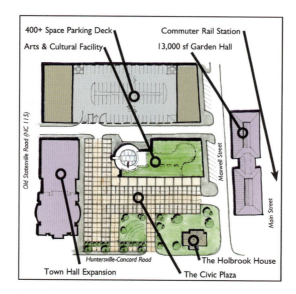

400+ Space Parking Deck

Arts & Cultural Facility

Commuter Rail Station

13,000 sf Garden Hall

Old Statesville Road (NC 115)

Maxwell Street

Main Street

Huntersville-Concord Road

Town Hall Expansion

The Civic Plaza

The Holbrook House

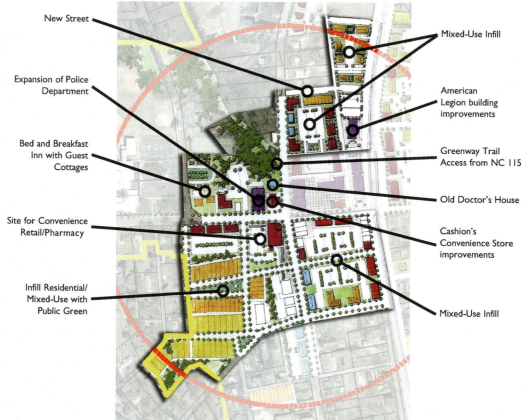

New Street

Expansion of Police Department

Bed and Breakfast Inn with Guest Cottages

Site for Convenience Retail/Pharmacy

Infill Residential/ Mixed-Use with Public Green

Mixed-Use Infill

American Legion building improvements

Greenway Trail Access from NC 115

Old Doctor's House

Cashion's Convenience Store improvements

Mixed-Use Infill

Figures 8.17 and 8.18 Civic Core Plan (top) and Town Center Plan (bottom), Huntersville Master Plan, 2004; The Lawrence Group, Town Planners & Architects. These two plans illustrate the redevelopment strategies for the heart of the downtown area. The corner site identified for a pharmacy became the actual site for the Discovery Place Kids museum and associated parking deck (see Figure 8.29).

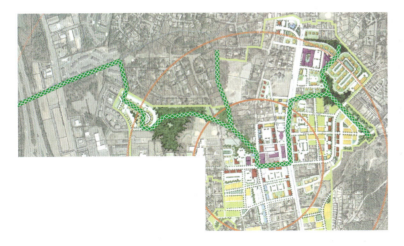

Figure 8.19 Greenway system, Huntersville Master Plan, 2004; The Lawrence Group, Town Planners & Architects. A connected system of pedestrian trails and bicycle path linking different parts of the planning area provides alternative transportation options for local citizens as well as an environmental resource.

Figure 8.20 Site for proposed new pharmacy and associated development as existing, Huntersville, NC. This simple patched panorama taken during the charrette provided the basis for the sketch of the proposed new development illustrated in Figure 8.21.

a market niche and provide much needed facilities for 'aging in place' (see Figure 8.22). The market study identified a potential gap in housing opportunities for active older adults and the elderly in the Huntersville area, and as the town continues to grow and mature, there will be a higher demand for these types of neighborhoods. The opening of the new Presbyterian Hospital in November 2004 within a mile of downtown supports this '55-plus' demographic age group with an important health care amenity.

The master plan provided a variety of such housing opportunities as part of this development on a site of just over 30 acres (12 hectares), including independent-living cottages and apartments, assisted-living apartments, and accommodation for skilled nursing care. The entire community is designed around a walkable network of new streets with a variety of traffic-calming

devices to slow down vehicle speeds. The site's proximity to the heart of downtown (less than a 10-minute walk) would provide residents with a comfortable destination for daily walks, with amenities such as shopping, civic and cultural activities, and the train station for easy access to Charlotte. Added security for residents would be provided by nearby police, fire and hospital emergency services. In its turn, a facility such as this can also become an employment center for the area.

(3) Encourage higher-density residential development on infill and redevelopment sites, especially around the proposed train station (see Figure 8.23). Fronting the rail corridor, development should occur as mixed-use, multi-story buildings close to the train station, transitioning to apartments and townhouses to the north. The old mill village was recommended for redevelopment simply by consolidating and resubdividing vacant and 'ripe' properties into denser configurations. Such redevelopment could include small lot single-family homes, townhouses, duplexes and small apartment buildings. The plan showed the retention of the existing homes which were stable, well maintained and owner-occupied at least until the current owners were ready to sell for redevelopment, at which time these small clusters of intact mill houses could easily be rehabilitated and used as homes or offices. Given the desire of this plan to densify near the transit station, the continued zoning in this area to permit manufactured homes could no longer be justified. Although manufactured housing in America is affordably low priced, it works only at low densities and tends to deflate surrounding property values, thereby discouraging high-quality urban infill. Affordable

Figure 8.21 Corner pharmacy and associated development as proposed, Huntersville Master Plan, 2004; The Lawrence Group, Town Planners & Architects. This new mixed-use development was intended to bring urban presence to an important downtown intersection and to promote a more contemporary style of architecture.

Figure 8.22 Anchor Mill detail plan, Huntersville Master Plan, 2004; The Lawrence Group, Town Planners & Architects. Facilities for 'aging in place' are much in demand by active older adults. Having choices of centrally located accommodation that supports them during the aging process allows older citizens to remain lively and involved in the community.

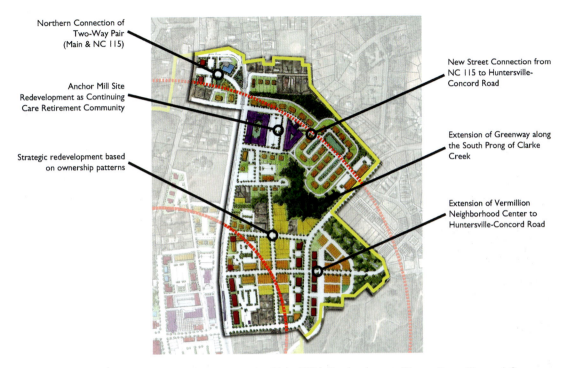

Northern Connection of
Two-Way Pair
(Main & NC 115)

Anchor Mill Site
Redevelopment as Continuing
Care Retirement Community

Strategic redevelopment based
on ownership patterns

New Street Connection from
NC 115 to Huntersville-
Concord Road

Extension of Greenway along
the South Prong of Clarke
Creek

Extension of Vermillion
Neighborhood Center to
Huntersville-Concord Road

Figure 8.23 Mill neighborhood, Huntersville Master Plan, 2004; The Lawrence Group, Town Planners & Architects. The design team struggled with the relationship between the location of the retirement community and the need for a connecting street network (with the consequent potential for disruptive cut-through traffic). Eventually it was decided to allow one connecting street to penetrate the elderly housing area, but to design it so that vehicle speeds would be strictly reduced for pedestrian safety by means of narrow traffic lanes, on-street parking, stop signs and aggressive speed bumps. In this way, the attractiveness of the street as a cut-through for motorists could be sharply reduced.

housing in the downtown needs to take more urban forms such as duplexes, town homes or apartments integrated with market rate housing.

The plan also proposed mixed-use buildings, town homes, and live-work units along the frontage of Huntersville–Concord Road in this same vicinity, with a new entrance street to Vermillion lining up with an existing street in the mill village. Buildings in this location should create a suitable street presence with significant architecture. In addition, the uses should encourage pedestrian activity by providing some local services such as dry cleaners, coffee shops, hair salons and doctors' offices. The new street connection would provide the Vermillion neighborhood with the easy access to downtown it has always lacked (see Figure 8.23). On other potential infill sites further away from the core, a mix of new small lot single-family homes and town homes should be considered, and configured

in ways that knit new homes and streets sensitively into existing neighborhoods (see projects 'L' and 'Q' in Figure 8.28).

In addition, small-scale office development should be encouraged throughout the downtown area as part of new mixed-use redevelopment, including new buildings and conversion of existing large homes as appropriate (see Figure 8.28). Typical spaces should be 3000–15 000 square feet (279–1393 square meters) in buildings from two to four stories.

Marketing and Branding Strategies

This work is not always included in master planning exercises, but in this case one of the main objectives of the project was to change citizens' perceptions of their old downtown to encourage reinvestment

Figure 8.24 Huntersville town logo, Huntersville Master Plan, 2004; The Lawrence Group, Town Planners & Architects. This new logo was adopted almost immediately by the town for its signs, vehicles and documents.

Budding Next Spring.

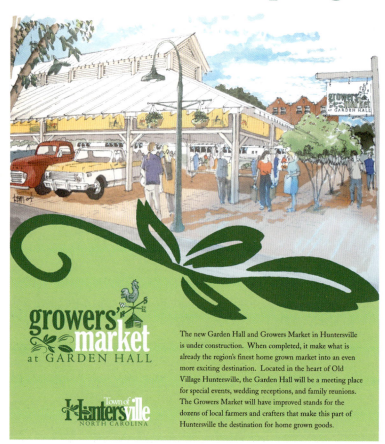

The new Garden Hall and Growers Market in Huntersville is under construction. When completed, it make what is already the region's finest home grown market into an even more exciting destination. Located in the heart of Old Village Huntersville, the Garden Hall will be a meeting place for special events, wedding receptions, and family reunions. The Growers Market will have improved stands for the dozens of local farmers and crafters that make this part of Huntersville the destination for home grown goods.

Figure 8.25 Hypothetical advertisement for the Growers' Market, Huntersville Master Plan, 2004; The Lawrence Group, Town Planners & Architects. Creative planning, robust architecture and neat graphic design all combine to build a new image for the town in general and the downtown area in particular.

and more intensive use. The were two main recommendations.

(1) Adopt a 'popular' logo for marketing and branding that gave a contemporary twist to the town's history (see Figures 8.24 and 8.25). Many charrette participants complained about a lack of identity for the downtown, and even for the town of Huntersville as a whole. It became clear to the team that the town possessed very little 'brand equity'; in the surrounding region many people still regarded the town as an old farming community that had rapidly suburbanized and

lost any character it once possessed. To compound this lost opportunity, the nearby Lake Norman Visitors' Center yielded brochures and information about Huntersville's neighbors (Cornelius, Davidson and Mooresville), but nothing about Huntersville. In addition, there was a more serious concern that the town's identity was being overridden by its shopping centers at Interstate-77 interchanges: Birkdale Village at Exit 25 (Figure 8.1) and Rosedale at Exit 23 (Figure 8.7) have become places identified more by their exit number than by their location within Huntersville.

Therefore, any marketing and branding plan for the downtown area must start with a community-wide approach, and then extend into its various shopping districts and neighborhoods. This strategy should be rooted in the heritage of the community, which has been deeply tied to the land; once a thriving 'farm-to-market' town, in 2006 Huntersville remained the horticultural center of the region. Large commercial horticultural businesses, one with over 2 million square feet under glass (over 18 hectares!), combined with multiple garden centers and landscape companies to provide the potential for a distinctive town image and marketing niche. This land-based heritage, coupled with the town's planning efforts that were sensitive to land preservation, made the marketing strategy even stronger. The result was a 'green' approach to the logo that used horticultural themes to relate to the town's heritage and a contemporary font to appeal to new residents, setting a progressive image and unique identity in the region.

(2) Implement a comprehensive 'wayfinding' and signage system (see Figure 8.26). Using the new logo and associated imagery, a system of directional signs and markers could direct visitors easily to key amenities. A true urban environment is differentiated from a shopping center by the level of detail that adorns the public realm, and many communities have incorporated fun and educational artwork into their sidewalks and public spaces, such as the Charlotte example illustrated in Figure 8.27. Whimsy should be encouraged as a way to enliven spaces and maintain a child-friendly focus. Programs could be devised with the local arts community and high schools for the creative placement of civic art within the sidewalks throughout the town. As examples, a brass two-dimensional fruit (for the Growers' Market) or train (for transit) could be embedded into the concrete of the sidewalk. This type of artwork is not expensive, can easily be expanded and adds interesting features for pedestrians.

Figure 8.26 Directional signs, Huntersville Master Plan, 2004; The Lawrence Group, Town Planners & Architects. Wayfinding signs add urban identity through well-designed street furniture.

Figure 8.27 The Writer's Desk, 2005; Larry Kirkland. This large piece of public art outside the downtown children's library in Charlotte, NC, honors a local newspaper editor and is very popular with families. (Photo by Linda Brown).

Environmental Protection

By their nature, downtowns are inherently urban, where the site coverage of buildings, parking areas and hardscape approaches 100 percent. If downtown Huntersville is to thrive as a pedestrian-friendly, mixed-use center, it must have wide sidewalks and buildings built close to the street and to each other. This urban setting presents little, if any, opportunity to manage stormwater ecologically on a site-by-site basis, or with Low Impact Development techniques (Sustainable Urban Drainage Systems in the UK) to retain and filter it on site to minimize polluted surface water run-off. If provided, stormwater retention would likely be handled underground, an expensive option.

Unfortunately, because a large part of downtown is located on the west side of the railroad tracks (the ridgeline), it falls within the protected watershed of adjacent lakes where rules limit the amount of impervious surface to 70 percent of a site – a condition not compatible with a dense urban core.

In order to permit the full build-out of the master plan, therefore, the downtown area must be relieved from the requirements of the watershed protection standards without sacrificing environmental stewardship. The best course of action would be to balance the urbanism of the downtown with a more open area nearby in the same watershed, specifically in this case the North Mecklenburg Park, located a couple miles north of downtown. Through deed restrictions or other similar legal mechanisms, the pervious soft landscape areas required but not achievable for the downtown could be offset by permanently protected undeveloped land in the park. By this means, development in the downtown area would simply need to manage the quantity and rate of water runoff and would be exempt from other water quality standards.

DEVELOPMENT ANALYSIS

The kind of development analysis carried out with each charrette depends largely on the level of detail and specificity of the master plan and its relation to the direct practicalities and economic context of the project. In this case study, figures were worked out in considerable detail, as the town was seeking ways to kick-start development in the study area by means of targeted public expenditures and policy changes. Figure 8.28 illustrates the location and content of the various public and private development opportunities,

and the economic breakdown of projects in the master plan, including their approximate construction cost and development value, is listed below. Figures used for costing are conservative and are illustrative only; the point of this exercise is to calculate the approximate value of new development in order to ascertain the increased tax revenue from new private development relative to the public costs for new civic buildings and infrastructure.

- 72 single-family detached homes each constructed for $100 000 (£53 300) gives a development value of $7 200 000 (£3 840 000)
- 94 duplex homes (semi-detached) each constructed for $80 000 (£42 700) gives a development value of $7 520 000 (£4 010 666)
- 173 town homes each constructed for $70 000 (£37 300) gives a development value of $12 110 000 (£6 458 666)
- 465 apartments or condominiums each constructed for $70 000 (£37 300) gives a development value of $32 550 000 (£17 360 000)
- 100 units of senior housing or assisted living accommodation each constructed for $70 000 gives a development value of $7 000 000 (£3 733 300) (this figure in particular is approximate for a specialized product)
- 292 925 square feet (27 214 square meters) of office space constructed for $110 per square foot (£631 per square meter) gives a development value of $32 221 750 (£17 172 034)
- 205 300 square feet (19 073 square meters) of retail space constructed for $90 per square foot (£516 per square meter) gives a development value of $18 477 000 (£9 841 668)
- Total construction value for major private projects: $117 078 750 (£62 416 334).

New private development totals more than $117 000 000 in potential investment value, which when added to the present day land values of these sites (almost $11 500 000 or £6 133 000) brings the Net Incremental Developable Tax Value of the downtown area to over $128 500 000 (£68 533 300). When this figure is added to the value of existing development left in place (almost $100 000 000 or £53 333 300) the total taxable value for the downtown area is approximately $228 500 000 (£121 866 600). At 2005 municipal tax rates, this total development figure would bring in approximately $640 000 (£341 330) per year or $6 400 000 (£3 413 300) over a 10-year

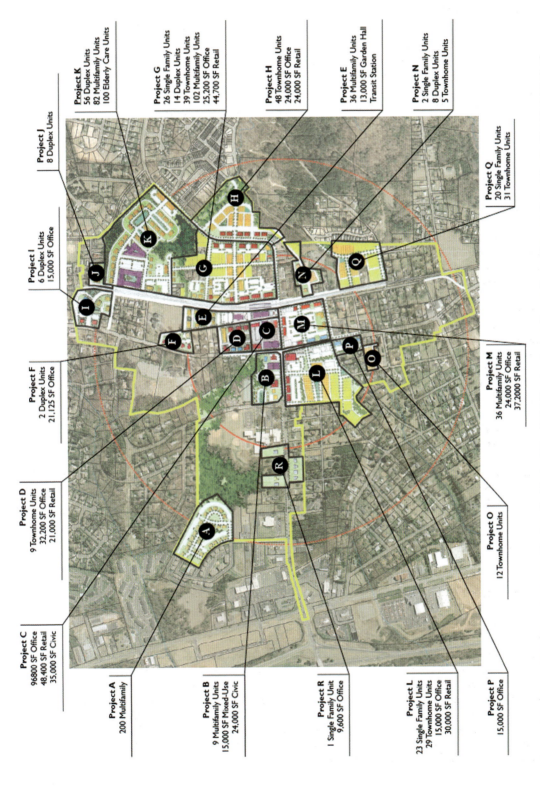

Project K
56 Duplex Units
82 Multifamily Units
100 Elderly Care Units

Project G
26 Single Family Units
14 Duplex Units
39 Townhome Units
102 Multifamily Units
25,200 SF Office
44,700 SF Retail

Project H
48 Townhome Units
24,000 SF Office
24,000 SF Retail

Project E
36 Multifamily Units
13,000 SF Garden Hall
Transit Station

Project N
2 Single Family Units
8 Duplex Units
5 Townhome Units

Project J
8 Duplex Units

Project Q
20 Single Family Units
31 Townhome Units

Project I
6 Duplex Units
15,000 SF Office

Project F
2 Duplex Units
21,125 SF Office

Project M
36 Multifamily Units
24,000 SF Office
37,2000 SF Retail

Project D
9 Townhome Units
32,200 SF Office
21,000 SF Retail

Project C
96800 SF Office
48,400 SF Retail
35,000 SF Civic

Project A
200 Multifamily

Project B
9 Multifamily Units
15,000 SF Mixed-Use
24,000 SF Civic

Project R
1 Single Family Unit
9,600 SF Office

Project L
23 Single Family Units
29 Townhome Units
15,000 SF Office
30,000 SF Retail

Project P
15,000 SF Office

Project O
12 Townhome Units

Figure 8.28 Development analysis plan, Huntersville Master Plan, 2004; The Lawrence Group, Town Planners & Architects. Keeping track of development numbers and the economic viability of design proposals is a vital task during charrettes of this type.

period. Figuring in a modest annual growth of the tax rate after 10 years, tax revenues from this new development could total in the region of $14 000 000 (£7 466 700) after 20 years. This potential income for the town is an important figure relative to the costs of the public projects in the plan.

Municipal projects would be paid for with tax dollars from the town's general fund or from the proceeds of municipal bonds, combined with other potential revenue sources. These include money from CATS for associated public improvements connected to the train station, and funds from the local Arts and Sciences Council for part of the costs of the cultural facilities building. The main public projects are:

- 59 000 square feet (5481 square meters) of civic space, comprising a 15 000 square foot expansion of the town hall, a 24 000 square foot expansion of the police station and a 20 000 square foot cultural facilities building constructed for $175 per square foot (£1004 per square meter) creates a building cost of $10 325 000 (£5 505 000); approximately $1 million should be added to this figure for the cost of acquiring the extra land needed for the expansion and extra parking, giving a total capital cost of approximately $11 325 000 (£6 040 000)
- 13 000 square foot (1208 square meter) Growers' Hall (constructed largely as an open shed with a small enclosed area for public toilets and train ticket kiosk) for $30 per square foot (£172 per square meter) creates a construction cost of $390 000 (£208 000) to which should be added $80 000 for a small amount of extra land required; this gives a total cost of $470 000 (£250 700)
- 27 600 square foot (2 564 square meter) Civic Plaza constructed for $800 000 (£426 700), plus the cost of acquiring adjacent land for full project implementation ($560 000 or £298 700); the total estimated project cost from public funds is approximately $1 360 000 (£725 400)
- 400-space car parking deck in the civic core area constructed for $4 800 000 (£2 560 000) with approximately $200 000 (£106 700) in land acquisition costs creates a further public cost of $5 000 000 (£2 666 700); this cost would be shared with CATS as the parking deck also serves the train station.
- The total cost of the public projects is approximately $18 155 000 (£9 677 800).

Against this public expenditure, not all of which would come from the town's funds, should be set the

$14 000 000 (£7 466 700) of anticipated future tax revenues from the private development potential of the plan. The town could reasonably expect contributions from CATS and the Arts and Sciences Council totaling $4 000 000–5 000 000 (£2 133 300–2 666 700) thus reducing municipal expenditure to the amount that could accrue to the town from the property taxes on new and existing downtown development. These figures do not include the cost of the new and improved road works noted earlier (see Figure 8.13), which would be financed separately in conjunction with the NC DOT.

These cost and income figures are approximate only, but they comprise an important component of this kind of detailed master plan; they demonstrate the financial viability of the plan's proposals, in particular how the tax revenue from new private development can offset the public expenditure on civic improvements. This is always an important equation for citizens, town staff and elected officials alike, and the implementation of a master plan often hinges on balancing these financial equations. These figures were worked out roughly at the end of the charrette and presented as working numbers as part of the final presentation. They were then refined for the final project report.

IMPLEMENTATION STRATEGIES

In order for the vision and recommendations encapsulated in the downtown master plan to be realized, specific implementation steps would need to be taken by the town of Huntersville, private property owners and other government bodies. The report outlined and prioritized the various actions necessary to create the conditions through which the master plan could be achieved; these included some minor amendments to the zoning code, targeted public investments, the development of appropriate programs and policies and sundry other activities. Table 8.1 excerpts a selection of these recommendations to illustrate the focus on implementation detail normal in a charrette project report of this type. A preliminary version of this information should always be included in the final PowerPoint presentation at the end of the charrette to convince citizens and elected officials of the plan's feasibility. Implementation priorities are indicated by the time period in which items should be completed. Year 1 items are the highest priority while a Year 10+ project could be completed as resources allow. In Table 8.1, 'town' means the town of Huntersville.

TABLE 8.1 Illustrative implementation Strategies excerpted from Project Report

Project task	Implemented by	Coordinated with	Year 1	Year 2–5	Year 5–10	Year 10+
Studies and plans						
Evaluate the location of the Police Station for future expansion and purchase land required	town		✓			
Establish final path and secure right-of-way for greenway system throughout downtown	town	property owners		✓		
Undertake Feasibility Study and preliminary engineering for implementing the N–S two-way pair street system	town, NC DOT		✓			
Plan commuter train platforms in location shown in master plan to integrate with new Growers' Market	CATS	town		✓		
Require new street connections for better block structure around downtown in all redevelopment plans	private developers	town		✓	✓	
Strategically manage parking lots around downtown until construction of new deck	town	property owners	✓	✓	✓	
Policy and ordinance amendments						
Encourage sensitive redevelopment and urban infill while permitting contemporary architectural styles	town	property owners	✓			
Require building within 800 feet (244 meters) of the Highway 115/Gilead Road intersection to be two stories	town	property owners	✓			
Remove the Manufactured Home overlay zone from the old mill village and rezone to Transit-oriented Dev. (TOD-R)	town	property owners	✓			
Capital improvements						
Acquire by purchase or long-term lease land around the town hall for civic expansion, parking deck and town plaza	town	property owners	✓	✓		
Plan, design and construct new civic plaza adjacent to town hall	town			✓		
Install 'green' roof systems on all new civic buildings	town			✓	✓	
Acquire right-of-way and construct the N–S two-way pair street connections and related improvements	town, NC DOT			✓		
Acquire property around the existing Farmers' Market for the expanded Growers' Market			✓			
Redevelop existing Farmers' Market into the Growers' Market at Garden Hall				✓		
Expand Police Station and Town Hall	town			✓		
Construct shared use parking deck for 400 spaces	town, CATS	private developers			✓	
Encourage the placement of public art throughout the downtown	town, public art commission	local artists and schools	✓	✓	✓	✓
Incorporate new logo and related graphics on all town signs and publicity materials	town		✓	✓	✓	✓

CRITICAL EVALUATION OF THE CASE STUDY

In professional terms, this master plan has been a success; it won the 2006 Smart Growth Award from the North Carolina Chapter of the American Planning Association. However, the more important evaluation is the extent to which the client body embraces the plan, and in these terms the report card is mixed but largely positive. The charrette took place in September 2004 and the full project report was completed 6 weeks later. The Huntersville Town Board approved and adopted the plan early in 2005 and set to work on several projects right away, the most immediate of which was the adoption of the new town logo on all street signs, town signs and promotional literature. However, the five-member Town Board adopted the plan on a split 3:2 vote, with two members dissenting on ideological grounds to the kind of public sector activism involved in partnering with private developers and property owners to achieve the community vision. These elected officials believed that such public-private partnerships were not a valid use of tax dollars; from their perspective, if a private development project is to succeed, it should do so 'on its own merits,' without any 'subsidy' of public money entering into the financial equations. When this view becomes a majority opinion, as it is in many American communities, coordinated planning for medium to long-term community goals becomes very difficult, and illustrates clearly the dimensions of the political chasm that exists between British local government operations and those of even their progressive American counterparts.

Despite these minority reservations, the town has moved forward on the two biggest elements in the master plan, i.e. the development of a cultural facility with a related parking deck and the creation of the 'two-way pair' of north–south streets. During the charrette, representatives of Discovery Place, a well-established natural history and science museum in Charlotte, participated in the proceedings as part of their own evaluation of possible plans to expand their facilities with a smaller, satellite facility in the fast-growing northern part of Mecklenburg County. These discussions were the kernel around which the proposal for a Huntersville cultural facility took shape, along with a new parking deck and civic plaza. Although the location shown in the master plan for this combination of facilities was always regarded as the best, because of its ability to integrate the train station, Growers' Market, the new cultural building and the expanded

town hall all together around a coherent sequence of public spaces culminating in the plaza (see Figure 8.13), this site presented some problems of land acquisition. The charrette team investigated an alternative site on the opposite corner of the main intersection, where the master plan ultimately illustrated a pharmacy as part of a comprehensive redevelopment of that quadrant (see Figures 8.18, 8.20 and 8.21). However, the report specifically noted the potential of that corner site for the Discovery Place facility due to the ability of land to be assembled quickly from willing sellers.

The potential for a new facility illustrated in the master plan, plus the eagerness of town officials to work with Discovery Place, persuaded that institution to choose Huntersville as their expansion site and to upgrade their plans from a small converted storefront operation into a larger educational venue housed in a new building. Negotiations continued between the parties during 2005, focusing on the alternative corner site, and by the spring of 2006 the Town Board approved a plan for that corner that included a mixture of cultural, commercial and residential uses, all in support of the original master plan (see Figures 8.29 and 8.30; compare Figure 8.29 to Figure 8.18, and Figure 8.30 to Figures 8.13 and 8.21).

The town has entered into a public–private partnership to buy the land for the future Discovery Place museum and future office space for the town. The project also includes a publicly owned parking deck, public streets, and privately owned retail and office space. An associated residential development created by a private developer would adjoin the site. The town would own the Discovery Place building and space on the third floor would include expansion space for town offices. The project should begin on site in 2007 and the town has budgeted approximately $16 million (£8.5 million) for the project plus a further $1 million (£533 300) in downtown street improvements. These figures are only a little higher than those sketched in by the master plan.

Comparing the proposed site plan of this new development with the master plan is instructive (see Figures 8.29 and 8.18). A new north–south street has been created closely following the line of one shown on the master plan and lined with high-density housing in accordance with master plan principles. Likewise, lower-density, single-family homes are tucked onto adjacent land as indicated on the master plan. The proposed new building also creates a small, inviting urban space on the street corner as noted for this location of the museum in the text of the report.

Figure 8.29 Discovery Place Kids mixed-use development site plan, 2006; Narmour Wright Creech Architecture PA. This plan is rotated 180° from the same area in the master plan (see Figure 8.18) but this new plan follows the main principles of the master plan with a major corner building, parking to the rear, a new street and infill housing. *(Reproduction courtesy of Narmour Wright Creech Architecture and the Town of Huntersville)*

Figure 8.30 Discovery Place Kids mixed-use development perspective, 2006; Narmour Wright Creech Architecture. Drawing by Risden McElroy. The architectural vision is very different from that envisaged in the master plan (compare with Figures 8.13 and 8.21), but the dynamic and positive impact of the development on the town center will likely be similar. *(Reproduction courtesy of Narmour Wright Creech Architecture and the Town of Huntersville)*

Easy and quick land assembly on the corner opposite the town hall was key to the Discovery Place project moving ahead, as opposed to complex and potentially lengthy land acquisitions on the site preferred in the master plan. Placing a small plaza in front of the entrance to the Discovery Place building is a good local urban design move, but that space cannot become the much-needed larger civic focus envisaged by the master plan. In other respects, the Discovery Place project is a great success, with integrated mixed civic, retail and office uses backed by high-density residential development in the right place.

In relation to the master plan's concept of the two-way pair of north–south streets, the town has hired a firm of transportation planners who are producing preliminary engineering studies for the project to facilitate the appropriate right-of-way acquisition and the relocation of utility lines prior to construction. The town is prepared to fund this project to a tune of $7.2 million (£3.84 million) from its own capital improvements program funds if necessary, but is also negotiating with the NC DOT for access to state money. In addition, town officials are in detailed discussions with a developer interested in the Anchor Mill site adjacent to the northern leg of the upgraded street about making a substantial contribution to the street improvements as a function of a negotiated planning approval for that site. Construction on the new road could begin as early as spring 2007.

The other main recommendations in the master plan have been accepted in principle by the town, but no concrete action has taken place to date by early summer 2006, due in part to recent doubts about the timing of the future commuter rail service linking Huntersville and adjacent towns with Charlotte. The federal government has recently stiffened its criteria for funding rail projects throughout the nation, and this has caused CATS to revaluate its proposals, level of service and timing. In an effort to maintain the impetus for the new rail line, local and regional developers with major investments tied to transit-oriented development along the rail corridor have begun to investigate the possibility of substantial private financing for the rail operation. This idea was in its infancy during the summer of 2006, but if some such initiative were to materialize, it would be the first instance of privately funded public transit in America for many decades. The importance of the train station in catalyzing private development in Huntersville's downtown cannot be overstated and private investors are waiting to see how the new uncertainty is resolved before committing money to new development in the area.

The clarity and high degree of detail in the master plan has served its purpose of raising interest in new development opportunities among property owners and elected officials. The design detail and specificity of proposals was necessary to spur the imaginations of stakeholders and the general public; without this fine grain the plan would fall flat. The detail illustrations and projects in the plan were not intended as fixed blueprints for future development, but as realistic catalysts for action. The vision was both clear and firm, but also flexible, as the Discovery Place example demonstrates.

But the events surrounding the new Discovery Place facility also illustrates the two main failures of the master plan – the attempts to move the town towards contemporary, sustainable architectural design and to create a sequence of civic spaces culminating in a new town square. In general terms, the urban design content of the master plan was rarely an issue during the charrette or since, due to the sophisticated design-based zoning ordinance that has been in place in the Huntersville community for the past 10 years. Many buildings and large developments have been constructed in the town during that 10-year period that follow the design principles set out in the ordinance (see Figures 8.1 and 8.7), and although the town's planning staff have to be constantly vigilant in maintaining design standards, the basic principles are no longer particularly controversial.

While the urban design goals of the plan met with partial success, the architectural design recommendations for more contemporary and ecologically responsive architecture were largely ignored. The master plan tried and failed to move the town and major developers beyond the pseudo-historical neo-classicism that has become the norm for both public and private sector buildings in the American South (see Figures 5.17, 8.31 and 9.24). While contemporary architecture is at least possible under the Huntersville ordinance (as noted in Chapter 5 the code was written to require only *compatibility* with older buildings without replicating their style) there is little discernible demand for progressive, sustainable buildings from the American public or elected officials outside some of the nation's major cities.

The well-liked and respected neo-classical architect from Charlotte responsible for the Discovery Place building had also designed the Huntersville Town Hall and Police Station across the road from the site of the new facility (see Figure 8.31), so there was a clear and understandable logic in the minds of town staff and elected officials to create a set of visually compatible neo-classical buildings as image generators for the downtown core. This locally generated logic overrode the alternative vision and recommendations of the master plan, and because the form-based zoning ordinance deals with urban form, not architectural style, it is appropriate in many ways for local wishes about building aesthetics to carry greater weight than outside professional taste. However, the matter of sustainable design goes deeper than aesthetics, and the author hopes fervently that this new

Figure 8.31 Huntersville town hall, 1997; David A. Creech, AIA, while with TBA2 architects. The town hall and adjacent police department share a neo-classical style in an attempt to bring a sense of civic presence to the faded downtown.

museum – poignantly showcasing science and the environment – will capitalize on sustainable building technology in its detailed design.

This episode illustrates clearly the difficulties faced by attempts to introduce sustainable, contemporary architecture into mainstream practice in many parts of America. At least the New Urbanist master plan made a bold case for contemporary and sustainable building design; this stands in contrast to most of the building styles illustrated in the following case study, for the nearby town of Concord, NC.

Whereas Huntersville citizens, planning staff and elected officials had reached a certain comfort level with the urban design principles embodied in the ordinance, allowing at least the possibility of more progressive architectural innovations to be introduced into the town's thinking, these same urban design concepts were new and relatively untested in the nearby town of Concord. As will be seen in the next chapter, the charrette team consciously took a more conservative architectural approach to rendering the master plan and its component buildings, believing that these progressive urban concepts would likely fail to generate public acceptance if they were illustrated through the medium of contemporary architecture. This conundrum illustrates one of the fundamental dilemmas for American architects and urban designers in developing master plans and design codes: these are rarely vehicles for progressive architectural design unless the client specifically supports innovative architecture. Where the client is a public authority, with elected officials answerable to the public-at-large, conservatism is generally the order of the day outside centers of architectural culture such as New York, Chicago and California. This is presently a fact of life in 2006, and if architects, like the author, chafe under these restrictions, we must remember always that the master plan is not ours; it belongs to the people – the public, the stakeholders and the elected officials of the community. The purpose of the plan is to energize and empower the community, not to boost architectural egos fed by the Fountainhead myth of architectural omnipotence in matters of taste.

Case Study II: Greenfield Urban Extension, Concord, NC

EXISTING CONDITIONS

Concord is a small city in Cabarrus County in the State of North Carolina with a population of just under 60 000, a figure that has dramatically doubled in size since 1990. It lies about 25 miles north of the major city of Charlotte and about 15 miles east of Huntersville. Settled in 1750 and the county seat since 1796, Concord has its roots in textiles and banking, which formed its economic base through the 19th century. Textiles then became dominant in the town's economy, which absorbed heavy economic blows during that industry's precipitous decline since the 1970s. However, economic activity has recovered well, based now on a mix of light manufacturing, health care, professional services and auto racing. The town is home to Lowes Motor Speedway, a huge NASCAR (National Association of Stock Car Auto Racing) race track just a couple miles south on the main Highway 29 (Concord Parkway) that crosses the project site; this facility is the region's second largest tourist attraction with the two main racing weeks each year drawing over 1 250 000 visitors between them (see Figure 9.1). Concord has undergone extensive residential growth within the booming economy of the greater Charlotte region, where it serves in part as a bedroom community to the big city, but only in the past few years has the town attempted to manage this growth in a constructive manner with new planning initiatives. Some useful form-based zoning provisions have recently been added to the conventional ordinance, but most regulations still reflect the standard, old-fashioned classifications by use with little urban design content.

The study area comprised 780 acres (315 hectares) located on the western edge of the city between the floodplain to a stream called Coddle Creek to the west,

extensive land holdings belonging to a large Philip Morris cigarette plant to the east and southeast, and two main roads, Weddington Road, a local thoroughfare to the north, and Concord Parkway (US Highway 29), an important regional route to the south (see Figure 9.2). Concord Parkway is a four-lane, median-divided major thoroughfare that provides important regional connections, carrying 25 000 vehicles per day.

Traversing the project site from north to south is Concord Farms Road, a two-lane road originally providing access to the agricultural activities that once took place on the site. Weddington Road to the north is currently two lanes wide, and collects sufficient traffic from adjoining neighborhoods to be classified as a minor thoroughfare with between 6500 and 8700 vehicles per day. The other local road of significance is Roberta Church Road, another small two-lane road carrying approximately 6400 vehicles per day that runs south from Highway 29 at the southeastern edge of the site.

When viewed in the regional context, the site is one of the last large undeveloped areas in western Concord. Low-density suburban residential neighborhoods surround the site on the west, north and east. This extensive suburban expansion has prompted plans for a major new road linked to Interstate-85, a few miles north of the site and moving south to intersect with Highway 29 on the project site and with another major regional road, Highway 49, several miles further south (see Figures 9.1 and 9.2).

This new highway is partly constructed at its intersection with the interstate north of the project site and is in the planning stages elsewhere; it is intended to thread through the western parts of the town, improving accessibility to existing developments and providing an alternative route for traffic that currently

Figure 9.1 Aerial view of site and surrounding area as existing, Concord, NC. Lowes Motor Speedway is the large oval in the bottom left-hand corner of the photograph. The smaller oval nearby is a related dirt-racing track. The project site is outlined in yellow, the floodplains are hatched in blue and the line of a proposed new highway is shown in red. The large Phillip Morris cigarette factory can be seen right of center, while Concord's downtown is 3 miles further east off the photograph to the right. State Highway 29 (Concord Parkway) bisects the site and the photograph on a diagonal. Interstate-85 can be glimpsed in the top left-hand corner.

traverses more central, built-up parts of town. The new road, while relieving some congestion, will also open up new land for further development with consequent increases in traffic. (The British concept of a by-pass, where no highway commercial development is allowed alongside the road, is barely known in America. Because American planners and communities lack either the legal ability or the political will to

restrict development along by-pass highways, new commercial and residential buildings spring up along their length, generating new traffic that limits their transportation function and efficiency.)

The alignment for this new highway runs down the eastern boundary of the project site, although specific engineering decisions had not yet been finalized at the time of the charrette. The default design is

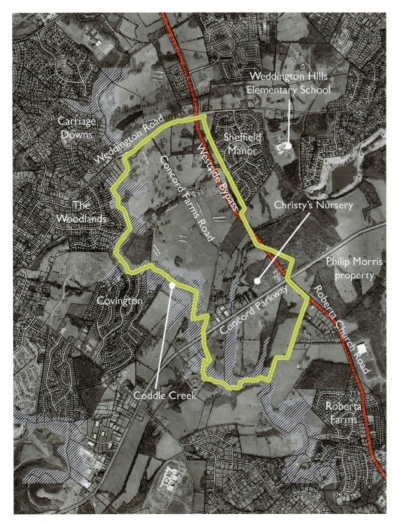

Figure 9.2 Detailed aerial view of site, Concord, NC. The site was an old poultry farm, now surrounded by disconnected suburban housing developments. The remnants of a historic wagon road can be seen in the fragments of hedgerows, within the site and beyond its boundaries, that form a broken line from southwest to northeast.

a five-lane road comprising four travel lanes with a continuous two-way-left-turn lane in the middle. No sidewalks or landscaping are normally included. This minimal design standard is widespread for state-funded road projects in North Carolina and elsewhere in America (and not unknown in Britain either); the only criterion considered by highway engineers seems to be the fastest travel of the greatest number of motor vehicles. Pedestrians, bicycles and the advantages of a walkable environment are rarely considered.

The site is mostly undeveloped and mainly flat with some gently rolling topography (see Figure 9.3). The main physical features comprise a number of small rock outcroppings, a few significant stands of trees

Figure 9.3 General site view of project area. The site comprises a bland but pleasant landscape.

217

and two farm-watering ponds. A garden supply and nursery business occupies approximately 20 acres (8 hectares) along the north side of Highway 29 between the road and a tributary of Coddle Creek, and the same family owns an additional 75 acres (30 hectares) immediately north of the garden center. The only other structures on the site are the last remnants of a once-thriving poultry farm and a few additional retail buildings scattered along Highway 29. On the south side of Concord Parkway are several tracts in corporate ownership with the same topography as the rest of the site, falling gently towards the creek.

To the east of the study area is the Weddington Hills Elementary School and the extensive campus of the Philip Morris Concord Plant (see Figures 9.1 and 9.2). This tobacco factory is surrounded by preserved open fields along both sides of Concord Parkway, which serves as a partial green belt to this portion of Concord, but sporadic suburban developments have increasingly compromised this positive aesthetic and environmental amenity.

The site area was identified in the 2004 Concord Land Use Plan as one of 10 Mixed-Use Districts, large designated areas at key intersections of major roads in high-growth areas where the infrastructure could support denser development. These districts promote the evolution of areas where people could live, work, shop and, in some cases, have immediate access to recreation facilities in the same general area. The intention is for uses to mix together as an integrated center allowing for pedestrian accessibility and connectivity. The Land Use Plan noted that good access to major highways makes this particular site ideally situated for office and light industrial uses, as well as retail and residential development.

The Concord Land Use Plan serves as the framework for the local or small area plans for the mixed-use centers, of which this master plan case study is one. The Land Use Plan establishes the context for the whole town, including major transportation infrastructure, green networks, concentration areas for employment, commercial activity and residential neighborhoods in much the same way as did the now obsolete English 'Structure Plans,' superceded since 2004 by more detailed spatial strategies and policies contained in each planning authority's Local Development Framework (LDF). The master plan in this case study acts as a small area plan within Concord's Land Use Plan and refines the recommendations of that larger plan by evaluating its goals on a site-specific basis and creating a local framework from which planners and elected officials can make specific decisions on new

development. While many of the technical aspects of the plans within these American and British systems are similar, it must be remembered that the American plans are more limited in legal authority than their English counterparts. American plans are advisory only, whereas English plans carry more procedural weight in terms of concrete proposals for the location, type and amount of future development (see Figure 3.7).

The study area for this master plan provides a clear illustration of the American divorce of planning from zoning discussed in earlier chapters. Whereas the Land Use Plan identifies a relatively straightforward vision for this site and its environs as mixed-use districts at major street intersections with the remainder as predominantly residential with some land set aside for office or light industrial development, the town's zoning map for the same area is markedly different, with no less than 12 different zoning districts incorporating nearly every land use category available in the town from agricultural to various types of housing to office and industrial.

EXECUTIVE SUMMARY

The conceptual master plan (see Figure 9.4), developed in a public design charrette held in early December 2004, focused on five key issues. First, it suggested a proposed alignment and design for the north–south George W. Liles Parkway extension. A number of alternative alignments were evaluated and ultimately the easternmost path was preferred. The plan recommended the construction of a true parkway with a wide median planted with trees and separate multi-use paths on both sides. Finally, the plan showed a ground level intersection with Concord Parkway, but preserved a trajectory for the future construction of a full grade-separated bridge interchange if future circumstances warrant this expense.

Second, the plan reserved locations for key civic structures including a church and a fire station. Additionally, outside but immediately adjacent to the eastern site boundary, an excellent site was identified for a middle school.

Third, to increase the opportunities for community parkland and alternative modes of transportation, and to minimize the ecological impact of the development, the plan incorporated extensive areas of open space throughout the site, especially the extension of a greenway along the Coddle Creek floodplain

The Neighborhood

Residential Lots – 90 units
Urban Residential – 1,040 units
Office – 334,800 sf
Civic/Institutional – 100,600 sf

Mixed-Use Campus

Mixed-Use – 1,483,800 sf
Civic/Institutional – 194,600 sf

The Great Wagon Road

Concord Farms Road South

Urban Residential – 350 units
Small Office/Retail – 112,200 sf
Office – 223,200 sf
Civic/Institutional – 14,200 sf

Weddington Neighborhood Center

Small Office/Retail – 86,400 sf
Retail – 66,400 sf

School Site

Concord Parkway Neighborhood Center

Retail – 124,000 sf
Mixed-Use – 150,800 sf

Southside Employment Campus

Office/Flex – 476,500 sf
Small Office/Retail – 28,800 sf

PLAN LEGEND

Single Family
Duplexes/Townhomes
Mixed-Use Employment
Mixed-Use Commercial
Parking

Park
School
The Great Trail
Creek/Greenway
Trees

Figure 9.4 Concord Parkway master development plan, 2004: The Lawrence Group, Town Planners & Architects. The line of the proposed new highway, the George W. Liles Parkway, runs along the eastern site boundary. An extensive greenway and park system follows Coddle Creek on the western edge of the site. North of the central mixed-use campus, a church or other institutional complex faces a small park.

Figure 9.5 Green infrastructure diagram, Concord Parkway Master Plan, 2004; The Lawrence Group, Town Planners & Architects. Presenting the green spaces as a simple figure-ground diagram communicates the size and structure of the landscape system as a positive design element.

as well as the preservation of key heritage sites. In particular, the little-known path of the 18th century 'Great Wagon Road' or 'Old Stage Route,' was preserved in the plan as an active interpretive trail. Additionally, the plan recommended a multi-use path system along the north side of Concord Parkway. Overall, more than 25 percent of the site was retained as various forms of open space (see Figure 9.5).

Fourth, the plan established the location of major activity centers. Towards the south of the site, a neighborhood center anchored by a grocery store or a large specialty retailer could be located on the north side of Concord Parkway (Highway 29). A second, smaller commercial node could be located at the intersection of the new George W. Liles Parkway and Weddington Road at the north end of the site. And, in the center of the area, the master plan recommended that development be organized as an urban, pedestrian-friendly mixed-use 'campus,' utilizing a grand boulevard as a generator of character and sense of place. This urban campus would be an excellent location for research and development companies, or major corporate offices.

Fifth and finally, the plan recommended the creation of new form-based zoning districts and design standards keyed specifically to this conceptual master plan. There should be adequate flexibility to accommodate shifts in market demand, but these standards should ensure a high level of quality for development in terms of both design and environmental sustainability.

Overall, the conceptual master plan illustrated a build-out of the following development potential (see Figure 9.4):

- 1 634 600 square feet (151 859 square meters) of mixed-use buildings (generally office with some street level retail and possibly apartments on some upper floors)
- 557 800 square feet (51 821 square meters) of typical class 'A' office space
- 476 500 square feet (44 268 square meters) of 'office/flex' space, a combination of single-storey office and warehousing or light manufacturing
- 226 600 square feet (21 052 square meters) of small office or retail space, typically one- and two-storey buildings with small floorplates. Their specific use depends on market conditions
- 188 000 square feet (17 466 square meters) of retail space
- 295 200 square feet (27 425 square meters) of civic or institutional space (not counting the school site outside the project boundaries)
- 1390 units of 'urban housing' – town homes, duplexes (semi-detached) and apartments
- 90 single-family detached homes.

DESIGN PROCESS – ANALYSIS

As a counterpoint to the generic quality of much recent development in the area, the designers paid special attention to the natural ecology and the cultural history of the site. In this way the team sought to create a specific 'sense of place' for the development, a desire noted also in many public comments, and it was from these public conversations that a significant historical fact was unearthed, i.e. the presence across the site of an old stagecoach route dating from the 18th century. Local history states that President George Washington traveled this historic highway, now marked only by a discontinuous series of hedgerows, on a tour of the newly independent states in 1791. Close attention was also paid to the market analysis to gauge the development potential of the site in the context of its sub-region, and to transportation issues, arising largely from the unresolved plans for the highway extension of the George W. Liles Parkway through the project site.

Public Input

A 5-day design charrette was used to guide the planning process with a similar timetable to the

Huntersville example (see Figure 8.10). A temporary design studio was set up in a city building (unfortunately nowhere near the site), but complete with drawing tables, meeting areas, computer equipment, and a presentation space. Many citizens and public officials participated during the 5-day period, and meetings were held to discuss various topics related to the area's future. Feedback from civic leaders, government representatives and residents suggested that Concord, like many American communities, clings to its historic roots and whatever small town character remains in the face of extensive and generic suburban development. The town's challenge, similar to Huntersville's, is to maintain and enhance this identity as it continues to grow, while creating a 'sense of place' within a community that has developed in a sprawling fashion along its highway corridors.

Citizens and local officials emphasized several specific points, especially the following:

- Opportunities exist for the town to enlarge its economic base, reducing its dependency on Charlotte and transitioning from a bedroom community.
- Business growth is especially targeted towards the motor sports and automotive industry along with new information and biotechnologies.
- This employment growth will drive demand for office and industrial uses.
- Population and income growth resulting from this economic development will drive demand for a mix of housing types, together with support services and retail.
- Plans should provide a range of opportunities for citizens to work, live and play locally.

Also discussed during the charrette was the *Community Assessment Report* prepared by the Centralina Council of Governments (COG). This provided an overview of the region's strengths, challenges and opportunities for improving its economy, and several findings supported creating a mixed-use campus focusing on business and research. The target industries included defense and security, automotive, software development and security, bioinformatics, optoelectronics, and fuel cell technology.

Historical Analysis

The public discussions during the charrette yielded the exciting but little known historical fact of an old wagon road, later a stagecoach route, which crossed the site from southwest to northeast. Known as the 'Upper

Road,' it was one fork of a multi-pronged system of wagon roads branching southeast from Philadelphia, PA and Fredericksburg, VA. Local sources and historical research revealed that this route was once part of an American Indian pathway system along the Appalachian Mountains from Pennsylvania to Georgia. In the early 1700s, progressive colonization brought the interconnected trail system under British control and the road whose remnants cross the project site became a principal highway into the colonial 'back country,' defining and supplying the 18th century frontier between Britain's dominions and the vast unexplored lands beyond their borders. The road became an important line of communication during the Revolutionary War of Independence (1775–1783) and several important battles were fought along its length through the Carolinas.

Today, the route across the site is marked by a fragmentary line of hedgerows that has been obliterated elsewhere by suburban development that unwittingly or uncaringly destroyed their segments of this historical artifact. The project team immediately decided that it was of the utmost importance to preserve and carefully enhance this wonderful physical trace of America's early history.

Market Analysis

Like Huntersville in the previous case study, Concord benefits from its proximity to Charlotte as the main driving force of an expanding economy. The town's working-class manufacturing history is reflected in part by a median household income of $46 094 (£24 583), much lower than Huntersville's and just above the national average, but this figure has risen substantially in the decade since the mid-1990s, establishing a positive trend of higher paying jobs. Expanding employment in non-manufacturing sectors demonstrates the community's transition from a manufacturing to a service–oriented economy, and this growth in white-collar jobs has stimulated demands for new office and retail space plus a variety of types and styles of housing. However, light-manufacturing employment remains an important part of the local economy, which together with the transportation of goods and materials creates a need for buildings that can flexibly accommodate office, light assembly and distribution uses.

Commercial space

Overall, the market study demonstrated that the anticipated demand for new office space totaled approximately 200 000–300 000 square feet of Class A and medical office space over a 5- to 10-year period, provided that job growth continues at an estimated 1500 jobs per year. Within this forecast, and possibly extending it, a unique opportunity presented itself for the study area due to its strategic location between two large hospitals, i.e. Northeast Medical Center in Concord, just a few miles from the site, and University Hospital adjacent to the University of North Carolina at Charlotte, approximately 12 miles south on Highway 29. Discussions revealed a demand for medical offices in this area, where both hospitals compete for market share. Additionally, the office space in the nearby Lowe's Motor Speedway complex is full and another demand exists for additional space for motor sports businesses.

Combined with offices, the market study noted a need for industrial 'flex' space for warehousing, distribution and light manufacturing. Typically these buildings comprise a large single-storey (18–22 feet or 5.4–6.7 meters) with loading docks at the rear and office or showroom space in the front. This building type suits a variety of high-tech and development industries such as pharmaceuticals and software, and is conducive to the clean technology or 'nano' type industries that local economic development agencies seek to encourage through partnerships with the nearby University of North Carolina at Charlotte. The motor sports industry could also utilize this type of space. By their nature, these warehouse type buildings with large floor plates and extensive truck access do not fit easily into an urban, pedestrian environment, and need a spatial layout that is more vehicle-oriented.

The largest growth segment of the commercial market has been retail, with a number of local and regional shopping venues. The largest of these is a mega-mall, Concord Mills Mall, some five miles from the project site with well over 1 000 000 square feet (92 903 square meters) of space. This shopping venue is North Carolina's biggest single tourist attraction, with over 3 500 000 visitors a year. With the construction of additional retail space near Concord Mills and other retail centers currently planned or under construction, the surrounding area (within a 5-mile radius of the study area) will provide over 3 000 000 square feet (278 709 square meters) of shopping, dominated by regional and national chain stores. Additionally, a 'power center' of major shopping outlets anchored by a Target store and totaling approximately 700 000 square feet (65 032 square meters) is planned at a nearby new interchange on Interstate-85. This future expansion of shopping opportunities, together with

Concord Mills and the University City shopping centers about 12 miles south around the campus of the University of North Carolina at Charlotte, severely limit the potential for major regional retail development in the study area.

However, the housing that currently surrounds the study area, combined with new housing on the project site, will create a need for neighborhood shopping, which could also serve people working in the office, warehouse and light industrial buildings likely to be developed within the study area. Sites along Highway 29 (Concord Parkway) to the south and Weddington Road to the north offer the best locations for new retail developments where these existing roads intersect with the new George W. Liles Parkway. Accordingly, the study recommended approximately 75 000–190 000 square feet (6970–17 650 square meters) of retail space be constructed in two phases, based on a 5- to 10-year absorption period. Appropriate uses include a grocery store with additional neighborhood services such as dry cleaners, restaurants, banks and other business to serve the basic needs of residents and employees.

Residential

Single-family homes have consumed 55 percent of the land area within Concord's city limits and annexed area. This significant proportion indicates a need to consider housing at higher densities to utilize the remaining land in the area more efficiently. With existing homes and new dwellings under construction or approved, local officials predict an oversupply of single-family houses in Cabarrus County by 5316 units. By contrast, multi-family units, town homes and apartments, will be under-supplied by 2108 units. This oversupply of single-family homes suggests caution about adding additional homes to the market until this surplus is at least partly consumed.

The shortfall in multi-family dwellings is largely due to younger, single renters and homeowners, and young families without children looking for alternatives to the suburban single-family house. Additional important market sectors include 'empty nesters' whose children are grown and who are looking to 'downsize' from their large family homes, and other active and retired adults. The study area presents an opportunity to create a variety of 'urban residential' housing types at higher densities and in a wide range of price points with only a small number of single-family homes in the mix.

DESIGN PROCESS – DEVELOPMENT STRATEGIES

Transportation

As part of the charrette process, a series of alternative alignments for the new George W. Liles Parkway were evaluated, exploring the possibility of shifting the alignment to the west and traversing the middle of the study area to open up easier access to developable land as opposed to following the eastern boundary. Careful examination of these options by the study team concluded that no significant benefits could be gained by departing significantly from the proposed alignment (see Figure 9.6). However, the team did make numerous recommendations regarding the detailed design of the new road. The master plan proposed protecting the adjacent residential neighborhood to the east by preserving the trees and other significant vegetation between the parkway and the neighborhood. This north–south corridor represents a prime opportunity for future public transit service as well as pedestrian and bicycle linkages, and the plan proposed a true parkway with significant landscaping, slightly narrower travel lanes to control vehicle speed (for pedestrians' and cyclists' safety), and protected multi-use paths for bicyclists and pedestrians on both sides (see Figure 9.7).

The anticipated traffic volume on the new parkway was estimated at just over 25 000 vehicles per day and the North Carolina Department of Transportation (NC DOT) recommended that the future intersection with Highway 29 be constructed as a grade-separated interchange. However, the projected future traffic volumes on both Highway 29 and the George W. Liles Parkway would not necessarily warrant this expensive interchange configuration; an 'at-grade' intersection would be less costly and still provide an efficient way to handle the traffic without the expensive land acquisition and construction costs for ramps and bridges. Avoiding a freeway-style intersection also reduces excessive vehicle speeds and slower speeds always increase the opportunities for alternative modes of transportation.

The charrette team thus illustrated an intersection of Highway 29 and the new parkway as a full movement, at-grade intersection controlled by traffic lights, and recommended that further study be conducted to determine the most appropriate design treatment for this intersection, making sure that vehicle speeds and convenience to through traffic are not the only determining criteria in the detailed design.

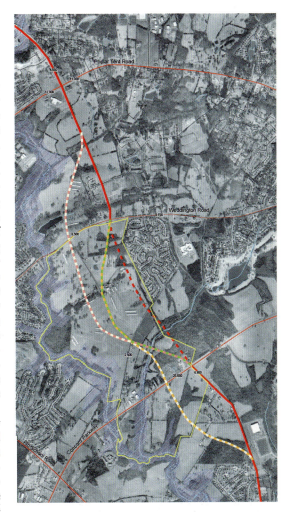

Figure 9.6 Alternative parkway alignments, Concord Parkway Master Plan, 2004; The Lawrence Group, Town Planners & Architects. Early thoughts that increased development opportunities would be opened up by a more central line for the new road were not borne out by quick design studies and the original boundary-hugging line proposed by the North Carolina Department of Transportation was confirmed by the master plan.

The other determining role the new parkway played in the development of the conceptual master plan was the location of intersections of new streets with the parkway. The spacing of these was determined by Department of Transportation regulations regarding intersections on major thoroughfares and Figure 9.8 illustrates the impact of these dimensions on the layout of the master plan. By establishing these

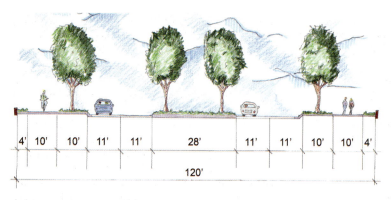

Figure 9.7 Proposed parkway section, Concord Parkway Master Plan, 2004; The Lawrence Group, Town Planners & Architects. The state highway engineers' design for the new parkway did not include urban elements such as sidewalks and bicycle paths. The road was conceived as a high-speed corridor for vehicles only, which would have been antithetical to the neighborhood character and scale of new development.

Figure 9.8 Street spacing on parkway, Concord Parkway Master Plan, 2004; The Lawrence Group, Town Planners & Architects. The location of streets leading into the new development were fixed by State highway regulations for the spacing of fully signalized intersections and unsignalized cross-overs. These dimensions had a determining effect on street pattern and block structure.

locations early in the process the overall area circulation pattern could be designed in a way that balanced the mobility needs of the region with the degree of local access necessary to accommodate future development. These major points of site access, together with carefully sited street connections with Weddington Road and Highway 29, provided opportunities to create an informal system of connected blocks for a well-organized and safe transportation network throughout

the project site – in contrast to the inefficient cul-de-sac systems of surrounding developments (see Figure 9.9). This interconnected system of streets with short blocks would disperse traffic and support future public transit, walking and bicycling. Streets should be designed with 10–11 feet (3.05–3.35 meters) wide travel lanes and a clearly defined pedestrian realm (typically accommodated by a planting strip for street trees and a minimum 5-foot (1.5 meter) wide sidewalk

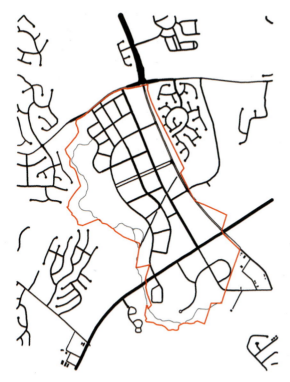

Figure 9.9 Street pattern and block structure, Concord Parkway Master Plan, 2004; The Lawrence Group, Town Planners & Architects. In contrast to areas surrounding the site, the pattern of streets and blocks was designed as a deformed grid with extensive connectivity, except the southernmost area where large warehouse-scaled buildings were set in park-like landscape between protected stream corridors and preserved landscape. The trail marking the historic wagon road is depicted by the broken diagonal line across the middle zone of the site.

on both sides) protected by on-street parking in most locations.

Design Evolution

The master plan evolved over a 3-day period prior to finalization and completion of the final drawings. Figures 9.10, 9.11 and 9.12 illustrate various stages in this process. Figure 9.10 shows the condition after the first day of design, with the site fairly crudely divided in three zones, matching housing to existing development on adjacent sites to the north and west, retail along Highway 29 and office uses in the middle portion of the site. The area south of Highway 29 had not yet received any consideration, and a flyover was assumed for the junction of the George W. Liles

Parkway and Highway 29, thus restraining potential development at that corner due to extensive ramps and gradients. The idea of an axial landscaped space as the organizing concept for the office park, turning it into a sort of campus was illustrated in outline form, and an interconnected street network was beginning to take shape along with parks and open spaces.

The plan from the second day (see Figure 9.11) showed some quite significant changes as alternative ideas were explored. The retail area along the north side of Highway 29 became a denser 'urban village' with a Main Street leading to an anchor store of some sort paralleled by a linear park alongside the small tributary stream to Coddle Creek. The organization of the middle office area had collapsed into rather a formless muddle, although some vestigial acknowledgement of the Great Wagon Road began to be evident as the first brief mention of this historical trace was casually made by a city employee. If the mid-section of the site had regressed, the northern area had developed into a more advanced mixed-use arrangement of commercial space, higher-density housing arranged around some preserved landscape with rock outcroppings and some single-family housing adjacent to the creek, which was now developing into a major greenway of preserved landscape, especially the tree-packed knoll on the western edge. The area south of Highway 29 had begun to emerge as a series of large commercial 'flex-space' buildings set in park-like landscape and screened by trees as far as possible. The team was still assuming a flyover at the main highway intersection.

The third day (see Figure 9.12) brought a revival of the axial concept for the main campus area, now shown with a mixture of uses with higher-density residential to north and south. Its location, and the spacing of other connections with the George W. Liles Parkway, was fixed by the required dimensions between major intersections defined from the transportation studies illustrated in Figure 9.8. The transportation studies had also convinced the team to push for an alternative arrangement to the flyover proposed at Highway 29 and illustrated instead an at-grade intersection. This freed up some land for a potential retail center along Highway 29, which became fronted by a more disciplined series of buildings on both sides, set back behind a landscaped buffer to preserve the parkway character of the road. The previous day's urban village in that location was abandoned as the market analysis indicated insufficient demand for that more expensive product. The area south of Highway 29 was also laid out in more formal fashion, interspersed with fingers of green space lining the small streams in

225

Figures 9.10–9.12 Design process drawing, days 1–3, Concord Parkway Master Plan, 2004; The Lawrence Group, Town Planners & Architects. These three consecutive drawings illustrate the dynamic design process characteristic of a public design charrette.

Figure 9.11

that area. The most northern part of the site remained unresolved and the importance of the line of the Great Wagon Road was not yet fully understood. However, the basic pattern of streets, blocks and connectivity was becoming clearer, and the western edge of the site was now consolidated as a major greenway and preserved parkland to protect the Coddle Creek floodplain.

The final plan illustrated in Figure 9.13 demonstrates how much design concepts are clarified and sharpened towards the end of any charrette process. In this example, the main east–west axis of the campus became fully established as the principal organizing device leading into the site from the main intersection with the George W. Liles Parkway. This axis was oriented to line up with the dominant knoll of trees behind the main building at the end of the boulevard. A zone of parking areas and decks necessarily separated this axis from development to north and south, but connectivity was enhanced by the alignment of a new north–south street that took over from Concord Farms Road as the main local street paralleling the new parkway. This street linked

developments from the southern extremity of the site where it connected with an existing stub street, all the way to Weddington Road at the north. The formal clarity and directness of this new street allowed other north–south streets to meander and interconnect into a deformed grid pattern fitted to the landscape.

The northern area became much more defined around a neighborhood park with an enhanced existing pond and rock outcrops, fronted by a new civic or institutional building such as a church, and lined by town homes and apartments on its other three sides. A small neighborhood retail center fitted in the corner of Weddington Road and the new parkway, while the remainder of the northern area was filled with medium-density housing to match the projections of the market study. A street of single-family houses backed up to the greenway along the western edge to match the existing subdivision across the creek. This matching of like to like is often a prerequisite to overcome automatic neighborhood opposition to higher-density housing near existing single-family developments.

The line of the Great Wagon Road also appeared as one of the organizing site geometries, and was preserved and enhanced as an interpretive walking and

Figure 9.12

Figure 9.13 Final master plan, Concord Parkway Master Plan, 2004; The Lawrence Group, Town Planners & Architects. This unified graphic communicates the pattern and scale of the buildings and spaces in a similar way to a figure-ground drawing. The spaces between the buildings are as important as the buildings themselves.

bicycling trail across the site linking with the greenway along the creek. The team felt this enhancement was very important even though it represented only a fragment of the original route. Either side of this preserved landscape feature, small-scale mixed-use buildings lined an informal network of streets defined by site geometries. Once the importance of the line of the Great Wagon Road was understood, it became apparent that a unique development opportunity existed immediately west of the site boundary where the Wagon Road was still visible in the field pattern. A piece of property the right size for a middle school and adjacent to the Weddington Hills elementary school to the north was potentially available, and this facility could be designed to include another section of the Wagon Road as an educational resource for both schools. Spacing of cross streets on the parkway enabled good access to be obtained, and a new local street extended around the edge of the school grounds to link up with the elementary school and Weddington Road to the north, thus providing safe and convenient access to school traffic.

Land north and south of Highway 29 was organized and connected more directly by means of the aforementioned new north–south street, which defined access to a retail and mixed-use center on the north side, anchored conventionally by a grocery store but framed around a local 'Main Street' of two-storey buildings. On the south side, the arrangement of large flexible space buildings evolved into a mix of formality facing the main streets, and informal geometries as the buildings fitted themselves into the existing landscape of woods and streams.

CONCEPTUAL DEVELOPMENT PROJECTS

The potential development projects that comprise the conceptual master plan are shown in Figure 9.4. Although definitively drawn and quantified, these projects are much more speculative than those shown in the preceding Huntersville example. This plan promotes a new, sustainable ethos to land development in Concord, and as such its main purpose is to demonstrate the economic and environmental potential of this new development pattern rather than promote specific developments on specific sites.

The key principles of sustainable development incorporated into the master plan included:

1. Mix land uses
2. Create compact and space-efficient building designs and layouts
3. Integrate a range of housing types, choices and price ranges
4. Foster a strong sense of place
5. Create walkable neighborhoods
6. Preserve open space and critical environmental areas
7. Utilize Sustainable Urban Drainage Systems (SUDS) wherever possible
8. Connect new developments with existing
9. Provide a variety of transportation choices
10. Encourage community and stakeholder collaboration in development decisions (Adapted from the *Principles of Smart Growth*; http://www.smartgrowth.org).

In addition to these development directives, the market study provided clear guidance regarding the content of the conceptual master plan, much of which differed from established patterns and existing zoning. As the master plan proposed types of development very different from the inward-looking single-family residential neighborhoods surrounding the site, the team recognized it was important to make transitions between new and existing as gentle as possible.

Along the northern edge of the study area, care was taken to provide smaller-scale buildings, areas of open space and uses similar to those existing nearby to relate to existing conditions as well as the potential development pattern of the vacant properties north of Weddington Road (see Figure 9.13). Along the eastern edge, the extension of George W. Liles Parkway itself created the transition. The master plan located the parkway to preserve a thin but significant stand of trees buffering the adjacent residential neighborhood to provide a better backdrop for the private spaces behind the homes in that community. To the west, a large expanse of wooded area and floodplain provided an expansive open space transition to the existing residential development. A significant stand of trees atop a knoll was specifically preserved on the greenway trail that followed the creek along this western edge.

The individual development projects are described as follows.

Northern Neighborhood Center
(see Figure 9.14)

Charrette team members walking along the Weddington Road noted a very hostile pedestrian environment with no sidewalks and high vehicle speeds; a new bridge recently constructed over Coddle Creek was clearly planned to accommodate a wider four-lane road in the future. Ironically, and somewhat tragically in regard to growing problems of child obesity in America, Weddington Hills Elementary School, just east of the study area and in direct proximity to a cluster of residential neighborhoods, is not considered to be in a 'walk to school zone' due to the dangerous traffic conditions on surrounding roads. Walking to school is not permitted and all children are driven the relatively short distance from their homes.

The master plan recommends a small mixed-use center located at the intersection of Weddington Road and George W. Liles Parkway. This capitalized on the development opportunities for the properties without bringing housing into close proximity with busy and potentially dangerous highways. Overall, the four quadrants of the neighborhood center should be planned to accommodate up to 150 000 square feet of

Figure 9.14 Northern neighborhood center, Concord Parkway Master Plan, 2004; The Lawrence Group, Town Planners & Architects. To create a sense of place while reaping a decent development potential from this site at the junction of two important roads efforts were made to save some significant stands of trees (seen in the distance in Figure 9.3).

office and some limited retail uses in relatively small buildings. The largest retail use envisioned was approximately 15 000 square feet (1394 square meters), the size of a typical national chain pharmacy. Limiting not only the amount, but also the type, of retail development here would allow Weddington Road and George W. Liles Parkway to operate at a successful level of service by not creating 'destination' retail which in turn would create more traffic. These larger stores would be better sited in the neighborhood center along Highway 29 at the south of the site.

Because Weddington Road lacked any pedestrian facilities, the team recommended that sidewalks should be added to both sides with a bicycle lane or widened street shoulders to accommodate bicyclists along the south side of the roadway connecting with a trailhead to the proposed greenway along Coddle Creek. As a final measure of traffic calming and pedestrian protection, on-street parking should be added on Weddington Road west of its junction with the new parkway. This would also provide convenient parking for businesses facing the street.

The North Neighborhood
(see Figure 9.15)

There was a clear public consensus during the charrette that residents from surrounding neighborhoods did not want the whole site to be developed as housing, which they saw as putting yet more demands on already overcrowded schools. City officials also did not desire extensive residential development as single-family housing was already in plentiful supply in the

Figure 9.15 North neighborhood, Concord Parkway Master Plan, 2004; The Lawrence Group, Town Planners & Architects. Rock outcroppings and an old farm pond are incorporated into a neighborhood park fronted by a church or school, and lined by housing to form a large green 'living room' for the community.

area, and this low-intensity use would remove land from other activities that could generate higher tax revenues for the city. At the same time, some residential development is a necessary component of any mixed-used project and the master plan followed the findings of the market analysis in recommending a higher-density 'urban residential' mix of housing types with only a small number of single-family lots.

The primary housing area of the master plan was located in the northwest corner of the study area, next to existing residential subdivisions. Encompassing approximately 135 acres (54.6 hectares), the conceptual plan for the northern quadrant included large and small single-family lots, town homes, loft apartments and condominiums as well as senior citizens' housing. The urban housing types were geared primarily to households with few or no children, thus limiting any impact on school overcrowding. The size of the neighborhood made it possible to provide housing at many different 'price points' to reach higher-income levels (particularly in locations backing up to the Creek) and integrate smaller homes that would be affordable to people with modest incomes.

Preserved open space and newly created parks served as the organizing armature of the area. A greenway trail and large natural area was preserved along the floodplain, town homes and apartments fronted on public lawns or squares that preserved some of the existing canopy trees, and a large, 10-acre (4-hectare) park preserved a stand of trees, rock outcroppings, and incorporated a rain garden or permanent detention pond for the area as sustainable site drainage.

This park also provided a key site for a major civic or institutional building, such as a church or a school, to overlook and define the open space. Like schools, most churches vie for sites in the urban fringe where the land is cheaper and more plentiful but which necessitate the whole congregation driving to services and other church activities. Historically, churches have served as the anchors for Concord's neighborhoods and provided for not only the spiritual needs of the community, but its civic needs as well with large meeting rooms and multi-purpose gymnasiums. Siting such a building in this location was strategic for a number of reasons:

1. It provided a unique and identifiable anchor for the neighborhood.
2. It fronted on a large park and provided a vibrant and active presence similar to the historic precedents of the squares in Savannah, GA or the New England Town Greens.

3. It was sited near the high point of the study area, enabling it serve as a visual anchor for the greater community.
4. It served as a transition use between the neighborhood and the Mixed-Use Campus.
5. Parking was adjacent to the commercial uses, permitting the shared use of the space using off-peak hours.
6. It was located on the first street connection into the area from the George W. Liles Parkway, giving the building full access and prominence from the developed areas to the north and east.

The conceptual master plan showed the design potential for about 1100 dwellings in this neighborhood at roughly 8 units per acre (20 dwellings per hectare). While higher density than the surrounding subdivisions, a neighborhood this size could help support and be supported by the adjacent vibrant mixed-use core. With the proposed intensity of development across the site including large employment areas and two neighborhood centers, this density provided realistic opportunities for residents to walk and bicycle to work and to the store rather than using their cars. In the jargon of transportation planners, it 'optimized internal trip capture (i.e. it maximized the number of journeys that begin and end within the same development), thus minimizing the overall transportation impact on the greater area.'

This density was also tempered by significant amounts of public open space incorporated in the site layout; nearly 30 percent of the area was designed as some type of open space. Higher densities were important in this regard because lower densities would not generate enough money for developers to set aside land for open space or important civic buildings.

As the neighborhood transitioned towards the new George W. Liles Parkway, residential uses gave way to a mixture of uses such as flexible office space and live-work units. Two- or three-storey buildings fronted the eastern edge of the large 10-acre (4-hectare) park, but the remaining buildings facing the parkway could be single-storey behind their landscaped buffer. Typical uses for this type of development include professional offices, medical offices or small tenant service businesses.

Mixed-use Campus

The central component of the conceptual plan was a mixed-use, walkable employment center with the capacity of up to 1.5 million square feet (139 354

Figure 9.16 Mixed-use campus, Concord Parkway Master Plan, 2004; The Lawrence Group, Town Planners & Architects. This is the central focus of the development plan. While the design team envisaged this as a high-tech, research-based corporate office area with retail and residential supporting uses, a more generic commercial mix of uses would be equally viable, perhaps with a concentration of medical functions.

square meters) (see Figure 9.16). Offices, the primary use, along with apartments and street-level retail were housed in three- and four-storey buildings lining a linear parkway forming an urban campus environment. This compact development pattern represented a new type of development for Concord, intended to attract high quality tenants looking for an urban atmosphere in a suburban location. Primary access to the site would be via a traffic signal at George W. Liles Parkway or by way of the several roads that parallel the new Parkway.

The centerpiece of this development was its environmental stewardship, a strategy that provided ecological leadership in the area and made good business sense by establishing a strong marketing niche and progressive ethos to differentiate it from competitors. The central boulevard included a sustainable urban

drainage system in its wide median in the form of a linear rain garden to serve as a dry detention and filtration area (see Figure 9.17). Most of the buildings in the campus would have frontage along this attractive, tree-lined boulevard.

The western terminus of the boulevard provided a prominent site backed by a significant stand of trees, the most conspicuous in the area, cresting a knoll and connecting directly to the planned Coddle Creek greenway. The location in front of this knoll should be reserved for a key anchor tenant such as the headquarters for a nationally prominent company. Alternatively, this site would be equally suitable for a school or other similar institutional or civic uses. Regardless of its use, the building that terminates the axis of the boulevard should have architecture that acknowledges its axial location and should be a minimum of three stories tall.

Figure 9.17 Sustainable Urban Drainage System (SUDS), Concord Parkway Master Plan, 2004; The Lawrence Group, Town Planners & Architects. Low Impact Development (LID) is beginning to influence American site design practices. This schematic depiction follows similar guidelines to SUDS in use in British developments such as Upton (see Figures 5.11 and 5.34).

Parking for the buildings lining the boulevard would be handled on-street and to the rear in surface lots or parking decks. The decision to use parking decks, which would be more costly, was a function of the size of the buildings in the campus and the potential density of employees in each building. Call centers, for example, have exceptionally high needs for parking, requiring as many as 16 spaces per 1000 square feet (93 square meters). Typical office uses are much lower ranging from four to six spaces per 1000 square feet (93 square meters). The use of parking decks also allowed the buildings to be set closer together – increasing the urbanism along the boulevard and encouraging greater pedestrian accessibility.

The Great Wagon Road

The remnants of the historic roadway followed old hedgerows that cut across the site and were partially visible on aerial photos (see Figure 9.2). Restoring the historic route was worthy of grant funding, particularly under the NC DOT's enhancement grant program. With or without such external funding, the master plan recommended preserving and celebrating this trail within the site, creating a 10–12 feet (3–3.6 meters) wide greenway path with planted sides and interpretive signage along its length. This path would tie into the Coddle Creek greenway that framed the western side of the site and connect to the new school

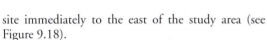

Figure 9.18 Great Wagon Road neighborhood, Concord Parkway Master Plan, 2004; The Lawrence Group, Town Planners & Architects. Remaining fragments of hedgerow marking the site of the old wagon road are stitched together in a linear extension of the extensive Coddle Creek park. The space is somewhat compromised by an existing cellphone tower (a small brown square at the midpoint of the hedgerow) and the line of Concord Farms Road (shown dotted). The line of this road was revised as part of the new street pattern and block structure.

Figure 9.19 School site, Concord Parkway Master Plan, 2004; The Lawrence Group, Town Planners & Architects. The drawing indicates the use of green roofs and the building's siting provides good solar potential on the remaining roof area. Although these ideas of sustainable design are not commonplace in school construction in the conservative Charlotte region, the master plan takes every opportunity to push a sustainability agenda.

site immediately to the east of the study area (see Figure 9.18).

Around the line of the old wagon route, the conceptual master plan showed buildings backing away from the path, to avoid creating spaces that were too urban. Mixed-use buildings of between one and three stories were arranged informally north of the old road to provide over 335 000 square feet (32 516 square meters) of mixed-use space to accommodate small flexible office, retail or service tenants. South of this area, along the small tributary to Coddle Creek, were sites suitable for approximately 350 apartments and town homes. This location took advantage of the creek as an amenity and preserved its frontage with a parkway, incorporating rain gardens as sustainable urban drainage systems wherever possible. Small-scale commercial development filled in the rest of the area fronting on Highway 29, with a small fire station located adjacent to the Coddle Creek greenway south of the Great Wagon Road to service the study area and nearby neighborhoods.

School Site

Immediately east of the site, and located between the Great Wagon Road path and the Philip Morris property, was a beautiful open field enclosed by hedgerows and forest stands. Because of its proximity to residential neighborhoods and to the existing elementary school, this 64-acre (26-hectare) site was well suited for a public middle school (see Figure 9.19). The playing fields and the remainder of the site not needed for school buildings or parking could easily function as a public park incorporating a stretch of the Great Wagon Road interpretive trail. The school itself was illustrated with a green roof as one means of integrating sustainable practices into its design.

This site could be accessed by a proposed full-movement intersection along the George W. Liles Parkway and should connect by a public street to the adjacent Weddington Hills elementary school. This would provide the elementary school with a second entrance, and the new school and park with access to

Figures 9.20 and 9.21 Concord parkway neighborhood center (left) and Main Street (right), Concord Parkway Master Plan, 2004; The Lawrence Group, Town Planners & Architects. The layout of the main retail center on the site is formed by a new pedestrian-friendly Main Street that screens the large parking areas needed for typical grocery stores and other uses in the suburban car-dominated environment.

Weddington Road, thereby improving the surrounding traffic network (see Figure 9.9). The plan also recommended a street stub to the Philip Morris tract to the south to accommodate any future development. Connectivity to future development is always an important element in any master plan.

Southern Neighborhood Center

The southern and larger of the two neighborhood centers was bounded by the George W. Liles Parkway to the east, Concord Parkway to the south and the Coddle Creek tributary to the northwest (see Figure 9.20). A new 'Main Street' provided access to the site from a signalized intersection at Concord Parkway. Mixed-use, commercial and office buildings faced this new street to create an urban gateway into the area (see Figure 9.21). On-street parking provided both convenience as well as safer sidewalks for pedestrians.

Buildings along Concord Parkway were set back about 100 feet (30.5 meters) to allow for a large linear swath of landscaped space that visually extended the parkway aesthetic from the Philip Morris property through the project site. This setback allowed tree planting to occur in more 'natural' clusters and also contained a 10-foot (3 meter) wide multi-purpose path that could extend for several miles in each direction beyond the site boundaries. The master plan contemplated the presence of a medium-sized anchor,

such as a grocery store, of at least 50 000 square feet (4645 square meters) within an overall development of nearly 275 000 square feet (25 548 square meters), typical for most neighborhood centers. The plan recommended that some of the original nursery or garden center operations be retained along Concord Parkway as part of this mixed-use center.

Southside Employment Area

Located on the south side of Concord Parkway, the Southside Employment Area comprised a variety of 'flexible use' buildings for office, research, warehousing and light industrial uses. Direct access to Concord Parkway via a signalized intersection and thence to George W. Liles Parkway leading directly to Interstate-85 made this portion of the plan ideal for larger industrial-type uses that required truck access and that were incompatible with mixed-use and pedestrian-friendly development. The plan illustrated the opportunity for over 500 000 square feet (46 452 square meters) of this flex space (see Figure 9.22).

As with the buildings located on the north side of Concord Parkway, structures to the south of the highway were set back approximately 100 feet (30.5 meters) to allow for the continuation of the landscaped parkway aesthetic. Some buildings lined the parkway, fronting over the landscaped space to create a signature presence on the highway and shield parking areas

Figure 9.22 Southside employment area, Concord Parkway Master Plan, 2004; The Lawrence Group, Town Planners & Architects. Under the Transect methodology, this area would be an Assigned or Special District.

from view with the aid of preserved stands of trees. The remaining buildings and their car parks were spaced to preserve the stream corridors and nestled within existing wooded areas.

Sustainable Design

The master plan pointed out that by their nature, mixed-use centers are inherently urban. That is, the coverage of building footprints, parking areas and impervious hardscape are much higher than in suburban or rural areas. As development occurs, protection of the floodplains in the area is critical. If this area is to thrive as a pedestrian-friendly, mixed-use center, it must have wide sidewalks, small lots, and buildings built close to the street and to each other. An important tool for managing stormwater and water quality in this context is the use of Low Impact Development (LID) standards. (This is very similar in concept to the British SUDS.) The goal of LID is to develop site design techniques and strategies to store, infiltrate, evaporate, retain and detain rain water run-off on the site, to simulate the water run-off characteristics of the land prior to development and to replicate as closely as possible the site's natural and unique hydrology. This limits the increase in pollutant loads caused by development and protects the water quality of streams and rivers. In urban areas, these techniques will range from

conventional underground retention to rain gardens, rain barrels and planted roofs.

The master plan also encouraged the use of the Leadership in Energy and Environmental Design (LEED) guidelines for certifying all new public buildings. Developed by the United States Green Building Council, the LEED Green Building Rating System is a national rating system for buildings designed to accelerate the development and implementation of ecological building practices. To further this goal, the plan urged the city of Concord to encourage the use of 'green' roofs such as planted gardens for all new construction, particularly for public uses such as fire stations and schools. Such roofing systems not only reduce energy costs on the buildings, but they can also be designed to capture and filter stormwater during rainstorms. This type of technology reduces the environmental footprint of a building and promotes sustainable development practices.

IMPLEMENTATION STRATEGIES

The implementation strategies for the Concord plan were very different from those in the Huntersville example. The Concord plan was a lot more speculative and illustrative of future changes to patterns of development in the community; it did not set out specific development projects for short to medium-term implementation in the same way as the Huntersville document. No attempt was made to cost out the various potential developments drawn on the master plan or relate them to public infrastructure costs and property tax income. Because this plan was the first of its type in Concord to incorporate such a high level of urban design detail into a small area plan, it was intended as a vehicle for city planners to demonstrate to developers and elected officials the kind of improved development standards that were possible and desirable, and the capacity of form-based zoning to contribute to these higher criteria. City planners hoped to build a vision that developers could embrace, but this depends ultimately on market conditions. If American developers perceive a market for this kind of mixed-use development, then they are likely to follow the plan; however, contrary to British practice, there is little political will amongst elected officials to use the plan to influence the market, let alone to direct it.

At the time of writing in early summer 2006, 18 months after completion of the charrette, the city council had not formally adopted the plan as a binding document. Currently it exists only as a guide for development in that location. Planning staff review any development proposals that fall within the small area plan to see if they are consistent with the plan's principles, but the layouts of proposed developments do not have to match the urban designs illustrated in the master plan. Planning staff tell developers that planning approval is likely to be easier if they follow the master plan, but there is no legal requirement for them to do so.

City planning staff did look into the possibility of adopting the small area plan as a map amendment to the official zoning map, but the council felt uneasy with that approach and the potential political ramifications. Even though local landowners had participated extensively in the charrette, several remained wary of any administrative zoning change to their property, apparently regarding it as government interference in their private property rights (even if such changes worked to their benefit). The city council became aware of these feelings and backed away from adoption of the master plan and the zoning changes associated with it.

Generally in the USA, owners of undeveloped land wait for interest in their property from developers and then seek a rezoning from the local council to whatever kind of use or uses sought by the developer. Individual landowners feel much more comfortable with this 'market-driven' rezoning approach: they perceive a zoning change that comes from short-term market forces as having more authenticity than one derived from any longer term master plan commissioned by government. This sentiment surfaces however well conceived the plan and however beneficial the recommended changes might be to affected individuals. This muddled thinking by landowners illustrates the difficulties faced by many American attempts at larger scale design-based planning.

As a way of obtaining some modest regulatory force to the master plan, Concord planners intend to dovetail the small area plan into the amended land use plan as they work to update the city's overall land use plan and take it back before council for adoption in 2007. In this way the small area plan would eventually be adopted by default; it would still act as guidance only, but the plan would have a few more teeth since it would then be a publicly adopted document, and willful deviations from it by elected officials would be open to active scrutiny and questioning by the public and the local press.

All told, it is very unlikely in this case study that actual development on the project site would follow the patterns set out in the master plan drawings, even though the master plan illustrates what the charrette team believe to be the best urban design layout for that large piece of land. Certain key provisions may be translated into actuality, particularly the preservation of the historic line of the Great Wagon Road, but everything else is likely to remain a picture of unrealized potential as there are few mechanisms in conventional American planning to translate the detail plan provisions into legally enforceable public policy, nor much political desire to do so, on the grounds that, as in this case, such action might unduly limit the perceived rights of property owners.

However, for progressive communities who do want to take more active charge of their development future, one way around the procedural hurdles placed in the way of adopting detailed design-based plans has been demonstrated by another town in the Charlotte region, Davidson, NC, west of Concord and north of Huntersville. Davidson's nationally recognized efforts at smart growth and the author's work in that town has been discussed elsewhere (Walters and Brown, 2004), and once again that progressive community has shown a way to implement more detailed urban design as a component of planning practice.

Davidson treated a similar small area plan like a large 'planned unit development,' normally a detailed design for a large project area, and amended their zoning map and existing form-based zoning ordinance to reflect the specific zoning and design content for each area in that master plan. This proactive procedure was an example of the political drive for smart growth shown by Davidson's elected officials over several years, and this kind of political authority is central to the success of detailed urban design as public policy. Without it, the urban design content of master plans remains advisory only, and relatively impotent. The Davidson example is not normal municipal practice in America; more usually, as in the case of Concord, developers who want to deviate substantially from the plan are allowed to make their case before the town's planning commission. Planners are always hopeful that their commission members will support the master plan, but this is by no means certain when there is political pressure to override it.

This illustrates once again that the power in American planning practice to push future development in positive directions lies with form-based zoning ordinances rather than master plans. Plans like this Concord example act as vehicles to decide what form-based zoning provisions should be created, rather than as concrete visions of future development. The form-based zoning derived from the plan benefits from the detailed study provided by the master plan in terms of its site specificity, and it is through the power of form-based zoning that the most immediate effects of this and other master plans will be felt.

New Zoning Districts

The master plan recommended creating mixed-use districts in the city zoning ordinance requiring a mix of uses and design standards for all areas so designated in the city's land use plan. All mixed-use districts would have design specifications regulating building form and placement, building façade treatment, mixture of uses, landscaping, parking and pedestrian amenities, all specified in a form-based code ready for adoption. The introductory chart for the mixed-use district zoning amendment, developed from form-based principles, is illustrated in Table 9.1, and incorporates the urban typologies of the Transect system described earlier. Figure 9.23 shows the Regulating Plan for these Transect zones applied to the project site. Although the Transect methodology was too radical a divergence from conventional zoning practice for Concord officials to incorporate it into their existing scheme of development control, planners did develop four new mixed-use districts based on the recommendations of the charrette report and master plan. These were added to the existing regulations available for use at a variety of locations when requested by developers; the city's policy is to encourage developers to use these regulations for developments within the small area plan, but it does not yet require them to do so.

CRITICAL EVALUATION OF THE CASE STUDY

The effectiveness of this project is hard to determine. The charrette process went smoothly, the urban design master plan has many strengths, and strikes a workable balance between market responsiveness and introducing progressive and sustainable design concepts to a community with little experience in that regard. Planning staff have supported the plan's concepts and tried to implement its recommendations, but in contrast to the Huntersville example, political action on the plan has been limited and developer interest lukewarm.

Lack of firm political endorsement of plans such as this example is, unfortunately, not unusual in mainstream American communities, where suspicion remains strong about coordinated public sector planning even when the desire exists to improve development practices. Even in progressive Huntersville, a minority of elected officials actively opposed adoption of the plan for ideological reasons, and in Concord, despite planning staff's recommendations, elected officials were unconvinced of the advantages of this kind of active growth management. The project site can play an important part in helping reduce the suburban sprawl that has engulfed the original historic town by providing a model of compact development within the town boundary rather than continually spreading beyond it, but it remains to be seen whether elected officials will take advantage of these possibilities.

The proactive planning that took place through this master plan process represents an opportunity to create a new place that is not entirely dependent on the automobile for every trip. The block structure, connectivity and street designs depicted in the conceptual master plan illustrate an infrastructure pattern supportive of mixed-use development, public transit and walkability. A firm and ringing endorsement of the plan by elected officials with zoning actions to match would have sent a strong, progressive message about standards required in future development. This has not happened. The determining ethos in Concord, as in most towns and cities across America, is to let the market decide where development should happen; the public sector's task is to facilitate that pattern. As an editorial in one of Charlotte's glossy magazines recently opined: '... politicians play a role in the [development] process, helping ... smooth whatever municipal pitfalls lie in front of developers and improv[ing] roads in and out of [their] establishments' (Trimakas: p. 4). Many Americans would agree exactly with that sentiment, which inevitably leaves planning and urban design to follow behind the market, trying to make the best of decisions already taken.

The charrette team paid very close attention to market forces in developing the conceptual master plan. This is common sense and important in all community design charrettes, but particularly so in Concord. Two primary strategies for economic development shared by the city of Concord and the regional Chamber of Commerce sought to promote small business growth and diversify the local economy, and the study area provided a perfect opportunity to advance these initiatives. Many components of the conceptual master plan presented opportunities to encourage entrepreneurial or small business growth as well as space to meet the demand for medical offices.

Table 9.1 Form-based standards by Transect zone

Building Type	T1	T2 Civic Institutional House	T3 Civic Institutional House Townhouse	T4 Civic Institutional House Townhouse Flat/Loft Mixed-Use Commercial	T5 Civic Institutional House Townhouse Flat/Loft Mixed-Use Commercial	T6 Civic Institutional House Townhouse Flat/Loft Mixed-Use Commercial
Permitted uses	agriculture	residential civic institutional	residential civic institutional	residential civic institutional retail office	residential civic institutional retail office	residential civic institutional retail office
Maximum density (units/acre)	not applicable	1	4	15	no maximum	no maximum
Minimum height	not applicable	none	none	none	none	2 stories or 20 feet
Maximum height	not applicable	50 feet	3 stories	3 stories	4 stories	none
Open space Dedication	not required	not required	yes	yes	yes	not required
On-street Parking	not applicable	occasional	occasional	dedicated	marked	marked
Lighting	not required	not required	regular spacing	pedestrian-scaled	pedestrian-scaled	pedestrian-scaled
Curb	not required	not required	Rolled/Valley or Standard	standard	standard	standard
Drainage	open swale	open swale	closed	closed	closed	closed
Street trees	not required	not required	40 feet average spacing in planting strip	40 feet average spacing in planting strip or tree wells	40 feet average spacing in planting strip or tree wells	40 feet average spacing in tree wells
Sidewalk	not required	multi-use path (10 feet minimum)	5 feet both sides	5–16 feet both sides	5–16 feet both sides	8–16 feet both sides

Colored columns relate specifically to Concord master plan. (See Figure 9.23).

Figure 9.23 Regulating Plan, Concord Parkway Master Plan, 2004; The Lawrence Group, Town Planners & Architects. (Read in conjunction with Table 9.1.) The five applicable zones of the Transect methodology are indicated as follows: *green* – T1, Natural Zone; *ochre* – T4, General Urban Zone; *brown umber* – T5, Urban Center Zone; *red-brown* – T6, Urban Core Zone; *gray* – Assigned or Special district (not shown on the transect diagram). These simple form-based categories provide all the necessary basic regulations for instigating and managing development.

Events subsequent to the charrette proved the team's analysis to be accurate about the demand and type of business activity suitable for the area, and about the effectiveness of a campus environment for attracting high-tech industries. But that kind of development interest in the project site was temporarily quashed when the same kind of development envisaged in the master plan was located, unexpectedly, just a few miles west of the project site in the adjacent town of Kannapolis, an old mill town contiguous with Concord. For years Kannapolis boasted a huge textile operation, but in 2003, the mills closed for good, laying off nearly 5000 workers and leaving derelict an industrial site of several hundred acres and nearly 6.5 million square feet (603 870 square meters) of old and obsolete industrial space.

This was a devastating blow to the local economy, with untold hardship for many working class families. The closure also left a huge brownfield site of abandoned buildings and contaminated ground. Salvation appeared in the form of a billionaire industrialist David Murdock who bought the site to realize his long-held dream of creating a new biological research campus for the advancement of medical and nutritional sciences in association with a consortium of local universities. On a site of more than 350 acres, Murdock's vision called for over 1 million square feet of office space housing biotechnology offices, research labs and medical offices, 350 000 square feet of retail and commercial space, and 700 housing units. For comparison, on the project site just over twice the size of the Kannapolis project, this case study master plan

239

provided over 2 million square feet of research labs and office space, over 400 000 square feet of retail and commercial, and nearly 1500 units of housing plus civic and institutional buildings. The two projects were thus very similar in scope and density; the charrette team read the market conditions accurately, but Kannapolis' gain was Concord's loss as the Murdock campus site will absorb the demand for the kind of high-tech industries envisaged in the case study master plan for several years to come.

The new buildings on the old industrial site in Kannapolis, beginning to be constructed in the summer of 2006, are arranged in a formal campus layout utilizing neo-classical architecture throughout. The aesthetic choices reportedly follow the dictates of the client, and when someone is investing many millions of their own money, their taste tends to dominate, but a marked preference for designing new academic and research buildings in neo-classical styles has been well-established across a multitude of American universities and colleges for many years, particularly in the southern states (see Figure 9.24). This popular taste for historicist architecture tends to be a pervasive factor in public discourse about new development in many regions of the USA and the charrette team tacitly acknowledged this in their various presentation drawings for the master plan on the Concord Parkway site.

While the agenda for sustainable design was carried in the text of the project report with specific recommendations for low impact site design and LEED certification for major buildings, and was also implicit in the urban design of the master plan, the three-dimensional images that carried this message were limited to those depicting urban spaces incorporating low-impact or sustainable urban drainage systems (see Figure 9.17) rather than illustrating contemporary buildings. Where buildings were shown, they were rendered either as background urban vernacular building types (see Figure 9.17) or as the standard commercial style for new retail and office developments (see Figure 9.21). This was a deliberate and tactical decision by the charrette team, who were able to gauge the mood and preferences of

Figure 9.24 Academic building, Central Piedmont Community College, Charlotte, NC, 2005; Little Diversified Architectural Consulting, Architects. Neo-classicism is the style of choice for many new academic buildings at American colleges. While many such buildings manifest a superficial nostalgia instead of rigorous adherence to neo-classical principles of design, this example does at least pay attention to some aspects of classical proportion and harmony.

charrette participants. In this conservative context, team members felt it was more important to persuade elected officials and developers of the merits of ecologically sensitive urban design, mixed-use and walkable neighborhoods than to advance an agenda for contemporary architecture to any degree that would obscure or divert attention from these main urban issues. Accordingly, all the graphics focused on urban design concepts, while the architecture remained generic and locally uncontroversial. As such, this case study epitomized the frustrating yet predominant condition in many American communities outside a few major cities with cultural appetites for architecture: sustainable urban design is slowly becoming an acceptable topic in civic discourse; however, its corollary of contemporary, energy efficient architecture has yet to capture the public's imagination or interest.

Afterword

The message of this book has been very simple: after several decades of absence, urban design has once again come to the fore in planning practice, and professional planners and urban designers in America and Britain share many concepts in common. Urban design professionals from both nations could cross over the Atlantic and pick up the threads of design practice in the opposite country with barely any hesitation or learning curve.

Compare once more the master plans from the Concord charrette and the Upton development at Northampton in the UK (Figures 5.28 and 5.29). The similarities are easy to see in their mutual concern for 'traditional urbanism' – well-defined urban space, enclosed 'urban rooms' of streets and squares with parking areas screened behind buildings, and the careful integration of natural areas of open space and civic buildings such as schools into the urban framework. Both plans stand out as urbane counterpoints to the formless suburban development around their borders.

There is certainly more space devoted to cars in the American version, due in part to a lack of transit options, and also a preponderance of commercial space in some parts of the Concord plan, which incorporates some realities of contemporary retail development while curbing its worst excesses with basic urban design principles of street patterns and spatial enclosure. But apart from these programmatic variations, the similarities are striking. The vocabularies of urban form and space, and the priorities for sustainable site design and attractive pedestrian environments are almost identical in the two examples from different countries. But the political contexts in which these designs are made could not be more different, and this has been the second major theme of the book.

As a British architect teaching and practicing in America, the author has benefited considerably from the genuine politeness and respect shown by most Americans for his English heritage. But there has been one disquieting common thread running through all 20-plus years of this professional experience in America: much like British attitudes in an earlier age of Empire, most Americans assume that because America is the most powerful nation on earth, the way Americans do things must be better than any other nation. From this perspective, the way American government operates, as decreed by the Constitution, must be the best; and within this framework, American planning, even with all its flaws, is regarded from a similarly blinkered perspective. The thought that other countries may be better at designing their cities and managing their environment rarely occurs to people outside the research arms of the design and planning professions.

To an extent these feelings of national superiority are natural, and every country manifests their own version as cultural and historical values are absorbed into generalized political views of the larger world. Most Britons would probably still hold their country and its systems of administration in equivalently high regard, and accept the British balance between private property rights and the public good as an appropriate one for a small and crowded island. In the author's experience, many Americans, when they understand more about the British system and its inherent communal bias regarding the limitations placed on the development rights of private property, have little hesitation in traducing such a system as 'socialist,' or even 'communist.' British values of communally planned and managed growth, that have been accepted as norms since World War II, trespass upon sacred American beliefs concerning private property and the expectation of property owners to develop their land at any time for almost any purpose, subject only to the push and pull of short-term market forces.

Political opinions about planning in America mirror the populist priorities of market forces over planned growth. While many people complain about ugly and poorly planned suburban environments in America, very few would accept the curtailment of property rights necessary to improve these conditions by developing coordinated area plans based on sound urban design principles and then making each property owner stick to the plan. The master plan for Upton is likely to be implemented in a manner very close to its original form, as developers follow detailed design codes that enforce the design content and standards of the planned layout with little variation. By contrast, the Concord plan has no chance of being implemented in the form in which it is drawn. There is no popular or political will to do so and no mechanism for enacting the design provisions. The best that the design team can hope for is that demonstrating the viability of sustainable urban design principles will spur the imagination of progressive developers, who could capitalize on the site's unique potential and develop it in stages as market conditions allow.

As neat and coherent as it sounds, there are many things wrong with the British planning system. For decades good, practical urban design guidance has been promulgated at a number of official and quasi-official levels, but most British suburban development during that time has been mediocre at best, downright ugly and wasteful at worst. From that frustrating perspective, the activism, coherence and missionary zeal of American New Urbanists offers an attractive model for progress, where urban design quality is directly encapsulated in design-based regulations that control the build out of each development. Since the mid-1990s, New Urbanist theory and practice has delivered a sharp shock to an American planning system that had all but forgotten that urban design existed. Now planners and planning students are scrambling to learn skills that have been absent from planning curricula for decades. A national conference for mid-career American planners in 2006 highlighted three areas of important continuing education: form-based codes, urban design and public participation techniques – the three main topics of this book.

In many ways, Upton, and new developments like it all over England, are direct descendants of Seaside, the Florida community that begat New Urbanism back in the early 1980s. But New Urbanist codes come in many shapes and sizes, depending whether they are publicly or privately administered, and in America, the movement is divided between its historicist wing, which incorporates traditional architecture into its principles, and its infrastructural wing, whose priorities are more generic and social, having to do with transit, ecology and social justice. Where aesthetics are concerned, this latter group demonstrates a general preference for contemporary architecture, but this is not their primary focus.

It seems clear that the complexities of New Urbanism are largely misunderstood or ignored in Britain, where uncritical analysis has defined the movement's aims and ambitions in terms of historicist tendencies alone. This book has in part tried to correct that mistake, and to draw attention to the realities of New Urbanist practice so that British readers can make more measured assessments of American precedents. To this end, the convergence of New Urbanist design theory and commercial development practice is unusual – but helpful. As recently as the 1990s, New Urbanist precepts were markedly in conflict with developers' ideas, and in 2006 it is still a little disorienting for urban designers to find themselves in harmony with members of the real estate industry who have traditionally been adversaries. At the beginning of the 1990s, to propose ideas of traditional urbanism in the context of American sprawl was to invite scorn and derision from developers and builders. This author was used to advocating changes in development practices to stony and unsympathetic audiences – or else the developers and real estate brokers found ideas of mixed-use and traditional urbanism so funny they could hardly stifle their mirth. But, by the end of the decade, the author often found himself on discussion panels with leading developers who recited New Urbanist principles word for word, claiming them as their own credo. This was an amazingly fast conversion, but these developers are the avant-garde of their profession and represent a relatively small minority. Unfortunately most developers in America are still producing conventional, outdated and unsustainable patterns of development despite changing demographics and lifestyle choices by consumers.

These outdated development practices persist despite the evidence that Americans who can afford it are paying small fortunes to live in traditional towns, places like Alexandria, VA, Charleston, SC, and Savannah, GA. Property prices are going through the roof as people vote with their wallets about the kind of places they prefer to live. And these homebuyers live 21st century lives in every respect; they want walkable neighborhoods with parks, well-designed urban spaces, and a variety of uses to enlarge their lifestyle choices and reduce their energy bills. The challenge in the USA is to produce enough new developments that provide these same attributes of sustainable urbanism while making them affordable to consumers from a wide range of income levels. Only when walkable, mixed-use neighborhoods become the normal condition of new development will prices come down to levels that are affordable to a wide spectrum of American families.

In terms of slowing the juggernaut of sprawl in America this embryonic alliance between theory and practice, and between planning, urban design and development, is an essential bond to be nurtured in every way possible. Architects and planners have relearned how traditional urbanism can help heal

American cities, and now is not the best moment for academics to disparage this practice and search instead for new theoretical forms of esoteric urbanism. While parts of American and British cities decay and the environment becomes more degraded, professionals on both sides of the Atlantic have their work cut out to improve and sustain the urban habitat before these problems reach unmanageable proportions. Academic architects and planners should resist fiddling while our cities burn.

Just as British professionals look to America for inspiration and New Urbanist precedents for improving the sad design quality of British suburbia, so do American planners and urban designers look enviously at Britain – a land where plans mean what they say and good urban design is a matter of public policy. American urbanists can only dream of a society where public good can hold sway over individual selfishness, and where communal standards of good design are legally enforceable without fear of lengthy and expensive legal challenge. But there is only so much that each side can learn from the other; the political divide is too great to be easily bridged. However, the struggles are similar, as are the means to make decent, attractive and sustainable places to live. This book has tried to improve each nation's understanding of the successes and failures of the other's processes of planning and urban design, and in so doing hold up a mirror to reflect one's own systems of belief, professional standards and methodologies. While British planners and designers work within a system, however imperfect, that provides a national framework for improving the design of towns and cities and protecting the countryside, and while their American counterparts struggle against a tide of political indifference and ideological opposition to these same objectives, both sets of professionals share an urgent concern for the future health of our planet and its urban culture. We have to win this battle for sustainable cities, and if, as the old adage goes, we do not succeed at first, we have to try and try again – before time runs out.

Essential attributes of form-based codes

This summary is adapted and extended from definitions and commentary by Paul Crawford, in *Form-based Codes: Implementing Smart Growth*, [California] Local Government Commission (www.lgc.org) and Craig Lewis, *Design-Based Codes* (2003).

In summary, form-based zoning codes must possess the following 12 essential characteristics:

1. Codes must focus on form, not use. Form-based codes de-emphasize the regulation of density and use in favor of rules for building form. They recognize that uses change over time but that buildings endure.
2. Form-based codes are organized around spatially defined districts, neighborhoods and corridors that manifest particular urban characteristics.
3. Form-based codes recognize the importance of well-defined and well-designed public spaces. This generally means that buildings in urban areas must be built close to the street to achieve this definition and help create a sense of place. Great attention must be paid to the design of the streetscape and the role of buildings in shaping that public realm.
4. As part of this definition of space and place, street level activity must be stimulated by mixing uses to create different rhythms of pedestrian activity during the day, the night and the week, and this ambience must be supported by pedestrian-friendly design of the lower stories of buildings. Building façades are very important, and the normative three-part design composition of base, middle and top can provide a useful design vocabulary. Where a contemporary design language is used for a building,

care must still be taken to provide a safe, attractive and meaningful pedestrian experience at street level with clearly observable windows and doorways while safeguarding the privacy of occupants.
5. Streets must be safe, convenient and attractive for pedestrians, cars, transit and bicyclists.
6. Parking lots must be concealed behind buildings and on-street parking provided for short-term use and for protecting pedestrian activity on the sidewalk from fast-moving traffic.
7. Neighborhoods should be compact, pedestrian-friendly, mixed-use, and provide a range of housing types. This brings workplaces, shops, schools, churches and parks into close proximity to housing and provides housing choices within a community that can meet the needs of many individuals at different times of their lives, especially with regard to older adults 'aging in place' and maintaining viable lives as part of the community.
8. Form-based codes are style neutral. This cannot be stressed enough, particularly in the context of much British misunderstanding of New Urbanism (see Chapter 6) where it is often mistakenly identified as inherently historicist or neo-classical. New Urbanist development in the USA can be found in many different kinds of styles, particularly in urban areas like Los Angeles. Only in certain regions such as the American South, where history and tradition weigh heavily on popular taste are New Urbanist developments predominantly historicist in nature.
9. Codes must be written in clear and concise language. Design standards should be tied to measurable purposes and outcomes. For example, ensuring infill

buildings are compatible with their context facilitates the creation of a convenient, attractive and harmonious community, and thus draws the 'essential nexus' between the regulations and a valid public purpose.

10. The codes must be presented in an easy to read format. This is nearly as important as the standards themselves. Standards should be clear in their narrative, as they will likely be tested in court by the interpretation of the text. Graphics, photos and illustrations should be included in generous quantities, but they should only supplement the text; they should not supplant it. Basic publishing rules apply – a readable typeface, consistent margins, balanced page composition and a thorough index are necessary. Communities in America should also consider the prevalence of codifying ordinances through web-based code clearing houses such as the Municipal Code Corporation. The format of the code should not be so rigid or over-sophisticated in its format so as to preclude publishing through these commercial companies.

11. The codes are produced through a design-focused process of public participation that assures discussion of urban form and land use issues. (This could most easily be a charrette that produces the detailed master plan for a limited and site-specific study area from which the code is derived, or from an extensive public process, as in the case of Huntersville, NC, where the whole zoning ordinance was completely rewritten.) This public process helps reduce conflict, misunderstandings and the need for lengthy, contentious hearings as individual projects are reviewed.

12. The most important tool in successful implementation of a form-based code is the facilitation of permits. Requiring developers to submit to design requirements, particularly in an area where such regulations are relatively new, and then sending their development application through an extensive public process is the equivalent of hitting them with two sticks and taking away the carrot. In general, developers are much more willing to abide by design standard and guidelines if they know that compliance will ensure a permit. Well-written design regulations ensure a sense of predictability for both developers and the public. If this can be combined with an expedited permitting process (most easily done on projects developed and controlled by a single master plan), design-based codes will also provide incentives to developers to spend money on important elements such as the building façades and better materials rather than on a prolonged public process and loan interest. (*Author note*: Surprisingly, one of the leading smart growth communities in America, Davidson, NC, fails miserably in this regard. Despite the details of the form-based code, planning staff and elected officials continually muddle the process and keep adding subjective requirements to projects that already meet the code and should be quickly approved. Behavior like this brings smart growth and form-based zoning into disrepute.)

References

Abercrombie, P. (1933). *Town and Country Planning*. London: Thornton Butterworth.

Abercrombie, P. (1945). *Greater London Plan 1944*. London: HMSO.

AJ (1966). 'House at Highgate.' *The Architects' Journal*, 23 March, 763–769.

AJ (1974). 'Stamford Hill supports house assembly kits.' *The Architects' Journal*, 28 August, 484–489.

AJ (1975). 'PSSHAK mark 2: flexible GLC housing takes a step forward.' *The Architects' Journal*, 21 May, 1070–1073.

Albrecht, J. and Lim, G.-C. (1986). 'A search for alternative planning theory: use of critical theory.' *Journal of Architectural and Planning Research*, Vol. 5, No. 3, 117–131.

Aldous, T. (1992). *Urban Villages: A Concept for Creating Mixed-use Urban Developments on a Sustainable Scale*. London: Urban Villages Group.

Aldous, T. (ed.). (1995). *Economics of Urban Villages: A Report by the Economics Working Party of the Urban Villages Forum*. London: Urban Villages Forum.

Alexander, C. (1966). 'A city is not a tree.' *Design*, No. 206, February, 46–55.

Alexander, C., Silverstein, M. and Ishikawa, S. (1977). *Pattern Language: Towns, Buildings, Construction*. New York: Oxford University Press.

Alexander, C., Neis, H., Anninou, A. and King, I. (1987). *A New Theory of Urban Design*. New York: Oxford University Press.

Altshuler, A. (1965a). 'The goals of comprehensive planning.' *Journal of the American Institute of Planners*, Vol. 31, 186–197.

Altshuler, A. (1965b). *The City Planning Process*. Ithaca, NY: Cornell University Press.

Ambrose, P. (1994). *Urban Process and Power*. London: Routledge.

American Institute of Architects (AIA). (2004). *R/UDAT – Planning Your Community's Future: A Guide to the Regional/Urban Assistance Team Program*. Washington, DC: AIA.

American Planning Association (APA), Morris, M. (ed.). (1996). *Creating Transit-Supportive Land-Use Regulations*. Planning Advisory Service Report No. 468. Chicago, IL, American Planning Association.

American Planning Association (APA). (2004). *Codifying New Urbanism; How to Reform Municipal Land Development Regulations*. Planning Advisory Service Report No. 526. Chicago, IL: Congress for the New Urbanism and the American Planning Association.

Arendt, R. (1994). *Rural by Design: Maintaining Small Town Character*. Chicago, IL: Planners Press.

Arendt, R. (1996). *Conservation Design for Subdivisions: A Practical Guide to Creating Open Space Networks*. Washington, DC: Island Press.

Arnstein, S. (1969). 'A ladder of citizen participation.' *Journal of the American Institute of Planners*, Vol. 8, No. 3, July. In: Stein, J.M. (ed.). (1995). *Classic Readings in Urban Planning*, 358–375. New York: McGraw-Hill.

Audirac, I. (1999). 'Stated preference for pedestrian proximity: an assessment of New Urbanist sense of community.' *Journal of Planning Education and Research*, Vol. 19, No. 1, 53–66.

Audirac, I. and Shermyen, A.H. (1994). 'An evaluation of neotraditional design's social prescription: postmodern placebo or remedy for metropolitan malaise?' *Journal of Planning Education and Research*, Vol. 13, No. 3, 161–173.

Baird, G. (2005). 'The Michigan debates on urbanism.' In: Fishman, R. (ed.). (2005). *New Urbanism: Peter Calthorpe vs. Lars Lerup. Michigan Debates on Urbanism, Vol. II*, 2–4. Ann Arbor, MI: The University of Michigan A. Alfred Taubman College of Architecture + Urban Planning.

Banfield, E.C. (1974). *Unheavenly City Revisited*. Boston, MA: Little Brown.

Banham, R. (1963). 'CIAM.' In: Hatjie, G. (ed.), *Encyclopedia of Modern Architecture*, 70–73. London: Thames and Hudson.

Barnett, J. (1974). *Urban Design as Public Policy: Practical Methods for Improving Cities.* New York: McGraw-Hill.

Barnett, J. (1982). *An Introduction to Urban Design.* New York: Harper & Row.

Barnett, J. (2003). *Redesigning Cities: Principles, Practices, Implementation.* Chicago, IL: Planners Press.

Barnett, J. (2004). 'New Urbanism and codes.' In: *Codifying New Urbanism: How to Reform Municipal Land Development Regulations.* Planning Advisory Service Report Number 526. Chicago, IL: Congress for the New Urbanism and the American Planning Association.

Barton, H., Grant, M. and Guise, R. (2003). *Shaping Neighborhoods: A Guide for Health, Sustainability and Vitality.* London: Spon Press.

Batchelor, P. and Lewis, D. (eds). (1985). *Urban Design in Action: The History, Theory and Development of the American Institute of Architects' Regional/Urban Design Assistance T (R/UDAT) Program Teams.* Raleigh, NC: The School of Design, North Carolina State University and the American Institute of Architects.

Beauregard, R.A. (1989). 'Between modernity and postmodernity: the ambiguous position of US planning.' *Environment and Planning D: Society and Space,* Vol.7, 381–395. In: Bridge, G. and Watson, S. (2002). *The Blackwell City Reader,* 502–512. Oxford: Blackwell.

Beauregard, R.A. (1991). 'Without a net: planning and the postmodernist abyss.' *Journal of Planning Education and Research,* Vol. 10, No. 3, Summer, 189–194.

Bentley, I., Alcock, A., Murrain, P., McGlynn, S. and Smith, G. (1985). *Responsive Environments: A Manual for Designers.* London: Architectural Press.

Bentley, I. (1999). *Urban Transformations: Power, People and Urban Design.* London: Routledge.

Biddulph, M. (2000). 'Villages don't make a city.' *Journal of Urban Design,* Vol. 5, No. 1, 65–82.

Biddulph, M., Franklin, B. and Tait, M. (2003). 'From concept to completion: a critical analysis of the urban village.' *Town Planning Review,* Vol. 74, No. 2, 165–193.

Blake, P. (1974). *Form Follows Fiasco: Why Modernism Hasn't Worked.* Boston: Little, Brown.

Bohl, C.C. (2000). 'New Urbanism and the city: potential applications and implications for distressed inner-city neighborhoods.' *Housing Policy Debate,* Vol. 11, No. 4, 761–819.

Bohl, C.C. (2002). *Place Making: Developing Town Centers, Main Streets, and Urban Villages.* Washington, DC: Urban Land Institute.

Bolan, R. (1980). 'The practitioner as theorist: the phenomenology of the professional episode.' *Journal of the American Planning Association,* Vol. 46, No. 2, 261–274.

Bosselman, F., Callies, D. and Banta, J. (1973). *The Taking Issue.* Washington, DC: US Government Printing Office.

Boyer, M.C. (1983). *Dreaming the Rational City: The Myth of American City Planning.* Cambridge, MA: MIT Press.

Brindley, T., Rydin, Y. and Stoker, G. (1989). *Remaking Planning: The Politics of Urban Change in the Thatcher Years.* London: Unwin Hyman.

Broadbent, G. (1990). *Emerging Concepts of Urban Space Design.* London: Van Nostrand Reinhold.

Broady, M. (1966). 'Social theory in architectural design.' *Arena: The Architectural Association Journal,* Vol. 81, No. 898, January, 149–154. Reprinted in: Gutman, R. (ed.). (1972). *People and Buildings.* New York: Basic Books.

Brooke, S. (1995). *Seaside.* Gretna, LO: Pelican.

Brower, S. (1996). *Good Neighborhoods.* Westport, CT: Praeger.

Brower, S. (2002). 'The Sectors of the Transect.' *Journal of Urban Design,* Vol. 7, No. 3, October, 313–320.

Brownhill, S. (1990). *Developing London's Docklands: Another Great Planning Disaster?* London: Paul Chapman.

CABE (Commission for Architecture and the Built Environment) and DETR (Department for Transport, Environment and the Regions). (2001). *The Value of Urban Design.* London: Thomas Telford Publishing.

CABE (2003a). *Protecting Design Quality in Planning.* London: CABE.

CABE (2003b). *The Councillor's Guide to Urban Design.* London: CABE.

CABE (2003c). *The Use of Urban Design Codes: Building Sustainable Communities.* London: CABE.

CABE (2004a). *Creating Successful Masterplans: A Guide for Clients.* London: CABE.

CABE (2004b). *Creating Successful Masterplans: A Guide for Clients (Executive Summary).* London: CABE.

CABE (2004c). *Housing Audit: Assessing the Design Quality of New Homes.* London: CABE.

CABE (2005a). *Making Design Policy Work: How to Deliver Good Design Through Your Local Development Framework.* London: CABE.

CABE (2005b). *Design Coding: Testing its Use in England.* London: CABE.

CABE (2005c). *Creating Successful Neighbourhoods: Lessons and Actions for Housing Market Renewal.* London: CABE.

Campbell, S. and Fainstein, S. (1996). *Readings in Planning Theory.* Oxford: Blackwell.

Calthorpe Associates (1992). *Transit-Oriented Development Design Guidelines.* San Diego, CA: City of San Diego.

Calthorpe, P. (1993). *The Next American Metropolis: Ecology, Community and the American Dream.* New York: Princeton Architectural Press.

Calthorpe, P. and Fulton, W. (2001). *The Regional City.* Washington DC: Island Press.

Calthorpe, P. (2005). 'New Urbanism: Principles or Style?' In: Fishman, R. (ed.). (2005). *New Urbanism: Peter Calthorpe vs. Lars Lerup. Michigan Debates on Urbanism, Vol. II,* 16–38. Ann Arbor, MI: The University of Michigan A. Alfred Taubman College of Architecture + Urban Planning.

Capo, J. (2004). 'CATS' Light Rail, Agenda 21, the UN & You.' *The Rhinoceros Times,* 20 May.

Carlo, G. de. (1948). 'The housing problem in Italy.' *Freedom,* 9/12, 2 and 9/13, 2.

Carmona, M., Heath, T., Oc, T. and Tiesdell, S. (2003). *Public Places, Urban Spaces: The Dimensions of Urban Design.* Oxford: Architectural Press.

Charlotte/Mecklenburg Planning Commission. (1992; codified through February 2006). *Zoning Ordinance: Urban Mixed Use District Regulations.* Charlotte, NC: Charlotte/ Mecklenburg Planning Commission.

Chase, J., Crawford, M. and Kaliski, J. (1999). *Everyday Urbanism.* New York: Monacelli Press.

Church, A. (1992). 'Land and property: the pattern and process of development from 1981.' In: Ogden, P. (ed.). (1992). *London Docklands: The Challenge of Development,* 43–51. Cambridge: Cambridge University Press.

Churchill, W. (1943). House of Commons Debate. *393 H.C. Deb. (5th series),* 403.

City of Salisbury (2001). *Salisbury Vision 2020 Comprehensive Plan.* Salisbury, NC: City of Salisbury.

Clark, J.P. and Martin, C. (eds). (2004). *Anarchy, Geography, Modernity: The Radical Social Thought of Elisée Reclus.* Lanham, MA: Lexington Books.

Coleman, A. (1985). *Utopia on Trial.* London: Hillary Shipman.

Coleman, R. (1978). *Attitudes towards Neighborhoods: How Americans Choose to Live.* Working Paper No. 49. Cambridge, MA: Joint Center for Urban Studies of MIT and Harvard University.

Collins, J. and Moren, P. (2006). *Good Practice Guide: Negotiating the Planning Maze.* London: RIBA Publishing.

Congress for the New Urbanism (1998). *Charter of the New Urbanism,* available at: http://www.cnu.org/charter.html.

Congress for the New Urbanism (2000). *Charter of the New Urbanism.* New York: McGraw-Hill.

Congress for the New Urbanism (2002). *Greyfields into Goldfields: Dead Malls Become Living Neighborhoods.* San Francisco, CA: Congress for the New Urbanism.

Conroy, S. (1998). 'Democracy, public space and civic life.' Transcript of radio program: *Radio Open Learning – The Good Citizen: Australian democracy and citizenship.* Transcript at: www.abc.net.au/ola/citizen/eps/ep09/texalone9.htm.

Conzen, M.R.G. (1968). 'The use of town plans in the study of urban history.' In: Dyos, H. (ed.), *The Study of Urban History,* 113–130. New York: St Martin's Press.

Cooke, P. (1988). 'Modernity, postmodernity and the city.' *Theory, Culture and Society,* Vol. 5, No. 3, 475–492.

Cooley, C. (1909). *Social Organization: A Study of the Larger Mind.* New York: Charles Scribner's Sons.

County Council of Essex (1973). *A Design Guide for Residential Areas.* Chelmsford: County Council of Essex.

Cowan, R. with the Urban Design Group and the Urban Design Alliance. (2002). *Urban Design Guidance: Urban Design Frameworks, Development Briefs and Master Plans.* London: Thomas Telford.

Crawford, M. (2005). 'Everyday urbanism.' In: Kelbaugh, D. (series ed.), *Everyday Urbanism, Margaret Crawford vs. Michael Speaks. Michigan Debates on Urbanism, Vol. I*, 16–32. Ann Arbor, MI: The University of Michigan A. Alfred Taubman College of Architecture + Urban Planning.

Crawford, P. (n.d.). 'What are form-based codes?' In: *Form-based Codes: Implementing Smart Growth.* Sacramento: [California] Local Government Commission, unpaginated. www.lgc.org.

Cullen, G. (1961). *Townscape.* London: The Architectural Press.

Cullen, G. (1967). 'Notation 1–4.' *The Architects' Journal (Supplements)*, 31 May, 12 July, 23 August, 27 September.

Cullingworth, J.B. (1993). *The Political Culture of Planning: American land Use Planning in Comparative Perspective.* New York: Routledge.

Cullingworth, J.B. (1997). *Planning in the USA: Policies, Issues and Processes.* London: Routledge.

Cullingworth, J.B. and Nadin, V. (1997). *Town and Country Planning in the UK*, 12th edn. London: Routledge.

Daniels, T. and Daniels, K. (2003). *The Environmental Planning Handbook for Sustainable Regions and Communities.* Chicago, IL: Planners Press.

Davidoff, P. (1965). 'Advocacy and pluralism in planning.' *The Journal of the American Institute of Planners*, Vol. 31, No. 4. In: Campbell, S. and Fainstein, S. (1996). *Readings in Planning Theory*, 305–322. Oxford: Blackwell.

Dear, M. (1995). 'Prologomena to a post modern urbanism.' In: Healey, P., Cameron, S., Davoudi, S., Graham, S. and Madani-Pour, A. (eds), *Managing Cities: The New Urban Context*, 27–44. London: Wiley.

Dear, M. (2000). *The Postmodern Urban Condition.* Oxford: Blackwell.

DeForest, R.W. and Veiller, L. (eds) (1903). *The Tenement House Problem: Including the Report of the New York State Tenement House Commission of 1900*, 2 vols. New York: Macmillan.

DETR (Department of the Environment, Transport and the Regions). (1995). *Planning Policy Guidance Note 1: General Policy and Principles.* London: DETR.

DETR. (2000). *Our Towns and Cities: the Future: Delivering an Urban Renaissance.* London: The Stationery Office.

DETR and CABE (Commission for Architecture and the Built Environment). (2000). *By Design: Urban design in the planning system: towards better practice.* London: DETR and CABE.

DCLG (Department for Communities and Local Government) [previously ODPM]. (2006). *Design Coding in Practice: An Evaluation.* London: DCLG.

DTLR (Department for Transport, Local Government and the Regions) [previously DETR] and CABE (Commission for Architecture and the Built Environment). (2001). *By Design: Better Places to live. A Companion Guide to PPG3.* London: HMSO.

Dittmar, H. (2005). 'Your place or mine?' *RIBA Journal*, Vol. 113, No. 7.

DoE (Department of the Environment). (1994). *Quality in Town and Country Initiative: A Discussion Document.* London: DoE.

DoE. (1995). *Quality in Town and Country Initiative: Urban Design Campaign.* London: DoE.

DoE. (1996). *Design Policies in Local Plans: A Research Report.* London: HMSO.

DoE. (1997). *Planning Policy Guidance Note 1, Planning Practice and Procedures.* London: HMSO.

DoE. (1999). *Transport and the Regions: Good Practice Guidance on Design in the Planning System.* London: HMSO.

Duany, A. and Plater-Zyberk, E. with Kreiger, A. and Lennertz, W. (eds). (1991). *Towns and Town-making Principles.* New York: Rizzoli.

Duany Plater-Zyberk & Co. (2002). *The Lexicon of the New Urbanism, Version 3.2.* Miami, FL: DPZ.

Duany, A. and Talen, E. (2002). 'Transect planning.' *Journal of the American Planning Association*, Vol. 68, No. 3, Summer, 245–266.

Duerksen, C.J. and Goebel, R.M. (1999). *Aesthetics, Community Character and the Law.* Planning Advisory Service Report Nos 489/490. Chicago,

IL: American Planning Association and Scenic America.

Dunphy, R. T., Cervero, R., Dock, F. C., McAvey, M., Porter, D.R. and Swenson, C.J. (2004). *Developing Around Transit: Strategies and Solutions That Work*. Washington, DC: Urban Land Institute.

Dutton, J.A. (2000). *New American Urbanism: Re-forming the Suburban Metropolis*. Milan: Skira.

Eisenman, P. (2005). 'Thoughts on the World Trade Center.' In: Kelbaugh, D. (series ed.), *Everyday Urbanism, Peter Eisenman vs. Barbara Littenberg and Steven Peterson, Michigan Debates on Urbanism, Vol. III*, 12–13. Ann Arbor, MI: The University of Michigan A. Alfred Taubman College of Architecture + Urban Planning.

Ellin, N. (1999). *Postmodern Urbanism*, rev. edn. New York: Princeton Architectural Press.

Ellis, C. (2002). 'The New Urbanism: critiques and rebuttals.' *Journal of Urban Design*, Vol. 7, No. 3, 261–291.

Engels, F. (1845). 'The great towns.' From: *The Condition of the Working Class in England*. In: LeGates, T. and Stout, F. (1996; 3rd edn 2003). *The City Reader*, 58–66. London: Routledge.

English Partnerships. (1999). *Space for Growth*. www.urcs-online.co.uk/.../background Documents/Document/Space%20for%20Gro wth%20-% 20Executive%20summary.pdf.

English Partnerships *et al.* (2005). *Upton Design Code (Version 2)*. London: English Partnerships.

Fainstein, S. (1995). 'Urban redevelopment and public policy in London and New York.' In: Healey, P., Cameron, S., Davoudi, S., Graham, S. and Madani-Pour, A. (eds), *Managing Cities: The New Urban Context*, 127–143. Chichester: Wiley.

Fainstein, S. and Fainstein, N. (1996). 'City planning and political values: an updated view.' In: Campbell, S. and Fainstein, S. (eds), *Readings in Planning Theory*, 265–287. Oxford: Blackwell.

Ferris, H. (1922). 'The new architecture.' *New York Times Book Review and Magazine*, 19 March.

Flax, J. (1987). 'Postmodernism and gender relations in feminist theory.' *Signs: Journal of Women in Culture and Society*, Vol. 12, No. 4, 621–643.

Florida, R. (2002). *The Rise of the Creative Class: And How It's Transforming Work, Leisure, Community and Everyday Life*. New York: Basic Books.

Foglesong, R.E. (1986). 'Planning the capitalist city.' In: Campbell, S. and Fainstein, S. (1996). *Readings in Planning Theory*, 169–175. Oxford: Blackwell.

Forester, J. (1989). *Planning the Face of Power*. Berkeley, CA: University of California Press.

Forgey, B. (1999). 'A breath of that old town atmosphere.' *Washington Post*, 13 March.

Forshaw, J.H. and Abercrombie, P. (1943). *County of London Plan*. London: Macmillan.

Friedmann, J. (1987). *Planning in the Public Domain*. Princeton: Princeton University Press.

Friedmann, J. (1989). 'The dialectic of reason.' *International Journal of Urban and Regional Research*, Vol. 13, No. 2, 217–236.

Friend, J. and Hickling, A. (1987; 2nd edn 1997). *Planning Under Pressure: The Strategic Choice Approach*. Oxford: Butterworth-Heinemann.

Gans, H. (1961). 'Some notes on physical environment, human behavior and their relationships.' In: Abrams, M. (1962). 'Planning and environment.' *Journal of the Town Planning Institute*, May.

Gans, H. (1962). *The Urban Villagers: Group and Class in the Life of Italian-Americans*. New York: Free Press.

Gans, H. (1968). *People and Plans*. New York: Basic Books.

Garreau, J. (2001). 'Face to face in the information age.' Unpublished conference paper: *City Edge 2: Centre vs. Periphery*. Melbourne, Australia.

Garvin, A. (1996). *The American City: What Works, What Doesn't*. New York: McGraw-Hill.

Garvin, E.A. and LeRoy, G.S. (2003). 'Design guidelines: the law and aesthetic control.' *Land Use Law and Zoning Digest*. Chicago, IL: American Planning Association, April.

Geddes, P. (1915). *Cities in Evolution*. London: Williams & Norgate. Reprinted (1971) as: *Cities in Evolution: An Introduction to the Town Planning Movement and to the Study of Civics*. New York: Harper & Row.

Gehl, J. (1987). *Life Between Buildings: Using Public Space*. New York: Van Nostrand Reinhold.

251

Gold, J.R. (1997). *The Experience of Modernism: Modern Architects and the Future City*. London: E & FN Spon.

Gómez-Ibáñez, J. (1991). 'A global view of automobile dependence – cities and automobile dependence: a source book.' *Journal of the American Planning Association*, No. 57, 376–379.

Gordon, P. and Richardson, H.W. (1989). 'Gasoline consumption and cities: a reply.' *Journal of the American Planning Association*, No. 55, 342–345.

Gosling, D. (1996). *Gordon Cullen: Visions of Urban Design*. London: Academy Editions.

Greenberg, E. (2004). 'From building to region: New Urbanist regulations in place.' In: *Codifying New Urbanism*. Planning Advisory Service Report No. 526. Chicago, IL: Congress of the New Urbanism and the American Planning Association.

Gutman, R. (ed.) (1972). *People and Buildings*. New York: Basic Books.

Haar, C.M. (1975). *Between the Idea and Reality: A Study in the Origin, Fate, and Legacy of the Model Cities Program*. Boston, MA: Little, Brown.

Haar, C.M. (1976). 'Assumptions and goals of city planning.' In: *Land-use Planning: A Casebook on the Use, Misuse and Re-use of Urban Land*. Boston, MA: Little, Brown.

Haar, C.M. (ed.). (1994). *Cities, Law and Social Policy: Learning from the British*. Lexington, MA: Lexington Books.

Habermas, J. (1987). *The Philosophical Discourse of Modernity*. Cambridge: Polity Press.

Hakim, B.S. (2001). 'Julian of Ascalon's treatise of construction and design rules from sixth-century Palestine.' *Journal of the Society of Architectural Historians*, Vol. 60, No. 1, March, 4–25.

Hall, P. (2002). *Cities of Tomorrow: an Intellectual History of Urban Planning and Design in the Twentieth Century*, 3rd edn. Oxford: Basil Blackwell.

Hall, R. (2003). 'Why the sprawl lobby has clout.' *The Charlotte Observer*, 19 May.

Hanchett, T. (1998). *Sorting Out the New South City: Race, Class and Urban Development in Charlotte, 1875–1975*. Chapel Hill, NC: University of North Carolina Press.

Harden, B. (2005). 'Anti-sprawl laws, property rights collide in Oregon.' *The Washington Post*, 28 February, A-1.

Harrison, P. (2002). 'On the edge of reason: planning and the futures of South African Cities.' Lecture delivered in October 2002 and published by Witwatersrand University, Johannesburg, SA. (Accessed at www.wits.ac.za/planning/January 2006).

Harvey, D. (1989). *The Condition of Postmodernity: An Enquiry into the Origins of Cultural Change*. Oxford: Basil Blackwell.

Harvey, D. (1997). 'The New Urbanism and the communitarian trap.' *Harvard Design Magazine*, Winter/Spring, 68–69.

Healey, P. (1992). 'Planning through debate: the communicative turn in planning theory.' *Town Planning Review*, Vol. 63, No. 2. In: Campbell, S. and Fainstein, S. (1996). *Readings in Planning Theory*, 234–257. Oxford: Blackwell.

Healey, P. (1997; 2nd edn 2006). *Collaborative Planning: Shaping Places in Fragmented Societies*. London: Palgrave Macmillan.

Healey, P. (2002). 'Collaborative planning: shaping places in fragmented societies.' In: Bridge, G. and Watson, S. (2002). *The Blackwell City Reader*, 490–501. Oxford: Blackwell.

Hebbert, M. (1998). *London: More by Fortune than Design*. Chichester: Wiley.

Her Majesty's Government (1944). *White Paper: The Control and Use of Land (Cmd 6357)*. London: HMSO.

Her Majesty's Government (2004). *The Planning and Compulsory Purchase Act*. London: The Stationery Office Limited. Online at www.opsi.gov.uk/acts/acts2004/20040005.htm.

Hoch, C. (1984). 'Pragmatism, planning, and power.' *Journal of Planning Education and Research*, Vol. 4, No. 2, 86–95.

Holden, A. and Iveson, K. (2003). 'Designs on the urban: New Labour's urban renaissance and the spaces of citizenship.' *City*, Vol. 7, No. 1, 57–72.

Homsy, G. (2006). 'Sons of Measure 37: Lessons from Oregon's property rights law.' *Planning*, Vol. 72, No. 6, June, 14–19.

Howard, E. (1898). *Tomorrow: A Peaceful Path to Real Reform*. London: Swann Sonnenschein.

Reprinted (1965) as: *Garden Cities of Tomorrow*. Cambridge, MA: MIT Press.

HRH The Prince of Wales (1988). *A Vision of Britain: A Personal View of Architecture*. London: Doubleday.

Hulse, J.W. (1970). *Revolutionists in London: A Study of Five Unorthodox Socialists*. Oxford: Clarendon Press.

Huxtable, A.L. (1997). *The Unreal America: Architecture and Illusion*. New York: New Press.

Huyssen, A. (1986). *After the Great Divide: Modernism Mass Culture Postmodernism*. Bloomington, IN: Indiana University Press.

Hylton, T. (2000). *Save Our Land: Save Our Towns*. Harrisburg, PA: Rb Books and Preservation Pennsylvania.

Ingersoll, R. (1989). 'Postmodern urbanism: forward into the past.' *Design Book Review*, 17, 21–25.

Innes, J. (1996). 'Planning through consensus building: a new view of the comprehensive planning ideal.' *Journal of the American Planning Association*, Vol. 62, No. 4, Autumn, 460–472.

Innes, J. (2000). 'Challenge and creativity in postmodern planning.' In: Rodwin, L. and Sanyal, B. (eds), *The Profession of City Planning: Changes, Images, and Challenges, 1950–2000*, 31–35. New Brunswick, NJ: Center for Urban Policy Research, Rutgers University.

Irving, A. (1993). 'The modern/postmodern divide and urban planning.' *University of Toronto Quarterly*, Vol. 62. No. 4, 474–487.

Isaacs, R.R. (1948). 'The neighborhood theory: an analysis of its adequacy.' *Journal of the American Institute of Planners*, Vol. 14, No. 2, 15–23.

Jacobs, J. (1961). *The Death and Life of Great American Cities*. New York: Vintage Books.

Jameson, F. (1984). 'Postmodernism or the cultural logic of late capitalism.' *New Left Review*, No. 146, 53–92.

Jencks, C. (1977). *The Language of Postmodern Architecture*. London: Academy Editions.

Jencks, C. (1992). 'The post-avant-garde.' In: Jencks, C. (ed.), *The Post-Modern Reader*, 215–224. London: Academy Editions.

Kaliski, J. (1999). 'The present city and the practice of city design.' In: Chase, J., Crawford, M. and Kaliski, J. *Everyday Urbanism*, 88–109. New York: Monacelli Press.

Katz, P. (1994). *The New Urbanism: Toward an Architecture of Community*. New York: McGraw-Hill.

Katz, P. (2004). 'Form first: the New Urbanist alternative to conventional zoning.' *Planning*, Vol. 70, No. 10, November, 17–21.

Kaufman, J.L. and Jacobs, H.M. (1987). 'A public planning perspective on strategic planning.' *Journal of the American Planning Association*, Vol. 53, No. 1. In: Campbell, S. and Fainstein, S. (1996). *Readings in Planning Theory*, 323–343. Oxford: Blackwell.

Keeble, L. (1959; 4th edn 1969). *Principles and Practice of Town and Country Planning*. London: Estates Gazette.

Kelbaugh, D. (ed.) (1989). *The Pedestrian Pocket Book*. New York: Princeton Architectural Press.

Kelbaugh, D. (1997). *Common Place: Toward Neighborhood and Regional Design*. Seattle, WA: University of Washington Press.

Kelbaugh, D. (2002). *Repairing the American Metropolis: Common Place Revisited*. Seattle, WA: University of Washington Press.

Kelbaugh, D. (series ed.). (2005). *Michigan Debates on Urbanism, Vols I, II and III*. Ann Arbor, MI: The University of Michigan A. Alfred Taubman College of Architecture + Urban Planning.

Kelly, K. (1998). *New Rules for the New Economy: 10 Radical Strategies for a Connected World*. New York: Viking.

Kent, T.J. (1964). *The Urban General Plan*. San Francisco: Chandler; (1991). 2nd edn. Chicago, IL: Planners Press.

Klaus, S.L. (1991). 'Efficiency, economy, beauty: the city planning projects of Frederick Law Olmsted, Jr 1905–1915.' *Journal of the American Planning Association*, Vol. 57, No. 4, 456–471.

Klosterman, R.E. (1985). 'Arguments for and against Planning.' *Town Planning Review*, Vol. 56, No. 1, 5–20.

Klotz, H. (1988). *The History of Postmodern Architecture*. Cambridge, MA: MIT Press.

Kolson, K. (2001). *Big Plans: The Allure and Folly of Urban Design*. Baltimore, MD: The Johns Hopkins University Press.

Koolhas, R. and Mau, B. (1995). *S,M,L,XL*. New York: Monacelli Press.

Kreiger, A, and Lennertz, W. (eds). (1991). *Towns and Town-making Principles*. New York: Rizzoli.

Kreiger, A. (2000). 'The planner as urban designer: reforming planning education in the new millennium.' In: Rodwin, L. and Sanyal, B. (eds), *The Profession of City Planning: Changes, Images, and Challenges, 1950–2000*, 207–209. New Brunswick, NJ: Center for Urban Policy Research, Rutgers University.

Krumholz, N. (1982). 'A retrospective view of equity planning: Cleveland, 1969–79.' In: Campbell, S. and Fainstein, S. (1996). *Readings in Planning Theory*, 344–362. Oxford: Blackwell.

Kucharek, C-J. (2006). 'Happiness per hectare.' *RIBA Journal*, Vol. 113, No. 5, May, 65–8.

Kunzmann, K.R. (1999). 'Planning education in a globalized world.' *European Planning Studies*, Vol. 7, No. 5, 549–555.

Lai, R.T. (1988). *Law in Urban Design and Planning: The Invisible Web*. New York: Van Nostrand Reinhold.

Lai, R.T. (1994). 'Can the process of architectural design review withstand constitutional scrutiny?' In: Scheer, B.C. and Preiser, W.F.E. (eds), *Design Review: Challenging Urban Aesthetic Control*. New York: Chapman & Hall.

Landecker, H. 'Is new urbanism good for America?' *Architecture*, Vol. 84, No. 4, 68–70.

Langdon, P. (2006). 'Louisiana on fast track to adopting new urban ideas.' *New Urban News*, Vol. 11, No. 2, March.

Ledgerwood, G. (1985). *Urban Innovation: The Transformation of London's Docklands 1968–84*. Aldershot: Gower.

Lee, D. (1973). 'Requiem for large-scale planning models.' *Journal of the American Institute of Planners*, Vol. 39, No. 3, 163–178.

Lefebvre, H. (1970). 'Reflections on the politics of space.' In: Peet, R. (1977). *Radical Geography: Alternative Viewpoints on Contemporary Social Issues*. Chicago, IL: Maaroufa Press.

Lefebvre, H. (1979). 'Space: social product and use value.' In: Freiburg, J. (ed.), *Critical Sociology: European Perspectives*. New York: Irvington.

Lefebvre, H. (1991). *Critique of Everyday Life*. London: Verso.

Lennertz, W. and Lutzenhiser, A. (2006). *The Charrette Handbook*. Chicago, IL: Planners Press.

Lewis, C. (2003). 'Design based codes.' *New Urbanism in Practice: The Newsletter of the New Urbanism Division of the American Planning Association*, Vol. 1, No. 2, Fall, 1, 3–4, 12.

Lewis, J. (2006). 'Battle for Biloxi.' *New York Times Magazine: The Architecture Issue*, 21 May, 100–108.

Lim, G.-C. and Albrecht, J. (1987). 'A search for an alternative planning theory: use of phenomenology.' *Journal of Architectural and Planning Research*, Vol. 4, No. 1, 14–30.

Lindblom, C. (1959). 'The science of "muddling through".' *Public Administration Review*, Vol. 19. In: Campbell, S. and Fainstein, S. (1996). *Readings in Planning Theory*, 288–304. Oxford: Blackwell.

Llewelyn-Davies. (1993). *The Gun Quarter: Planning and Urban Design Framework*. Birmingham: Birmingham City Council.

Llewelyn-Davies (in association with Alan Baxter and Associates). (2000). *Urban Design Compendium*. London: English Partnerships and the Housing Corporation.

Lloyd, R. and Clark, T.N. (2001). 'The city as entertainment machine.' In: Gotham, K.F. (ed.), *Critical Perspectives on Urban Redevelopment. Research in Urban Sociology*, Vol. 6, 375–378. Oxford: JAI Press/Elsevier.

Local Government Commission [California] (n.d). *Form-Based Codes: Implementing Smart Growth*. Sacramento, CA: [California] Local Government Commission. www.lgc.org/freepub/land_use/factsheets/form_based_codes. html.

Logan, J.R. and Molotch, H. (1987). *Urban Fortunes: The Political Economy of Place*. Berkeley, CA: University of California Press.

Lyall, S. (2006). 'The Future of Cities: The AR's recent London conference on masterplanning and the character of cities provided much food for thought.' *The Architectural Review*, Vol. CCXIX, No. 1310, 80–81.

Lynch, K. (1981). *A Theory of Good City Form*. Cambridge, MA: MIT Press.

Lyotard, J.-F. (1988). *The Postmodern Condition*. Minneapolis, MN: University of Minnesota Press.

MacCormac, R. (1973). 'Housing form and land use: new research.' *RIBA Journal*, November, 549–551.

Malpass, P. (1979). 'A re-appraisal of Byker, Parts 1 and 2: magic, myth and the architect.' *The Architect's Journal*, 19/1979 and 20/1979.

Marshall, T.H. (1965). *Class, Citizenship, and Social Development*. New York: Anchor.

McDougall, I. (2000). 'The new urban space.' In: *City Edge Transcripts, Proceedings of the City Edge Conference: Private Development vs Public Realm*, 29–35. Melbourne, Australia.

McKean, J.M. (1976a). 'Walter Segal.' *Architectural Design*, May, 288–295.

McKean, J.M. (1976b). 'Walter Segal – pioneer.' *Building Design*, 20 February, 10–11.

Mearns, A. (1883). *The Bitter Cry of Outcast London: An Inquiry into the Condition of the Abject Poor*. London: James Clarke. Also at: http://www.attackingthedevil.co.uk/related/outcast.php.

Meck, S. (1997). 'Rhode island gets it right.' *Planning*, Vol. 63, No. 11.

Mehrotra, R. (2005). 'Introduction.' In: Kelbaugh, D. (series ed.), *Everyday Urbanism, Margaret Crawford vs. Michael Speaks, Michigan Debates on Urbanism, Vol. I*, 12–13. Ann Arbor, MI: The University of Michigan A. Alfred Taubman College of Architecture + Urban Planning.

Mellor, H. (1990). *Patrick Geddes: Social Evolutionist and City Planner*. London: Routledge.

Miller, J. (2004). 'Smart Codes Smart Places.' *On Common Ground*. Summer. National Association of Realtors®.

Ministry of Health, Central Housing Advisory Committee. (1944). *The Design of Dwellings* [The Dudley Report]. London: HMSO.

Ministry of Housing and Local Government. (1969). *People and Planning. Report of the Committee on Public Participation in Planning* [The Skeffington Report]. London: HMSO.

Mitchell, W.J. (1999). *E-Topia: Urban Life, Jim – But Not As We Know It*. Cambridge, MA: MIT Press.

Moore Milroy, B. (1991). 'Into postmodern weightlessness.' *Journal of Planning Education and Research*, Vol. 10, No. 3, 182.

Mumford, L. (1946). 'The garden city idea and modern planning.' Introduction to: Howard, E. (1965). *Garden Cities of Tomorrow*. Cambridge, MA: MIT Press.

Mumford, L. (1954). 'The neighborhood and the neighborhood unit.' *Town Planning Review*, Vol. 24, No. 4, 257–270.

Mumford, L. (1961). *The City in History*. New York: Harcourt, Brace and World.

Mumford, L. (1962). 'The sky line: Mother Jacobs' home remedies.' *New Yorker*, 1 December. Republished in: Mumford, L. (1968). *The Urban Prospect*, 182–207. New York: Harcourt, Brace and World.

Murphy, J.W. (1989). *Postmodern Social Analysis and Criticism*. New York: Greenwood Press.

Murrain, P. (2002). 'Understand urbanism and get off its back.' *Urban Design International*, Vol. 7, No. 3–4, 131–142.

NAHB (National Association of Homebuilders). (n.d.). *The Truth About Property Rights*. Washington, DC: NAHB.

Nairn, I. (1955). *Outrage*. London: Architectural Press.

Nairn, I. (1957). *Counter-attack against Subtopia*. London: Architectural Press.

Newman, P. and Kenworthy, J. (1989). 'Gasoline consumption and cities: a comparison of US cities with a global survey.' *Journal of the American Planning Association*, No. 55, 24–37.

Newsom, M. (1996). 'A Mecklenburg miracle: how regional citizens are having a say on growth.' *The Charlotte Observer*, 1 June, 14.

Nylund, K. (2001). 'Cultural analyses in urban theory of the 1990s.' *ACTA Sociologica*, Vol. 44, 219–230.

ODPM (Office of the Deputy Prime Minister). (2005a). *Delivering Sustainable Development PPS1*. London: The Stationery Office.

ODPM. (2005b). *The Future for Design Codes. Further Information to Support Stakeholders' Reading Draft PPS3*. London: The Stationery Office.

ODPM (2005c). *Sustainable Communities: People, Places, Prosperity*. London: The Stationery Office.

Owen, G. (2006). 'In dark waters: opportunity and opportunism in the reconstruction of New Orleans.' *Journal of Architectural Education*, Vol. 60, No. 1, September, 7–9.

Pawley, M. (1971). *Architecture versus Housing*. London: Studio Vista.

Peirce, N. (2006). 'Reforming American politics: a "one-stop" guide.' *The Charlotte Observer*, 17 July, 13A.

Pellin, M.E. (2006). 'A planning bloc for mass transit.' *The Rhinoceros Times*, Vol. V, No. 14, 6 April, 1 and 14.

Perry, C. (1929). *Regional Survey of New York and its Environs, Vol. 7.* New York: Committee on Regional Plan of New York and its Environs.

Pettinger, R. (2006). 'We aren't changing climate: let's avoid snap judgments and wishful thinking on warming trend.' *The Charlotte Observer*, 5 February, 24A.

Popper, F.J. (1988). 'Understanding American land use regulation since 1970.' *Journal of the American Planning Association*, Vol. 54, No. 4, 291–301.

Porritt, J. (2003). 'Foreword.' In: Barton, H., Grant, M. and Guise, R., *Shaping Neighborhoods: A Guide for Health, Sustainability and Vitality*, ix. London: Spon Press.

Plater-Zyberk, E. (1994). 'Foreword.' In: Scheer, B.C. and Preiser, W.F.E., *Design Review: Challenging Urban Aesthetic Control*. New York: Chapman & Hall.

Punter, J. (1999). *Design Guidelines in American Cities: A Review of Design Policies and Guidelines in Five West Coast American Cities*. Liverpool: Liverpool University Press.

Punter, J., Carmona, M. and Platts, A. (1996). *Design Policies in Local Plans: A Research Report.* London: Department of the Environment.

Pyatok, M. (2000). Comment on Charles C. Bohl's 'New Urbanism and the city: potential applications and implications for distressed inner-city neighborhoods – the politics of design: the New Urbanists vs. the Grass Roots.' *Housing Policy Debate*, Vol. 11, No. 4, 803–814.

Ravetz, A. (1976). 'Housing at Byker, Newcastle-upon-Tyne.' *The Architects' Journal*, 14 April, 735–742.

RIBA (Royal Institute of British Architects). (2006). *Practice Bulletin*, No. 339, 2 March.

Reclus, E. (1892). 'Quelques mots d'histoire, Suivi de Préface à la Conquête du Pain de Peter Kropotkine.' In: Clark, J.P. and Martin, C. (eds). (2004). *Anarchy, Geography, Modernity: The Radical Social Thought of Elisée Reclus*. Lanham, MA: Lexington Books.

Rogers, R. (1997). *Cities for a Small Planet*. London: Faber.

Rouse, J. (2002). 'Foreword.' In: Cowan, R. with the Urban Design Group and the Urban Design Alliance, *Urban Design Guidance: Urban Design Frameworks, Development Briefs and Master Plans*, 7. London: Thomas Telford.

Rouse, J. (2004). 'Foreword.' In: *Creating Successful Masterplans: A Guide for Clients*, 3. London: CABE.

Rowland, I.D. and Howe, T.N. (eds). (1999). *Vitruvius. Ten Books on Architecture*. Cambridge: Cambridge University Press.

Rowley, A. (1994). 'Definitions of urban design: the nature and concerns of urban design.' *Planning Practice and Research*, Vol. 9, No. 3.

Rudlin, D. and Falk, N. (1995). *21st Century Homes, Building to Last: A Report for the Joseph Rowntree Foundation*. London: Urban and Economic Development Group.

Rudlin, D. and Falk, N. (1999). *Building the 21st Century Home: The Sustainable Urban Neighborhood*. Oxford: Architectural Press.

Rutherford, P. (2005). 'Saving suburbia: mixed-use and smart planning: the keys to the white picket fence.' RTKL (ed.). RTKL Associates Inc. http://www.rtkl.com/docs/rtkl-savingsuburbs.pdf (accessed 5 October 2005).

Rybczynski, W. (1995). 'This old house: the rise of family values in architecture.' *New Republic*, May, 14–16.

Safdie, M. (1997). *The City After the Automobile*. New York: Basic Books.

Sandercock, L. (1998). *Towards Cosmopolis: Planning for Multicultural Cities*. Chichester: Wiley.

Sandercock, L. (1999). 'Expanding the "language" of planning: a meditation on planning education for the twenty-first century.' *European Planning Studies*, Vol. 7, No. 5, 533–544.

Sandercock, L. (2000a). 'Café society or active society?' In: *City Edge Transcripts: Proceedings of the City Edge Conference: Private Development vs Public Realm*, viii–xi. Melbourne, Australia.

Sandercock, L. (2000b). 'When strangers become neighbours: managing cities of difference.' *Planning Theory and Practice*, Vol. 1, No. 1.

Sandercock, L. (2004). 'Sustainability: a dialectical take.' http://www.scarp.ubc.ca/faculty%20pro-files/leonoesustst.html (accessed 19 February 2006).

Santayana, G. (1905). *Life of Reason, Reason in Common Sense*. New York: Scribner's.

Schmitz, A. and Scully, J. (2006). *Creating Walkable Places: Compact Mixed-Use Solutions*. Washington, DC: Urban Land Institute.

Sexton, R. (1995). *Parallel Utopias: Sea Ranch and Seaside: the Quest for Community*. San Francisco: Chronicle Books.

Simonsen, K. (1990). 'Planning on "postmodern" conditions.' *Acta Sociologica*, Vol. 33, 51–62.

Shane, D.G. (2005). *Recombinant Urbanism: Conceptual Modeling in Architecture, Urban Design, and City Theory*. Chichester: Wiley.

Smart, B. (1992). *Modern Conditions, Postmodern Controversies*. London: Routledge.

Smith, D. (2006). 'NoDa next stop in rail-line boom?' *The Charlotte Observer*, 5 April, 4D.

Sorkin, M. (ed.) (1992). *Variations on a Theme Park*. New York: Hill and Wang.

Snyder, K. (2006). 'Putting democracy front & center: technology for citizen participation.' *Planning*, Vol. 72, No. 7, July, 24–29.

Soja, E. (1989). *Postmodern Geographies*. London: Verso.

South Hams District Council. (2005). *South Hams Local Development Framework: Statement of Community Involvement*. Totnes: South Hams District Council.

South Hams District Council. (2006). *South Hams Local Development Framework: Core Strategy*. Totnes: South Hams District Council.

Southworth, M. (1989). 'Theory and Practice of contemporary urban design – a review of urban design plans in the United States.' *Town Planning Review*, Vol. 60, No. 4, 369–402.

Southworth, M. (1997). 'Walkable suburbs? An evaluation of neotraditional communities at the urban edge.' *Journal of the American Planning Association*, Vol. 63, No. 1, 28–44.

Southworth, M. (2003). 'New Urbanism and the American metropolis.' *Built Environment*, Vol. 29, No. 3, 210–26.

Southworth, M. and Ben Joseph, E. (1997). *Streets and the Shaping of Towns and Cities*. New York: McGraw-Hill.

Speaks, M. (2005). 'Every day is not enough.' In: Kelbaugh, D. (series ed.), *Everyday Urbanism, Margaret Crawford vs. Michael Speaks. Michigan Debates on Urbanism, Vol. I*, 34–42. Ann Arbor, MI: The University of Michigan A. Alfred Taubman College of Architecture + Urban Planning.

Stein, J.M. (ed.) (1995). *Classic Readings in Urban Planning*. New York: McGraw-Hill Inc.

Steuteville, R. and Langdon, P. (2003). *New Urbanism: Comprehensive Report & Best Practices Guide*, 3rd edn. Ithaca, NY: New Urban Publications.

Storper, M. (2001). 'The poverty of radical theory today: from the false promises of Marxism to the mirage of the cultural turn.' *International Journal of Urban and Regional Research*, Vol. 25, 155–79.

Sudjic, D. (1992). *The 100 Mile City*. San Diego, CA: Harcourt Brace.

Symes, M. and Pauwells, S. (1999). 'The diffusion of innovations in urban design: the case of sustainability in the Hulme Development Guide.' *Journal of Urban Design*, Vol. 4, No. 1, 97–117.

Talen, E. (1999). 'Sense of community and neighborhood form: an assessment of the social doctrine of New Urbanism.' *Urban Studies*, Vol. 36, 1361–79.

Talen, E. (2000). 'The problem with community in planning.' *Journal of Planning Literature*, Vol. 15, No. 2, 171–83.

Talen, E. (2002). 'Help for planning: the Transect strategy.' *Journal of Urban Design*, Vol. 7, No. 3, 293–312.

Talen, E. (2005). *New Urbanism and American Planning: The Conflict of Cultures*. New York: Routledge.

Talen, E. and Duany, A. (2002). 'Transect planning.' *Journal of the American Planning Association*, Vol. 68, No. 3, 245–66.

Talen, E. and Ellis, C. (2004). 'Cities as art: exploring the possibility of an aesthetic dimension in planning.' *Planning Theory and Practice*, Vol. 5, No. 1, March, 11–32.

Taylor, N. (1974). *The Village in the City*. London: Maurice Temple Smith.

Taylor, N. (1999). 'Anglo-American town planning theory since 1945: three significant developments but no paradigm shift.' *Planning Perspectives*, Vol. 14, 327–345.

The Lawrence Group (2002). *Master Plan: Haynie-Sirrine Neighborhood.* Davidson, NC: The Lawrence Group and the City of Greenville, SC.

The Lawrence Group (2003/4). *The Renaissance Plan.* Davidson, NC: The Lawrence Group and the Town of Wake Forest, NC.

Thornley, A. (1991). *Urban Planning under Thatcherism: The Challenge of the Market.* London: Routledge.

Thorpe, K. (2004). 'Urban and sustainable communities: plan policies driving mixed-use.' Presentation at: *Maximising Returns from Mixed-Use: The Estates Gazette Mixed-Use Development Conference,* London.

Tibbalds, F. *et al.* (1990). *Birmingham Urban Design Study.* Birmingham: City of Birmingham Planning Department.

Tibbalds, F. (1992). *Making People Friendly Towns: Improving the Public Environment in Towns and Cities.* Harlow: Longmans.

Tiesdell, S. (2002). 'New urbanism and english residential design guidance.' *Journal of Urban Design*, Vol. 7, No. 2, October, 353–376.

Tocqueville, A. de. (1957; originally published *c.* 1848). *Democracy in America.* New York: Vintage.

Towers, G. (1995). *Building Democracy: Community Architecture in the Inner City.* London: UCL Press.

Town of Davidson. (1995). *Davidson Land Plan: Part I, Policy Guide.* Davidson, NC: Town of Davidson.

Town of Davidson. (2000). *Zoning Regulations.* Davidson, NC: Town of Davidson.

Town of Huntersville. (1996; as amended through 18 July 2005). *Zoning Ordinance.* Huntersville, NC: Town of Huntersville.

Tracy, S. (2003). *Smart Growth Zoning Codes: A Resource Guide.* Sacramento, CA: Local Government Commission.

Triangle J Council of Governments (TJCOG). (2001). *High Performance Guidelines.* Raleigh, NC: TJCOG.

Trimakas, T. (2006). 'Letter from the Editor.' *Uptown Magazine*, June. Charlotte, NC: Collier Bing, LLC.

Turner, J.F.C. (1965). 'Lima's *Barriadas* and *Corralones*: suburbs versus slums.' *Ekistics*, Vol. 19, 152–155.

Turner, J.F.C. (1976). *Housing by People: Towards Autonomy in Building Environments.* London: Marion Boyars.

Turner, J.F.C. and Fichter, R. (eds). (1972). *Freedom to Build: Dweller Control of the Housing Process.* New York: Macmillan.

Unwin, R. (1912). *Nothing Gained by Overcrowding! How the Garden City Type of Development May Benefit both Owner and Occupier.* London: P.S. King.

Unwin, R. (1920/1). 'Distribution.' In: *Town Planning Institute: Papers and Discussions, Vol. 7.* London: Town Planning Institute.

Urban Design Associates. (1999). *The Baxter Pattern Book: Architectural Guidelines for Residential Neighborhoods.* Pittsburgh, PA: Urban Design Associates.

Urban Design Associates. (2003). *The Urban Design Handbook: Techniques and Working Methods.* New York: Norton.

Urban Design Associates. (2004). *The Architectural Pattern Book: A Tool for Building Great Neighborhoods.* New York: Norton.

Urban Land Institute. (2006). 'Urban land: being green – high performance development across the board.' *Urban Land*, Vol. 65, No. 6, June.

Urban Task Force. (1999). *Towards an Urban Renaissance.* London: DETR.

Urhahn, G. and Bobic, M. (1994). *A Pattern Image: A Typological Tool for Quality in Urban Planning.* Bussum: Thoth.

US Department of Housing and Urban Development (HUD). (1997). 'HUD awards $90.8 million in grants and loan guarantees to create homeownership zones in Baltimore, Buffalo, Cleveland, Louisville, Philadelphia, and Sacramento.' Press Release No. 97-43, April 8. Washington, DC: US Government Printing Office.

Vale, L.J. (2000). 'Urban design for urban development'. In: Rodwin, L. and Sanyal, B. (eds), *The Profession of City Planning: Changes, Images, and Challenges, 1950–2000*, 220–223. New Brunswick, NJ: Center for Urban Policy Research, Rutgers University.

van Eyck, A. (1962). 'Team 10 primer.' In: Jencks, C. and Kropf, K. (eds). (1997). *Theories and Manifestoes of Contemporary Architecture*, 27–29. Chichester: Academy Editions.

Venturi, R., Scott-Brown, D. and Izenour, S. (1972). *Learning from Las Vegas*. Cambridge, MA: MIT Press.

Walters, D. and Brown, L. (2004). *Design First: Design-based Planning for Communities*. Oxford: Architectural Press.

Wakeford, R. (1990). *American Development Control: Parallels and Paradoxes from an English Perspective*. London: HMSO.

Wates, N. (ed.) (1996). *Action Planning: How to Use Planning Weekends and Urban Design Action Teams to Improve your Environment*. London: The Prince of Wales' Institute of Architecture.

Wates, N. (ed.) (2000). *The Community Planning Handbook: How People can Shape their Cities, Towns and Villages in any Part of the World*. London: Earthscan.

Webber, M.M. (1963). 'The urban place and the non-place urban realm.' In: Webber, M.M. (ed.), *Explorations into Urban Structure*, 71–54. Baltimore, MD: Johns Hopkins University Press.

Webber, M.M. (1964). 'Order in diversity: community without propinquity.' In: Wingo, L. Jr (ed.), *Cities and Space: the Future Use of Urban Land*, 23–153. Philadelphia: University of Pennsylvania Press.

Webber, M.M. (1968/9). 'Planning in an environment of change.' *Town Planning Review*, Vol. 39, 179–195, 277–295.

Wilmott, P. (1962). 'Housing density and town design in a new town: a pilot study at Stevenage.' *Town Planning Review*, Vol. 33, No. 2, 115–127.

Wilms, P. (2005). 'NCHBA scores major victories in 2005 legislative session.' *North Carolina Builder*, October, 7.

Woodcock, G. (1980). 'Misreading radical history: the anarchist way to socialism.' Review of Fleming, M. *The Anarchist Way to Socialism*, Croom Helm, Rowan and Littlefield. *The New Leader*, 28 January, 21. New York: New Leader Publication Association.

Woolf, M. (2006). 'Demolition Dave (Or how the Tory leader wants to knock down "dull little boxes" and build modern villages).' *The Independent on Sunday*, 13 August, 27.

Index

References to illustrations are shown in italics.